MW01629775

CAMP FIRES OF GEORGIA'S TROOPS,
1861 - 1865

By
William S. Smedlund

43

The author invites comments, corrections, and additional information from the readers. Any additional information will be acknowledged in any future editions and would certainly be appreciated. Correspondence can be sent to the author at the address shown below.

Additional copies of this book can be ordered from:

William S. Smedlund
1666 Glen Arm Drive
Lithonia, Georgia 30058-5513

Deluxe Edition $63.50 plus $3.50 shipping, U.S. funds

Library of Congress Cataloging in Publication Data

Date of Publication, August 1994

Grant provided by the R. J. Taylor, Jr. Foundation.

ISBN 0-9635861-2-2

Printed in the United States of America. First edition.

This Book is dedicated to the men and boys
from Georgia who endured the hardship of
the camp and made the ultimate sacrifice
for their home and country.

Acknowledgements

I wish to acknowledge a number of people and organizations for their assistance or information they provided which made this project possible. Without the letters, images or maps provided by these people the project would be incomplete. Many "thanks" to all of you. I hope you enjoy the finished work as much as I enjoyed putting it together.

First, I would like to thank the R. J. Taylor, Jr. Foundation for their grant which assisted in the printing of the book.

Secondly, I wish to thank Carl Anderson for the use of his microfilm reader, microfilm and research assistance.

Finally, I want to thank the many people listed below who submitted items or assisted in making this book possible.

Tom Aderhold
Carl Anderson
Fran Beckemayer
James W. Bell
Timothy Bradshaw, Jr.
Robert S. Brandt
Jack & Debbie Buchert
Elliott Butler
Brant Calvit
John Carroll
C. Pat Cates
Gene Chatham
Anne R. Clayton
Richard A. Clayton
Joe Cliett
J. Brad Coker III
David Cole
Jerry Coody
Susan Hawkes Cook, C.G.
Lori Nash Cosgrove
Robert S. Davis, Jr.
Jimmy Dodd
Gary Doster
Bob Edmondson
Kerry Elliott
Gene Eubanks
Dickey Ferry
The Florida State Archives
Robert W. Ford
Jo B. Gladney
Scott T. Glass
George M. Glover
Georgia Department of Archives and History
Steve Griffith
Edward H. Hahn
Emmett Hall
Michael Hannon
Earl Harris
Dorothy A. Herring
Elmer Hogue
Dixon Hollingsworth
H. Grady Howell
Charles Jackson
Greg Jamison
Lee Joyner
Diane Smedlund Jones
Jeff Jones
Martha Julian
Wallace P. Julian
Danny Kuykendall
Dave Larson
Martha Clayton Lee
Rabun A. Lee, Jr.
William Leigh, Jr.
John Lines
Craig Lloyd
Bob Lurate
Norman Malone
Alan J. Marshall
L. C. Mathis, Jr.
Richard M. McMurry
Jack W. Melton, Jr., photography
Mississippi Department of Archives and History
Pierce Moore
Lanny W. Morgan
Patricia Mullinax
Steve E. Mullinax
Charles Nash
Nan Nash
R. E. Nevill
Clifford Orth
Lawrence E. Pawl, M. D.
Sanford Pentecost
Charlotte Ray
Dr. Richard J. Reid
Elizabeth W. Roberson
Mark Royal
William R. Scaife
Steve Scott
Joey Seguin
John Sexton
Stan Sheram
Romulus Skaggs, Jr., artwork
Carl Smedlund
David Smedlund
Erika Smedlund
Maxine Smedlund
Everett R. Smith
James L. Speicher
C. Willard Spivey, Jr.
Robert Sprayberry
Edith Clayton Stephens
Chris Taras
David Vaughan
Dr. Scott Walker
George H. Watkins
Dick Wescott
Dr. Max E. White
George S. Whiteley IV
David Windham
Earl Young

TABLE OF CONTENTS

Table of Abbreviations

The following are the abbreviations of sources used in the book.

ADC&S, *Augusta Daily Chronicle & Sentinel* newspaper, Augusta, Georgia

AGLB, Adjutant General's Letter Books, at the Georgia Department of Archives and History

AHB, *Atlanta Historical Bulletin*, published by the Atlanta Historical Society, Atlanta, Georgia

AHC, Atlanta History Center, Atlanta, Georgia

AP, *Albany Patriot* newspaper, Albany, Georgia

ASB, *Athens Southern Banner* newspaper, Athens, Georgia

ASW, *Athens Southern Watchman* newspaper, Athens, Georgia

C&CNMPL, Chicamauga & Chattanooga National Military Park Library

CDT, *Columbus Daily Times* newspaper, Columbus, Georgia

CE, *Columbus Enquirer* newspaper, Columbus, Georgia

CG, *Central Georgian* newspaper, Sandersville, Georgia

CR, *Columbus Recorder* newspaper, Columbus, Georgia

CSR, Compiled Service Records

CU, *Confederate Union* newspaper, Milledgeville, Georgia

CV, *Confederate Veteran* magazine

DU, Duke University, Durham North Carolina

ECN, *Early County News* newspaper

EU, Emory University, Atlanta, Georgia

FU, *Federal Union* newspaper, Milledgeville, Georgia

GDAH, Georgia Department of Archives and History, Atlanta, Georgia

GHQ, *Georgia Historical Quarterly*

GHS, Georgia Historical Society, Savannah, Georgia

GJ&M, *Georgia Journal & Messenger* newspaper, Macon, Georgia

KMNBPL, Kennesaw Mountain National Battlefield Park Library

KDR, *Knoxville Daily Register* newspaper, Knoxville, Tennessee

MJ&M, *Macon Journal & Messenger*, Macon, Georgia

MR, Muster Rolls

Ms., Manuscript

MSR, *Milledgeville Southern Recorder*

MT, *Macon Telegraph* newspaper, Macon, Georgia

O.R., *War of the Rebellion, Official Records of the Union and Confederate Armies*

PC, Private Collection

RWC, *Rome Weekly Courier* newspaper, Rome, Georgia

SC, *Southern Confederacy* newspaper, Atlanta, Georgia

SDMN, *Savannah Daily Morning News* newspaper, Savannah, Georgia

SFU, *Southern Federal Union* newspaper, Milledgeville, Georgia. Previously the *Federal Union*

SR, *Savannah Republican* newspaper, Savannah, Georgia

TWC, *Tri Weekly Courier* newspaper, Rome Georgia

UDC, United Daughters of the Confederacy

UGA, University of Georgia, Athens, Georgia

UNC, University of North Carolina, Chapel Hill, North Carolina.

USC, University of South Carolina, Columbia, South Carolina.

WL, Washington Library, Macon, Georgia.

TABLE OF ILLUSTRATIONS

TABLE OF PHOTOGRAPHS

INTRODUCTION

Volumes of books have been written on the War Between the States. The most notable and referenced work is the *War of The Rebellion. Official Records of the Union and Confederate Armies.* Unit histories, company histories, biographies, reminiscences, books on battles, a day by day history, periodicals, reference books of all types, bibliographies, compendiums, price guides on these books and collectibles, even a civil war dictionary can be found on the shelves of the serious researcher and student of the great American conflict. With all of these works relating to the War Between the States, not one is designed to record the camps of the men who spent most of their time in bivouac or encampments. More men died in the various camps of disease and wounds from battle than died on the battlefield. Try to find the words bivouac or encampment defined in *The Civil War Dictionary.* The history of the camps has been largely overlooked.

Thousands of letters were written in these camps. Many have survived fires, floods and the indifference of generations since they reached the homes of the anxious relatives and friends. Their value is no less today than when they were received during those trying times. They record family history, the battles, the mood of the army, troop movements, activities in camp, the sickness, the death, and the sad and happy times whenever a letter was received from home. The camp names from the letters and records can be used by genealogists, researchers, Universities and Archives to identify the Georgia unit of the writer, identify the county in which the writer lived, the location of the camp, or help trace the movement of the unit. The letters written to relatives and friends or published in newspapers are a major source for this history.

This book is an attempt to record the camps of Georgia's troops that were named in honor of the martyrs for the lost cause, prominent citizens, past and present leaders and those who gave of their time and resources to assist the men and boys in camp. Some were named for their location, and others reflected their moods or environment.

It is also intended to give basic information on how a company was formed and outfitted. A number of excerpts from letters and newspaper articles or ads are included to give the reader an example of the variety of activities in camp or daily events which would not occur to us today. Several maps of these camps are included; some are drawn by Georgia soldiers. A few photographs are included to give the reader an idea of the variety of uniforms worn by Georgia soldiers. The stern expression on their faces reflects the seriousness of their mission. Many of them believed that death was their fate. They were resolved to fight until death for their rights.

It is intended to satisfy the curiosity of the novice or serious researcher about the camps of Georgia's Troops in the most terrible war this country has ever experienced.

The Honorable J.M. Mason addressed the Maryland Troops in Virginia with these truthful words, " The true duty of the soldier is not merely to fight battles or kill the enemy. He has also to endure the trials of the camp: the vigilance of the day and night, the restraints of discipline and patience to bear with his discomforts and disappointments. This is the real test of courage, and he who comes out of the war with the reputation of having thus done his duty through sunshine and through storm is the true man and the thorough soldier."[1]

Additional information has been received since the cut-off date for the listing of camps in the indexes. An addendum has been added in order to share this information.

---

[1]   *Rome Weekly Courier,* August 9, 1861

Chapter I

How to Use This Book to Help Determine the County
Origin of Your Georgia Ancestor

There are several ways to identify the Georgia unit of your ancestor. If he was in the infantry, you would look in the *Roster of The Confederate Soldiers of Georgia, 1861-1865,* by Lillian Henderson. [Hereafter refered to as Roster or Georgia Roster.] The *Roster* does contain errors and omissions, which makes it necessary to check the compiled service records as well. Assuming you find his name in the *Roster*, you can then determine which Georgia county or counties supplied men for his company. The Georgia county or counties that supplied men for a particular company are listed with each company shown in the *Roster*. Only the infantry of Georgia's Confederate troops is covered in this six volume roster. If your ancestor has a common name or was in the Confederate artillery or cavalry from Georgia, or one of the units organized by the State of Georgia, it is much more difficult to identify his unit. With the exception of The Georgia State Line, sometimes referred to as Georgia State Troops, there is no roster published for the Confederate artillery or cavalry as a unit, or any of the other Georgia State units. There is a project underway to partly fill this void. The roster for the Georgia State Line can be found in the book, *Joe Brown's Army,* by William Harris Bragg. There are very few histories of Georgia's artillery or cavalry units which include the rosters. The few that have been published are difficult to find.

Other ways to identify the unit in which your ancestor served is to methodically look for his name on the microfilm rolls and the compiled service records, or check the alphabetical index of Georgia soldiers, also on microfilm. These records are at the Georgia Department of Archives and History in Atlanta, Georgia, or at the National Archives in Washington, D.C.. If you know he served in the artillery, you would look at each roll of microfilm for the artillery. Once his name is located, you would then need to find where his unit organized. Generally, if his name appears on the compiled service records, it will indicate in which county he signed up. If you cannot determine the county of his origin by the compiled service records, check the names of other members of his company. Generally each company is recruited from the same county or surrounding area.

This book gives you one more alternative to the above and many times is used in conjunction with the *Georgia Roster*. To identify the Georgia unit with this list of camp names, you must either have a letter from your Georgia ancestor with a camp name and date, or know a specific camp name in which he served or trained. From the name of the camp and date on the letter, go through the alphabetical list of camp names, locate that camp name and the Georgia unit will be listed along with the camp name. If the date on your letter varies more than a few days from the camp name in the book, it is possible this is not the camp. I am sure there are many other named camps that were not discovered for this edition. Every effort was made to find the inclusive dates of each camp. Unfortunately many of the camp names come from a single source with this camp name. If there are several camps of the same name, use the date from your letter as a process of elimination to narrow down the possibilities for the proper camp. Often the letter will also give the location of the camp along with the camp name. Use this information with the camp name and date to select the proper camp. Again, the Georgia unit or units occupying this camp will be listed. If you have other letters with a camp name, go through the same process with each letter that has a camp name, and by process of elimination you will be able to determine the Georgia unit of your ancestor. If no other letters have camp names, use the locations and dates from the letters, go to the index by unit, and find all the camps of this unit. Then compare the locations and dates from the other camps to help determine the unit. In other words, compare the itinerary from the dates and information in the letters with the chronological list of camps from the book.

If you know he trained at Camp McDonald, there are twenty-two recorded units who trained in this camp at various times. Then if you know he served in Tennessee, Mississippi, or in Virginia, this reduces the list of twenty-two units down to a more manageable number of units in which to search for his name. Part of the troops that trained at Camp McDonald went to Virginia, others went into the Army of Tennessee, and a few of these went on to serve in the Vicksburg campaign. This would also apply to the two other major training camps, Camp Stephens and Camp Davis. Family histories or information that has been passed down from those who served in the War Between the States can be very helpful as a process of elimination to determine the Georgia unit.

There are times you will need to use the *Georgia Roster* along with the list of camp names. As an example, your letter is signed by James Davis from Camp Hatton. The *Roster* alone will not determine the unit of James Davis. There are forty-one names in the *Roster* with either James Davis or J. Davis. Now look up Camp Hatton. You will find there were three Georgia units in Camp Hatton, the 36th Regiment, 39th Regiment, and the 43rd Regiment Georgia Volunteer Infantry. Next, write down from the *Roster* the volume and pages for these three regiments. Then go to the index to see how many James and J. Davis' there are in these three regiments. You will find there was only one James Davis in the three Georgia units listed in Camp Hatton. You will now know this James Davis was in Company F, 36th Regiment Georgia Volunteer Infantry. Go back to the *Georgia Roster* and you will find that Company F, organized in DeKalb County, Georgia. To investigate further, check the compiled service records for the 36th Ga. Vol. Inf. and you will find James Davis transferred to Company E, 7th Regiment Georgia Volunteer Infantry, and there is a Robert Davis in this company. Robert very likely is his brother or a close relative and was the reason James transferred to the 7th Ga. Vol. Inf. Further investigation will reveal the answer. This is an actual example from a letter at the Dekalb County Historical Society in Decatur, Georgia.

As mentioned earlier, there were three major training camps in Georgia for troops serving in the Confederate army. They were Camps Davis in Guyton, McDonald at Big Shanty, and Stephens near Griffin. In February of 1862, the State of Georgia received a Requisition from the Confederate Government to raise twelve more infantry regiments. Georgia was able to raise thirteen infantry regiments and two infantry battalions, easily surpassing their requirement. There were companies that organized and had to be turned away because they could not furnish their own arms. Many of these companies during the next few months offered their services to other States and were accepted. During this period Georgia had companies join regiments in Alabama, Tennessee, North Carolina, and South Carolina.

Adjutant and Inspector General, Henry C. Wayne, issued GENERAL ORDER No. 2, dated February 13, 1862, which relates to the Requisition of the Confederate Government upon the State of Georgia for twelve regiments. The following Regulations prescribe which Military Divisions of Georgia were to report to these three camps and form the twelve required regiments. The apportionment of men to be furnished from each county was forwarded to the Clerk of the Superior Courts, who would communicate the same to the respective Commanders of Regiments, Battalions, or Independent Companies on the day they were to march.

Item 10 of GENERAL ORDER No. 2 states:

"Volunteers and drafts throughout the State will report to the camps of instruction as follows:

Those from the 1st, 2nd, 6th and 13th Military Divisions, at Camp Davis, on the Central Railroad, thirty miles above Savannah.

Those from the 3rd, 5th, 8th and 10th Military Divisions at Camp Stephens, near Griffin.

Those from the 4th, 7th, 9th, 11th and 12th Military Divisions at Camp McDonald, seven miles above Marietta on the Western and Atlantic Railroad."[1] These orders applied only to the thirteen regiments and two battalions which reported to these three camps of instruction as a result of GENERAL ORDER No. 2. The regiments which trained at these three training camps as a result of this order were: at Camp Davis, 47th, 48th, 49th, 50th and 51st Regiments Georgia Volunteer Infantry; Camp Stephens, 44th and 45th Regiments, and 10th Battalion Georgia Volunteer Infantry; Camp McDonald, 39th, 40th, 41st, 42nd, 43rd and 52nd Regiments, and 9th Battalion Georgia Volunteer Infantry.

The companies from each Georgia County reported to the three training camps according to the Military Divisions of Georgia,[2] which were:

First Division
First Brigade - Chatham, Bryan, McIntosh, Camden, Wayne, Liberty, Effingham, Glenn, Charlton
Second Brigade - Scriven, Bulloch, Montgomery, Tattnall, Burke, Jefferson
Second Division
First Brigade - Richmond, Columbia, Warren, Glascock
Second Brigade - Washington, Hancock, Taliaferro
Third Division
First Brigade - Morgan, Putnam, Baldwin
Second Brigade - Greene, Oglethorpe
Fourth Division
First Brigade - Wilkes, Lincoln, Elbert, Hart
Second Brigade - Jackson, Franklin, Madison, Banks
Fifth Division
First Brigade - Jones, Jasper
Second Brigade - Henry, Fayette, Butts, Clayton
Sixth Division
First Brigade - Wilkinson, Pulaski, Twiggs, Laurens
Second Brigade - Telfair, Irwin, Appling, Ware, Lowndes, Clinch, Brooks, Coffee, Colquitt, Echols, Berrien, Pierce
Seventh Division
First Brigade - Habersham, Hall, Rabun, White
Second Brigade - Forsyth Lumpkin, Union, Towns, Dawson
Eighth Division
First Brigade - Bibb Crawford, Houston, Dooly, Worth
Second Brigade - Monroe, Upson, Pike, Spalding
Ninth Division
First Brigade - Merriwether, Troup, Heard
Second Brigade.- Coweta, Campbell, Carroll
Tenth Division
First Brigade - Harris Muscogee, Chattahoochee, Stewart, Taylor, Webster
Second Brigade - Talbot, Sumter, Macon, Marion, Schley

---

[1]   *Savannah Daily Morning News*, February 21, 1862

[2]   *Savannah Republican*, February 27, 1862

Eleventh Division

First Brigade - Dekalb, Cobb, Paulding, Polk, Fulton, Harralson
Second Brigade - Newton, Walton, Gwinnett

Twelfth Division

First Brigade - Bartow, Cherokee, Gilmer, Gordon, Fannin, Whitfield, Catoosa, Pickens, Milton
Second Brigade - Floyd, Murray, Walker, Chattooga, Dade

Thirteenth Division

First Brigade - Decatur, Early, Randolph, Clay, Terrell
Second Brigade - Baker, Thomas, Mitchell, Lee, Calhoun, Dougherty, Quitman, Miller, Wilcox

A similar order was issued by John B. Weems, Lt. Col. & A.A.G.., Commanding Camps of Instruction, State of Georgia. This order is as follows:

Headquarters, Camp Randolph, Decatur, Ga.

November 21, 1862. - GENERAL ORDERS, No. 7. - I. On and after Monday, the 24th, my Headquarters will be established at Camp Cooper, near Macon, Ga. Enrolling officers in the 1st, 2d, 3d, 4th and 7th Congressional (not Military) Districts, will communicate directly with me, and will order all Conscripts (draftees) from those Districts to report to me at Camp Cooper.

II. Maj. CHARLES S. HARDEE is assigned to the command of Camp of Instruction known as "Camp Randolph," near Decatur, Georgia. Enrolling officers in the 5th, 6th, 8th, 9th and 10th Congressional Districts, will communicate directly with Major Hardee for information connected with their duties, and will also order all Conscripts from those Districts to Report at his Headquarters.

Jno. B. Weems, Lt. Col. & A.A.G.,
Comd'g Camps of Instruction State of Georgia.[3]

The differences between this order and the previous GENERAL ORDER No. 2, is that Camps Cooper and Randolph were for conscripts or draftees and not volunteers. In other words the men that trained in these two camps most likely were drafted into the army and had not volunteered for military service. Also, the men who were drafted into these training camps could have served in any Georgia unit, artillery, cavalry, or infantry. A number of Georgia units sent recruiting officers to these camps to replace the men who had died or were discharged. The records show that there were possibly a few units that trained at Camp Cooper near Macon, and the Georgia Militia used this camp briefly when they passed through Macon in late 1864. The list of counties within the ten congressional districts is not nearly as beneficial in determining the home county of your ancestor since you can only eliminate about one-half of Georgia's counties. The counties within the ten congressional districts are as follows:

Congressional Districts

First District

Appling,, Bryan, Bulloch, Camden, Charlton, Chatham, Clinch, Coffee, Effingham, Emanuel, Glynn, Liberty, McIntosh, Montgomery, Pierce, Scriven, Telfair, Tattnall, Ware, Wayne

Second District

Baker, Berrien, Brooke, Calhoun, Clay, Colquitt, Decatur, Dooly, Dougherty, Early, Echols, Irwin, Lee, Lowndes, Mitchell, Miller, Randolph, Terrell, Thomas, Wilcox, Worth

---

[3] *Augusta Chronicle & Sentinel,* November 25, 1862

Third District

Chattahoochee, Harris, Macon, Marion, Muscogee, Quitman, Schley, Stewart, Sumter, Talbot, Taylor, Webster

Fourth District

Baldwin, Bibb, Crawford, Houston, Jasper, Jones, Laurens, Pulaski, Putnam, Twiggs, Wilkinson

Fifth District

Burke, Columbia, Glascock, Hancock, Jefferson, Johnson, Lincoln, Richmond, Warren, Washington, Wilkes

Sixth District

Clark, Elbert, Franklin, Greene, Hart, Madison, Morgan, Newton, Oglethorpe, Taliaferro, Walton

Seventh District

Butts, Clayton, Fayette, Henry, Merriwether, Monroe, Pike, Spalding, Troup, Upson

Eighth District

Campbell. Carroll, Cobb, Coweta, DeKalb, Fulton, Haralson, Heard, Paulding, Polk

Ninth District

Banks, Cherokee, Dawson, Forsyth, Gwinnett, Habersham, Hall, Jackson, Lumpkin, Milton, Pickens, Rabun, Towns, Union, White

Tenth District

Cass, Catoosa, Chattooga, Dade, Fannin, Floyd, Gordon, Gilmer, Murray, Walker, Whitfield

There are always factors which make it more difficult to trace the unit of a Georgia soldier by the camp names. One of these is when he writes a letter from a hospital camp. Occasionally these are named such as Camp Winder. It must be determined if the soldier is sick or wounded and writing from a hospital camp. These letters must be eliminated when you try to trace the Georgia unit using the camp names. A Georgia soldier could transfer from one Georgia unit to another, or to a unit in another State, or from a unit in another State to a Georgia unit. All of these situations occurred. Fortunately they were the exception and not the rule.

Off to war

Chapter II

Organizing and Outfitting a Regiment

The wartime governor of Georgia, Joseph E. Brown, didn't waste any time organizing an army and ordering equipment once he felt there would be a conflict with the United States. He ordered guns and other items from manufacturers in the north. The ship *Star of the South* arrived in Savannah's port on January 13, 1861, with $72,000 worth of arms, principally Maynard rifles and revolvers.[1] Some of the Northern manufacturers turned him down immediately and others began to fill his orders before they were stopped by President Lincoln. One order of guns was seized in New York in February, 1861, just before they were loaded aboard a ship for Georgia. Governor Brown retaliated by impounding northern ships in the Savannah harbor and finally released the ships one month later after the guns in New York were loaded on board a ship.[2] In April, 1861, waist belt plates and side belt plates intended for many of the southern States including Georgia were seized at the manufactory of James S. Smith in New York. They were destroyed along with the dies for these plates.[3] It didn't take long for manufacturers in Georgia to receive contracts for the various items needed to outfit and arm the men and boys from Georgia. Governor Brown began to convert the old flintlock muskets in Georgia's arsenal to the more modern and reliable percussion style rifles. This was done both by prisoners at the State Armory in Milledgeville and by gunsmiths throughout the state. Cannon, rifles, sabers, pikes, knives, caissons, saddles, wagons, tents, knapsacks, bridles, spurs, waist belt plates, uniforms, military buttons for the uniforms, hats, shoes, oil cloths, ammunition of all types, powder, and many other items were made in Georgia.

The state of Georgia supplied Georgia's troops with uniforms and shoes early in the war, then later whenever the Confederate government was unable to do so. When cloth for making uniforms or the leather for shoes and other leather goods came in short supply, the state of Georgia had to look elsewhere. Georgia then imported these items from England and other countries to fill this need. More and more items had to be imported to meet the demands of the war. Georgia purchased cannon and the ammunition for the cannon to protect the Georgia coast. Nearly every item came in short supply and had to be purchased outside of the Confederate States. The United States blockaded the Confederate harbors with gun boats, making it difficult to bring the necessary supplies into the southern ports. Running the blockade was dangerous and many supply ships were sunk just as they were approaching the harbors. In 1862 the Confederate government seized 4,800 Enfield rifles which Governor Brown purchased for Georgia's state troops. This created a great deal of controversy between Governor Brown and the Confederate government. A number of these guns were sent by the Confederate government to arm Georgia's Confederate troops in Tennessee.

On January 16, 1861, the same day Georgia's Secession Convention met, the Rattlesnake Club of Savannah paraded through Savannah's principal streets, the band playing the Marseillaise and carrying a banner. "On one side is represented Mason and Dixon's line, with Abe Lincoln in the act of slipping over it from North to South. His progress is met however by a huge rattlesnake, who keeps Abraham on the other side of Jordan. On the reverse are the words: Rattlesnake Club of Savannah - Don't Tread on Me."[4] The excitement moved like wildfire from community to

---

[1]   *Savannah Daily Morning News*, January 15, 1861
[2]   *Savannah Republican*, March 19, 1861
[3]   *Georgia Journal and Messenger*, May 8, 1861
[4]   *Savannah Daily Morning News*, January 16, 1861

community once Georgia's Secession Committee voted to secede. In February, 1861, Jefferson Davis was elected President of the Confederate States of America. The move toward a war was accelerating. The need for an army and navy to defend the Confederacy was now a matter of urgency. Military companies were forming. The majority of Georgia's young men had no military training and depended on the few with military experience or those who wished to take on the responsibility of organizing and training a company. Southern men at West Point Military Academy returned home to help their friends and neighbors organize military companies. Most of the early war companies relied on one of the few available military manuals to instruct them in the various commands and maneuvers necessary to discipline an army. There was a moderate supply of the *Gilham's Manual* (William Gilham, Commandant of Cadets at Virginia Military Institute) at the Georgia arsenal. In response to the many requests, Governor Brown had Adjutant General Henry C. Wayne freight enough manuals for each of the officers of a company to the nearest railroad station where they would pick them up and begin their training. The supply soon gave out requiring the companies to find their own manuals until they could be reprinted. A variety of military manuals including Gilham's could then be found advertised for sale in Georgia newspapers.

The organization and training began in earnest, and those who volunteered and signed up for a company were ordered out to the local fairground, schoolyard or field where they would begin to learn these commands and maneuvers. Often they would meet two or three times a week to drill. A camp was soon established near the drill ground where they would begin to learn about camp duties and drill two or three times a day. A number of these camps were named such as Camp Brown near Talbotton, Camp Linwood in Columbus, or Camps Liberty and Independence in Wilkinson County. By the definition of training camp, these were the earliest training camps.

Governor Brown received a Requisition for 2,000 troops from President Davis on March 16, 1861. The Confederate States Government required a minimum of 65 men and not more than 110 for a company. Their ages had to be between 18 and 45. These restrictions changed as the war continued with fewer men available to fight. A regiment required at least ten companies, and a battalion was less than ten companies. The officers of a regiment were called field officers. The first in command was the colonel, followed by the lt. colonel and major. The staff officers consisted of an adjutant, who assisted in administrative duties, an aide-de-camp who acted as the field officer's confidential assistant and secretary, the doctor, or any other officer acting in an advisory capacity. The commisioned officers of a company usually consisted of a captain, 1st, 2nd and 3rd lieutenants. The non-commisioned officers were 1st, 2nd and 3rd sergeants, and 1st, 2nd and 3rd corporals. Occasionally there were additional sergeants and corporals. A battalion was commanded by either a lt. colonel or a major depending on the size of the battalion. Usually seven to nine companies were commanded by a lt. colonel, and a major commanded two to six companies.

To fill the initial requisition of 2,000 men, Governor Brown ordered a number of companies to rendezvous at Camp Oglethorpe in Macon, on April 3, 1861, to organize and move quickly to Pensacola, Florida. These companies formed the 1st Independent Battalion of Georgia Volunteers, who subsequently became Villepigue's 36th Regiment Georgia Infantry, along with Ramsey's 1st Regiment Georgia Volunteer Infantry. The Washington Artillery from Augusta also arrived on April 3, 1861. The *Macon Telegraph* of April 4, 1861, describes the previous days events:

CAMP OGLETHORPE.

The streets and avenues leading to Camp Oglethorpe were filled with pedestrians, gents on horseback and carriages at an early hour yesterday, and as the day wore along towards the hour fixed for the review, the whole area of the Camp was densely packed with thousands to witness the imposing sight of so many armed men in battle array. But the review by the Governor was postponed, as the election of officers of the Regiment took up so much time that it was found to be impossible to carry out the original programme.

The election passed off in a very quiet manner, as the men voted by companies; that is, each man deposited his vote as his name was called. We give the result in another place. The best of good feeling exists among the different companies, and after their regular drills, merriment is the order of the day. The Oglethorpe Infantry were provided with the new muskets yesterday, in place of the arms which they brought with them. Several other companies were also furnished with the same style musket, although some prefer their old arms; but we understand that this change is made to ensure uniformity in equipment.

The drilling of the different companies was an exciting scene to witness, and sometimes their sudden wheeling was the cause of great confusion, as they would march full upon some unsuspecting crowd of spectators.

THE DRILL

The Washington Rifles, Capt. Jones, were out, and presented an amount of solid material that will strike terror into the hearts of assailants. Capt. Jones has three sons in the company, one whom is Lieutenant. The Bainbridge Independents, Capt. Jno. W. Evans, is a hardy looking lot of men, who will make some folks see sights if war ever does come. They marched sixty miles in a day and a half, under the scorching rays of a Southern sun. If that is not hard to beat we don't know what is.

The Southern Rights Guard, Capt. Houser, were the "observed of all observers" as they marched out to drill, preceded by the Houston Brass Band, which discoursed excellent music while the company was drilling. All the other companies were out, but want of space forbids an extended notice.

The review of the Regiments by the Governor this evening, will undoubtedly draw out a large crowd of spectators.

The 5th Regiment Georgia Volunteer Infantry rendezvoused at Camp Oglethorpe on May 7, 1861, filling the requisition for 2,000 men. They began moving to Pensacola, Florida on May 9.

The election of officers for these companies had taken place earlier at the courthouse of the counties in which they organized, where they would be witnessed by a county official. The captain would then mail a copy of his roster to Governor Brown to accept or reject the company as was needed. The information submitted included the number and type of arms in the company, if the company was uniformed, and in the case of artillery, the number and type of guns and horses. Similar information was submitted for the cavalry companies. Companies which had formed prior to 1861 were accepted first since they were outfitted and trained. Naturally, the expense to the state of Georgia was less for these companies.

The uniforms for the early companies were made both at home and by tailor shops who advertised for their services in the local newspapers. Later they were made by mills such as the Roswell Factory in Roswell, Georgia or the New Manchester Mill at Sweetwater. Occasionally a wealthy citizen or the captain would pay for the uniforms and other supplies needed by the company. The company would then honor the citizen or captain by naming the company after him. The state of Georgia supplied these early troops with modern weapons, many in exchange for their old rifles or muskets. By June, 1861, the supply of guns was nearly gone, and Governor Brown had to stop issuing weapons. The companies which did not have their own arms were rejected. They took their services to other states which had not filled their requisition for troops and were armed by that state.

In October, 1861, Governor Brown organized the Georgia State Troops for the protection of Georgia's coast. They were mustered in for six months and mustered out after their term expired. These companies were accepted only if they brought their own rifles or muskets. When they arrived at their training camps, Camp Harrison or Camp Satilla, a part of them were offered more modern weapons in exchange for their country rifles. At the end of their term they were required to turn in these rifles. The old guns received by the state, were sent to the Georgia arsenal in Milledgeville to be converted to percussion style rifles. After they were converted, they were distributed to portions of the 30th Regiment Georgia Volunteer Infantry, the 8th Battalion Georgia Volunteer Infantry and Smith's Legion. Later the Georgia legislature reimbursed those soldiers who exchanged their old style guns.

Governor Brown and the Confederate government attempted to transfer the Georgia State Troops into Confederate service, but the men voted it down. They joined the state army to protect the state from invasion and did not want to leave the State. As a result of their refusal to be converted to Confederate service, the conscript law was passed which allowed the State to draft eligible men into the Confederate army. Governor Brown and President Davis did not want to lose these men who had been trained and outfitted. As their term expired in March and April, 1862, they began to head home when Ft. Pulaski was attacked on April 10, 1862. Little did the United States realize they were doing Georgia and the Confederate States a service by arousing the southern patriotism once again. Georgia was now under attack. Most of these men now joined the Confederate army as Georgia had just received a requisition for twelve additional regiments. (See information on this requisition in Chapter I, page xx.)

Many supplies were needed such as cooking pots, lanterns, blacksmith tools, axes and other tools. Many of the men brought a folding camp stool. The colonel of the regiment would often have a small desk. Tents were obtained; wagons and horses were required to haul all of their supplies along with their provisions. On occasion they needed to carry enough food for a full regiment of one thousand men to sustain them for a week or longer. Tents were manufactured in Augusta, Georgia, by Stovall, McLaughlin & Co. as early as August of 1861. The following article appeared in the *Augusta Daily Chronicle and Sentinel* on July 13, 1861: "The tents for a single regiment cost not far from $4,000. Twenty-five wagons are required, costing $150 each. The entire expense of equipping a regiment does not fall short of $50,000."

In 1863, Mr. Hargrove of Floyd County submitted to Governor Brown, a calculation of the expenses of a regiment for one year. This applied to a regiment in state service. (A regiment in Confederate service would cost more.)

<pre>
Pay of Colonel and Staff $15,402
Pay of Captains 15,600
Pay of First Lieutenants 10,800
</pre>

Pay of Second Lieutenants	19,200
Pay of Orderly Sergeants	11,600
Pay of other non-commisioned officers	20,640
Pay of 900 Privates, including rations	384,600
Cost of wagons and horses	17,400
Cost of tents	2,500
Cost of guns, ammunition and transportation	229,000

Total $726,742

Mr. Cabaniss, another representative, stated that from information he had obtained in military quarters, the cost of maintaining a Regiment of 1,000 men, for pay and subsistence, was $872,955 per annum.[1]

An article from the *Southern Confederacy* Newspaper of Atlanta, dated January 7, 1862, described the wagon train of the 24th Regiment Georgia Volunteer Infantry. "This regiment, made up of companies from North-East Georgia, and under the command of Col. Robt. McMillan, of Habersham, rendezvoused here last August. Our citizens will no doubt recollect that long train of 75 wagons, mostly from Habersham county, that brought their arms and baggage to this place."

Another article from the *Southern Confederacy* dated November 19, 1862, taken from the *Abington Virginian*, Abington, Virginia, told of the expense of the 9th Battalion Georgia Light Artillery.

> Ninth Georgia Battalion. - This Battalion of artillery, under command of Maj. Leyden, left this place on Tuesday last, for a distant field of operation: It was really an imposing sight to see the long line of guns, caissons and forges, each with six horses attached, followed by a long train of ambulances and baggage wagons -- stretching out at least a mile. Some idea of the immense expense of an army may be arrived at, when an Artillery Battalion, comprising only about 200 men, requires 60 bushels of corn and 1400 pounds of hay per day for its horses.

Every wagon required a driver and men to repair them when they broke down; the horses needed reshoeing. Before long there were men who could not march due to illness or injury and had to be carried by a wagon. It was not uncommon for a wagon to break down, an axle broke or the horses were too exhausted to pull the wagon. The wagon trains moved through rain storms, snow, or in the dry weather stirred up dust clouds that could be seen for miles. Occasionally the mud would come up to the axles, and the men would have to push the wagons along, many men losing their shoes in the mud. As the wagons broke down, something had to be left behind. Usually the tents were the first item to be disposed of. On occasion all of the tents were burned because the wagons were needed to carry the ammunition, sick and wounded, and burning kept the tents from the enemy. There were times the men had to clear a place in the snow to rest or sleep for lack of tents. A bush arbor became a favored spot to protect themselves from the snow and wind. If they had a blanket or oil cloth, it might be their only means of protection from the elements.

---

[1]   *Rome Weekly Courier*, May 1, 1863

Now, let it rain!
Camp Fires of the Confederacy, Edited by Ben LaBree

As the war continued it became increasingly difficult to raise companies and regiments. Ads were placed in local newspapers. Posters were placed around the towns by prospective captains asking that volunteers sign up at the local newspaper office or some other business establishment. The following ad came from the *Augusta Daily Chronicle and Sentinel*:

A SECOND

OGLETHORPE ARTILLERY

COMPANY

MORE RECRUITS WANTED

The Oglethorpe Artillery

Have been authorized by proper
authority, to raise a second AR-
TILLERY COMPANY, to be attached to Major Capers' Artillery Battalion, now in Camp at Augusta.
Officers to be elected. Applications must be made to

J. V. H. ALLEN, Capt.

Office in rear of Jas. Miller's Dry
Goods Store.

Once a soldier was mustered into the Confederate army, it became the responsibility of the Confederate government to arm him if he did not possess a weapon, furnish his ammunition, train him, clothe him, provide the necessary provisions and proper leadership. Georgia assisted the

Confederate government in virtually all of these areas when it was apparent the men needed assistance. Governor Brown   addressed   the state Senate and House of Representatives on November 6, 1862. One of the items he addressed was the clothing for the Georgia troops which he read:

> Information of the most authentic character has been received from the army, which verifies the report that many of the Georgia troops in Confederate service are almost destitute of clothing and shoes and must suffer terribly this winter if speedy relief is not afforded. This suffering should not be permitted by the people of the State as long as we are able to raise a dollar for their relief. I have recommended the Georgia Relief and Hospital Association to draw and expend for clothes and shoes for the most destitute, the remaining portion of the appropriation which they have not had the occasion to use for hospital purposes.

He further recommended if satisfactory arrangements could not be made with the proprietors of Georgia's factories and tanneries, that the state seize them until a good pair of shoes and a suit of clothes be furnished the destitute soldiers.[1]

The towns and communities of Georgia organized soldiers' aid societies and sent train car loads of clothing, blankets and provisions for the soldiers from their communities. There was the Soldiers' Way - Side Home in Union Point, Georgia which gave aid to soldiers passing through Georgia. Some of them were sick or wounded. The following is one example of the many that were published in Georgia's newspapers. This list of donations is very similar to the list of donations to the soldiers aid societies. This article appeared in the *Augusta Daily Chronicle and Sentinel* of October 30, 1862.

Weekly Contributions

To Wayside Home, Union Point, ending Sunday, Oct. 26th, 1862.

Mrs. Jas. Dolvin, 1 doz. candles, 1 doz. eggs, 1 basket tomatoes.
Mrs. W.B. Dolvin, 1 basket potatoes.
W.M. Mandeville, Athens, $1.
J. Wilkerson,   " $1.
Albon Chase,   " $1.
Hon. Junius Hilyer, Athens. $5.
Vice Pres't. A.C. Stephens, Athens. $20.
J.J. Martin, Tuskeegee, Ala., $10.
Mr. James, 5 chickens.
Mrs. R.G. Carlton, 1 qr. lamb.
W. A. Corry, 1 shoat.
Mrs. P. Thornton. 1 loaf bread, 1 basket pies.
Mrs. Fred Devant, 1 doz. chickens.
Alfred Grant, cash, $2.
Wm. Daniel, 1 bag rice.
Mr. Asa Rhodes, 1 basket potatoes, 1 bacon ham.
Mrs. Laura Malone, Penfield, 1 jar butter.
Mrs. John Dolvin, 6 chickens, 1 doz. eggs.

---

[1]   *Augusta Daily Chronicle & Sentinel*, November 9, 1862

Mrs. Johnson Boswell, 1 bucket lard, 1 doz. eggs.
Mrs. Wm. Brooks, 3 chickens.
Miss. Julia Wagnon, 1 loaf light bread.
Miss. Wildred Sanford, 1/2 doz. candles and catsup.
Miss Georgia Sanford, 1 bag dried fruit.
Mrs. Dan'l. Sanford, 1 pillow, 1 bag flour.
Hon. Joshua Hill, Madison, cash, $5.
Col. L.J. Gartrell, Rome, cash, $10.
J.M. Briton, $2.
Col. M.C. Fulton, 1 bacon side.
Brig. Gen'l. M. Jeff Thompson, $10.
Mrs. Dr. T.P. Jones, Penfield, 50 lbs. flour, 1 bush. meal, 20 lbs. lard, 14 lbs. butter, 1 bag fruit, 1 1/2 bush. potatoes, 1/2 bush. peas, 1 doz. cabbage, 2 doz. ears green corn, 1 basket tomatoes, 1 ham, 5 lbs. sugar, 1/2 lb. black tea.
Mrs. B.A. Davis, 6 chickens.
Mrs. H.M. Houghton, 1 loaf bread.
Mrs. Spencer, Penfield, 2 pr. socks, 2 shirts, 1 pr. drawers, 1 bdle. bandages.
Miss. Susan Goodman, 1 pr. socks.
Mrs. Henry English, 1 pr. socks, 1 bdle. bandages, 1 towel, 1 basket apples, 1 basket tomatoes.
Mrs. Tiller, Woodville, 2 chickens, 1 basket potatoes, sage and pepper.
Miss. A.H. Newsome, 1 pr. socks.
Mrs. Sarah Cox, 2 chickens.
Mrs. T.R. Thornton, 1 bucket butter.
Mrs. E.C. Bowden, 1 qr. lamb, 1 basket potatoes.
Mrs. Spencer, 1 lot wine.
Mrs. Wm. Daniel, 1 loaf bread.
P.W. Printup, half doz. Catawpa wine.
Mrs. P.W. Printup, 1 basket cake, loaf bread.
Gen. Howell Cobb, $50.
Hentierson, cash $4.
Mrs. R.G. Carlton, 1 bag Irish potatoes.
Miss Sallie F. Shackelford, Lexington, 1 jar pickles.
Mrs. George Moore, Oglethorpe County, 1 basket cooked provisions.
Mrs. Haynes, Oglethorpe, 2 bottles wine and pies.
Mrs. Henry Edmondson, 1 basket provisions, 1 quilt, 1 jug milk.
Master W.A. Shackelford, Lexington, 50 cents.
Mrs. Rebecca E. Shackelford, Lexington, $1.
Miss Mary E. Shackelford, Lexington, 50 cents.
Master Charles P. Shackelford, 50 cents.
Master Floyd S. Shackelford, 50 cents.
Mrs. D.P. Parham, 1 pr. sheets, 1 jar pickles, 2 doz. eggs, 1 gal. vinegar.
A wounded Tennessean, $5.
Capt. John D. Ferrell, $2.
W.F. Mattox, 50 cents.
Judge Brightwell, Oglethorpe County, $10.
Mrs. Wm. Gunn, Taliaferro County, 1 loaf bread.
Thompson & Vincent, 10 lbs. beef.
Mrs. F.M. Leverett, 4 chickens, 2 doz. eggs.

Mrs. L.D. Carlton, 1 qr. lamb.

Mrs. H.C. Peek, 1 bottle honey.

Mrs. Wm. Brooks, 1 bottle wine, 1 bag fruit, 1 bucket lard, 1 basket potatoes, 2 loaves
bread, 1 bundle linen, 1 bundle bandages.

Mrs. H.F. Bunkley, 20 lbs. flour, 20 lbs. beef, 1 bottle wine, 1 bag potatoes.

Mrs. Cocroft, 16 lbs. beef, 6 chickens, 1 ham, 1 roll bandages.

Mrs. Joel Early, 1 bag flour, 1 jar lard.

Mrs. Billingsles, Greensboro, 1 bag meal, 1 bag potatoes, 1 doz. eggs, 1 basket chickens, 2
pitchers milk.

Mrs. C.W. Gill, 1 basket potatoes.

————

Union Point, Oct. 27, 1862.

Mr. Editor.: - Will you please to publish our weekly contribution list in your journal, also some resolutions, and letters that you will find enclosed. During the past week we have administered unto 803 of our way-worn and war-worn soldiers.

Yours Truly,

Jenny Hart, Sec'y and Treas'r.

Nearly everyone was involved in trying to raise money or assistance for the men at war or in the hospitals in Virginia or elsewhere. Concerts or tableaux were held at a number of concert halls or schools all over Georgia. In March of 1864, the Temperance Hall in Columbus offered the Confederate Nightingales to entertain for the benefit of the Nelson Rangers, and on June 30th, 1864 offered Madam Ballini and Little Ella Montgomery for the benefit of the sick and wounded soldiers. The following ad appeared in the *Central Georgian*, Sandersville, Georgia, on September 18, 1861.

**Grand Entertainment for the Soldiers'
Fund.**

By request of our Ladies Association, Prof. J.J. Gorres will give a grand and fine entertainment at Washington Institute, Linton, Hancock County, on Thursday, September 26th, at 6 o'clock, P.M.

PROGRAMME.

Performance of the Linton Brass Band.

Solos and Duetts for Piano and Violin.

Solos, Duetts, and chorus in vocal music.

Tableaux, Dialogues and Declamation.

Grand Battle, Soldiers' dress parade.

Tableaux of Bull Run - Cannonading and illuminative Comic Scene - Washington taken - Lincoln and his Cabinet - Old Scott scared to death and taken Prisoner (with illumination) - Grand Victory.

Tableaux closing with chorus song Dixie, accompanied by the Brass Band.

A particular programme will be seen in the Institution.

Persons from a distance will be accommodated in the village by the ladies of the society.

Admission 50 cents - Children 25 cents.

Mrs. E.V. Adams,
Mrs. M. Reaves,
Miss A. Stone,   Com'te.
Miss V. Adams,

The list of contributors diminished as the war grew longer, and food was in short supply at home even though many farmers changed from planting cotton to planting food crops. The demand for medical supplies increased as the battles were devastating to Georgia's young men.

As early as late 1863, the stories in the letters told of regiments having as many as one-half of their men without shoes. They left blood-stained footprints in the snow and ice in northeast Tennessee when they were with General Longstreet. Similar occurrences were reported in the Army of Northern Virginia. Their clothes were tattered and patched so many times you could not find any remnants of the original garment. The supply of clothes, shoes and blankets was nearly gone. The few that became available were distributed by drawing names. On May 9, 1864, Governor Brown wrote President Davis asking clearance for the steamer *Little Ada*, loaded with 300 bales of cotton. He had purchased 30,000 blankets for the state of Georgia and was sending the cotton to pay for them. The blankets were in the islands below Florida.[1] It is believed that these blankets never reached Georgia or were used by any of Georgia's troops.

By 1864, the only men available to answer the call for the Georgia militia, and assist the Confederate troops defend Georgia, were young boys, old men and Confederate soldiers who had been discharged from the Confederate army because they were too sickly or disabled. The workers in Georgia's military factories who were previously exempt from military service were organized into companies and regiments. The Arsenal Battalion from Columbus helped defend Atlanta, and returned to their factories within a couple of weeks to continue making guns and military supplies.

Sherman's campaign in Georgia effectively ended the majority of the manufacturing in Georgia. There were typically only fifteen to twenty-five battle-worn and ragged men left in a regiment of a thousand proud men to answer the roll call at Appomattox.

---

[1] *War of the Rebellion, Official Records of the Union and Confederate Armies*, Series IV, Volume 3, p. 402

Chapter III

Where the Names of Georgia's Camps Originated

The names of Georgia's camps began with every letter in the alphabet except the letters Q, U, and X, beginning with Camp Adams and ending with Camp Zollicoffer, both of these camps being in Chatham County, Georgia. There was no other place where Georgia troops had such a concentration of named camps. Most of these camps are now in residential areas or under industrial developments, as are the majority of the camps listed in this book.

Georgia's first camp of the Southern Confederacy was Camp Farley, named for Mr. James A. Farley in Montgomery, Alabama, who allowed the Columbus Guards to camp on his property while they were attending President Jefferson Davis's inauguration. The earlier camps could certainly be considered Confederate camps beginning with the date Georgia seceded.

The source of most camp names is obvious, others are only speculative and may never be known such as Camp Terrell near Orange Courthouse, Virginia, camp of the 44th Regiment Georgia Volunteer Infantry. Could it have been named for Dr. Terrill who had a farm near Orange Courthouse or named after one of the prominent Terrell families of Georgia?

The majority of the camp names came from military leaders and political leaders living or dead. President Davis had fourteen camps named in his honor, with General W.H.T. Walker having eleven in his name. General Thomas (Stonewall) Jackson had twelve camps named in his honor, with nine Camp Lees, and eight Camp Bartows. General Francis Bartow probably was the most admired Georgia military leader. These are all camps which Georgia troops occupied. There were many other camps named after these leaders that were occupied by troops from other States. Many of the camp names in this book were named after property owners or plantations such as Camp Adams or Camp Bonna Bella in Chatham County, Georgia.

There were many camps named for the location of the camp such as Camp Knoxville, Camp Mason's Hill or Camp Waller's Tavern. Some of these camp names may not have been the official names given to the camps, but they were taken from a letter or document and were recorded as such.

A number of camps were named for women. No doubt some were named for wives of the commanders and others for family members. General Howell Cobb named several camps in honor of women in his family. Camp Jenny Hart was named for the secretary and treasurer of the Wayside Home at Union Point, Georgia. Camp Paulina was named after the secretary of the Ladies Volunteer Association in Athens, Georgia.

The mood of the troops certainly was a factor for camp names such as Camp Despair, Dismal, Hardship, Hardtimes, Miserable, Pleasant, Precarious or Camp Trouble.

There were a few with humorous names such as Camp Fanny H___, Grease Gut, Pinch Gut, or Polecat. Another was the Camp Chickabiddy Chokee.

Apparently the British found the reports after the Battle of Manassas on July 21, 1861, a bit humorous. This article was published in the *Augusta Daily Chronicle and Sentinel*, August 29, 1861.

    Punch's Account of the "Change of Base." --
A copy of the London Punch, lately received, contains the following veritable account of McClellan's grand strategic movement:

Punch's Office, No. 85 Fleet St.,
July 26, 1862.

(Latest American Dispatch -- By Horsemarine Telegraph.)

Camp Chickabiddy Chokee, Monday afternoon.

The Federal troops have won another splendid victory. Seeing that the rebels were approaching in great force at 6 A.M., this morning, I issued my directions for a general advance, an order which our brave fellows were prompt to carry out. The advance was made in the identical direction as that in which the rebel army were proceeding, and was achieved, I need not say, with the most success. Astonishing to say, the whole of our front line escaped without a hurt, and, with the exception of a few slight wounds and bruises in the rear, I really have no casualties worth mention to report. A good deal of baggage and some few hundred stand of arms we left upon the field for a strategic purpose; and we likewise abandoned about a score of field pieces, which were found to impede the rapid movement of our troops.

My next dispatch will probably be dated from Richmond, which I intend to take at half past 5 o'clock precisely on Saturday morning next.

(Signed)   Bunkum, Gen'l Com'g.

To the Secretary of War, Washington.

If you are researching camps for other States, you will find Georgia camp names will not always apply for troops from other States occupying the same camp. Information shows Camp Allegheny to the Georgia troops was named Camp Baldwin by the Virginia troops.[1] Camp Willcoxon at Bluffton, South Carolina was Camp Jackson to the 4th Regiment South Carolina Cavalry.[2]

You will find many of the camps listed in the book will have the source of the camp name identified with it's history, or will be obvious from the description of the camp's location.

---

[1] 1966 thesis of Edward M. Keller, Wheeling College

[2] *Saddle Soldiers*, by Lloyd Halliburton

Chapter IV

Types, Sizes, and Durations of Camps

There seems to be a great deal of misunderstanding of the various types of camps. I will cover ten different types of camps in alphabetical order and define them as I perceive them. The different types of camps have been derived from my observations and study and are not from a military manual. This information is not definitive and as any serious student knows, there could be, and were, any combination of these camps. Quite often the type of camp will dictate the size and duration of the camp. The theater of operation also dictated the size of the camp.

Bivouac:
A bivouac is a temporary camp, generally without the use of tents. This is the simplest of all camps. An army or even a company would move over great distances, making it impractical to pitch a tent every night. Typically they would move from eight to twenty-five miles in a day. A march of one hundred miles could take from four days to as many as seven or eight. The weather, condition of the roads and health of the men would dictate the distance.

A bivouac would be located immediately next to the road, and on occasion the men would sleep on the road. Wood and water, the two major considerations for the location of any camp, would not be as important as in any other type of camp. Water could be obtained each day as they crossed a stream, or they would dip water from a well on the side of the road. Three days rations would have been prepared prior to making a long march, so the wood necessary for cooking would not be a factor. If the movement of the troops lasted longer than three days, the consideration for wood and water, would become a factor.

The size of the camp would be dictated by the troop movement and generally would not last more than a few days.

Conscript Camps:
Georgia had two conscript camps as described in Chapter I, Camp Cooper, also known as Camp of Instruction No. 1, in Macon, and Camp Randolph, also known as Camp of Instruction No. 2, in Decatur, Georgia. These camps were intended to train soldiers who were drafted, or conscripted into military service. Georgia troops did not organize or train as a unit in these camps as a general rule. Recruiting officers of various Georgia units would be sent to these camps from their regiments in Virginia or elsewhere. They would try to replace the men lost to the regiment due to illness or death. These camps were also used by troops passing through these areas as a temporary camp.

Since these were permanent camps, the location would be important. Wood and water were major factors for its location as was also proper drainage. A gentle slope on firm ground would be selected. The sinks would be located one to two hundred yards downwind from the camp.

The size of the camps varied from only a few men to a full regiment in the camp. Camp Cooper was established on November 24, 1862, and the 1st Regiment Georgia Light Duty used the camp as late in the war as October 26, 1864. Camp Randolph was established on November 21, 1862, and records show it was used as late as March of 1864.

Camp of Convalescents:

These camps were also used as exchange camps. Men who had been wounded in battle and could convalesce without surgery would use this type camp. It would also be used by men who had surgery and were now recovering to the point they needed very little assistance.

This item from the *Knoxville Register* of October 15, 1862, describes one purpose of the camp.

HEADQUARTERS, Department E. Tenn.
Knoxville, Sept. 28th, 1862.

General Orders No. 3.

I. All officers and soldiers within the limits of this Department, who have been captured and paroled by the enemy, will immediately report in person, to Captain Kain, commanding Camp of Convalescents at this place to have their exchange perfected.

By command of: Maj. Gen. S. Jones.

Chas. S. Stringfellow, A. A. G.

Camp Lee at Richmond was also used for this purpose. Many of the soldiers who were captured at Champion Hill or Vicksburg ended up at Camp Lee after their parole and exchange. A number of letters with the caption of Camp Lee, Richmond, Va., were written by soldiers who were from the Army of Mississippi or Army of Tennessee.

The size of the camp varied as men arrived and were discharged according to their physical condition. This camp probably lasted about one year.

Camp of Direction:

After a general movement by an army, a camp was established to assist the various departments of the army and keep it organized. It was also used to help soldiers who had become separated from their command to make contact and rejoin their unit. There is evidence of several Camps of Direction.

This order published in the *Chattanooga Daily Rebel*, on September 26, 1862, clearly describes the purpose of this type camp.

Orders Commander of the Post.
Headquarters C.S. Forces,
Chattanooga, September 23d, 1862.

SPECIAL ORDERS,
No. 1.

I. In order to facilitate officers and soldiers anxious to join their commands it is ordered as follows:

II. All officers and soldiers arriving at Chattanooga will report to Major St. Paul, at the camp of "Direction," Surgeons and assistants will report to Surgeon Flewellyn, Medical Director. Quartermasters and assistants will report to Major Thomas, Post Quartermaster. Commissarys and assistants will report to Capt. Francis, Post Commissary.

III. The men in Camp of Direction will be divided into three temporary divisions to wit:

Those belonging to Buckner and Anderson's divisions will constitute the right wing; those belonging to Withers, Cheathams and Kirby Smith's divisions will constitute the left wing. The cavalry, mounted and dismounted, and the artillery will constitute the reserve.

IV. Captains or Lieutenants of Companies, belonging to either of these two divisions, will upon reporting to the commander of Camp Direction, be authorized to enroll from amongst the men of these respective divisions of not less than 120 men, and report the names of the officers of said companies to the Camp Commander.

V.   As soon as said companies are formed, they will be armed and equipped, and forwarded to Knoxville, there to report as follows:

Those belonging to the right wing to the officer commanding the right battalion of the light brigade commanded by Lt. Col. Whitfield, and those belonging to the left wing to the officer commanding the left wing of said brigade.

VI.   The artillery and cavalry will report to Lieut. Col. Whitfield for further orders.

VII.   A commissioned officer will be detailed to examine the passes of all persons leaving Chattanooga by the different railroads. Any officer or soldier leaving without a pass from these headquarters will be arrested and ordered to report to the Provost Marshall.

By command of Alex. McKinstry, Col. Commd'g.
JOHN L. CHANDLER,
A. A. G. Gen'l.

The size of this camp varied as men were directed to their commands. This camp lasted less than a year.

Encampment:

An encampment is a temporary camp where the soldiers would pitch their tents or build some type of shelter if tents were not available. Buildings such as barracks might be used as was the case at Camp Winder in Richmond, prior to their being converted to a hospital. There were times that a tent or any type of cover was not available to protect them from the weather.

One of the major misconceptions of most students on the War Between the States is that a camp would be in a concentrated area. The map of Camp Bartow on the Greenbrier River is a good example. Both the 1st and 12th Regiments Georgia Volunteer Infantry called this Camp Bartow even though their camps were over one mile apart. In the case of Camp Hatton in Tennessee, the camp was spread out over several miles. A letter from a soldier at Camp McDonald said the camp was strung out over six miles with tents pitched on any ground large enough to hold a tent.

The site selected would have access to water, and wood was necessary for cooking and shelters. The camp might be close to the major road or set back away from the road as much as a quarter of a mile. If the camp was close to a town, the site selected would generally be a mile or more from the citizens in the town. It would not be easily exposed to view from the main road since the men could be rowdy or noisy. The ground would typically be on a gentle slope to allow water to drain easily.

The tents or shelters would be aligned, arranged by companies, with named streets. Campfires would be built in front of each tent, or in a designated cooking area, to prepare their provisions and to keep the men warm. These campfires would allow the men to write their letters at night when the activity of the camp had ceased. If water was not immediately available, wells would be dug at the end of each row of tents.

In colder weather a fireplace might be built next to the tent from stones or sticks covered with mud. A barrel might be used for the chimney. A fire could be built in the tent by digging a hole and placing the fire in the hole. A trench would run from the fire over to the fireplace or chimney, and the trench would then be covered with rocks.

To protect the men from wet weather, they might build a mound as high as six to twelve inches and pitch their tent on it. A trench might be dug around the tent to allow the water to drain away. If boards were available, the tent would have a wood floor. The wood planks would become prized possessions and occasionally moved from camp to camp if room was available on the wagons. In Savannah, wagons would be sent back to the old camps to retrieve the planks used as flooring.

Stalls would be built for the horses from logs or boards taken from a nearby barn or vacated building.

Drilling or training did not stop once they were in camp. Recruits needed to learn the commands, but most importantly, it was a mean of controlling or keeping discipline in the camps. The roll was called each time they were drilled to see if any of the men had taken French leave or deserted.

An encampment in Virginia could contain nearly a whole army of 20,000 to 40,000 men and last for a few days or a few weeks. An encampment on the coast of Georgia could contain only a company of less than one hundred men to as many as 5,000 men and last from a few days to several months. The longest encampment recorded in these records was Camp Jackson in Virginia, of the 4th Regiment Georgia Volunteer Infantry. It lasted nearly one year.

Extracts from letters describing the camps will be scattered throughout the list of camps.

Hospital Camp:

The hospital camp was one of the most dreaded camps of all. The men often wrote home that they would rather be in battle than go to the hospital. When an arm or leg was hit by a bullet or shell fragment, the arm or leg was usually amputated. The chance of recovery was slim.

The hospital camp would usually get the best tents. A wall tent was the most common. Later in the war any type of tent was acceptable. The men with contagious diseases would be separated from the wounded or those convalescing from a minor illness.

Water was a major consideration for the location of a hospital camp. Wounds were washed daily to keep down infection.

The hospital camps varied from a few tents to as many as three or four barracks in Richmond, Virginia. The hospital camps were used throughout the war.

Camp of Instruction:

Just as the name infers, this is the camp where the men were trained. Officers with military experience would teach the men the maneuvers necessary to control the men in battle or simply move around from one place to another. They would also learn camp duties which were new to many of the young men.

The men who trained at Camp McDonald or Camp Stephens in Georgia, also organized their battalion or regiment in these camps. Many Georgia units were ordered to rendezvous in Atlanta and organize. They would vote for the officers of the regiment, organize the unit, and immediately be assigned to one of the training camps in Virginia such as Camp Lee in Richmond, or Camp Davis in Lynchburg.

The earliest training camps in Georgia had less than one hundred men in the camp. The largest training camps, Camp Davis, Camp McDonald and Camp Stephens would have as many as about 4,500 men in the camp at one time. Camp Davis was used as a training camp for about six weeks. Camp McDonald was used for training a little over one year, and Camp Stephens was used for training just under one year. Later in the war these camps were also used for temporary camps as troops passed through the areas.

Picket Camp:

The purpose of a picket was to prevent the enemy from attacking the army by surprise or preventing parties of the enemy from observing the movements and defenses of his army. On the coast of Georgia the pickets would also alert the plantation owners and help prevent their slaves from escapimg to the enemy where they could advise the enemy of troop strengths, movements and defenses.

A picket station on the coast of Georgia would consist of one cavalry officer and five or six cavalrymen. In Virginia an entire regiment could be used as pickets. These are the extremes and could vary anywhere in between. Some of the picket posts on the coast were used for nearly the whole war, where in Virginia they would be used as long as the army was in the area.

The pickets were in the most dangerous position of all. Quite often they were within sight of the enemy and would occasionally converse with the picket of the enemy. There were times they would challenge each other to see which man was the best shot. Occasionally a picket was killed by playing this game. Some of the most interesting stories are told by the men at these stations.

The following stories involve Georgia soldiers in Virginia. The first is an extract of a letter dated August 18, 1862, to the editor of the *Augusta Chronicle & Sentinel*. It was written by an unidentified member of the Richmond Hussars, Co. B, at New Market Heights, Virginia, and appeared in the Augusta newspaper August 20, 1862.

> We have a very agreeable time now with the enemy's pickets, as the practice of shooting at one another while on post has been stopped, by mutual agreement. At two points on our line, the pickets are not more than 50 yards apart, and some times engaged in conversation. While on post there yesterday, the Yankee picket sang several songs for our benefit, and then called for one from some of our boys. Sergent Wm. H. Jones responded, and gave them the "Bonnie Blue Flag," which they greeted with applause.

The second story was reported by a correspondent of the New York *Tribune*.

> Sport Among the Pickets. - A correspondent of the N. Y. *Tribune,* in McClellan's army, relates the following:
> During the first day's skirmish on our right, two soldiers, one from Maine, the other from Georgia, posted themselves each behind a tree, and indulged in sundry shots, without effect on either side, at the same time keeping up a lively chat. Finally, that getting a bit tedious, Georgia calls out to Maine, "Give me a show," meaning step out and give an opportunity to hit. Maine, in response, pokes out his head a few inches, and Georgia cracks away and misses. "Too high," says Maine. "Now give me a show." Georgia pokes out his head, and Maine blazes away. "Too low," sings Georgia. In this way the two alternated several times, without hitting. Finally Maine sends a ball so as to graze the tree within an inch or two of the ear of Georgia. "Cease firing," shouts Georgia. "Cease it is," responds Maine. "Look here," says one. "we have carried on this business for one day. 'Spose we adjourn for rations?" "Agreed," says the other. And so the two marched away in different directions, one whistling "Yankee Doodle," the other "Dixie."

Picket Support Camp:

The picket support camp would be located within a few miles of the pickets. From my observations, they were about five to six miles away, or where they could easily respond or support the pickets. The response time is the key. The cavalry might be located a little further from the picket post. When General Wheeler was moving ahead of the Union Army in South Carolina, he ordered his men to camp two miles from the videttes. This way his men could respond quickly and easily support his men on picket duty.

Another purpose for this camp was to rotate the pickets daily or on a regular basis with men who were rested.

The size of the picket support camp would vary in proportion to the size of the picket post. One company would generally support six or seven men on the coast of Georgia, while a regiment would support a company on picket in Virginia.

Winter Camp:

As the roads became impassable in the colder weather, the army had no choice but to slow down. The wagons would mire up in the mud and the artillery became useless. Most of the fighting done in the winter was done by the cavalry in minor skirmishes. The fighting continued in Florida and in the warmer climates.

Since the men could not move around it became necessary to built more substantial quarters for the men and better stalls for the horses. The only difference in a winter camp from an encampment is that the men would build log huts to protect them from the cold winter air and snow. The major troop movements would come to a stop for about two or three months or as long as the weather dictated. The daily drills would be reduced as weather permitted.

The winter camps varied in size from the western theater to the eastern theater. In Virginia a winter camp would commonly have a brigade of three to five regiments in the same camp, while in Georgia the winter camp may have as many as three regiments in the same camp. During the Georgia campaign of 1864, the winter camps in Dalton would be as large as brigade size.

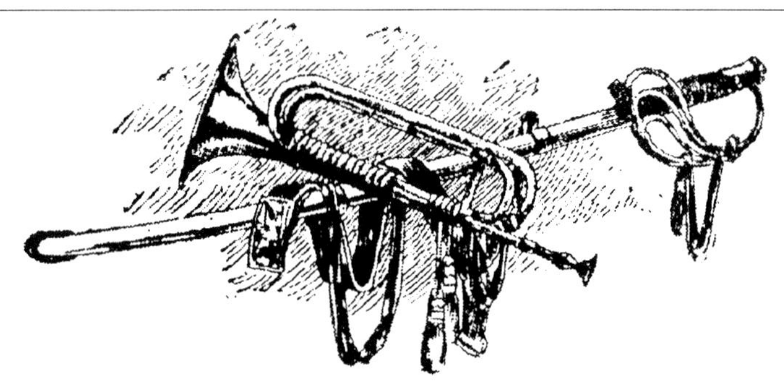

Chapter V

Camp Activities

One of the more important activities in camp was to organize the company, battalion or regiment. Electing the officers was the first task of the company or unit. A description of the organization of a regiment or battalion was described in Chapter II in the article on Camp Oglethorpe. As in any organization, the results did not always satisfy everyone. On occasion the discontented might try to stir up trouble in the unit which might result in a court-martial for those involved. If the commanding officer felt the offense was serious enough, the soldier could be drummed out of the unit. The most serious offenses could result in the soldier being shot by a firing squad.

As the men became more accustomed to each other they would organize baseball games, play chess from the chess pieces carved from bullets, play checkers, or if playing cards were available, play one of the many card games. Gambling was discouraged, and in most camps outlawed. Most men had a pocket knife and carved a number of items from the trees in the area, or from bullets. Rings were the most popular item sent home. Books from home were passed around until the pages were so ragged they could not be read. Newspapers from home were also passed around from one tent to another. The news from the battlefields of Arkansas to the battlefields of Virginia might take a few days or two to three weeks if the trains were delayed. Many of the men wrote letters to the editors of their newspapers to let the people from home know how many of the men were sick, who had died, or the latest outcome from a battle. A number of extracts from these letters are included in the chapter on camps. Most of the men remained anonymous when they wrote to the newspapers, since there were orders to keep the men from revealing their position or the strength of the army in their letters home. Mail trains were captured on occasion.

When it was time to elect the governor of the state of Georgia, the men would write their vote on a piece of paper, and drop the vote in a hat as their name was called from the roll. The results were sent to the local newspaper and printed in the earliest issue.

Once or twice a day, and when weather permitted, the men were on the parade ground learning the orders necessary for controlling a large group of men when their movements were most important in battle. Drilling was a daily affair, and served several purposes. Roll was generally called to make sure there had not been any desertions or men on French leave. Punishment for these offenses varied with the degree of the offense. The offender might be required to serve extra guard duty or was shot by a firing squad if caught deserting to the enemy.

The procedure for an execution was to march the men from the unit of the man to be executed into what was termed a "hollow square." Three sides of a square were lined with the men of the unit, with the man to be executed in the center of the fourth side. The names of twelve men were drawn to become the firing squad. The twelve men each chose a rifle, of which six were loaded with a bullet, and six loaded with blanks. None of the men knew if he had a rifle with a ball. The man to be executed had the choice of a blindfold, and could be tied to a tree, standing on the edge of his grave or sitting on the edge of the box in which he was to be buried. A minister would say a prayer for the condemned man. Orders were given: Ready-- Aim-- Fire! The condemned was no more.

Early in the war, when the Army of Northern Virginia lived in tents, an occasional keg of 'juniper juice' was sent to the Georgians by considerate friends at home, and in camp eternal vigilance was the security of the "fire-water." The soldiers of the -th Louisiana often drank this liquor in their own quarters. They managed to get possession in this way: One of their number, who was remarkable for a chronic black eye and a battered nose was known as the *sacrifice man.* His business was to make a bold effort to steal the liquor from the front of the tent, in which, of course, he would be detected, and while he patiently received his well-deserved punishment his confederate would roll out the keg from the rear of the tent.

The sacrifice man
Camp Fires of the Confederacy, Edited by Ben LaBree

Cooking in camp might be done by a servant, if the soldier was wealthy, or typically it was done by one of the men in the mess. The duty of cooking might be rotated on a weekly basis or one of the mess could volunteer to cook in exchange for another man in the mess taking the cook's picket duty or camp guard duty.

The food sent from home was usually divided among the men in the mess. Food was also sent to the men from one of the several soldiers aid societies and divided as were the clothes and the many other items. If the camp was close enough to a large creek or river, and permission given, fishing would often produce a meal or two. On the coast the men would gather oysters or clams and prepare them in a number of ways. Hunting for deer or other game fed a number of men for several days.

As the war continued, it became more difficult to feed the Army. Shortages of food were commonplace as early as the second year of the war. Wagons to transport the food were difficult to obtain. Horses and mules were used to move the more essential items of warfare, ammunition and cannon. Foraging for food was a necessity for the survival of many. Orders were given to try to prevent the foraging, but overlooked on many occasions. A number of the foragers would bribe the officers to keep from being punished. Many times a farmer would come to the camp to try to recover a missing pig. The pig was most likely killed and buried in the woods. Anything edible was fair game to the forager. Occasionally guards were provided to a farmer.

A COMMON OCCURRENCE IN THE CONFEDERATE CAMP.
Two of the mess have been out foraging for roasting ears. One fellow has landed a bagful; the other was driven off before he got any; he is coming in, with an empty sack, looking very much crestfallen, while his successful companion is telling of their escapade.
Camp Fires of the Confederacy

During the winter camps there was a great deal of time for writing letters, telling stories, or snowball fights. An occasional battle in the winter disturbed the winter camp. The following are several examples of the stories told in camp and sent to the newspapers back home.

WOULDN'T WAIT TO BE BURIED. -- As one of the hospital wagons was proceeding slowly toward the grave yard the other day with a load of coffins, the driver was disturbed in his chant, (he was whistling "Dixie" to the time of a dead march) by a rattle in his rear. He turned and looked in some trepidation upon the long, narrow boxes. Rap! Rap! The reins fell from his hand. Thump! Thump! Then a voice cried out: "Hallo! Ho There!" Driver was sorely frightened and replied: "What's the matter? Can't you rest quietly and peaceably? -- What's the use o' takin' it so hard for? "But I'm not dead!" returned the voice, making a desperate effort, and wrenching out two screws from the lid. "The devil you say!" "No I'm not, let me out of this." "Oh go along! You'd better be quiet, we'll be there presently." "Be where?" "Why to the grave." Another prodigious plunge and three more screws out. -- Lid by this time half off and one arm and part of a leg protruded. "Oh Lord" roared the terrified driver, "don't! they'll lay the whole of it to me." "Well let me out then." The driver cracked his whip, the horses dashed forward and away went the dead and the semidead and the wouldn't-stay-dead and all, at a gallop, the coffin of the obstreperous corps creaking, and rocking to and from, and the voice of its inmate crying, "Wait till I get out o' here and if I don't give you ------!" At length the grave yard was reached, where the poor fellow was relieved by the workmen and sextons present. He was full of fight and swore roundly against the "darn'd rascal that wanted to bury him dead or alive," but on explanation and expostulation he agreed to be pacified, and rode back to town sitting upright in his own coffin. He is now well and will join his command in a day or two. -- *Chattanooga Rebel*

THE LAST YANKEE INVENTION OUT. -- It is stated that a genius down East intends applying for a patent for a machine, which, he says, when wound up and set in motion, will chase a hog over a ten acre lot, catch, yoke and ring him; or, by a slight change of gearing, it will chop him into sausage, work his bristles into shoe brushes, and manufacture his tail into a cork screw.
Augusta Daily Chronicle & Sentinel, August 19, 1863 - Augusta, Georgia

---

A RICH BURLESQUE

Our special correspondent at "the front" furnishes us the following highly amusing satire upon the system of issuing orders indiscriminately by many general officers. It was written by a private soldier; is a very happy hit, and will be duly appreciated by those who, like him have become well nigh demented, trying to "keep the fun of them."

HEAD'QRS RESERVE BRIGADE,
February 20th, 1864

General Orders No. 30,127
In view of the numerous orders on the subject of furloughs from Army, Corps and Division Headquarters, and in order the more effectually to guard against the possibility of

any soldier obtaining a furlough or leave of absence, the following regulations in reference thereto are published, and will be strictly observed in this command:

I. In all applications under General Orders No. 227, 15, 6, 18, 10 and 20 the certificates of company commanders must show --

1st. That "Order is Heaven's first law."

2nd. That none are absent or desire to be absent on furlough or otherwise.

3d. That every man in the Company has re-enlisted for the war, and has signed a pledge to re-enlist again for the same length of time, under the late military law.

4th. That the applicant has been a "gallant and meritorious soldier," and has slain at least seven or eight Yankees in single combat. Scalps must be forwarded with application, or the certificate of a Medical Board who saw the same taken in action.

5th. In order that the above paragraph may be fully carried out, and only the meritorious receive furloughs, a certificate is required that applicant has been chosen by lot.

6th. The number of barefooted men must be given, together with the condition of the camps, and the number of cases of camp itch.

7th. "The vulgar fractions of each company will be aggregated with the extra duty men,: wagons and ambulances, the square root extracted, and nine wagons out of every ten furloughed.

II. When a recruit is furnished, certificate of the mother of recruit must show that he was lawfully begotten and piously brought up; that he is not subject to desertion, inclined to calvary, and that he is not now and never has been a minor or nitre bureau. (Family Bible will in all such cases, be enclosed with the application.)

III. In case of officers applying for leaves of absence, certificate must show --

1. That applicant is alive and well and hopes Col. Geo. Win Brent, A.A.G., is enjoying the same blessing.

2. That applicant has never been tried by General Orders or General Court Martial.

3. That he fully and entirely understands all orders upon furloughs and leaves of absence, as well as all other orders whatsoever, that may have been or will be hereafter issued.

4. No such plea as a desire to marry, or attend to important business, or to visit a dying wife, father or mother will be considered. In the present crisis of our affairs, no person of command patriotism will entertain the idea of dying neither will it be allowed. They must quietly wait their turn under General Orders.

5. No application for furlough or leave of absence will be entertained unless folded according to form prescribed in G.O. No. 5, and neatly secured with 6 yards of red tape.

VI. The following persons are excluded from the benefits and operations of the foregoing order:

1. All men who have been executed under sentence of a court martial.

2. All married men who have either visited home or written their wives within twelve months preceding the battle of Missionary Ridge.

3. All unmarried men who have at any time during the period of six months next preceding the 18th of January, entertained the idea of a matrimonial alliance.

VII. No furloughs or leaves of absence will be granted in any case whatever.

By Order of

BRIG. GEN. VIDETTE

Jerry <u>Sosews</u>, Active Expectant Gen.

Southern Confederacy - Atlanta, Georgia

CAMP FUN. -- The Richmond Whig has a correspondent in Jackson's corps, who furnishes the following specimens of soldiers wit:

It is when idle in camp that the soldier is a great institution; yet one must be seen to be appreciated. Pen cannot fully paint the air of cheerful content, hilarity, irresponsibility loungings, and practical spirit of jesting that "obtains" ready to seize on any odd circumstances in its licensed levity. A "calvaryman" comes rejoicing in immense top boots, for which in fond pride he had invested fully forty dollars of pay; at once the cry from an hundred voices follows him along the line -- "Come up out'er them boots! come out! -- too soon to go into winter quarters! I know you're in thar! -- I see your arms stickin' out!" A bumpkin rides by in an uncommonly big hat, and is frighted at the shout -- "Come down out'er that hat!" Come down! 'taint no use to say you aint up thar! I see your legs hangin' out!" A fancy staff officer was horrified at the irreverent reception of his nicely twisted moustache -- as he heard from behind innumerable trees -- "take them mice out'er your mouth! take 'em out! no use to say they aint thar -- see their tails hangin' out! -- Another, sporting immense whiskers, was urged to "Come out of that bunch of har! I know you're in thar! I see your ears a workin'!" Sometimes a rousing cheer is heard in the distance, it is explained -- "boys lookout! here comes old Stonewall" or an old hare, "one or tother." -- they being about the only individuals who invariably bring down the house.

Rome Weekly Courier, December 19, 1862 - Rome, Georgia

A SAD INCIDENT IN CAMP.

The following is an extract of a letter from an officer of our army in Tennessee, writing to his family.

A sad thing occurred near my camps yesterday. A soldier in the 1st Georgia Regiment had been claiming himself sick for several days, and was regularly excused from duty by the Surgeon every morning. Yesterday morning, when the sick call was made, he went before the Surgeon to be excused. The Surgeon thought that he had been playing "Old Soldier" long enough, and returned him to duty. He was immediately ordered on guard, to which he protested, saying the Surgeon was mistaken in his case. After finding that his protest would avail nothing, he offered ten dollars, "all the money he had," for some person to take his place. This right was also refused, and the poor fellow was placed on guard. About two o'clock he fell dead at his post, without any assistance.

It is strange to relate, but true, that only a few moments after his death was announced, his brother (who had a short time since heard that his brother was a member of the regiment) reached the Brigade and inquired for the 1st Georgia Regiment, stating that he had a brother in it that he had not seen before for more than six years. When he was told the whereabouts of the Regiment, he left with a proud heart and fond hopes that he would in a few moments clasp the hand of his long absent brother. As he was making his way to the regiment, he had to pass the post his brother was guarding when he breathed his last. Here he saw a corpse surrounded by a few men who were preparing it for its resting place. He halted and commenced inquiring what caused the death. - Upon inspection he thought he recognized the features of the brother that he so fondly expected soon to meet. After examining, he found letters that proved to him that there lay the remains of the object of his trip. It is useless to attempt to describe the emotions of this brother, after finding his brother dead.

Augusta Daily Chronicle & Sentinel, June 28, 1863 - Augusta, Georgia

STORIES HEARD AROUND THE CAMP FIRE.

Nothing to Eat.
        Said a hungry Confederate to the lady who met him at the door, when out foraging one day, "Madam, will you please give me something to eat: I haven't had a mouthful for three days -- to-day, to-morrow and next day."
Camp Fires of the Confederacy

HOW TO WARM A TENT. -- A hole is dug in the centre of the tent, about two feet in depth and diameter. This is walled with stones laid in soft clay, and covered at the top, with the exception of a small aperture for the introduction of fuel. For this apperture there must be a close fitting door or cover, which can be opened and closed at pleasure. Across one side of the tent a trench is laid and covered with wood and earth, through which the cold air is conveyed freely to the bottom part of this subterranean fire place. From the top of the same, and across the opposite side of the tent, is another trench inlaid and carefully covered with stone and earth, through which the smoke and surplus heat is carried off. This is the whole machine. The merits of it are obvious.
Columbus Daily Times, December 3, 1861 - Columbus, Georgia

Some Indian soldiers on a scout in the mountains of Georgia, came to a house occupied by an old woman. "Well old lady, what are you? Secesh?" said the leaders. "No." she said. "What then?" "Baptist," said she promptly, "and always was."
Savannah Republican, July 21, 1864 - Savannah, Georgia

AN INCIDENT ON THE RAPPAHANNOCK - The following extract of a letter from Fredericksburg by an officer in Gen. Lee's Army, relates a pleasant incident in camp life, which no doubt helped materially to relieve its monotony.
        I must tell you of an agreeable episode in our camp life, which occurred a few days since. It is acknowledged that the Federals, with all their faults, have some capital bands in their ranks. - Recently one of these organizations came down to the river side opposite Fredericksburg, and favored our boys (who had gathered in large numbers to listen) with a variety of popular pieces, in the best style. Applause from the audience on each side followed. The band then struck up "Dixie," and executed it in a credible manner. At its conclusion, our soldiers sent up such a shout as made the welkin ring. This was followed by "Yankee Doodle," when a burst of applause from the Federals followed. Finally, the band played "Home Sweet Home," a melody which all could feel and appreciate; and when it was finished, such a shout went up from both armies as I doubt has ever been heard on earth. I looked around me, and saw tears coursing down many a furrowed and battle worn cheek, and if the frantic cheers that went up from the other side of the river were any criterion, our neighboring enemies were as much affected.
Augusta Daily Chronicle & Sentinel, March 21, 1863 - Augusta, Georgia

---

[ARMY CORRESPONDENCE OF MORNING NEWS]
Battle of Rappahannock Academy,
Camp Near Port Royal, VA.
February 25th, 1863

Dear News: It becomes my duty to chronicle a spirited engagement which took place here yesterday. Our division, as you have probably heard, has lately been reorganized. General Early has been promoted to the Command left vacant by the continued disability of the gallant Ewell. Gen. Trimble, formerly commanding a brigade of this division, composed of the 12th and 21st Georgia and two regiments of North Carolinians, has been promoted to the command of Jackson's old division -- the 12th and 21st Georgia regiments have been transferred to Dole's brigade, Hill's division, and two regiments of North Carolinians added to Trimble's old brigade, and the brigade placed under the command of Col. Hoke, now promoted Brigadier General. Our division now has one brigade of Louisianians, one of Georgians, one of Virginians, and one of North Carolinians. I was not aware that these dispositions had created jealousies among the troops, at least to the extent of producing a hostile demonstration, and was therefore slowly picking my way along the road towards the Academy yesterday morning, when I met several mounted couriers and stragglers flying at the top of speed. In terrified accents they stated that Gen. Hoke's brigade was then on the march, and not more than a quarter of a mile distant, and that the object of the expedition was to attack and drive our brigade from their camp. I continued my walk, however, thinking to watch the enemy, and ascertain, if possible, his intentions. I had not gone far before I descried the head of the column approaching. It will probably be proper here to give a sketch of the ground on which this memorable conflict occurred. About half a mile from the Rappahannock Academy, a road makes off from the main road leading from Guinea Station to Port Royal. The latter road leads eastwardly -- the former due north, and the one our principal remarks will apply to. This road is skirted on the west side by a field three hundred yards from its junction with the main road to a ravine. On the north side of this ravine is the camp of Lawton's brigade. The ravine terminates near the road. The brigade is encamped in a line perpendicular to the road, in the following order -- 31st, 38th, 60th, 13th, 26th and 61st -- the camps of the first being about one hundred yards from the road, and the others still beyond, in succession. When I first deserted the forces of the enemy they were in the field first mentioned, and were soon halted. Gen. Hoke and staff then rode forward, accompanied by a company of cavalry, improvised from old artillery horses, drivers and gunners, to reconnoitre our position. It must however, be stated for the honor of a soldier that he had, in true knightly style, sent an intimation of his purpose to Col. Stiles, commanding our brigade. Having closely scanned our position, by the aid of a *strong glass*, he devised his plan of attack with a master's skill. Discarding the idea of attempting to cross the ravine by a flank march and then deploy in line on the other side, he determined to move his whole force by the flank along the road; and at once threw out his skirmishers, who marched along the edge of the woods at their proper intervals on his left flank, which would become his front when the column should reach its distance and be faced into line. Thus, formed, his brigade was in the order of battle, with skirmishers out and all ready before our first regiment had got into position. Any one by noting this disposition, can readily comprehend that if the North Carolinians advanced before all our regiments had conformed to the new direction, they could easily fall upon and demolish us in detail. Such indeed was the fact. Ere the 31st and 38th had formed in line, the enemy gave the order to charge. Their right thus overlapped and flanked our left, and though these two regiments stood their ground manfully for a time, they were compelled to fall back and change front like Beauregard at Manassas. Col. Stiles and his Adjutant then rapidly brought the 60th and 13th into line -- the 26th and 61st were on picket. The fighting now became *pelting* and severe in the extreme, and with varied success. At one time the enemy had nearly got to our Headquarters, and had captured our Adjutant General. Finally, they began to fall back and were hotly pressed by our columns, who were momentarily reinforced by stragglers, staff officers, Quartermasters and Commissary employees and every other available recruit. The tide of battle had now fairly turned. We were driving the enemy fast and furiously -- soon we captured their General and a Major. We were driving them out of the encampment, across the road, through the adjoining field and pell-mell into a ravine to the left of the Guinea Station road. Here, however, alas! like Beauregard at Manassas, we lost by too much prudence the result of our brilliant success. Instead of following the shattered forces of the enemy and entering their camp pell mell at their heels, we must needs halt our forces, reform and hold a council of war as to the best means of reaping the fruits, like the waters of Tautalus, were eluding our grasp, while we were discussing the best means of securing them! We finally determined not to follow the enemy across the ravine, but to march round by the road. This gave them time to collect and reform in front of their camp. -- When we came in sight they were drawn up in battle array -- flags were waving and officers riding along the lines escorting the men, shouting and waving handkerchiefs. We were marching by the flank. Here, again, we committed a blunder. Instead of prolonging our column in a direction parallel to the enemy's front, and then, when we had reached our ground, facing to the front and marching forward, we resorted to the formation "on the right by file into line," thus subjecting ourselves to the danger of being fallen upon, before our lengthy column had untangled, thrown into confusion and routed. This calamity did not actually befall us, but the soldiers saw the danger and were so much fluttered by it, that they could not recover their self-possession - an important thing in battle. We finally got our column in line and advanced with a shout - but a new mistake precipitated the catastrophe. The "Tar-heels" had provided themselves with haversacks filled to the brim with ammunition - whereas we only had a ball or two in our possession. When these were exhausted, of course, we had to improvise for the occasion, while our foes could pelt us mercilessly with an unremitting *hail* and thus interfere materially with the process of manufacturing ours. Under these circumstances our plan of attack should have been to charge furiously to a distance of five paces of the Van Winkle, fire one volley and then charge again, making the contest a hand to hand one. Had we done so, I have no doubt we would have swept the encampment. But on the contrary we charged up very near and then halted and commenced to fire. The consequence was that our ammunition was soon exhausted, while that of the Rips was only lightened enough to expedite their movements. This state of things could not long continue - our line gradually wavered, then broke and fled. In endeavoring to rally the color company, I was captured by a six foot Winkler, who cast me to the earth and commenced the process of white-washing. I bleated lustily, but he would not notice my signals. I then bethought myself and asked for a chew of tobacco - this at once opened his heart. He helped me up, brushed my clothes, and asked me if I was hurt. He promised me I should soon be paroled, and asked me what part of North Carolina I came from. I told him that I was not a North Carolinian. "Why, did I not understand you to ask me for a chew of tobacco?" I told him that I did, but it was only a ruse and that every thing was fair in war. Our colors, our Adjutant and the commander of the color company had all been captured, and the shout and defiance of persuer and persued could just be heard in the distance as I brushed my clothes and arranged to return to our lines. I was carried before the proper authorities, paroled, sworn not to attempt to burn Tar river, nor be guilty of any other set of incendiarism towards the "Old North State" till duly exchanged, and then dismissed to return to our lines. The road as far as the Academy was lined with the jaded heroes of the combat, resting against the fences, or returning from the pursuit of our flying legions. We were greeted with many a jest on account of our capture, but we replied that it was more honorable to be taken prisoners than to run away.

Thus ended one of the most memorable combats of the war. A part of it was witnessed by Gen. Jackson and staff. I wish the old faded uniforms could have participated in it. I want to throw one *snow-ball* at Stonewall Jackson. - I had neglected heretofore to state that, like Hohenlinden, this battle was fought on ground covered to the depth of twelve inches in snow - and that the snow was "all bloodless" both before and after it, but awfully trampled.

E. T. C.

Savannah Daily Morning News, March 5, 1863 - Savannah, Georgia

Chapter VI

Some Explanations

There are a number of explanations that need to be covered to assist the reader or researcher to better understand the information in this book. A number of things were discovered about the naming of camps, some have been covered in other chapters. Occasionally it would appear that a Georgia unit occupied two or more camps at the same time. Several reasons are discussed for this phenomenon. Rather than leaving the guesswork to the reader it is my opinion these things should be explained. I will cover each category in the listing of the camps, that is: camp name, state, county, description of the camp location, Georgia unit, date(s) in the camp, sources, and maps.

Camp names:

The camp names were taken from letters, the compiled service records, which were a compilation of information from the muster rolls and requisitions, morning reports, orders, newspapers, diaries, both published and unpublished, private collections of Georgia letters and Georgia unit histories. All camp names are reported. Whenever the letter or document began with Camp, then gave a name, it was reported. I suspect there are some names which are not official camp names. Some of the camp names which are named for towns or place names are highly suspicious. However, I have been surprised several times by seeing these camp names reported from more than one source.

The writers of these letters would not use the camp names on all of their letters. Probably less than five percent of the writers were consistent in reporting the camp name on their letters. Then about fifty percent of the time, once a camp name was given on a set of letters from a specific camp, the writer would use the camp name only a few times, or on less than twenty percent of the letters from the camp. Generally if the camp name was used at all, it was used early in the camp. This leaves thirty or forty percent of letter writers who never mentioned a camp name on any of their letters. It is my opinion that the more literate the writer, the more the camp name would appear on the set of letters from the writer. The higher the rank, the more the camp name was reported. The reason for this is that the official camp name was generally chosen by the highest ranking officer in the camp. I suspect some soldiers never knew or cared about the camp name.

There seems to be a misconception among many researchers and Civil War buffs that when a camp name was assigned to a brigade or regimental camp, that the camp was in a concentrated area. The brigade may be spread out over several miles with each regiment using the same camp name. The same correlation can be given for a regiment. Note the letter written by a citizen about Camp Randolph in Gordon County, Georgia. The name Camp Randolph was apparently assigned to all of the camps in the Calhoun, Georgia, area.

The researcher must also be aware of errors in camp names from transcribed letters. Misspelling of camp names and phonetic spelling must be mentioned.

The use of camp names diminished as the war grew longer. My belief is that the attitude toward the war was changing, and when the excitement and romanticism toward the war declined, they were less likely to assign a camp name. Also, the men who enlisted early in the war were more patriotic than those who were conscripted. As the war continued, there were fewer of these patriotic men due to attrition. Many of these early patriots were killed by both the bullet and diseases. Those who were wounded beyond useful Confederate service returned home to serve in the Georgia Militia and local defense troops or served in hospitals. It can be noted that a high percentage of the Georgia Militia used and reported camp names on their letters in 1864.

States and Counties:
   The reporting of the state and county is based on the present boundaries as best as can be determined. Unfortunately there are a number of sources that made it difficult or impossible to determine the accurate county name for these camps, especially when the best description was "near Petersburg" or "near Richmond." The beginning researcher must be aware of the separation of West Virginia from Virginia in 1861. Although the state of West Virginia did not officially become a state until June 20, 1863, it was referred to as West Virginia as early as late 1861. The early letters and battle reports from Greenbrier River and other sites in what is now West Virginia were reported as being in Virginia.
   Many counties have changed boundaries and names since the war years. Those reported during this time may have changed.

Descriptive Location:
   Nearly all of the descriptive locations used in this book come from the letters or reports used by the soldiers. This descriptive location would most often be described in the first letter written from a new camp.
   One soldier may write that he was two miles from Richmond. The second letter may state that he was south of Richmond. The third may say he was on Darby Town Road. The information used in this section comes from the compilation of this information. Orders issued early in the war discouraged the soldiers from identifying his location for fear the enemy might capture the mail wagons.
   It is understandable why the soldiers used the word "near" as often as they did. When you place a soldier from Georgia in the state of Virginia or any other state, he probably has no idea where he is. Many of the letters reflect this and so the word "near" was used as the description for the camp location. Near is only relative to the area the soldier was in. On the coast of Georgia, near described the closest settlement or post office, and could be seven to ten miles away from his actual camp location.
   Directions such as north, south, east or west were occasionally off by as much as 90 degrees or more. A compass was rare, and these directions were often incorrect. Corrections were made when the proper directions were known.

Georgia Troops:
   The identity of the Georgia unit or units in these camps was for the most part not difficult. However, there were a few records which misidentified the unit, and corrections were made. Early in the war there was a great deal of confusion between the Confederate designations for the Georgia units and the designation given the unit by Governor Brown. I will not attempt to list these differences, but have reported the final designation within the book. The following article from the *Rome Weekly Courier* of August 16, 1861, gives you an idea of a few of these differences.

The Georgia Regiments. - There seems to be no little confusion in the numbers by which the Georgia regiments are designated. An irregularity that may lead to important, if not unjust, mistakes in history. For instance:

Col. Conner's Regiment is known in Virginia as the Twelfth Georgia, while in Governor Brown's list Col. Thomas' Regiment, also in Virginia, is set down as the Twelfth.

Col. Bartow's Regiment is known in Virginia, and will be in all of history, and known gloriously, as the Eighth Georgia, while the Executive schedule puts down the Independent Volunteer Regiment of Savannah, whose title is fixed by law and cannot be altered except by the legislature, as the Eighth.

These discrepancies should not exist, and especially for the reason that created them - Executive punctillio. Only think of the glorious Eighth being rejected by Governor Brown from the list of Georgia soldiers simply because it was tendered directly to the President and not through His Excellancy first aforesaid.

For the honor of the State and in justice to our gallant troops, we hope all the Georgia regiments will be properly classified, as they are known to the world, and then a complete list published under the authority of the Governor.

There are several camps of Confederate cavalry units listed in the book. There are a number of Georgia men in these units, and letters from these camps could exist. The reason the unit was identified as Confederate was because the regiment was represented by more that one state, and its designation could not be identified as from a single state.

Dates:

It was rare that a letter with a camp name did not have a date on the letter. Dates of the camps can be confusing.

How can a unit be in two or more camps at the same time? I have found five reasons to explain this.

The first is the most obvious. A regiment may have one or more companies detached from the regiment on a special assignment or picket duty. Each of these companies may name their camp. This often occurred in the Savannah, Georgia, area or on the coast of Georgia or South Carolina where picket posts were manned by a company or as few as five or six men. Most often this company or a part of a company on picket duty would name their camp. It would then be reported as a camp of the regiment at the same time the majority of the regiment would be in the main camp or headquarters camp.

The second is easily explained but not as easily discovered. Quite often when a regiment, battalion or any unit left a camp, they left behind the sick who could not be moved at the time, due to the shortage of wagons, or due to the seriousness of the wound or sickness. These men left behind would often write letters from the old camp of the unit. The sick could be in this old camp for several weeks. The reporting of the dates for the camps were for the period of time the major portion of the unit was in the camp as best as could be determined.

Another reason for the overlapping of dates from two camps is due to the unit taking several days to move out of one camp into another. Generally the reason for this is due to the lack of transportation; either there was a shortage of wagons or train cars to move the entire unit at once.

In Virginia, a brigade would often be broken up due to the lack of transportation. In a movement from Richmond to Orange Court House, a regiment or two may take the train and would then be in a new camp in a day or two. The balance of the brigade may have to march the entire distance taking four to six days before they could write their letters from a new camp.

The fourth was discovered in a letter from "Camp White within Camp Stephens." This may explain why there are two camps of a regiment reported at the same time. The Upson Guards, Company K, of the 5th Regiment Georgia Volunteer Infantry was the first company of the regiment to arrive in Pensacola. When they arrived, they named their camp "Camp White." When the rest of the regiment arrived, the official name used by the regiment was "Camp Stephens." The Upson Guards continued to use the camp name "Camp White," and "Camp White within Camp Stephens."

The fifth reason is when the name of a camp was changed. Both the old name was used, along with the new name. The most confusing camps to discern were when Gen. Henry Rootes Jackson ordered five different camps of the Georgia State Troops be renamed "Camp Lee." A few of them had three different names.

You can now begin to understand the reasons for two or more camps of a single unit being reported during the same time period.

Many of the camps are shown to be only one day camps. There is no doubt these camps existed longer than one day. If more information is found, this will be shown in a future edition.

Sources:

You will see a combination of abbreviations and numbers as follows: GDAH, CSR, 254/43. Refer to the abbreviations table in the front of the book and you will see the information came from the Georgia Department of Archives and History, Compiled Service Records. The numbers can be interpreted to be microfilm drawer 254, roll 43. All rolls of microfilm from the Compiled Service Records are based on the locations at the Georgia Department of Archives and History.

I began collecting information on Georgia camps about 1987. Unfortunately I did not realize the importance of documenting the source of my information until two or three years later. I never intended to publish this list of camp names. This explains why there are two or three camp names without a source noted. I discovered a list of about two hundred camp names at the Georgia Department of Archives and History about 1989. The person who compiled this list included the name of the camp, whatever was known about its location, the dates during which it was known to have been in existence, and the Georgia troops known to have been camped at it. Again, no source was given for these camps. I have been able to provide the sources for all but three or four of these camp names. All camp names were used since I feel it is more important to document them rather than leave them out due to the lack of a source.

The major sources used are documented with each camp. Many other sources were researched to determine troop movements and assist in verifying information.

The spelling and grammar in the articles and letters in this book are left as they originally appeared. I do not attempt to change them.

Some maps in the book have been "cleaned up" due to the difficulty in reading them.

Hopefully, I have anticipated and answered the many potential questions on each of the sections within the information for each camp.

1   **Camp Adams**
Chatham County, Georgia
The camp was located one-half mile from Adams house on the south end of Skidaway Island, and three miles from the fortifications on Green Island.
Georgia Troops:
31st Regiment Georgia Volunteer Infantry, Co. D, 11/3/1861-11/14/1861
Source:
GDAH, 283/27, William. W. Head

2   **Camp Advance**
Wayne County, North Carolina
The men were quartered in the stalls at the racetrack near Goldsboro.
Georgia Troops:
3rd Battalion Georgia Volunteer Infantry, 10/26/1861-11/7/1861
Cherokee Artillery, 10/26/1861-11/7/1861
Sources:
RWC, 11/8/1861 & 11/22/1861

3   **Camp Advance**
Fairfax County, Virginia
The camp was located at Falls Church. Other Regiments used this camp also. Picket duty was rotated from the Regiments in Camp Pine Creek.
Georgia Troops:
2nd Regiment Georgia Volunteer Infantry, 9/23/1861-9/30/1861
Sources:
CV, XXXII, 464; GDAH, CSR, 254/100

4   **Camp Advance**
Henrico County, Virginia
The camp was located at the breastworks on Williamsburg Road, five to six miles from Richmond.
Georgia Troops:
4th Regiment Georgia Volunteer Infantry, 6/1/1862-6/27/1862
22nd Regiment Georgia Volunteer Infantry, 6/26/1862
Sources:
4th GVI, EU, #363, David Read Evans Winn; GDAH, CSR, 254/128
22nd GVI, SC, 1/2/1862

5   **Camp Aiken**
Bibb County, Georgia
The camp was located near Macon.
Georgia Troops:
Findlay's Battalion, Home Guards, 12/30/1863-5/1/1864
Sources:
GDAH, 283/48, Bibb County File; MT, 12/24/1863

Camp Allegheny
Pocohantas County, West Virginia

The camp was located on the Parkersburg-Staunton Turnpike, near the summit of Valley Mountain. Also referred to as Camp Yeager. There was a battle in the camp on December 13, 1861.

Georgia Troops:

12th Regiment Georgia Volunteer Infantry, 8/2/1861-8/13/1861 & 11/16/1861-4/2/1862

Sources:

EU, #20, John Levi Griffin; *A Post of Honor, The Pryor Letters, 1861-1863*, Edited and narrated by Charles R. Adams, Jr.

Map: 1966 Thesis of Edward M. Kelleher, Wheeling College, Wheeling, West Virginia

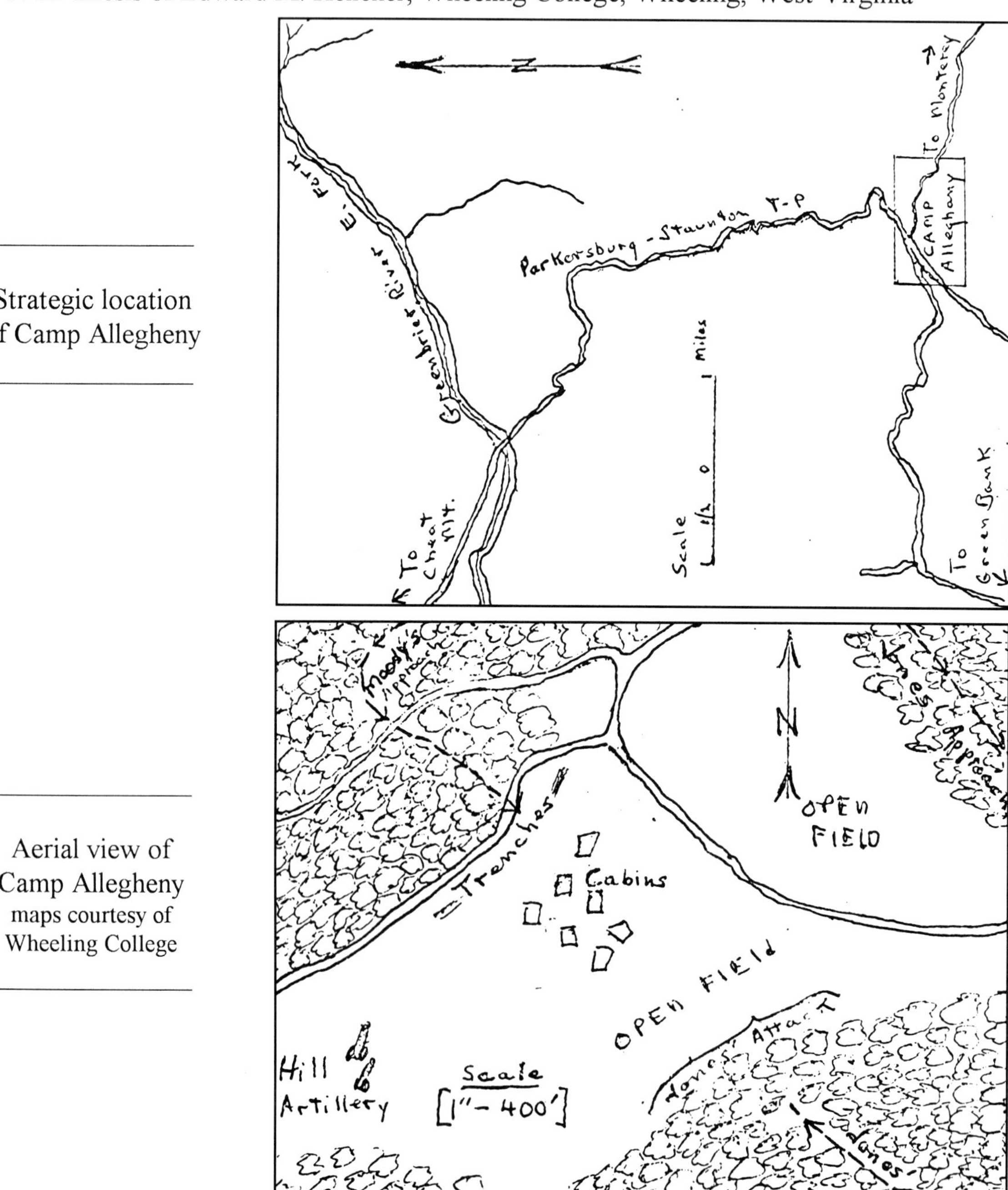

Strategic location
of Camp Allegheny

Aerial view of
Camp Allegheny
maps courtesy of
Wheeling College

7   **Camp Allen**

Beaufort County, South Carolina

The camp was located about 10 miles below Hardeeville on the road to Savannah (Screven Ferry Road,) and about one and one-half miles below Cook's Battery.

Georgia Troops:

47th Regiment Georgia Volunteer Infantry, 4/1863-5/8/1863

Phillips' Legion, four infantry companies, A, D, E & F, and cavalry battalion, 6/8/1862-6/15/1862

Sources:

47th GVI, GHS, #296, 47th GVI papers; DU, Benjamin S. Williams

PL, GDAH, CSR, 251/42; 283/16, James R. Andrews

8   **Camp Allston**

Roane County, Tennessee

The camp was located near Kingston

Georgia Troops:

1st Regiment Georgia Volunteer Cavalry, 6/12/1862-6/30/1862

Source:

GDAH, CSR, 253/74; Dekalb County Historical Society, 1st Ga. Cav.

9   **Camp Anderson**

Macon County, Georgia

The camp was probably near Andersonville prison. See Camp Sumter.

Georgia Troops:

3rd Regiment Georgia Infantry Reserves, 5/29/1864

Source:

GDAH, 171/39, Thomas J. Hand

10   **Camp Anderson**

Chatham County, Georgia

The camp was located on Wildhorn Plantation, one and one-half miles below Station No. 1 on the Savannah, Albany and Gulf Railroad, and on the west side of Grove River. See Camp Miller of the Columbus Artillery.

Georgia Troops:

1st Battalion Georgia Sharpshooters, four companies, 9/27/1862-2/15/1863

29th Regiment Georgia Volunteer Infantry, Companies A & G, 9/1862

Sources:

1st Bn Ga SS, GDAH, CSR, 254/96, ADC&S, 12/29/1862

29th GVI, GDAH, CSR, 256/79

11   **Camp Anderson**

Liberty County, Georgia

The camp was on St. Catherines Island.

Georgia Troops:

1st (Olmstead's) Volunteer Regiment of Georgia, Company A, Republican Blues, 9/1861

Source:

GDAH, CSR, 254/81

12   **Camp Anderson**

Caroline County, Virginia

The camp was located within one-half mile of Guinea's Station, and twelve miles south of Fredericksburg.

Georgia Troops:

45th Regiment Georgia Volunteer Infantry, 4/23/1862-5/28/1862

Sources:

GDAH, 227/10, Marion Hill Fitzpatrick; GHQ, Vols. 46 & 55, Charles A. Conn

13   **Camp Anna**

Spotsylvania County, Virginia

The camp was six miles from Fredericksburg.

Georgia Troops:

16th Regiment Georgia Volunteer Infantry, 4/13/1863-5/27/1863

Sources:

GDAH, CSR, 255/115; 20/76, William L. Smith; 65/54, James David Williams

14   **Camp Anners**

Suffolk County, Virginia

The camp was located near Suffolk. See Camp Hunter.

Georgia Troops:

16th Regiment Georgia Volunteer Infantry, 3/12/1862-3/22/1862 (On March 22, 1862, the regiment moved to Goldsboro, North Carolina.)

Sources:

In Care Of Yellow River, By Elizabeth Whitley Roberson; GDAH, 283/17, William T. Bailey

15   **Camp Ansley**

Hamilton County, Tennessee

The camp was located near Chattanooga, and named in honor of Capt. Edwin W. Ansley, mortally wounded at Murfreesboro.

Georgia Troops:

2nd Battalion Georgia Sharpshooters, Cos. A & C, (Oglethorpe Infantry, Co. B,) 1/28/1863-5/22/1863

Sources:

ADC&S, 2/5/1863, & 5/30/1863

16   **Camp Antioch**

Twiggs County, Georgia

The camp was located near Antioch.

Georgia Troops:

Faulk Invincibles, 8/13/1861 (Later became Co. E, 26th [Styles] Regiment Georgia Volunteer Infantry.)

Source:

MT, 8/20/1861

17   **Camp Arnold**

Bryan County, Georgia

The camp was on Dr. Arnold's Plantation, on the west side of the Ogeechee River, five miles from Staves Landing. The battery moved to Staves Landing on 4/22/1863. See map of Savannah area. See Camp Rogers.

Georgia Troops:

Howell's Battery Georgia Light Artillery (prev. Martin's Battery), 11/2/1862-4/22/1862

Sources:

GDAH, CSR, 254/55; SDMN, 3/4/1863; *Memoirs of a Confederate Veteran 1861-1865*, By I. Hermann, C.S.A.

18   **Camp Ashby**

Chatham County, Georgia

The camp was at White Bluff in a pine grove, within sight of the Vernon River.

Georgia Troops:

Terrell Light Artillery, Brook's Battery, 3/1863-4/11/1863

Chatham Artillery, 8/7/1862-8/16/1862, 1/1/1863

Sources:

Brook's Btry., GDAH, CSR, 254/47; 283/39, Wm. B. Safford

Chatham Arty., *Historical Sketch of The Chatham Artillery during The Confederate Struggle for Independence*, by Charles C. Jones, Jr.; SR, 1/5/1863

19   **Camp Atkinson**

Camden County, Georgia

The camp was on Big Cumberland Island.

Georgia Troops:

13th (Styles) Regiment Georgia Volunteer Infantry, Co. B, Camden Rifles, 8/1861-11/6/1861

Sources:

GDAH, CSR, 256/59; SDMN, 10/24/1861

20   **Camp Augusta**
Jackson County, Alabama
The camp was near Grahams, on the Nashville & Chattanooga Railroad.
Georgia Troops:
12th Battalion Georgia Light Artillery, 7/25/1862
The 34th and 56th Regiments Georgia Volunteer Infantry and Jackson's Artillery were here with
Ledbetter's Brigade. No documentation with this camp name has been found for these two units.
Sources:
GDAH, CSR, 254/32; FU, 7/29/1862

21   **Camp Avery**
Lincoln County, Tennessee
The camp was located at Fayetteville.
Georgia Troops:
23rd Batallion Georgia Cavalry, 1/22/1863
Shortly after this, the Battalion became a part of the 4th (Avery's) Regiment Georgia Cavalry.
Source:
CR, 1/29/1863

22   **Camp Bailey**

Fulton County, Georgia

This camp, located near Fairburn, is where the 30th Georgia organized and trained.
Georgia Troops:
30th Regiment Georgia Volunteer Infantry, 9/1861-12/16/1861
Source:
Brief History of the Thirtieth Georgia Regiment, By Augustus Pitt Adamson

23   **Camp Bald Head**

Fayette County, Georgia

The camp was located near Lovejoy, seventeen miles north of Griffin. See Camp Lovejoy.
Georgia Troops:
Georgia Militia, 10/31/1864-11/18/1864
Sources:
Johnny Cobb: Confederate Aristocrat, By Horace Montgomery; *Howell Cobb's Confederate
Career*, By Horace Montgomery, Confederate Centennial Studies, Number Ten

24   **Camp Banks Ford**

Spotsylvania County, Virginia

This camp was at Banks Ford on the Rappahannock River, four and one-half miles above
Fredericksburg. See Atlas Plate XXXIII, 1.
Georgia Troops:
Phillips' Legion, Infantry Battalion, 5/5/1863-5/10/1863
Source:
KMNBPL, Diary of Marcus L. Green

25   **Camp Barkuloo**

Chatham County, Georgia

The camp was located four miles from Savannah on the Central Railroad.
Georgia Troops:
54th Regiment Georgia Volunteer Infantry, 5/11/1862-6/1/1862
The 54th Georgia became the 57th Regiment Georgia Volunteer Infantry, in January, 1863, while
in Jackson, Mississippi.
Sources:
GDAH, 283/22, Edwin T. Davis; 283/30, John L. Keen; 283/45, Vinson Wright

26   **Camp Barrow**

Leon County, Florida

The company was on provost duty while in this camp near Tallahassee.
Georgia Troops:
29th Battalion Georgia Cavalry, Co. H, 2/24/1864-3/8/1864
Source:
ECN, 3/23/1864

27   **Camp Bartow**
Camden County, Georgia

   The company was in command of a battery on the south end of Cumberland Island while in this camp.
Georgia Troops:
13th (Styles) Regiment Georgia Volunteer Infantry, Co. A., Brunswick Riflemen, 9/29/1861-2/27/1862
Sources:
GDAH, CSR, 256/59; SDMN, 11/20/1861

28   **Camp Bartow**
Chatham County, Georgia

   The camp was located on Pembrook plantation, five and one-half miles below Savannah, on the Skidaway Rd., and on the edge of a lake. Also described as being at the Skidaway narrows.
Georgia Troops:
30th Regiment Georgia Volunteer Infantry, 6/12/1862 (Also, see Camp Pembroke.)
Wright's Legion, 11/18/1861-3/23/1862 (Wright's Legion changed denomination to the 38th Regiment Georgia Volunteer Infantry on January 9, 1862 while in this camp.)
Jo Thompson Artillery, Co. M, Wright's Legion, 11/18/1861-12/16/1861 &
12/27/1861-1/25/1862 (Jo Thompson Artillery was detached from Wright's Legion, 6/6/1862, along with the Chestatee Artillery.)
Sources:
30th GVI, GDAH, MR, 279/83
WL, RWC, 11/29/1861; GDAH, CSR, 256/121; *Atlanta Historical Bulletin*, "War Diary of Cornelius R. Hanleiter," Edited by Elma S. Kurtz

29   **Camp Bartow**
Habersham County, Georgia

   The camp was located near Clarksville.
Georgia Troops:
Independent Volunteers, Thomas Guards, White Marksmen, Hiawassee Volunteers, McMillan Guards, 8/6/1861 (These companies later became Companies A, B, C, D & K, 24th Regiment Georgia Volunteer Infantry.)
Source:
ASB, 8/7/1861

30   **Camp Bartow**
Muscogee County, Georgia

   The camp was east of the cemetery in Columbus.
Georgia Troops:
Columbus Volunteers, later became Co. C, 17th Regiment Georgia Volunteer Infantry, 8/12/1861.
Source:
CDT, 8/12/1861

Camp Bartow

Fairfax County, Virginia

The camp was located two miles from Fairfax Courthouse, on the road to Manassas.

Camp Bartow near Fairfax Court House   Sept'r 21st 1862

My Dear Wife:

In haste I seat myself to drop you a few lines this morning, which leaves me very well and I hope it may find you and my little boy well and doing likewise.

I have waited very anxiously for a letter from you But I have not received one since I sent one to Greensboro to be mailed to you.

I have no news of any importance to write this morning. The regiment is moving today a few miles nearer Washington. They just got back from picket duty. A day or two ago, they went to a place called Mason's Hill from which they had a grand view of Alexandria and Washington and say they could see the Yankees drilling at those places. Some of our boys went over and talked with them and they say we gave them a decent whipping at Manassas but they are going to get us the next time. They told our boys when they parted that they had met in peace and they never wished to meet them any other way. They say their officers told them they were whipped their last time and had made their last retreat but I doubt it very much myself, for our boys don't know what it is to be whipped. They are most too brave at times.

I never got to go with the boys as I had the mumps when they left and I am on guard duty today.

I want you to write me a long letter and give me all the news about Georgia. Tell the old lady I really wish I was there and could get a good cup of coffee and some biscuit for I am hungry for something to eat.

Our men are in a right smart stir this morning and are all moving forward, no telling for what purpose. There is a Kentucky regiment passing by now and among them I see some women; wives of the soldiers, I suppose they have come to share their fates together, but that's too bad. They don't seem to be in their proper places, at least I don't think they are.

There is a great deal of sickness in camps at this time, mostly Typhoid Fever, but through the mercy of God I am yet spared.

Puss, you don't know how bad I want to see you and Willie and be with you all again. Time appears long since we parted but I hope we will soon be permitted to meet again on earth. I can't describe my feelings to you for it is impossble.

I have seen and learned a heap since I left you and must admit I never knew the sweets and pleasures of home 'till I left and have been away so long, and now there is but one point I dread and that is taking the city of Washington, for I know for certain there is going to be oceans of blood shed in the attempt and our officers seem to be honor-seeking and we will be pushed into it, no doubt.

I need not attempt to paint to you the horrors of the battlefield for I can no more than touch at them in a way of description but it makes the heart of the most savage shudder now to look over the plains of Manassas and see already the fields white with the bones of the enemy, but I must stop.

Give my best wishes and respects to all the family and tell the girls I would like to hear from some of them. Tell Tyre he must write to me again. Also my compliments to William and Lucy and tell them I want to see them.

Your Devoted Husband

S.J.G. Brewer

Georgia Troops:
7th Regiment Georgia Volunteer Infantry, 9/15/1861-9/21/1861
8th Regiment Georgia Volunteer Infantry, 9/15/1861 & 9/19/1861-9/21/1861
9th Regiment Georgia Volunteer Infantry, 9/15/1861-9/21/1861
11th Regiment Georgia Volunteer Infantry, 9/15/1861-9/21/1861
Sources:
SFU, 10/8/1861; GDAH, 283/18, Samuel J. G. Brewer

Thomas G. Wood, drummer boy, Co. H, 11th Regiment Georgia Volunteer Infantry. Joined July 3, 1861, and died of disease in Richmond, Virginia, November 20, 1861.

photo courtesy of Jerry Coody

32   **Camp Bartow**
Pocahantas County, West Virginia

Near the Greenbrier River. (See map.) The camp was refered to as Camp Greenbrier for a few days before the name was changed to Camp Bartow.

The activities of the camp were described in a letter published in the *Augusta Daily Chronicle and Sentinel,* October 8, 1861. The letter was written by a member of the 1st Georgia.

We have been kept busy for the last week or two, entrenching and fortifying our camp, building "masked batteries," and clearing woods around the camp.

Our present location being too much exposed, we have been clearing up a camp ground up on the mountain, about a mile back of where we are now, in a much stronger position.

We had a very severe rain storm here last Friday which flooded everything in our camp - there was not a dry tent on the ground. This morning there was a heavy white frost and considerable ice. You can imagine from this what kind of weather we are having. Our boys as a general thing stand it very well, and I wonder that there are not more of them sick - as we had to sleep, for the last three or four days in wet or damp blankets on the cold ground, and our tents afford but little protection from the cold or the heavy dews at night. I do not know how we shall stand the winter if we stay here.

Gen. Jackson has moved his quarters over to the right of our regiment - we being on the extreme right of the camp, and will move back with us when we change our camp. He has selected our regiment for his "body guard" so we are told.

On October 3, 1861, the Union troops attacked Camp Bartow. The following is a report of that battle.

Camp Bartow, Greenbrier River,   October 3, 1861.

The enemy attacked us at 8 o'clock this morning in considerable force, estimated at 5,000, and with six pieces of artillery of longer range than any we have. After a hot fire of four and a half hours, and heavy attempts to charge our lines, he was repulsed, evidently with considerable loss. We had no cavalry to pursue him on his retreat. The loss on our side has been inconsiderable. A fuller report (see *Official Records*, Volume V, p. 224.) will be given through the regular channels, but for several days my correspondence with General Loring has been interupted. The enemy's force was much superior to ours, but we had the advantage in position.

H. R. JACKSON,
Brigadier-General, Commanding,

Secretary of War.

The men continued to improve their defences at Greenbrier River and moved Camp Bartow about one mile from the Greenbrier River to the head of Travelers Repose Valley, fully expecting another attack on their camp. They began to prepare for the winter by building fireplaces in their tents. This letter from a member of the Walker Light Infantry describes the more pleasant aspects of camp life.

Camp Bartow, Nov. 17th, 1861.

Dear Friend:- We are having a cold time now, the ground being covered with snow and ice. But few of our regiment have ever seen such cold weather; but the boys enjoy it and suffer no one to pass, not even the Colonel, without pelting the passer with snow balls. Colonel Clark and our surgeon are enjoying themselves with this pleasant sport. Joe Taliaferro is sitting in the corner reading "Valentine Vox;" Capt. Crump and Fred. Stoy are talking over the adventures of the latter in the mountains; Russell is writing; Hood and Charley Doughty have gone on the Alleghaneys to hunt provisions; Gibson, Deas, Bugg and Bowden are on picket guard; Larus has gone with a requisition for blankets and shoes, while the other members of the company are either keeping warm by the fire, or cooking their dinner.

The men enjoy good health, but I fear that many will suffer much with cold if we are not ordered soon to go into winter quarters. I do not think that any but insane men can approve of prosecuting an active campaign in North Western Virginia this winter.

In our tents we are quite comfortable, having a fire-place. It is made by digging a trench which is covered with rock, one end being in the tent, in which we build a fire, a barrel with both heads knocked out is our chimney: but even with the fire my hands are so cold I can hardly write.

Monday.- I was interupted in writing by Col. Clark bringing up the Regiment, armed with snowballs to take our battery. After a desperate fight, they suceeded.

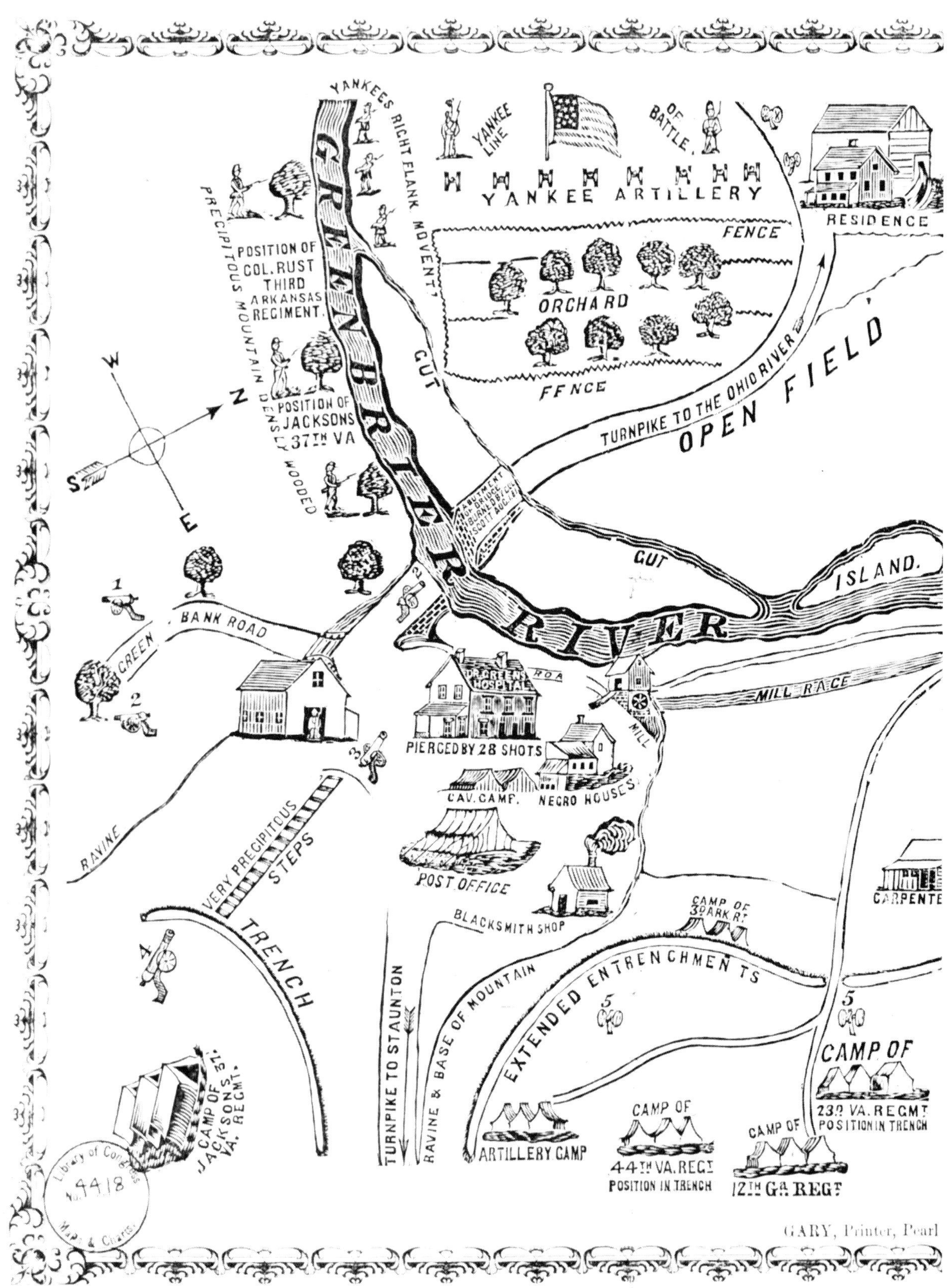

Map of the battleground of Greenbrier River, drawn and published by A. T. McRae, Quitman

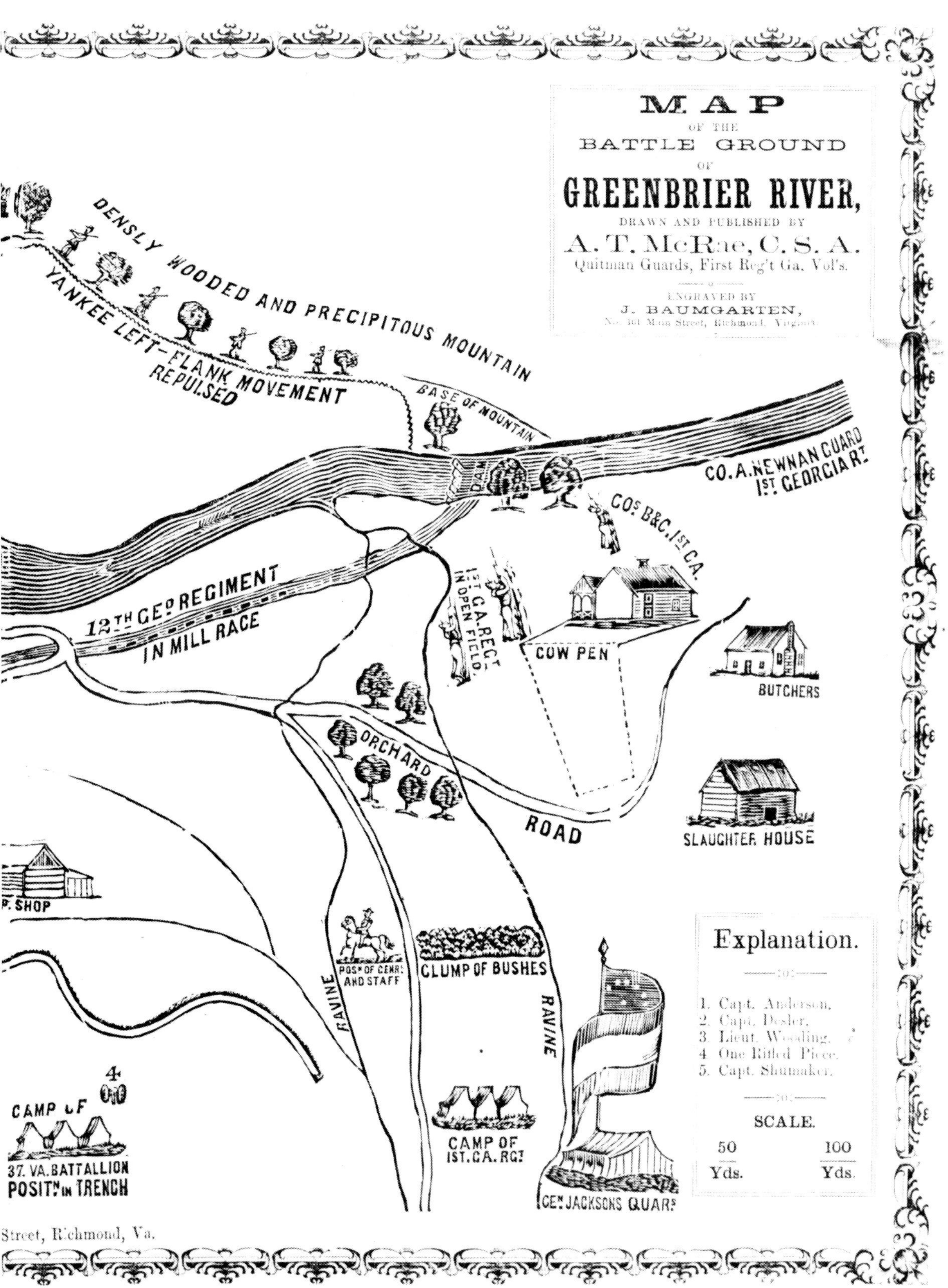

Guards, Co. K, 1st (Ramsey's) Regiment Georgia Volunteer Infantry, showing Camp Bartow.

Yesterday Henry J. Sibley arrived with blankets, &c. He gave to our company each man a blanket, undershirt and pair of socks. He also gave articles to the Oglethorpe Infantry and other companies.

An order has just been received for us to march to Staunton on Thursday, there to receive other orders. We are ordered to send our trunks and all extra baggage to-morrow.

As it is so cold I can hardly hold my pen, you will excuse brevity. The company are all well.

Yours, &c.   W.

Georgia Troops:
1st (Ramsey's) Regiment Georgia Volunteer Infantry, 9/9/1861-11/22/1861
12th Regiment Georgia Volunteer Infantry, 8/14/1861-11/21/1861
Sources:
1st GVI, GDAH, CSR, 254/91; UNC, #2292, William Oliver Fleming
12th GVI, GDAH, CSR, 254/91; 283/16, James Atkins; *A Post of Honor, The Pryor Letters, 1861-1863*, Edited and narrated by Charles R. Adams, Jr.

33   **Camp Bartow**
Prince William County, Virginia

The camp was located two and one-half miles northeast of Manassas near the Smith's house and the railroad.

Georgia Troops:
7th Regiment Georgia Volunteer Infantry, 7/30/1861-9/11/1861
8th Regiment Georgia Volunteer Infantry, 7/30/1861-9/11/1861
9th Regiment Georgia Volunteer Infantry, 8/31/1861-9/11/1861
11th Regiment Georgia Volunteer Infantry, 8/1/1861-9/11/1861
20th Regiment Georgia Volunteer Infantry, 8/1/1861-8/7/1861
Sources:
7th GVI, GDAH, CSR, 255/33; 283/33, Fernando D. McMillan
8th GVI, GDAH, CSR, 255/44
9th GVI, GDAH, CSR, 255/56
11th GVI, GDAH, CSR, 255/77
20th GVI, EU, #20, Lewis Groce, Jr.

34   **Camp Bartow**
Spotsylvania County, Virginia

The camp was located near Fredericksburg.

Georgia Troops:
14th Regiment Georgia Volunteer Infantry, 3/10/1862-3/21/1862 (With Hampton's Brigade)
19th Regiment Georgia Volunteer Infantry, 3/10/1862-3/21/1862 (With Hampton's Brigade)
Sources:
14th GVI, *War of the Rebellion, Official Records of the Union and Confederate Armies*, Series 1, Vol. 5, p. 533. Hereinafter refered to as O.R.'s, and will be Series 1 unless noted otherwise.
19th GVI, GDAH, CSR, 256/7

35   **Camp Battalion**
Henrico County, Virginia
The camp was located three miles north of Richmond.
Georgia Troops:
Cobb's Legion, Cavalry Battalion, 7/4/1862
Source:
UNC, #3353, Noble John Brooks

36   **Camp Battalion**
Rockingham County, Virginia
Probably located near Harrisonburg. No location was given in the compiled service records, but the cavalry battalion was in this area during this time.
Georgia Troops:
Cobb's Legion, Cavalry Battalion., Co. C, 2/1863 (The Infantry and Cavalry of Cobb's Legion permanently separated in February of 1863.)
Sources:
GDAH, CSR, 258/8; ADC&S, 3/8/1863

37   **Camp Battery Harrison**
Chatham County, Georgia
The camp was located one-half mile north of Battery Harrison, and three and one-half miles from Savannah on White Bluff Road. The 32nd Regiment Georgia Volunteer Infantry was mustered in at this camp April 11, 1861. Battery Harrison was also two and one-half miles from Camp William Duncan Smith at the rear of the city park. John Carswell wrote February 23rd, 1862, "We are not far from Gen. (Col.) W's (Wilson's) brigade."
Georgia Troops:
3rd Regiment Georgia State Troops,
2/21/1861-4/7/1861
32nd Regiment Georgia Volunteer Infantry,
4/11/1861-5/27/1861
Sources:
3rd GST, GDAH, 91/64, Thomas W. Shine;
GDAH, 43/79, John D. Carswell
32nd GVI, SDMN, 4/12/1862 & 5/27/1862

Private Bryant G. Phillips, Co. A, 32nd Regiment Georgia Volunteer Infantry. Enlisted in 1862, and was a member of the band.

photo courtesy of Lee Joyner

38   **Camp Bay Spring**
Bibb County, Georgia

Located at the Bay Spring school house. The following is a portion of the letter to the editor of the *Macon Telegraph.*

Mr. Editor: On Monday last, the Warrior Rifles left their parade ground and took up the line of march for Bay Spring school house, five miles distant, for a week's encampment. Notwithstanding the day was oppressively hot, and the road a portion of the way through deep sand, the soldiers seemed not to be wearied, but so soon as the camp was pitched, commenced playing leap frog, running races, &c., although a meridian sun was pouring down its intensest rays.

Bay Spring camp is a delightful place for a military encampment. On an elevated level is a commodious school house, and breaking out from the foot of this elevation on several sides of it are bold never failing springs. Separated from the encampment by a bold stream of pellucid water (a delightful bathing place) is the parade ground - an old field of more than 40 acres of sufficient slope to relieve the monotony.

Here shortly after dinner our drill commenced, Capt. Shelton of Macon our drilling officer. We remained until this (Saturday) morning, drilling regularly every day, A.M. and P.M. The best of feeling prevailed, and when off the drill the company was engaged in athletic sports never evincing weariness or fatigue.

On Thursday we were visited by large numbers of friends and neighbors from fifteen miles around, and at noon were enlivened by a patriotic soul-stirring speech from Col. J.H.R. Washington of Macon in reference to the present struggle and our duties as patriots. The Warrior Rifles is composed of as good material as can be found in the Southern Confederacy. Rough, tough and active, they seem to endure hardship with fortitude, and labor without weariness. Our Corps is commanded by Capt. Cicero A. Tharp - is composed of 54 men rank and file, anxious for a chance at the rail splitting minions.

Before they were dismissed, several resolutions were adopted.
Georgia Troops:
Warrior Rifles, 8/1/1861-8/8/1861
Source:
MT, 8/7/1861

39   **Camp Beall**
Chesterfield County, Virginia

The camp was located at Drewry's Bluff.
Georgia Troops:
Confederate States of America Marines, 11/17/1862-1/22/1863
Sources:
GDAH, UDC Books, Vol. VI, Henry L. Graves

40   **Camp Beasley**
Floyd County, Georgia
Located seven and one-half miles north of Rome. See map of Rome on page 303.
Georgia Troops:
Second Regiment Georgia State Guards, Cavalry, 12/16/1893-1/20/1864
Source:
GDAH, CSR, 253/86

41   **Camp Beaulieu**
Chatham County, Georgia
The camp was located at Beaulieu plantation on the Vernon River, ten miles south of Savannah.
The plantation was owned by David Cole, Sheriff of Chatham County.
Georgia Troops:
8th Battalion Georgia Volunteer Infantry, 6/11/1862-7/5/1862
31st Regiment Georgia Volunteer Infantry, 5/20/1862
Sources:
8th Bn GVI: GDAH, CSR, 255/52
31st GVI: GDAH, 215/40, Curry Hill plantation

42   **Camp Beauregard.**
Columbia County, Florida
The camp was located on the Olustee River, 13 miles from Lake City, between Barber's and
Lake City.
Georgia Troops:
28th Battalion Georgia Siege Artillery, 2/13/1864-2/21/1864
Chatham Artillery, 2/13/1864-2/21/1864
Guerards Light Battery, 2/13/1864-2/21/1864
1st Regiment Georgia Regulars, 2/13/1864-2/21/1864
6th Regiment Georgia Volunteer Infantry, 2/13/1864-2/21/1864
19th Regiment Georgia Volunteer Infantry, 2/13/1864-2/21/1864
23rd Regiment Georgia Volunteer Infantry, 2/13/1864-2/21/1864
27th Regiment Georgia Volunteer Infantry, 2/13/1864-2/21/1864
28th Regiment Georgia Volunteer Infantry, 2/13/1864-2/21/1864
32nd Regiment Georgia Volunteer Infantry, 2/13/1864-2/21/1864
64th Regiment Georgia Volunteer Infantry, 2/13/1864-2/21/1864
Sources:
ASB, 3/2/1864; O.R. Vol. 35, Pt.1, 331, 346

43   **Camp Beauregard**
Camden County, Georgia
Location not known. The companies were on picket duty.
Georgia Troops:
4th (Clinch's) Georgia Volunteer Cavalry, Companies C & H, 6/1863
Source:
GDAH, CSR, 253/94

44   **Camp Beauregard**
Garrard County, Kentucky
See Camp Dick Robinson.

45   **Camp Beauregard**
New Hanover County, North Carolina
The camp was located near Wilmington.
Georgia Troops:
47th Regiment Georgia Volunteer Infantry, Company B., 12/18/1862-1/3/1863
Source:
GDAH, CSR, 257/42

46   **Camp Beauregard**
Richland County, South Carolina
The camp was located near Columbia.
Georgia Troops:
32nd Georgia Volunteer Infantry, Company F, 2/21/1864
Source:
GDAH, 160/10, W.R. Harrison

47   **Camp Bee**
Chatham County, Georgia
   The camp was located near White Bluff at Vernonsburg, on the Vernon River. The name was probably named after Gen. Barnard E. Bee who was killed at the battle of the 1st Manassas.
Georgia Troops:
32nd Regiment Georgia Volunteer Infantry. 7/1/1863-10/1/1863
Sources:
GDAH, CSR, 256/96; 90/36, SDMN, 7/7/1863 & 7/8/1863

48   **Camp Belcher**
Chesterfield County, Virginia
   The camp was near Mechanics cotton factory on Swift Creek, two and one-half miles above Petersburg. See Atlas Plate LXXVII, 3.
Georgia Troops:
4th Regiment Georgia Volunteer Infantry, 5/22/1862-5/28/1862
Sources:
GDAH, CSR, 254/128; AHC, Ms. 51f, Richard Memminger Campbell diary

49   **Camp Bellfield**
Greenville County, Virginia
   The camp was located near Bellfield.
Georgia Troops:
Cobb's Legion, Cavalry Battalion. 1/12/1865
Source:
GDAH, 283/29, William Thomas Huff

50
Camp Belton
Bradley County, Tennessee
The camp was located near Cleveland, Tennessee.
3rd Regiment Confederate Cavalry, Co. E, 8/31/1862
Source:
GDAH, CSR, 258/64

51
Camp Ben Hill
Chesterfield County, Virginia
The camp was located on Falling Creek below Richmond.
Georgia Troops:
3rd Regiment Georgia Volunteer Infantry, 6/15/1862-8/8/1862
Sources:
GDAH, CSR, 254/114; ASB, 8/27/1862

52
Camp Benning
Muscogee County, Georgia
The camp was located near Columbus, and named after General Henry Benning of Columbus.
Georgia Troops:
Dawson Artillery, 8/11/1864-8/13/1864
Source:
CDT, 8/13/1864

53
Camp Berrien
Chatham County, Georgia
The camp was located near the toll gate at White Bluff Road and Lovers Lane.
Georgia Troops:
1st Regiment Infantry Georgia Army, Co. D, 3/10/1862-3/17/1862
2nd Battalion Georgia Cavalry, 10/24/1861-10/28/1861, 11/10/1861-1/18/1862 & 1/13/1863-1/22/1863 (The 2nd Bn. Ga. Cav. became a part of the 5th Regiment Georgia Volunteer Cavalry on 1/22/1863.)
5th Regiment Georgia Volunteer Cavalry, 1/22/1863-5/5/1863 & 5/15/1864-5/17/1864
Savannah Volunteer Guards, 4/4/1862
Sources:
1st RGA, UGA, #25, Margaret Branch Sexton Collection
2nd Bn GC, EU, #12, John H. Ash; SR, 10/25/1861 & 10/28/1861
5th GC, GDAH, CSR, 253/87; EU, #12, John H. Ash; SR, 5/16/1864
SVG, SR, 4/5/1862

54   **Camp Berryville**
Clark County, Virginia

The camp was located near Berryville.
Georgia Troops:
14th Regiment Georgia Volunteer Infantry, 10/1862
Source:
GDAH, CSR, 255/101

55   **Camp Bethel**
McNairy County, Tennessee

The camp was located twenty miles above Corinth, Mississippi, near Bethel Springs. See Camp Maxey.
Georgia Troops:
5th Regiment Georgia Volunteer Infantry, 4/15/1862-4/23/1862
Sources:
DU, William McCoy; GDAH, 160/57, John C. Curtwright

Major William Lewis Salisbury, 5th Regiment Georgia Volunteer Infantry. Retired at reorganization, May 8, 1862. Elected Colonel 5th Regiment Georgia State Guards Infantry.

photo courtesy of David Vaughn

56   **Camp Bethesda**
Chatham County, Georgia

The camp was located at the Bethesda Orphanage, ten miles below Savannah and two miles from Camp Philips.
Georgia Troops:
7th Battalion Georgia Volunteer Infantry, 3/19/1862-5/26/1862
Source:
GDAH, CSR, 257/113

57
Camp Bethlehem
Washington County, Georgia

The camp was probably at the Bethlehem Academy, which was the meeting room of the Jackson Guards. Bethlehem Academy was in the immediate vicinity of Bethlehem Church. When they went into camp, they invited other companies from Washington County and adjoining counties to join them. On October 1, 1861, they passed through Sandersville on their way to Camp Harrison.

Georgia Troops:
Jackson Guards, 7/29/1861-8/2/1861 (They later became Company B, 1st Regiment Georgia State Troops.)
Sources:
CG, 7/17/1861 & 8/7/1861

58
Camp Beulah
Knox County, Tennessee

The camp was located near Knoxville.
Georgia Troops:
1st Regiment Georgia Volunteer Cavalry, 2/28/1863
Source:
GDAH, MR, 279/64

59
Camp Big Creek Gap
Claiborne County, Tennessee

The camp was located at Big Creek Gap on the Kentucky-Tennessee state line, just west of Cumberland Gap.
Georgia Troops:
1st Regiment Georgia Volunteer Cavalry, part of regiment, 5/30/1862-6/8/1862
36th (Glenn's) Regiment Georgia Volunteer Infantry, 6/1/1862
Sources:
1st GVC, GDAH, 187/12, James M. Pepper
36th GVI, GDAH, CSR, 256/112

60
Camp Big Hill
Madison County, Kentucky

The camp was located near Big Hill. See map accompanying Camp Dick Robinson for the location of Big Hill.
Georgia Troops:
55th Regiment Georgia Volunteer Infantry, 10/15/1862
Source:
DU, Daniel Printup

61   **Camp Big Level**
Lexington County, South Carolina
The camp was located fifteen miles southwest of Columbia.
Georgia Troops:
66th Regiment Georgia Volunteer Infantry, 2/18/1865.
Source:
AHC, Ms. #78f, Jones Porter Crane

62   **Camp Big Savannah**
Dawson County, Georgia
The camp is located in the southeast part of Dawson County.
Georgia Troops:
11th Regiment Georgia Militia Cavalry, 11/7/1864
Source:
Athens Southern Watchman, 11/30/1864

63   **Camp Bird**
Chatham County, Georgia
The camp was located in the rear of the Medical College in Savannah.
Georgia Troops:
2nd Battalion Georgia Cavalry, Co A, 5/1862-1/16/1862
5th Regiment Georgia State Troops, Co H, 4/23/1862
Sources:
2nd Bn GC, GDAH, CSR, 253/87; SR, 1/20/1863
5th GST, SR, 4/24/1862

64   **Camp Bivouac**
Madison County, Mississippi
The camp was located about one mile south of Vernon.
Georgia Troops:
46th Regiment Georgia Volunteer Infantry, 6/14/1863-6/17/1863
Sources:
GDAH, CSR, 257/35; GHS, #874, Claudius C. Wilson

65   **Camp Black**
Gordon County, Georgia
Located at Blackwood Springs, four miles east of Calhoun. The 8th Battalion Georgia Volunteer
Infantry organized and trained in this camp.
Georgia Troops:
8th Battalion Georgia Volunteer Infantry, 10/3/1861-11/5/1861
Sources:
GDAH, CSR, 255/52; ADC&S, 11/7/1861: *A Short Sketch of the PAST HALF CENTURY by an
old Confederate soldier*, By T. T. Bell

66   **Camp Black**
Jackson County, Tennessee
The camp was located two miles from Bridgeport.
Georgia Troops:
1st Confederate Regiment Georgia Volunteers, 2nd Battalion, 7/10/1863-7/13/1863
Source:
Civil War Regiments, "From Santa Rosa Island to Chickamauga," C. Pat Cates

67   **Camp Blanchard**
Portsmouth County, Virginia
The camp was located in an old field three miles southwest of Portsmouth on the western branch of the Elizabeth River, also, six miles east of Camp Vincent. While in this camp the men would march to the James River, some six miles, and watch naval battles on Hampton Roads.
Georgia Troops:
22nd Regiment Georgia Volunteer Infantry, 12/1861-2/22/1862 & 4/1/1862-4/20/1862
Sources:
GDAH, CSR, 256/28; 65/54, Col. Robert H. Jones; RWC, 2/21/62

68   **Camp Blois**
Beaufort County, South Carolina
Not certain as to its location. Possibly on New River or Red Bluff.
Georgia Troops:
Oglethorpe Siege Artillery, Lieut. Theodore Blois, 2/3/1862
Source:
SDMN, 2/4/1862

69   **Camp Blue Spring**
Dougherty County, Georgia
Located at Blue Spring near Albany.
Georgia Troops:
Mitchell Independants, 5/15/1861-5/23/1861 (Later they became Co. F, 6th Regiment Georgia Volunteer Infantry.)
Sources:
AP, 5/16/1861 & 5/30/1861

70   **Camp Bolton (Belton)**
Fulton County, Georgia
Located near Atlanta, probably near Bolton Station on the Western and Atlantic Railroad.
Georgia Troops:
Georgia Militia, 6/17/1864-7/9/1864
Source:
Letters of Jonathan Bridges, a Confederate Soldier of Stewart County, Georgia, by Richard M. Patchin and Deborah Dean Patchin

71   **Camp Bonna Bella**
Chatham County, Georgia
Located on the Bonna Bella plantation below Savannah.
Georgia Troops:
20th Battalion Georgia Cavalry, most companies, 12/1862-3/20/1863
Sources:
GDAH, CSR, 254/6; SDMN 3/19/1863

72   **Camp Bradford**
Leon County, Florida
Located twelve miles north of Tallahassee, near Bradfordville.
Georgia Troops:
Georgia Militia, 11/11/1864-11/25/1864
Source:
GDAH, 283/30, Jack H. King

73   **Camp Bragg**
Glynn County, Georgia
Located fourteen miles from Camp Wayne.
Georgia Troops:
4th (Clinch's) Georgia Volunteer Cavalry, Co. K, 11/1862 & 12/1862
Source:
GDAH, CSR, 253/94

74   **Camp Brailsford**
Liberty County, Georgia
The camp was probably located at or near Sutherland Bluff.

On November 7, 1862 , the Union gunboat *Potomska*, proceeded up the Sapelo River and stopped at each of the plantations along the river. One of the plantations, located on Sutherland Bluff was owned by Captain William Brailsford of the Lamar Rangers (Lamar Mounted Rifles.) The Union report stated,

> Under the guns of the *Potomska* we landed at Colonel Brailsford's, drove in a company
> of pickets from his regiment, and destroyed all the property on the place, together with all
> the most important buildings.

Captain Brailsford responded in a letter to the editor of the *Savannah Daily Morning News*, published November 19, 1862. It read,

> I see in the *News and Republican* a great deal said about very little, with regard to the
> Yankees coming up the Sapelo River, and the two fights that is said to have taken place;
> and as the writer has put my name in his publication, and not wishing even our abolition
> enemies to suppose I am afflicted with the epedemic which is so prevalent both South and
> North, which is not being able to tell the truth, and being an eye witness to the whole
> affair, I will give you the facts as they occured: I rode down to one of my pickets stationed

at Sutherland Bluff, which is the first land upon the main. Two steamboats - one a propeller, the other the old *Darlington*, I think - came up the river about eight o'clock in the morning. The boats stopped about five minutes, and I expected them to shell, but they did not. The boats went up the river to Belville (Plantation), Colonel Hopkins' place, landed some men for a few minutes, then went on to Mr. King's place (Mallow Plantation), stopped, landed a negro company, which they have had stationed at St. Simon's Island, and took all of Mr. King's negroes, with a few exceptions, and would have taken the old gentleman if his daughter had not clung to him as she did. The propellor stayed there, and the old *Darlington*, with her negro company and one gun, proceeded up the river to Mr. McDonald's place. As they passed White Bluff, Captain Hopkins' Company fired on the boat with their small arms; when the boat could bring her gun to bear she fired four or five guns at the bluff. I had my men conceiled about two hundred yards from the river, and took my position in the yard so as to see them when they landed. They shelled for one hour and a half, and the trees under cover of which my men were conceiled, were riddled. All we did was to lay down and dodge shot and shell, and I think the only blood that was spilt on either side during the day, was a little bull calf of mine that was knocked down by a shell.

Georgia Troops:
1st Battalion Georgia Cavalry, Lamar Mounted Rifles, Captain Brailsford's Company, 11/11/1862-2/1/1862 (The company became Co. H, 5th Regiment Georgia Volunteer Cavalry, when the regiment organized on 1/22/1863.)
Sources:
GDAH, CSR, 253, 79 & 101; O.R., Vol. XIV, 192

75   **Camp Brandy Station**
Culpeper County, Virginia
  The camp was located at Brandy Station. See Atlas Plate XLIV, 3.
Georgia Troops:
13th Regiment Georgia Volunteer Infantry, 10/20/1863
Source:
UNC, #3348, W.R. Redding

76   **Camp Brighton**
McIntosh County, Georgia.
  The camp was located near Darien.
Georgia Troops:
20th Battalion Georgia Cavalry, Company C, 6/1863-8/1863
Source:
GDAH, CSR, 254/6

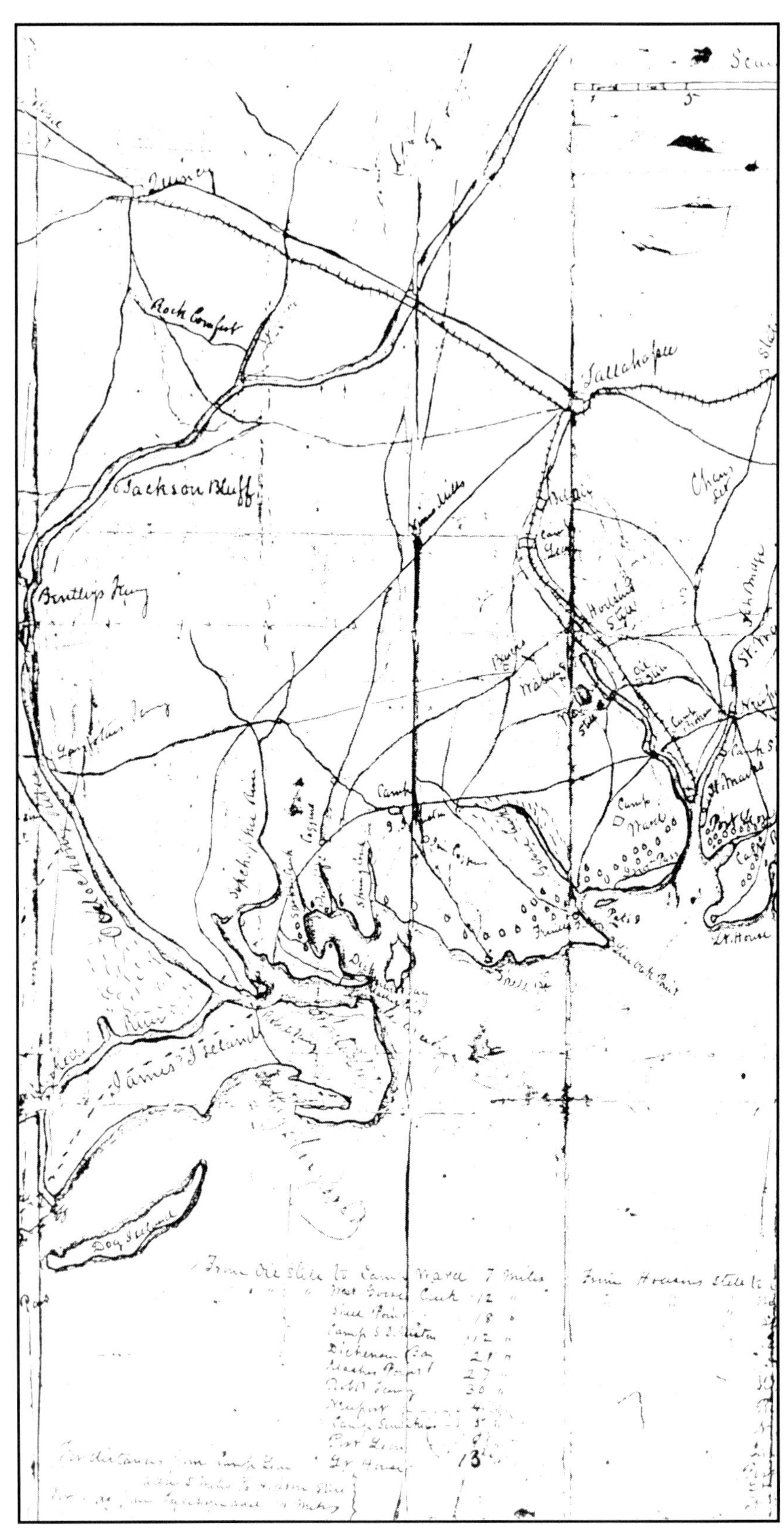

Map of the Tallahassee-St. Marks area showing the locations of

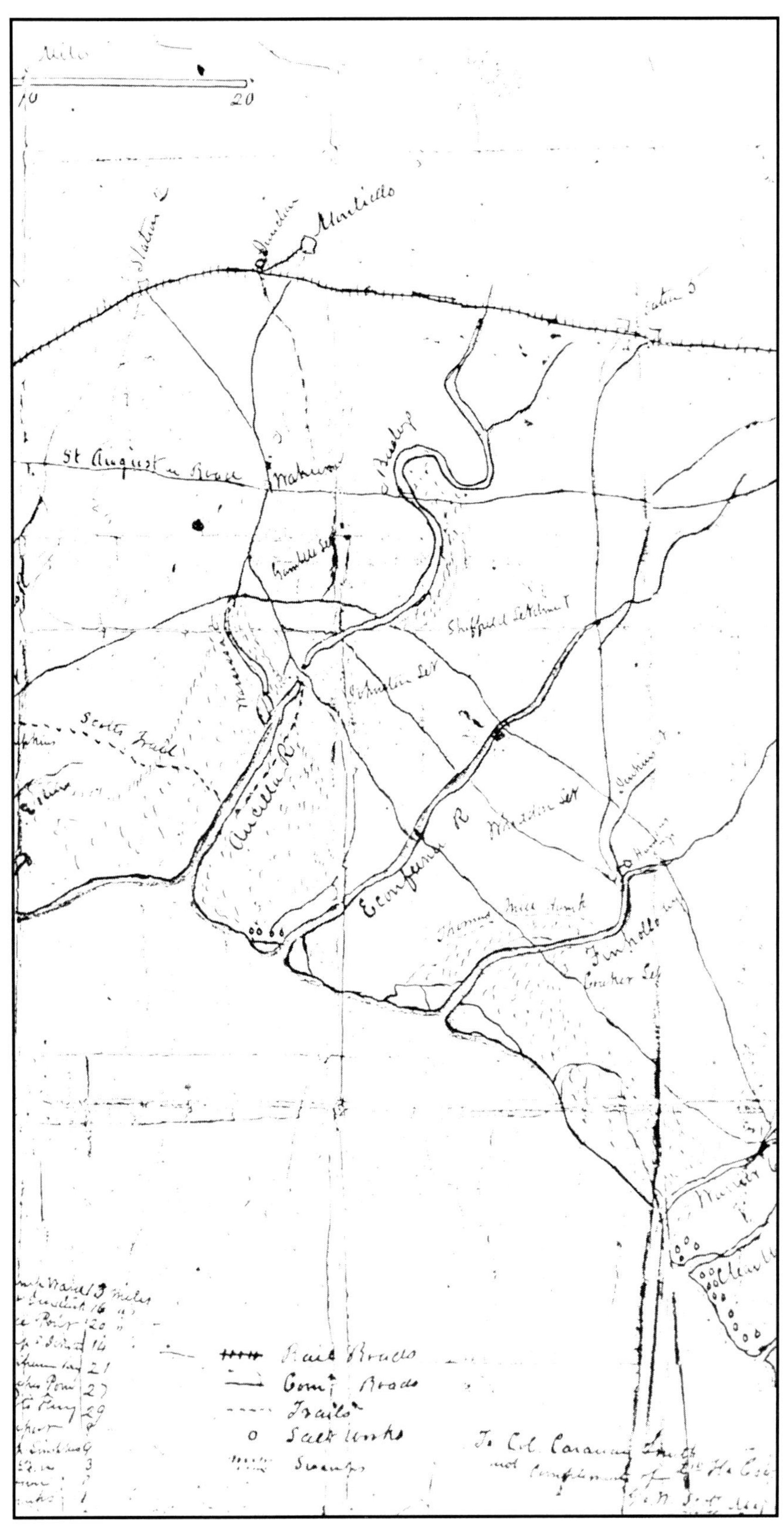

Camps Brokaw, Leon and Simpkins.
Map courtesy of The Florida State Archives

77   **Camp Brokaw**
Wakulla County, Florida
    Located about three miles from St. Marks and one to two miles west of Newport. (See map on
pages 72 & 73.)
Georgia Troops:
Echols' Light Artillery, Capt. Tiller's Co., 4/1/1863-5/28/1863
Capt. Cullen's Independent Company of infantry, 2/23/1863-3/24/1863
Sources:
ELA, GDAH, CSR, 254/63; PC, James Jewell letters; EU, #20, James Jewell
CCIC, GDAH, CSR, 258/5

78   **Camp Brookfield**
Glynn County, Georgia
    The general location is not known.
Georgia Troops:
4th (Clinch's) Georgia Volunteer Cavalry, Co. D, 9/1862-2/1863
Source:
GDAH, CSR, 253/94

79   **Camp Brooks**
Chatham County, Georgia
    This is a picket post east of Savannah.
Georgia Troops:
5th Regiment Georgia Volunteer Cavalry, Companies D & G, 7/13/1863-7/20/1863
Sources:
GDAH, CSR, 254/9; SDMN, 7/22/1863

80   **Camp Brown**
Bibb County, Georgia
    The camp was located near Macon. There may be two Camp Browns near Macon. One named
after Governor Joseph Brown, the other after Col. Jack Brown of the 59th Regiment Georgia
Volunteer Infantry.
Georgia Troops:
Muckalee Guards, later Company A, 12th Regiment Georgia Volunteer Infantry,
6/10/1861-6/14/1861 (The Muckalee Guards left for Richmond on 6/14/1861.)
59th Regiment Georgia Volunteer Infantry, 6/13/1862-8/31/1862 (The 59th Georgia was formed
from the 7th Regiment Georgia State Troops.)
Sources:
MG, EU, #20, John Levi Griffin.
59th GVI, GDAH, CSR, 257/99; 91/64, Vincent Montgomery

81   **Camp Brown**
Chatham County, Georgia

The camp was located in the rear of the Catholic (Cathedral) Cemetery, near Fort Brown. This was the headquarters of the 2nd Brigade Georgia State Troops at this time.

Georgia Troops:
2nd Brigade Georgia State Troops, 3/7/1862-4/16/1862
4th Regiment Georgia State Troops, 2/14/1862-4/18/1862
7th Regiment Georgia State Troops, 3/20/1862-3/27/1862
Irish Jasper Greens, Co. B, 2/2/1862-4/30/1862
Georgia Light Artillery, 2/23/1862-3/30/1862
50th Regiment Georgia Volunteer Infantry, 5/1862-7/19/1862

Sources:
2nd Brig GST, DU, CSA Papers
4th GST, *Saddle Bag and Spinning Wheel*, Edited by George Peddy Cuttino
7th GST, SDMN, 3/26/1862; MT, 3/31/1862
IJG, Co. B, SDMN, 2/24/1862 & 4/30/1862
GLA, WL, William H. Hill; CG, 2/26/1862
50th GVI, GDAH, CSR, 257/63

82   **Camp Brown**
Cobb County, Georgia

Located about five miles below Marietta on the Smyrna campground. It was originally referred to as Camp Smyrna. Cadets from the Georgia Military Institute in Marietta were used as drill masters. See Camp McDonald for the organization of the 4th Brigade of Georgia Volunteers.

> Camp Brown, Near Marietta,
> Georgia, April 30th 1861

My Dear Wife,

I am happy to inform you that my health & strength are fully & I trust permanently restored - I never recovered health & strength faster in my life than since I left home - I have not been off my post of duty a single moment day nor night rain or sunshine since I arrived here.

I am now more stronger & more vigorous than I have been for several years. I have always thought that an Army life would be best for me & I am now convinced of the fact. My men are all well & in the highest spirits - The Governor is now in Camps with us. He arrived last night - and will leave this evening after Review.

The greatest possible enthusiasm pervades every breast here. Troops are daily passing out Camp in route for the seat of war. Several Companies from the encampment have already left. We will probably not be called into the field under two or three weeks. No Company in the encampment are making more rapid improvement in the art of war than mine. My Company and the Hart County Company are looked upon as the Stoutest & hardest soldiers in the Brigade.

Tell Mrs. Pace that she might never to regret that Mr. Pace joined the volunteers. There is not a better soldier on the American Continent nor one who will discharge his duty better & with more credit to himself & country.

Mr Pace will write to morrow.

We will start for home in a few days. We will perhaps remain at home a few days or weeks at furthest, before taking up our line of march for the enemy's camp. I regret very much indeed that Dr. Young did not obey the order to this encampment.

When I arrived here, I made arrangements with Gen'l. Phillips to give to Dr. Young the appointment of Assistant Surgeon of the Brigade and with that determination, we were anxiously awaiting his arrival when I received a letter from him which I fear will be the means of the appointment falling upon an other man.

Governor Brown told us to day that we need have no fear of our volunteers disbanding or backing out while we are absent, that if they do, we shall be required to fill up the ranks immediately by draft for a longer term of service - that he has in safe keeping Eight thousand of the best arms on the Continent with which we are to be supplied when called into the field - that the guns he sent us, was only for us to learn to drill with -

If you should have any chance to send Mrs. Jones any word you may tell her also that R. A. Jones is well & in finest spirits.

Mr Lester is also well pleased with camp, Jane.

It is necessary for me to attempt to write you the news from the seat of war - as you will keep posted by the news papers. The ladies of Marietta gives us a dinner to morrow.

I beg you not to feel uneasy about me - be cheerful & happy. Tell the children and your Ma to be cheerful & contented that I make the sacrifice & endure the trial through a sense of duty & that it will all return to our mutual future happiness & prosperity - Kiss them all for me, God bless you all - I hope to be with you in a few days. Most devotedly

as ever   W. T. Millican

Colonel William T. Millican began his military service as Captain of the Tugalo Blues of the 4th Brigade of Georgia Volunteers. The Tugalo Blues later became Co. B, 15th Regiment Georgia Volunteer Infantry. He was elected Lieutenant Colonel, May 1, 1862 and Colonel, July 22, 1862. He was wounded and captured at Sharpsburg, Maryland, September 17, 1862. He died at David Smith's Farm, Virginia on September 17, 1862, and is buried in the Confederate Cemetery at Hagerstown, Maryland.

photo courtesy of Lee Joyner

Georgia Troops:
4th Brigade of Georgia Volunteers, 4/23/1861-5/9/1861
Georgia Military Institute Cadets, 4/23/1861-5/9/1861
Sources:
RWC, 5/3/1861 & 5/17/1861

83   **Camp Brown**

Fulton County, Georgia

The camp was located about three miles north of Atlanta. The following is an extract of a letter of Captain Henry Mitchell, Co. E., 5th Regiment Georgia Militia.

> Since I wrote you the other day we have moved our camps, three miles north of Atlanta and about six miles from our old camp (Camp Georgia). We are camped near the railroad going to Marietta. We are fifteen miles below Marietta.

Georgia Troops:
Georgia Militia, 6/9/1864
Source:
GDAH, 283/23, Dickey Family Letters

84   **Camp Brown**

Talbot County, Georgia

The camp was located near Talbotton, and fourteen miles from Geneva.
Georgia Troops:
Captain Little's Co., later Co. E, 29th Battalion Georgia Cavalry, 7/29/1863-9/29/1863
Sources:
GDAH, CSR, 254/13

85   **Camp Brucetown**

Frederick County, Virginia

The camp was located near Brucetown, north of Winchester.
Georgia Troops:
50th Regiment Georgia Volunteer Infantry, 8/1864 & 9/29/1864-10/18/1864
Source:
GDAH, CSR, 257/63

86   **Camp Bryan**

York County, Virginia

The camp was located near Grafton Church about three miles south of Yorktown on Newport News Road.

The following are excerpts from a letter signed by J.R.N. of Col. Howell Cobb's Regiment that were published in the November 6, 1861, *Southern Banner* describing the trip from Camp Cobb to Camp Bryan.

> On Saturday morning, the 19th inst. 4 1/2 o'clock, we struck our tents and came forty miles by railroad to West Point on the York river. There we took passage on the steamer *Logan*. Our trip down the York river was delightful. A bracing sea breeze kept the surface of the water ruffled as the steamer ploughed her way through it. Many of us stood out on the deck and feasted our eyes on the rich scenery around us. The river is from two to three miles wide. The houses and villages dotting the hills and valleys for miles away in every direction; the white pools behind where the water had been lashed into foam by the wheels of the steamer; the waves in every direction rushed together and throwing up their white

caps; the oyster boats occasionally seen gliding about with their sails swelling before the breeze; the water fowls circling around through the air; the sharp report of rifles and the singing of minnie balls that would be seen every few minutes whizzing at the birds; and the music of our brass band that would occasionally throw a charm over everything as it floated over the waters, made the time pass pleasantly.

We landed at Yorktown about dark, and marched half a mile to a grove of little scrubby cedars on the bank of the river, leaving our tents and baggage to be brought to us in wagons, We laid off our knapsacks but a few steps from the old Revolutionary fortifications, ate our cold rations from our haversacks, and soon were stretched on the wet ground, sleeping as soundly as the nature of our beds would admit of. - When the baggage and tents arrived, late at night, a few pitched their tents, but most of the regiment continued to sleep in the open air. The next morning we took up our line of march for this place, which is on the direct road from Yorktown to Newport News. But before leaving, some of us gratified the curiosity we had, to see the place where Cornwallace surrendered to Washington. This spot is now marked by a marble monument, about a quarter of a mile from the river. Relics of Revolutionary times can yet be picked up about the old fortifications. We had in our hands a thirty pound cannon ball that had been dug up, and also a piece of bomb shell. The village of old brick houses are now there that were there eighty years ago. On some of them the prints of balls may be now seen. Age dilapidation and decay mark everything in the village. Rotten enclosures, mostly worm-eaten door facings, crumbling walls, and old fashioned architecture are the chief characteristics of the residences. As we look out from where we camped down the channel of the river, no land can be seen. The river widens for seven miles where it loses itself in the bay. The vast extended sheet of water seems to rise in the distance, and away off on the topless waves, could be seen the Federal blockading vessels. At first glance they would escape notice, but by close observation they appear to the naked eye like chips riding on the waves.

Between our present camp and Yorktown, stands the house in which the treaty was drawn up after the surrender of the British; and also the house which LaFayette used as his headquarters.

We are encamped in a clover field and are surrounded by a forest of ripe chesnuts, chinquepins, summer grapes, muscadines and walnuts. --- Wild turkeys are heard around our camp every morning. Cobb's Legion is encamped three miles from us towards Newport News. We have oysters here in the greatest abundance. -- The men are generally very fond of them. They go down to the creeks a few hundred yards off, and to the river about a half a mile distant, and gather their haversacks full, and bring them back to shell at their leisure. The first day we were here, it was a novel sight to see the men huddeled about in squads all over the encampment, cracking oysters. They prepare them in various ways. Some roast them in the shell, others make soup of them; some season them and eat them raw, others mix them in corn meal and dough and fry the mixture. ----

While in Richmond we experienced the worst trials incident to camp life, which are the camp diseases that generally go through every regiment. -- The regiment is now restored to health and great jollity prevails, as we go out into active service. I don't believe nine hundred and twenty happier men can be found together on the globe. -- We do not know at what moment we may be ordered out to battle. We keep cartridges in our boxes and one day's rations cooked ahead. The enemy are at Big Bethel and Newport News, and it is thought that they will land a large force on this Peninsular soon. Thirty war vessels are now to be seen off the coast below here.

Georgia Troops:
16th Regiment Georgia Volunteer Infantry, 10/20/1861-12/12/1861
Sources:
GDAH, CSR, 255/115; 20/76, W.G. Smith; ASB, 11/6/1861

87 **Camp Buckingham**
Buckingham County, Virginia

The camp was located forty miles from Lynchburg, and not more than fifty miles from the North Carolina State line.
Georgia Troops:
Phillips' Legion, Cavalry Battalion, 4/8/1863-5/13/1863
Source:
GDAH, 283/41, John T. Swan

88 **Camp Buckner**
Carter County, Tennessee

The camp was located near Elizabeth Station on the East Tennessee and Georgia Railroad.
Georgia Troops:
6th Regiment Georgia Cavalry. 8/20/1863
Source:
RWC, 8/28/1863

89 **Camp Buist**
Chatham County, Georgia

The camp was located near Savannah. Named after Major George Lamb Buist, commanding Siege Train Battery Artillery, composed of Guerard's and Daniel's Batteries Georgia Artillery and two South Carolina batteries.
Georgia Troops:
12th Battalion Georgia Volunteers, 3/3/1863
Sources:
GDAH, CSR, 254/33; *Georgia Artillery Units*, compiled by Willard E. Wright

90 **Camp Bumpass Station**
Louisa County, Virginia

The camp was located at Bumpass Station, about halfway between Louisa Court House and Hanover Junction.
Georgia Troops:
Phillips' Legion, Infantry Battalion, 8/31/1863-9/1/1863
Source:
KMNBPL, Marcus L. Green

91   **Camp Bunker Hill**
Frederick County, Virginia
The camp was located at Bunker Hill.
Georgia Troops:
8th Regiment Georgia Volunteer Infantry, 6/16/1861 & 6/17/1861
12th Regiment Georgia Volunteer Infantry, 9/23/1862-10/13/1862
21st Regiment Georgia Volunteer Infantry, 8/20/1864-8/22/1864
Sources:
8th GVI, RWC, 6/28/1861
12th GVI, *A Post of Honor, The Pryor Letters, 1861-63*, Edited and narrated by Charles R. Adams, Jr.
21st GVI, GDAH, CSR, 256/21

92   **Camp Bush Arbor**
Floyd County, Georgia
The camp was located nine miles southwest of Rome and nineteen miles from Camp Yeiser, probably at Bush Arbor Church.
Georgia Troops:
Floyd's Legion, State Guards, 9/1863
Source:
GDAH, CSR, 258/41

Macon Telegraph 8/6/61

RELICS -- In excavating the trenches at Yorktown the soldiers found an old magazine, the wooden walls entirely decayed, and within it a number of nine inch shells, the fuses rotted off, but charged with buckshot and with powder which is still alive and mischievous. The shells are of the description used in the last war with Great Britain, none of that caliber being known in the revolution. One of them was sent to Richmond for the inspection of President Davis.

---

93   **Camp Calhoun**
Chatham County, Georgia

The camp was located six miles below Savannah, near the Isle of Hope, and in twenty yards of the marsh.
Georgia Troops:
4th Battalion Georgia Volunteer Infantry, 4/5/1862-4/25/1862 (The 4th Battalion became a part of the 60th Regiment Georgia Volunteer Infantry on April 25, 1862.)
60th Regiment Georgia Volunteer Infantry, 4/25/1862-6/6/1862
Sources:
4th Bn GVI, SR, 4/9/1862 & 4/11/1862
60th GVI, GDAH, CSR, 257/105

94   **Camp Calhoun**
Gordon County, Georgia

The camp was located three miles east of Calhoun.
Georgia Troops:
3rd Regiment Georgia Volunteer Cavalry, 6/19/1862
Source:
KMNBPL, GA-26, William N. Thornton

95   **Camp Calhoun**
Hinds County, Mississippi

The camp was located near Calhoun Depot, about five miles north of Jackson.
Georgia Troops:
46th Regiment Georgia Volunteer Infantry, 5/15/1863-5/17/1863
Sources:
GDAH, CSR, 257/35; SC, 6/3/1863

96   **Camp Calhoun**
Jasper County, South Carolina

The camp was located in the "piney woods" near Pocataligo. The troops had to send four miles for cartridges.
Georgia Troops:
46th Regiment Georgia Volunteer Infantry, 3/28/1862-4/6/1862 (The 46th Georgia returned to the Pocataligo area on November 2, 1862.)
51st Regiment Georgia Volunteer Infantry, 3/28/1862-5/1862
Sources:
46th GVI, GDAH, 283/30, William R. King
51st GVI, GDAH, 283/43, William C. Ware

97   **Camp Callaway**
Chesterfield County, Virginia

   The camp was located on Swift Creek.
Georgia Troops:
Troup Artillery, Callaway Battery, 11/15/1864
Source:
EU, Charles James Oliver, Civil War journal

98   **Camp Candler**
Chatham County, Georgia

   The camp was located near Savannah.
Georgia Troops:
2nd Regiment Georgia Volunteer Infantry, Co. A, Banks Co. Guards & Co. E, Joe Browns,
4/1861-5/7/1861
Sources:
SDMN, 5/9/1861

99   **Camp Canoochee**
Bryan County, Georgia

   The camp was located near the Canoochee River.
Georgia Troops:
24th Battalion Georgia Cavalry, Co. B, 4/1863
Source:
GDAH, CSR, 254/11

100   **Camp Capers**
Chatham County, Georgia

   The camp was located five miles above Savannah on the Central Railroad. The name of the
camp was changed to Camp Lee on January 10, 1862. See the reference to this change described
in Camp Jasper.

STRAYED,

From Camp Capers, five miles above Savannah, on Central Railroad, a deep BAY STALLION, heavy mane, bob tail; very heavy neck and shoulders. Any information respecting his whereabouts left at Freeman & Henderson's stables, or at the camp of the Seventh Regiment, will be thankfully received, and a liberal reward given for his delivery at either of the above places.

Jan 28   tf

Georgia Troops:
7th Regiment Georgia State Troops, 1/27/1862-1/28/1862
Sources:
SDMN, 1/10/1862 & 1/27/1862; SR, 1/29/1862

101   **Camp Capes Baley**

Chatham County, Georgia

This was a picket post, located near Savannah, four to five miles from the regiment.

Georgia Troops:

Georgia State Troops. 7/29/1861

Source:

GDAH, 80/57, Truston B. Adams

102   **Camp Caroline**

Spotsylvania County, Virginia

The camp was located between the Rappahannock River, and the headwaters of the Mattaponi River, in hilly country.

Georgia Troops:

Cobb's Legion, Cavalry Battalion, 5/16/1862

Source:

GDAH, UDC Books, Vol. X, 166

103   **Camp Caroline**

Caroline County, Virginia

The camp was located near Chesterfield.

Georgia Troops:

Milledges Battery Georgia Light Artillery, 1/25/1863-4/1863

Source:

GDAH, CSR, 254/59

104   **Camp Carrington**

Wayne County, Georgia

This camp was probably located at or near Camp Satilla. It was named in honor of Mr. LaFayette Carrington.

Georgia Troops:

Milledgeville Grays, independent company of the 2nd Brigade Georgia State Troops, 1/10/1862

Source:

SFU, 1/21/1862

105   **Camp Carrollton**

Carroll County, Georgia

The camp was probably located near Carrollton. See Camp Ivor.

Georgia Troops.

7th Regiment Confederate Cavalry, Co. B, 6/10/1862-6/18/1862 (They later became Co. B, 10th Georgia Cavalry.)

Source:

GDAH, CSR, 258/69

106   **Camp Carswell**
Fulton County, Georgia

The name was changed from Camp Lick Skillet on June 24, 1864. See Camp Lick Skillet for location.
Georgia Troops:
Georgia Militia, 6/23/1864 & 6/24/1864
Sources:
GDAH, M87-019; AHC, Ms. 116, A.T. Holliday

107   **Camp Carteret**
Glynn County, Georgia

The camp was located at Carteret Point above Ridgeville.
Georgia Troops:
1st Battalion Georgia Cavalry, Lamar Mounted Rifles, 10/31/1861 (They later became Co. H, 5th Regiment Georgia Volunteer Cavalry.)
4th (Clinch's) Regiment Georgia Volunteer Cavalry, Co. A, 6/1862-9/1862
13th (Styles') Regiment Georgia Volunteer Infantry, Brunswick Riflemen, 10/1861
Sources:
LMR, GDAH, MR, 279/65
4th GVC, GDAH, CSR, 253/94
13th GVI, *South Georgia Rebels,* By Alton J. Murray

108   **Camp Causton's Bluff**
Chatham County, Georgia

The camp was located near Causton's Bluff on the St. Augustine Creek, four miles east of Savannah.

The 13th Regiment Georgia Volunteer Infantry and Phillips' Legion were transferred to the southern coast from General Floyd's Brigade in West Virginia. The following is extracted from the December 14, 1861 inspection report of Assistant Inspector-General, George Deas.

> I would recommend that the Thirteenth Georgia Regiment, Phillips' Legion, and the Twentieth Mississippi Regiment be ordered into a milder climate. The severe winters of Western Virginia will be fatal to those Southern men.

Phillips' Legion was transfered to the Hardeeville, South Carolina area, and the 13th Regiment Georgia Volunteer Infantry was sent to Savannah.
Georgia Troops:
13th (Ector's) Regiment Georgia Volunteer Infantry, 12/20/1861-6/7/1862
25th Regiment Georgia Volunteer Infantry, 6/17/1862-10/22/1862 & 10/24/1862-12/13/1862
(The 25th Regiment left for North Carolina on 12/13/1862.)
29th Regiment Georgia Volunteer Infantry, 4/16/1862-8/26/1862
47th Regiment Georgia Volunteer Infantry, 4/30/1862-6/4/1862
Columbus Artillery, Croft's Battery Georgia Light Artillery, 12/26/1861-6/1862

Sources:
13th GV, GDAH, 283/34, Richard W. Milner; 39/70, Charles L. Howard
25th GVI, GDAH, CSR, 256/49; *Letters & Papers of Archibald P. Thompson and James S.
Thompson, Two Confederate Soldiers from Screven County, Georgia*, Compiled by Rabun A Lee,
Jr.; GHS, #874, Claudius C. Wilson
29th GVI, RWC, 5/2/1862 & 8/29/1862
47th GVI, GDAH, CSR, 257/42; 199/74, Eli C. & Jonas W. Proctor
CA, CE, 12/30/1861; SDMN, 2/25/1863; GDAH, CSR, 254/50

109   **Camp Cedar Bluff**
Chatham County, Georgia
George C. Amason, described the location of the camp in his reminiscences.

Our first camp was about four miles this side of Savannah on the Central Railroad, in
the forks of this railroad and the railroad leading to Charleston, South Carolina. Afterward
we moved below the city, about 3/4 of a mile, and in plain view of the city. This camp was
called Cedar Bluff, from cedars that grew on a bluff that separated the higher land from a
piece of low land that intervened between us and the city.

Georgia Troops:
2nd Battalion Georgia State Troops, Taylor's Battalion, 1862
25th Regiment Georgia Volunteer Infantry, Co. G, 7/19/1862-8/3/1862
Sources:
2nd Bn GST, GDAH, 283/16, George C. Amason
25th GVI, GDAH, CSR, 256/49

110   **Camp Cedar Run**
Prince William County, Virginia
The camp was located on Cedar Run.
Georgia Troops:
17th Regiment Georgia Volunteer Infantry, 10/23/1862
Source:
GDAH, CSR, 255/121

111   **Camp Centreville**
Fairfax County, Virginia
The camp was located immediately in front of Centreville.
Georgia Troops:
21st Regiment Georgia Volunteer Infantry, 9/15/1861-9/18/1861
Source:
RWC, 10/4/1861

                              Camp Centreville
Fairfax County, Virginia

The camp was located on Braddock Road, on a low flat woodland between Centreville and Fairfax. Although no documents or letters have been found with the name Camp Centreville on them for the 8th and 9th Regiments Georgia Volunteer Infantry, records do indicate the Brigade was in the the same camp and it was customary that all regiments in the brigade use the same camp name.

The picket station for this camp was located at Mills Cross Roads, a place on the road from Fairfax Court House to Falls Church, five and one-half miles from the former and two and one-half miles from the latter. This is about four miles from Mason's and Munson's Hills. The location of the bivouac was in the skirt of a pine thicket on the margin of an old field.

This poem was written while on picket and appeared in the *Columbus Daily Times* of November 9, 1861.

Camp of the 8th Ga. Regiment
Near Centreville, Va., Oct., 29, 1861.
Lines written on Picket, and Dedicated to one who will recognize initials.
By J. M. G. of the "Macon Guards."
I'm alone in the gloom of the woods, to night,
For the beautiful day is done,
And I watched the stars as they trembled forth,
'Pon the bright sky, one by one;
and I drew my cloak still closer to me,
As I tho't of our home of flowers,
And I sighed for the balm of her fragrant winds,
And the light of her laughing bowers.

And my heart went out like a bird set free,
For it longed to look down once more
'Pon the orange groves of my native South,
Ere life's dull day was o'er;
And it hover awhile 'neath a clinging vine,
And whispered a word for me.
For a beautiful spirit lay nestled there -
A being of purity.

And it told her of how my soul had yearned,
For the light of her darling eye,
And the murmur of words that are with me yet
For their echoes cannot die:
And oft in the midnight shadows deep -
On my sentinel post I stand,
And long for the light of other day's,
And dream of that sunny land,
Where I shall meet again with the loved and lost,
And only remember my sentinel post.

Georgia Troops:
7th Regiment Georgia Volunteer Infantry, 10/1/1861-1/22/1862
8th Regiment Georgia Volunteer Infantry, 10/1/1861-1/22/1862
9th Regiment Georgia Volunteer Infantry, 10/1/1861-1/22/1862
11th Regiment Georgia Volunteer Infantry, 10/1/1861-1/22/1862
Sources:
7th GVI, GDAH, CSR, 255/33
8th GVI, RWC, 10/11/1861
9th GVI, no source
11th GVI, GDAH, CSR, 255/77; *Georgia Boys with "Stonewall" Jackson,* By Aurelia Austin

113   **Camp Chafin's Farm**
                                   Henrico County, Virginia
   The camp was located on Chafin's Farm near Richmond.
Georgia Troops:
Phillips' Legion, Infantry Battalion, 8/6/1862-8/11/1862
Sources:
GDAH, 283/23, John C. Reynolds; UNC, #3015, John Alexander Barry

114   **Camp Chalmers**
                                   Escambia County, Florida
   The camp was located near Pensacola.
Georgia Troops:
36th (Villegipue's) Regiment Georgia Infantry, Cos. G, H & I, 10/1861-2/5/1862
Source:
GDAH, CSR, 256/116

115   **Camp Charleston**
                                   Bradley County, Tennessee
   The camp was located on the railroad at Charleston.
Georgia Troops:
37th Regiment Georgia Volunteer Infantry, 9/1/1863-9/2/1863
Sources:
GDAH, UDC Books, Vol. VI, Isaih V. Moore; ASB, 1/13/1864

116   **Camp Chehaw**
                                   Colleton County, South Carolina
   The camp was located one mile from Tar Bluff on the Combahee River, probably at the
Middleton house.
Georgia Troops:
5th Regiment Georgia Volunteer Cavalry, Cos. D & I, 12/30/1863-12/31/1863
(Company I left 12/31/1863 to picket at Warren's Point.)
Source:
GDAH, CSR, 252/101

117   **Camp Chickamauga Station, Tennessee**
Hamilton County, Tennessee
The camp was located at the Chickamauga Station on the Western & Atlantic Railroad.
Georgia Troops:
9th Regiment Georgia Volunteer Infantry, 10/19/1863
Source:
GDAH, CSR, 255/56

118   **Camp Christian's Farm**
Henrico County, Virginia
The camp was located on Mrs. Christian's farm northeast of Richmond. See *The Official Military Atlas of the Civil War*, Pl. XX, 1. Also, see Camp Comfort.
Georgia Troops:
Cobb's Legion, 6/6/1862-6/11/1862
Sources:
GDAH, 160/74, Joel Crawford Barnett; ASB, 6/25/1862

119   **Camp Clark**
York County, Virginia
The camp was located several miles down river from Camp Washington, and two or three miles from Winn's Mill on the Warwick River.
Georgia Troops:
16th Regiment Georgia Volunteer Infantry, 12/1861
Source:
GDAH, UDC Books, Vol. VI, 136

120   **Camp Clark's Mountain**
Orange County, Virginia
This winter camp of Gordon's Brigade was just to the northeast of Clark's Mountain, nine miles from Orange Courthouse, about a mile from the Rapidan River and about one and one-half miles from the Sommerville Ford on the Rapidan River. See Atlas Plate LXXXVII, 4, for camp of Gordon's Brigade. Picket duty assignments during this time were at the several fords on the Rapidan River, since the Union Army was camped on the other side of the river.
Georgia Troops:
13th Regiment Georgia Volunteer Infantry, 12/8/1863-4/30/1864
26th Regiment Georgia Volunteer Infantry, 12/8/1863-4/30/1864
31st Regiment Georgia Volunteer Infantry, 12/8/1863-4/30/1864
38th Regiment Georgia Volunteer Infantry, 12/8/1863-4/30/1864
60th Regiment Georgia Volunteer Infantry, 12/8/1863-4/30/1864
61st Regiment Georgia Volunteer Infantry, 12/8/1863-4/30/1864
Sources:
All, ASB, 12/23/1863; UNC, #3348, W.R. Gladding
61st GVI, GDAH, 179/79 John Terrell Erwin

Camp Cleghorn
Chatham County, Georgia

The camp was located on Bulloch's old lot on the Isle of Hope.

Georgia Troops:

Chatham Artillery, 9/28/1861-4/23/1862

Sources:

The Children of Pride, Edited by Robert Manson Myers; *Historical Sketch of The Chatham Artillery during The Confederate Struggle for Independence*, By Charles C. Jones, Jr.; Map: GHS, Savannah, Ga.

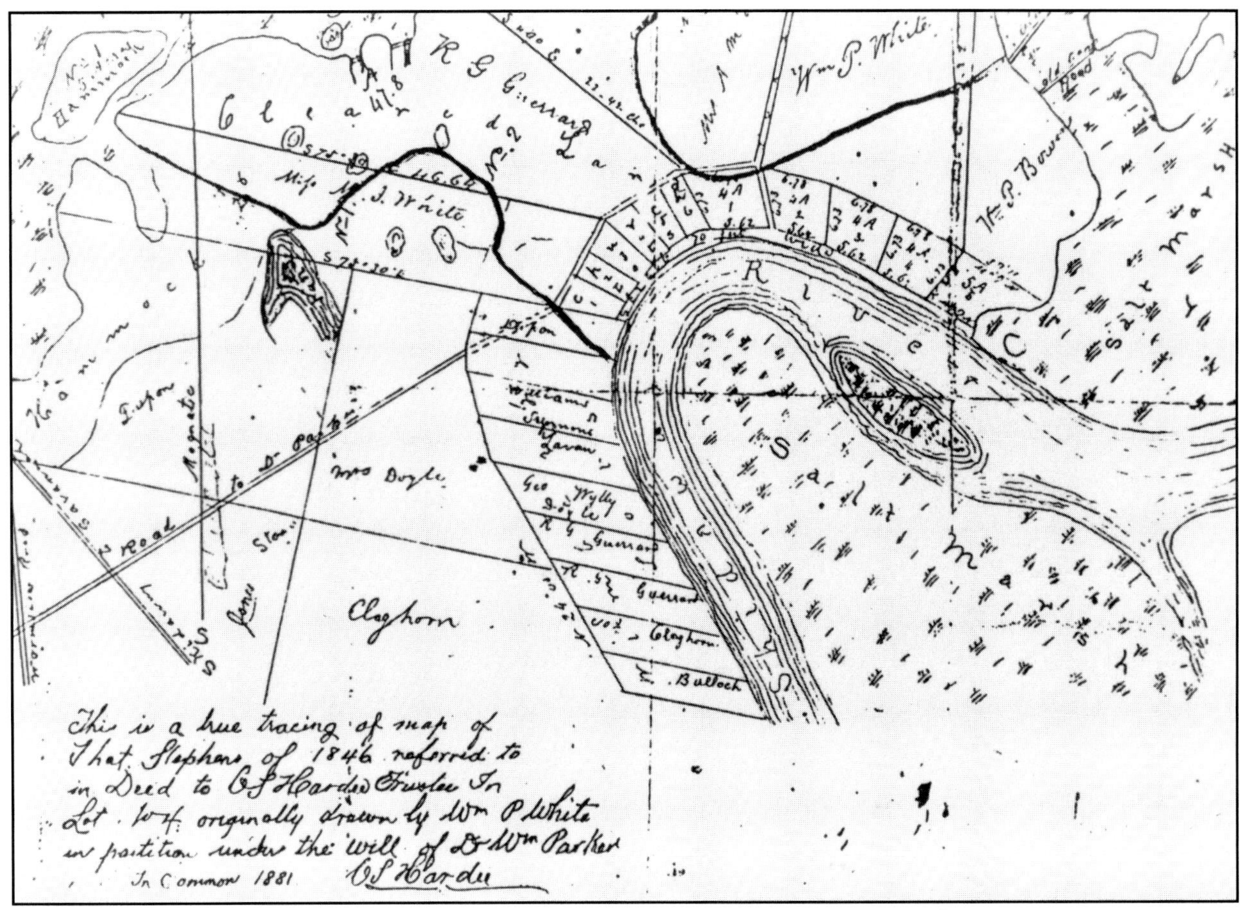

Map of a portion of the Isle of Hope showing the location of Bulloch's old lot.
Map courtesy of the Georgia Historical Society, Savannah, Georgia

Camp Clinch
Glynn County, Georgia

Location not known.

Georgia Troops:

4th (Clinch's) Regiment Georgia Volunteer Cavalry, Co. D, 6/1862-9/1862; Co. G, 10/1862-2/1863, 5/29/1863

Sources:

SDMN, 6/10/1862; GDAH, CSR, 253/94; AGLB, #15

123   **Camp Duncan L. Clinch**
Long County, Georgia

The camp was located behind Lake Bluff battery on Morgan's Lake, an oxbow lake on the Altamaha River.
Georgia Troops:
4th (Clinch's) Regiment Georgia Volunteer Cavalry, Co. K, 6/1863
Source:
GDAH, CSR, 253/94

124   **Camp Clingman**
New Hanover County, North Carolina

The camp was located two miles from the railroad station at Wilmington, and probably named after Thomas L. Clingman, Commissioner of North Carolina to the Confederate States.
Georgia Troops:
25th Regiment Georgia Volunteer Infantry, 12/19/1862-12/31/1862
29th Regiment Georgia Volunteer Infantry, 12/19/1862-12/31/1862
30th Regiment Georgia Volunteer Infantry, 12/19/1862-1/1/1863
Sources:
25th GVI, GHS, # 874, Claudius C. Wilson
29th GVI, GDAH, CSR, 256/85
30th GVI, GDAH, MR, 279/83; *Brief History of the Thirtieth Georgia Regiment*, By Augustus Pitt Adamson

125   **Camp Clinton**
Hamilton County, Tennessee

The camp was located near Chattanooga.
Georgia Troops:
36th Regiment Georgia Volunteer Infantry, 5/13/1862
Source:
SC, 5/18/1862

Private Napoleon Bonaparte Landers, Co. K, 36th Regiment Georgia Volunteer Infantry. Enlisted May 13, 1862, and died July 26, 1863.

photo courtesy of
Elizabeth Whitley Roberson

126   **Camp Clover**
Chesapeake County, Virginia

The same as Camp Ross. Located one to two miles west of Gosport Navy Yard and six to seven miles from Hodges Bridge over the west branch of Elizabeth River. See *The Official Military Atlas of the Civil War*, Pl. XXVI, 4.
Georgia Troops:
4th Regiment Georgia Volunteer Infantry, 5/18/1861-5/22/1861
Source:
See Camp Ross

127   **Camp Clover**
Henrico County, Virginia

The camp was located on the south bank of the Chickahominy River, about four miles from Richmond and about equidistant below the Mechanicsville bridge.
Georgia Troops:
16th Regiment Georgia Volunteer Infantry, 5/26/1862-6/12/1862
24th Regiment Georgia Volunteer Infantry, 5/26/1862-6/12/1862
Cobb's Legion, 5/26/1862-6/12/1862
Source:
Howell Cobb's Confederate Career,
by Horace Montgomery, Confederate
Centennial Studies No. Ten

Private John Park Macklin, Co. F, 24th Regiment Georgia Volunteer Infantry. Enlisted August 24, 1861, and died in Richmond, Virginia, July 25, 1862.

photo courtesy of Michael G. Kelly

128   **Camp Cobb**
Bibb County, Georgia

The camp was located near Mr. Napier's home, near the railroad, near Macon. The unit moved to Lovejoy Station from here.
Georgia Troops:
5th Regiment Georgia Infantry Reserves, Headquarters, 6/8/1864-10/21/1864
Sources:
WL, F.H. Bozeman; GDAH, CSR, 255/18; 283/48, Bibb Co. file; 283/27, W.B. Henslee

129   **Camp Cobb**
Chatham County, Georgia

   The camp was located on Whitmarsh Island, "in Whitman's Retreat, about seven miles from Savannah."
Georgia Troops:
1st (Olmstead's) Volunteer Regiment of Georgia, Headquarters, 4/20/1864-4/24/1864
Sources:
GDAH, CSR, 258/6; 283/28, Asbury W. Hodges; SR, 4/28/1864

130   **Camp Cobb**
New Hanover County, North Carolina

   The camp was located three miles east of Wilmington.
Georgia Troops.
46th Regiment Georgia Volunteer Infantry, 1/13/63-2/11/63
Source:
GDAH, CSR, 257/35

131   **Camp Cobb**
Henrico County, Virginia

   Located about one mile from the State House in Richmond, on the racetrack of the old Richmond fairgrounds.

Col. Howell Cobb's Regiment
Camp Cobb, Oct. 4, 1861.

Editors Southern Banner;

   It might not be uninteresting to your readers to hear from this Regiment especially as there has been so much said by others as to how we are situated &c. We were very much surprised a short time since, to learn from Georgia that we were shut up in a camp quite disagreeable to our feelings, on account of its locality, and pent up condition, thus causing the great calamity of our sickness. We were sorry to learn that such an opinion prevailed among the relatives of the soldiers, knowing that it caused much unnecessary uneasiness. No less we were displeased to hear that our commander (Hon. Howell Cobb) was the object of much abuse, for suffering such a state of things to hang over his command. We propose, therefore, in a few words to give a detail of the facts concerning this matter, by a simple and common sense view of our camp life, situation &c. My company arrived about the 27th of July and was conducted to Camp Reservoir at which place we remained until the Regiment was formed. While there the measles, mumps, &c., began the history of our sickness. Finding our quarters objectionable on account of filth, locality and so on, diligent inquiry was made for a more agreeable situation. This place was chosen and for many reasons is one of the most pleasant encampments at or near Richmond. Our convenience to the city affords many advantages which we could not otherwise enjoy, such as carts for police duties &c. These conveniences tend greatly to lighten the burden of a soldiers work. Our camp is considered a healthy point by all who have spoken to us about it - and by the way, there is not a single argument to the contrary. The water is excellent, and the place sufficiently elevated to cause falling water to run off immediately. The breezes have been almost constant.

   When we were sickening and dying the Surgeons were sent out in search of a better and more healthful location, but failed in every instance, claiming that we could better our condition by a change of place: and in point of medical talent and attention, ours is as well represented as any regiment about Richmond. As to our sickness, we must consider that the recruits composing this body were brought up from the country, and consequently have been able to escape measles and mumps and c. These diseases were greatly aided in their fatality by a cool wet spell of weather in the midst of their attack, and before Hospital tents had been secured for the Regiment. A few weeks presented quite a different condition. After the measles began to die out a more rapid convalescence has never been seen by the writer than our sick have experienced. Many appeared alarmed for a few weeks as one by one our brave comrades fell by our sides. Soon, however the hearty cheers of the well and good humored jokes of the sick told a better story to our visitors and friends. A livelier and better contented Regiment in all probability cannot be found in the service, than ours is at this time. Other Regiments have suffered more than ours, and still Col. Cobb must be blamed with the whole of our casualties, as if we had the power to arrest the hand of death and by a mighty miracle restore health and comfort to his command. It is almost unnessary to offer a defence for him, as his friends at home know more of his life and character as a gentlemen, than to believe such statements. In a word, we might say that he has done all that he could to render our condition comfortable. During our distress, we heard him frequently lamenting the condition of his men. His conversation and countenance upon the subject were evidences of the deepest interest of feeling for us, that anxious solicitude could paint, and still he was accused of neglecting his command. That argument sets him above controversy -- that is, he struck his tent among us and scarcely took a meal anywhere else during our illness. By a steady course of discipline, he has won both the confidence and respect of all, and in point of morality, the change if any has been favorable. An editor who visited our camp a short time since, remarks through his paper, that he has never heard a harsh or profane word during his stay with us. Drunkeness and other evils so common in camp-life have been restrained with such energy that he is troubled very little in controlling the Regiment at present: and if he does not deserve credit instead of abuse, we are at a loss to know the reason. The officers and privates so far as I have been able to ascertain, are not only satisfied with Col. Cobb and Bryan, but proud of them: and should the Government order us to the field under their command, we expect to leave our mark upon the head of the enemy.

Capt. M. (J.D.H. McRae)
Com. F, 16th Reg. Ga.

Georgia Troops:
16th Regiment Georgia Volunteer Infantry, 8/20/1861-9/19/1861
Cobb's Legion, 8/1/1861-9/15/1861
Cobb's Legion, Cavalry Battalion, left for Yorktown on 9/15/1861
Sources:
16th GVI, ASB, 10/16/1861, & 11/6/1861
CL, GDAH, 21/29, Jno. William Rheney, Jr.; ADC&S, 8/6/1861

132   **Camp Lamar Cobb**
Gadsden County, Florida

Located one to two miles below Quincy, in an old field convenient to a very bold spring.
Georgia Troops:
29th Battalion Georgia Cavalry, 10/7/1863-2/1864
64th Regiment Georgia Volunteer Infantry, 4/28/1863-5/26/1863
66th Regiment Georgia Volunteer Infantry, 9/7/1863-10/7/1863
Echols' Light Artillery, 1/15/1863-3/7/1863 & 5/31/1863-8/8/1863 (On 3/7/1863, part of the battery left for Camp Leon, while the balance remained in this camp.)
Sources:
29th Bn GC, GDAH, CSR, 254/13; ECN, 2/17/1864
64th GVI, GDAH, CSR, 257/126; SC, 5/5/1863
66th GVI, GDAH, 239/60, William R. Hurst
ELA, PC, James Jewell letters; EU, #20 James Jewell

133   **Camp Cogdell**
Liberty County, Georgia

The camp was located near Darien.
Georgia Troops:
McIntosh County Guards, 9/5/1861-9/16/1861 (The company later became Co. M, 26th [Styles] Regiment Georgia Volunteer Infantry.)
Sources:
SR, 9/11/1861; SDMN, 9/16/1861

134   **Camp Cogdell**
McIntosh County, Georgia

The camp was located eighteen miles from Johnson's Station (now Ludowici,) and two miles from Ft. Barrington on the Altamaha River.
Georgia Troops:
5th Regiment Georgia Volunteer Cavalry, Cos. D & G, 6/27/1863
Terrell Light Artillery, Brooks Battery, 6/27/1863
Sources:
5th GVC, GDAH, CSR, 253/101
TLA, GDAH, CSR, 254/47

135   **Camp Colquitt**
Jasper County, South Carolina

The camp was located six miles below Grahamville.

The following extract from a letter dated April 27th, 1862, by William Bonner McDowell, tells about the regiments move from Camp Colquitt to Grahamville.

> We moved our camp yesterday six miles nearer the railroad. We are now in a quarter of
> a mile from Grahamville which is about two miles of the railroad. I like this place much
> better than our former one. It is a level old field which has not been cultivated for some
> time. The people about here are planting some sea island cotton with the few hands which

are allowed to remain here. The majority of the plantations containing thousands of acres cleared will this year be uncultivated.

Georgia Troops:
46th Regiment Georgia Volunteer Infantry, 4/26/1862
Sources:
GDAH, CSR, 257/35; UDC Books Vol. II, 568

136   **Camp Colquitt**
Charleston County, South Carolina

The camp was located on James Island, 100 yards below Camp Wheaton, and immediately south of the road from Camp Wheaton to Artillery crossroads.
Georgia Troops:
Chatham Artillery, 4/30/1864-12/5/1864 & 1/5/1865-2/2/1865
Sources:
GDAH, CSR, 254/64; SR, 5/12/1864; *Historical Sketch of The Chatham Artillery during The Confederate Struggle for Independence*, By Charles C. Jones, Jr.

137   **Camp Colquitt**
Norfolk County, Virginia

The camp is located one-half mile directly east of Sewell's Point in a beautiful grove, three-fourths mile from the bay and three-fourths mile from Hampton Roads.
Georgia Troops:
2nd Independent Infantry Battalion of Georgia, 6/7/1861-9/6/1861
Sources:
GDAH, CSR, 254/107; MT, 6/15/1861, CDT, 6/17/1861; SDMN, 6/26/1861

138   **Camp Colston**
Chatham County, Georgia

The camp is probably located on the parade grounds behind the city park. An ad in the *Savannah Daily Morning News* dated December 23, 1863, for a strayed horse from the camp of the 57th Regiment Georgia Volunteers, asks that the finder return the horse to the camp of the 57th Ga. Vols. in rear of the park. See Camp Lawton.
Georgia Troops:
57th Regiment Georgia Volunteer Infantry, 12/14/1862
Sources:
GDAH, CSR, 257/95; SDMN, 12/23/1863

139   **Camp Columbus**
Chatham County, Georgia

Near the Isle of Hope and two miles from Skidaway Island.
Georgia Troops:
Terrell Light Artillery, Brooks Battery, 3/17/1862-5/31/1862
Source:
GDAH, CSR, 254/47

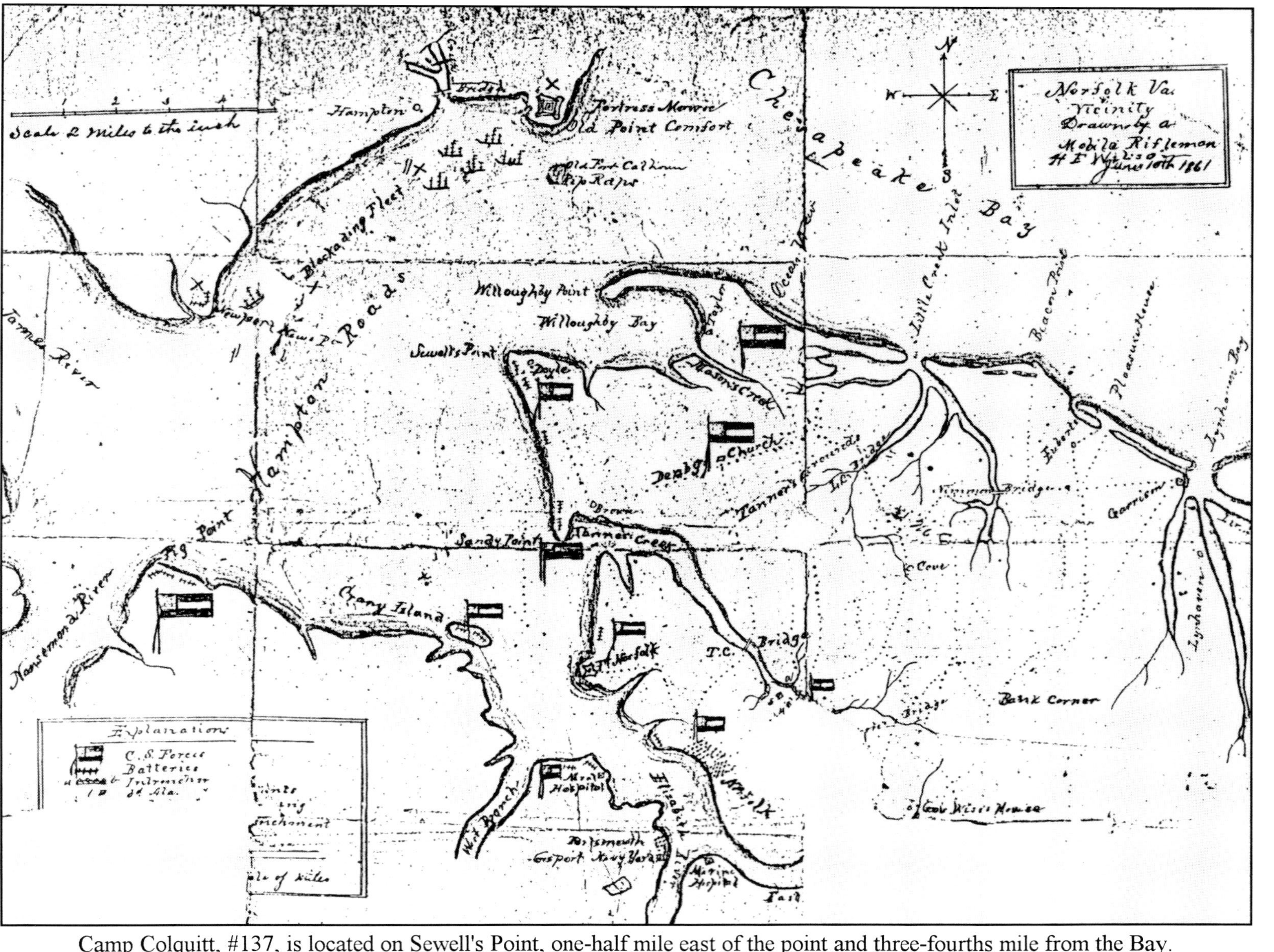

Camp Colquitt, #137, is located on Sewell's Point, one-half mile east of the point and three-fourths mile from the Bay. Map from the Alabama Department of Archives and History

140   **Camp Comfort**
Henrico County, Virginia

The camp was located at Burnt Tavern on Nine Mile Road, four miles east of Richmond, and two miles from Mrs. Christian's farm.
Georgia Troops:
16th Regiment Georgia Volunteer Infantry, 6/12/1862-6/28/1862
24th Regiment Georgia Volunteer Infantry, 6/12/1862-6/28/1862
Cobb's Legion, Infantry Battalion, 6/12/1862-6/28/1862
Sources:
Howell Cobb's Confederate Career, By Horace Montgomery, Confederate Centennial Studies No. 10; GDAH, 160/74, Joel Crawford Barnett

141   **Camp Cone**
Jasper County, South Carolina

The camp was located near Hardeeville.
Georgia Troops:
47th Regiment Georgia Volunteer Infantry, Cos. A & B, 4/19/1863-5/4/1863
Source:
DU, Benjamin S. Williams

142   **Camp Conley**
Fairfax County, Virginia

The camp was located near Fairfax Courthouse. An extract from a letter published in the *Augusta Daily Chronicle & Sentinel* on October 19, 1861, reads:

> We are now encamped a few miles from the enemy, and can at times distinctly hear them practicing with their artillery. Our boys are enjoying excellent health, and are in fine spirits, eager and anxious for a chance to open the "races" on the *Fairfax Race Course*; for I have no idea they have yet forgotten what excellent time the Yankees made from Manassas. --- By way of explaination I would add that our Captain has named this, our second camp, after our estimable fellow citizen, Mr. Benjamin Conley, whom to know is to admire.   (signed)   Junius.

Georgia Troops:
Blodget Flying Artillery, 10/9/1861-10/13/1861 (The battery later became Milledge's Battery Georgia Light Artillery.)
Source:
ADC&S, 10/19/1861

143   **Camp Convalescence**
Knox County, Tennessee

Located on the fairgrounds, about one mile above Knoxville and within half a mile of the river. Men who had been wounded in battle and could convalesce without surgery would use this type camp. It would also be used by men who had surgery and were now recovering to the point they needed very little assistance. Refer to Chapter IV, for General Order No. 3, from Camp Convalescence.

Georgia Troops:
3rd Battalion Georgia Volunteer Infantry, 7/8/1862-8/8/1862
Sources:
CE, 7/22/1862 & 8/19/1862; KDR, 10/15/1862

144   **Camp Cooper**
                                              Bibb County, Georgia
   The camp was located near Macon, and refered to as Camp of Instruction No. 1.
Georgia Troops:
64th Regiment Georgia Volunteer Infantry, 4/5/1863-4/8/1863
66th Regiment Georgia Volunteer Infantry, 8/1/1863-9/1/1863
12th Regiment (Robinson's) Cavalry, Georgia State Guards, 1/27/1864
1st Regiment Georgia Light Duty, 10/26/1864
Macon Light Artillery, Co. B, 10/7/1863
Moughon Infantry, 8/17/1863
Sources:
64th GV, GDAH, CSR, 257/126
66th GV, GDAH, CSR, 258/3
12th Cav GSG, GDAH, CSR, 253/125
1st GLD, GDAH, CSR, 254/73
MLA, Co. B, SDMN, 10/12/1863
MI, GDAH, 283/48, Bibb Co. file

145   **Camp Cosby**
                                            Hinds County, Mississippi
   The camp was located on the Vernon Road near Brownville, two miles from the Clinton and
Vernon crossroads, near the Texas Brigade.
Georgia Troops:
Columbus Artillery, Croft's Battery Light Artillery, 11/11/1863-12/4/1863
Source:
Fighting With Ross' Texas Cavalry Brigade, C.S.A., Edited by Homer L. Kerr

146   **Camp Courtis**
                                              York County, Virginia
   The camp was located eleven miles below Yorktown near Bethel Church.
Georgia Troops:
6th Regiment Georgia Volunteer Infantry, 6/16/1861-6/19/1861
Source:
GDAH, UDC Books, Vol. VI, Francis Goulding Woods

147   **Camp Courtnay**
Charleston County, South Carolina

The camp was located on James Island.
Georgia Troops:
46th Regiment Georgia Volunteer Infantry, Cos. H, I & two others, 3/6/1863-3/12/1863
Source:
GDAH, CSR, 257/35

148   **Camp Cox**
Cobb County, Georgia

The camp was located behind Johnston's river line, which was between Nickajack River and the Chattahoochee River.
Georgia Troops:
4th Georgia Militia, Co. D, 6/29/1864-7/1/1864
Source:
GDAH, 80/56, Thomas S. Warren; 283/20 T. S. Campbell

149   **Camp Craig**
Gordon County, Georgia

Located near Resaca. Upon arrival at Resaca these troops reported to Gen. Jackson.
Georgia Troops:
1st Regiment Infantry, Georgia State Guards, Cos. A & G, 9/9/1863-11/1863
Source:
GDAH, CSR, 254/77

150   **Camp Croft**
Chatham County, Georgia

Located on Grove River at Cheves Landing, three miles below Camp Miller and sixteen miles from Savannah.
Georgia Troops:
Columbus Artillery, Croft's Battery Georgia Light Artillery, 9/17/1862-11/17/1862
Source:
GDAH, CSR, 254/50

151   **Camp Sam Crump**
Chatham County, Georgia

Located on the Isle of Hope. Every newspaper in Georgia printed ads from friends and fellow soldiers who had lost a relative or friend due to sickness or injuries from the war. No one was untouched.

The following tribute was published in the Augusta Daily Chronicle & Sentinel on June 4, 1863.

Tribute of Respect.
Camp Sam Crump,
Isle of Hope, May 17th, 1863.

At a meeting held this day by the Capers Light Guards, Lt. J.B. Allison having been appointed chairman, and S.A. Howard, Secretary, a committee consisting of C.E. Clark, Jno. M. Stephens, and W.M. Hitt were appionted to draft resolutions expressive of the regret of the Company at the death of Nelson Gibbs. The following preamble and resolutions were adopted:

Whereas, We the members of the Capers Light Guards, 12th Battalion Georgia Volunteers, having been called to mourn the untimely death of one of our late members, Nelson Gibbs, who by the accidental discharge of a gun, fell in the full vigor of manhood's prime: Therefore, be it

Resolved, That in his early demise we profoundly lament the loss of one whose excellent character as a gentleman, and high qualities as a soldier, ever commanded the esteem, and challenged the admiration of all with whom he mingled.

Resolved, That while we drop a tear to his memory, although we cannot countermand the irrevocable decrees of an Omniscient and overruling Providence, and wake him from his sepulchral response, we will ever strive to emulate his many virtues and imitate his noble example.

Resolved, That we tender to his distressed family our deep and heartfelt sympathy in their poignant anguish and sore bereavement.

Resolved, That in honor to his memory a blank page be left in our Roll Book - that a copy of these resolutions be sent his widowed mother, and that they be published in the Augusta papers.

The meeting then adjourned.

Lt. J. B. Allison, Ch'n.

S. A. Howard, Sec'y.

Georgia Troops:

12th Battalion Georgia Volunteers, 5/5/1863-7/10/1863 (On July 10, 1863, the 12th Battalion Georgia Volunteers moved to Charleston, South Carolina.)

18th Battalion Georgia Volunteer Infantry (Savannah Volunteer Guards), 5/28/1863

Sources:

12th Bn, GDAH, CSR, 254/31; EU, #12, John H. Ash; ADC&S, 6/4/1863

18th Bn, SR, 6/17/1863

152   Camp Cumming

Mobile County, Alabama

The camp was located a few miles from Mobile.

Georgia Troops:

1st Confederate Regiment Georgia Volunteers, Cos. C, D, G, I & K, 2/28/1863 (Previous designation was Villipigue's 36th Regiment Georgia Infantry.)

Source:

1st Confederate Regiment, compiled by C. Pat Cates

153   **Camp Cumming.**
Chatham County, Georgia.
   The camp was located near the Isle of Hope Church, seven and one-half miles from Savannah.
Georgia Troops:
2nd Battalion Georgia Cavalry, Cos. B, C & E, 10/1861-5/5/1862
2nd Battalion Georgia Cavalry, Co. D, 1/18/1862-3/2/1862
Sources:
GDAH, CSR, 253/87; SDMN, 1/27/1862; SR, 1/29/1862; EU, #12, John H. Ash

$20 REWARD.

Strayed away from Camp, on the 16th inst, a Sorrel MARE, about 14 hands high; has a white face and one white foot. The above reward will be paid to any one who will return her to me; at Camp Cumming, near the Isle of Hope Church, seven and a half miles from the city.
                                                  W. H. WILTBERGER,
jan 25   3   Captain G. H.

154   **Camp Cumming**
Washington County, Virginia
   The camp was located near Abingdon.
Georgia Troops:
9th Battalion Georgia Light Artillery. 9/1/1862-11/20/1862
Sources:
Letters to Lucinda, 1862-1864, By James Addison McMurtrey; SC, 11/19/1862 & 11/20/1862

155   **Camp Cutts**
Prince William County, Virginia
   The camp was located one mile east of Manassas Junction, and named in honor of Captain Allen S. Cutts of the Sumter Light Artillery.
Georgia Troops:
11th Battalion Georgia Light Artillery, 7/28/1861-9/7/1861
Source:
PC, Letters of Joseph M. Little

156   **Camp Cuyler**
Bibb County, Georgia
   The camp was located in Macon.
Georgia Troops:
5th Regiment Georgia Infantry Reserves, Headquarters, 7/4/1863
Source:
MT, 7/7/1863

157   **Camp Darby**

Wakulla County, Florida

The camp was located twenty miles from Camp Jackson, and probably at Darby Still.

Georgia Troops:

29th Battalion Georgia Cavalry, 9/14/1864

Echols' Light Artillery, 8/25/1864

Sources:

29th Bn GC, GDAH, CSR, 254/13

ELA, EU, #20, James Jewell; PC, James Jewell; GDAH, 283/33, Richard Butler Mathews

158   **Camp Davant**

Chatham County, Georgia

The camp was located at the Wymberly plantation, the home of Col. J. H. Estill, on the Isle of Hope.

Georgia Troops:

2nd Battalion Georgia Volunteer Cavalry, 10/28/1861 (The 2nd Battalion Georgia Cavalry became a part of the 5th Regiment Georgia Volunteer Cavalry on January 22, 1863.)

5th Regiment Georgia Volunteer Cavalry, Headquarters, 5/5/1863-10/26/1863

Sources:

2nd Bn GVC, SDMN, 10/28/1861

5th GVC, GDAH, CSR, 253/101; EU, #12, John H. Ash; CV, XIV, 564

159   **Camp Davis**

Jackson County, Alabama

The camp was located at Moore Spring in Hog Jaw Valley, four miles south of Bridgeport. See *The Official Military Atlas of the Civil War*, Pl. LXXX, 12.

Georgia Troops:

54th Regiment Georgia Volunteer Infantry, 7/7/1862-8/1/1862 (The 54th Georgia changed it's designation to the 57th Regiment Georgia Volunteer Infantry at Jackson, Mississippi, in January, 1863.)

Sources:

GDAH, CSR, 283/45, Vinson Wright; CG, 11/5/1862

160   **Camp Davis**

Chatham County, Georgia

The camp was located near Savannah.

Georgia Troops:

21st Battalion Georgia Cavalry, Co. C, 3/4/1862

Source:

GDAH, CSR, 254/9

161   **Camp Davis**

DeKalb County, Georgia

The camp was located near Decatur.

Georgia Troops:

13th (Ector's) Regiment Georgia Volunteer Infantry, 7/18/1861-7/25/1861

Source:

GDAH, 283/34, Richard W. Milner; MT, 7/18/1861

162   **Camp Davis**

Effingham County, Georgia

E. C. Corbett's letter comes from the letters to Governor Brown at the Georgia Department of Archives and History.

Whitesville, No. 3, C.R.R

Col. Wm. T. Thompson

Dear Sir   according to promise I here furnish a Skeleton description of the Locality of Camp Davis which has been selected on C.R.R. between the 32 & 33 mile posts and consists of three or four successive elevated ridges of land interspersed with a plentiful growth of oak and pine with the prospect of an abundant supply of wood and water. There are two flush branches of water - one below and the other just above this Site and the grounds are so that the 4 Regiments can all be encamped within a 1/4 of a mile of each other. Convenient to the whole is an open old field large enough for 5,000 men to drill on.

Respectfully
E C Corbett
Maj of 4th Bat'n

To his Exelency Jos. E. Brown Gov'n & c.

The undersigned Citizens of Whitesville (Guyton) at No. 3 C R R respectfully call your Exelency's notice to the above location for Camp Davis, and beg leave to say we recommend the site as the best in this vicinity for the Camp.

J. Toole M.D.	E. J. Bird, M.D.
L.L. Westman Jr.	The. Bourguine
Todd L. Toole Atty at Law	J. Loahn

An extract from a report dated March 24, 1862, from W.T. Thompson, Col. & A.D.C., Commanding Camp Davis, to Henry C. Wayne, Adjutant and Inspector General, states:

I appointed Maj. E.C. Corbett a resident of Whitesville familiar with the grounds to lay off the camp in regimental encampments, and to assign the companies and squads to positions in their respective divisions.

Georgia Troops:

11th Battalion Georgia Volunteer Infantry, 3/13/1862-4/1862 (The 11th Bn. Ga. Vol. Inf. became the 47th Regiment Georgia Volunteer Infantry while in this camp.)

48th Regiment Georgia Volunteer Infantry, 3/11/1862-3/24/1862

49th Regiment Georgia Volunteer Infantry, 3/11/1862-4/12/1862
50th Regiment Georgia Volunteer Infantry, 3/4/1862-4/21/1862
51st Regiment Georgia Volunteer Infantry, 3/11/1862-3/24/1862
54th Regiment Georgia Volunter Infantry, 5/6/1862 (The regiment probably organized here, then went to Camp Way for training.)
Sources:
Letter of Maj. Edmund C. Corbett, GDAH, Letters to Governor Brown
Letter of Wm. T. Thompson, GDAH, Letters to Henry C. Wayne, Adj. Gen. & Insp. Gen.
48th GVI, SFU, 4/1/1862; SDMN, 3/25/1862
49th GVI SFU, 4/15/1862
50th GVI, GDAH, 283/30, William M. Jones; 283/45, Cicero Holt Young; SR, 4/10/1862
51st GVI, SFU, 4/1/1862; SDMN, 3/25/1862
54th GVI, GDAH, CSR, 257/83

163 **Camp Davis.**

Hancock County, Georgia.

The camp was located on the Sparta fairground.

Georgia Troops:
Hancock Confederate Guards, later Co. K, 15th Regiment Georgia Volunteer Infantry, 6/8/1861
Source:
CG, 6/12/1861

164 **Camp Davis**

Muscogee County, Georgia

The camp was located in the rear of the Opelika Depot on the outskirts of Columbus.

Georgia Troops:
Ivey Guards, later Co. G, 20th Regiment Georgia Volunteer Infantry, 7/12/1861-7/21/1861
Terrell Artillery, 9/13/1861-10/17/1861
Sources:
IG, CDT, 7/13/1861, & 7/22/1861
TA, CDT, 9/13/1861 & 10/16/1861

165 **Camp Davis**

Pike County, Georgia

The camp was probably located in Pike County where the Pike County Volunteers organized.

Georgia Troops:
Pike County Volunteers, 6/12/1861 (Later they became Co. H, 44th Regiment Georgia Volunteer Infantry.)
Source:
GDAH, 284/40, William M. Speights

166   **Camp Davis**
Spalding County, Georgia

The camp was located about five miles from Griffin. The Berry Infantry was ordered to this camp to join Col. Underwood's Regiment. However, it disbanded and they were ordered to Savannah.
Georgia Troops:
Berry Infantry, 9/18/1861-9/30/1861 (Later they became Co. I/D of the 29th Regiment Georgia Volunteer Infantry. There was another company in this camp from Franklin County.)
Georgia Militia, 3/10/1862
Sources:
BI, RWC, 9/27/1861 & 10/11/1861
GM, CE, 2/27/1862

167   **Camp Davis**
Sumter County, Georgia

The camp was located three miles from Americus.
Georgia Troops:
Americus Volunteer Guards, 6/1861 (Later they became Co. K, 9th Regiment Georgia Volunteer Infantry.)
Source:
Americus Newspaper

168   **Camp Davis**
Whitfield County, Georgia

The camp was located near Dalton.
Georgia Troops:
4th Battalion Georgia Volunteer Infantry, 9/28/1861-10/2/1861
Source:
SR, 10/3/1861

169   **Camp Davis**
Pender County, North Carolina

The camp was located seven miles east of the town of Topsail Inlet.
Georgia Troops:
23rd Regiment Georgia Volunteer Infantry, 7/31/1863-8/8/1863
Source :
GDAH, 283/25, William W. Fisher

170   **Camp Davis**
Campbell County, Virginia

This was a major training camp in Virginia. Troops from most all Southern states were trained in this camp. Located on the fairgrounds, two miles west of Lynchburg.
Georgia Troops:
1st Regiment Georgia Volunteer Infantry, 3/2/1862
19th Regiment Georgia Volunteer Infantry, 8/15/1861-9/15/1861

24th Regiment Georgia Volunteer Infantry, 9/1861
Georgia Artillery Battalion, 8/11/1861-10/22/1861 (Later they became the Cherokee Artillery and 3rd Battalion Georgia Volunteer Infantry.)
Phillips' Legion, Infantry Battalion and Cavalry Battalion, 8/22/1861-10/7/1861
Source:
1st GVI: GDAH, *Letters Written by Lavender R. Ray of Newnan, Georgia During the War Between the States*, Compiled by Ruby F. Ray
19th GVI, GDAH, CSR, 256/7-9
24th GVI, SC, 1/7/1862
GBA, RWC, 8/30/1861 & 11/1/1861
PL, GDAH, CSR, 258/42; 57/65, John F. Milhollin; 9/79, Boyd & Sitton Collection

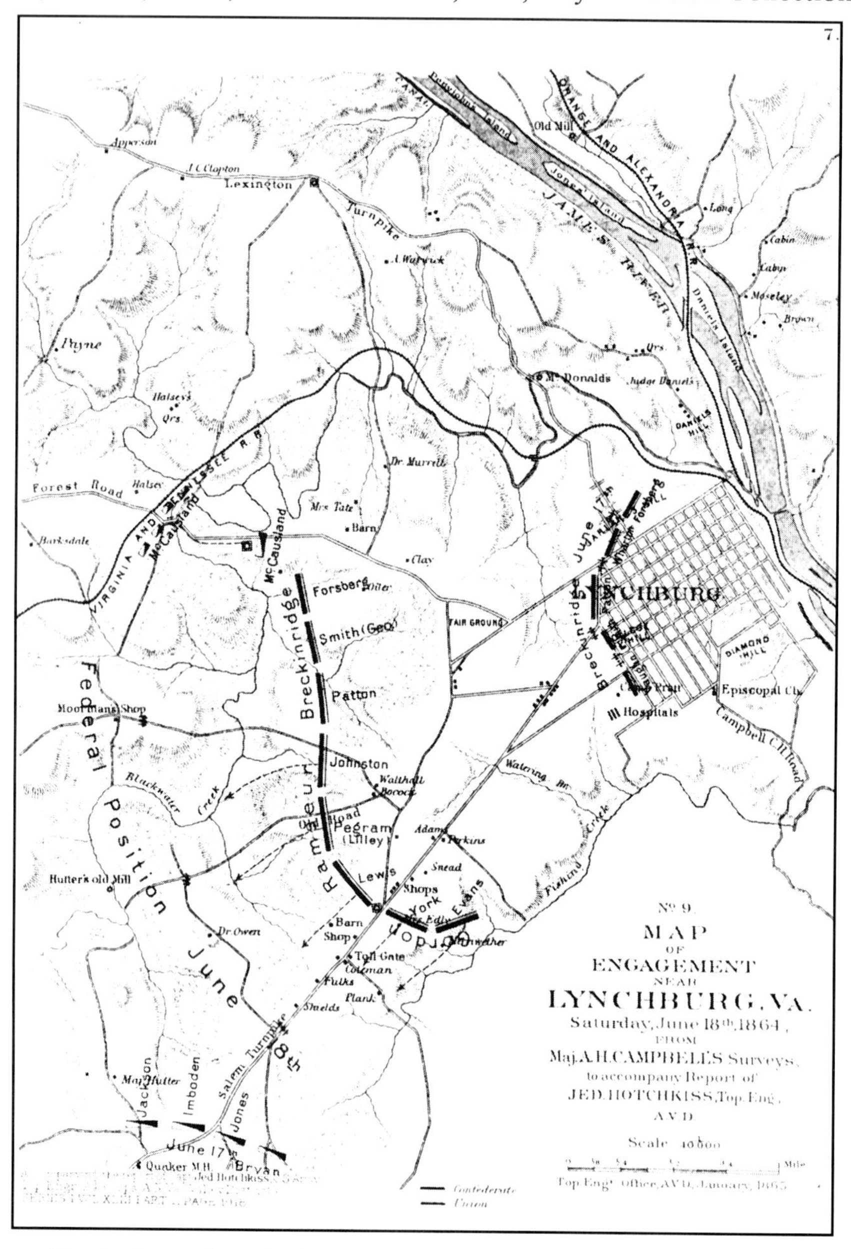

Camp Davis, located on the fairgrounds two miles west of Lynchburg, Virginia
Map from the *Official Military Atlas of the Civil War*, Plate LXXXIII, 7

171   **Camp Davis**

Henrico County, Virginia

This was a camp of instruction located near Richmond.

Georgia Troops:

13th (Ector's) Regiment Georgia Volunteer Infantry, 7/31/1861-8/25/1861

Sources:

GDAH, 39/70, Charles L. Howard; 171/40, Richard W. Milner

172   **Camp Davis**

Prince William County, Virginia

The camp was located on the Occoquan River, about two miles from Bull Run.

Georgia Troops:

14th Regiment Georgia Volunteer Infantry, 12/1861-2/22/1862

Sources:

GDAH, 283/37, Franklin Poor; MT, 3/10/1862

on left, pvt. Robert N. Rogers, Co. E, 14th Regiment Georgia Volunteer Infantry. He enlisted July 4, 1861, elected Jr. 2nd Lieut. May 1863, and Captain June 30, 1864.

on right, pvt. William E. Rogers, Co. E, 14th Regiment Georgia Volunteer Infantry. He enlisted July 4, 1864, was wounded at Seven Pines, Virginia on May 31, 1862. He was killed at Willow Creek, Cobb County, Georgia in 1864.

photo courtesy of James W. Bell

173   **Camp Debtford**

Chatham County, Georgia

The camp was located on the Debtford Plantation, east of Savannah and near Lee Battery.

Georgia Troops:

13th (Styles') Regiment Georgia Volunteer Infantry, Co. A, 3/5/1862-3/16/1862 (The regiment reorganized May 10, 1862, and became the 26th Regiment Georgia Volunteer Infantry.)

29th Regiment Georgia Volunteer Infantry, 5/1862-7/1862 (While in this camp, pickets of this regiment rotated duty in Camp MacKey.)

1st (Olmstead's) Volunteer Regiment of Georgia, Co. A, Irish Jasper Greens, 4/14/1862
Sources:
13th GVI, GDAH, CSR, 256/59
29th GVI, GDAH, CSR, 256/79
1st VRG, SDMN, 4/15/1862

174   **Camp Decatur**
DeKalb County, Georgia
   The camp was located seven miles from Atlanta on the Augusta Road.
Georgia Troops:
13th (Ector's) Regiment Georgia Volunteer Infantry, 7/17/1861
Source:
GDAH, 283/34, Richard W. Milner

175   **Camp Defiance**
Chatham County, Georgia
   The camp was located two miles below Savannah, and two miles from the Savannah River.
Georgia Troops:
4th Regiment Georgia State Troops, 2/10/1862
2nd Battalion Georgia State Troops, Taylor's Battalion, 2/11/1862
Source:
4th GST, *Saddle Bag and Spinning Wheel*, Edited by George Peddy Cuttino
2nd Bn GST, WL, Loc. 05-31 90-19, Dumbleton, Jeanne Humphries Collection, Thomas K. Campbell letters

176   **Camp Defiance**
Frederick County, Virginia
   The camp was located four miles from Winchester.
Georgia Troops:
8th Regiment Georgia Volunteer Infantry, 6/17/1861-6/20/1861 (Bartow's Brigade organized on 6/17/1861.)
Sources:
RWC, 6/28/1861 & 7/5/1861

177   **Camp Defiance**
Fayette County, West Virginia
   The camp was located on the western top of Big Sewell Mountain. A part of the regiment stood picket at Bald Mountain during this time.
Georgia Troops:
13th (Ector's) Regiment Georgia Volunteer Infantry, 9/24/1861-10/13/1861
Sources:
GDAH, UDC Books, II, 92-95, Charles E. Milner; 39/70, Charles L. Howard; *The Civil War in Fayette County West Virginia*,
By Tim McKinney

private James A Ogletree, Co. I, 13th Regiment Georgia Volunteer Infantry. Enlisted July 8, 1861, in Spalding County, Georgia. Died of wounds sustained at the battle of Sharpsburg September 21, 1862, four days after being wounded.

photo courtesy of Jerry Coody

178 **Camp Defiance**
Fayette County, West Virginia
   The camp was located in a wheat field on a hill to the rear of Boliver. Also, about three-fourths mile from the armory and about one mile from Harper's Ferry. See Atlas Plate XLII, 1.
Georgia Troops:
8th Regiment Georgia Volunteer Infantry, 6/9/1861-6/15/1861
Source:
RWC, 6/21/1861 & 6/28/1861

179 **Camp Dens**
Chatham County, Georgia
   The camp was located near Savannah.
Georgia Troops:
32nd Regiment Georgia Volunteer Infantry, 6/24/1863 & 10/31/1864
Source:
GDAH, 194/3, MR of Co. A

180 **Camp Despair**
Beaufort County, South Carolina
   This picket post is located twenty miles below Hardeeville, and two and one-half miles below Bluffton.
Georgia Troops:
Phillips' Legion, Infantry Battalion, Co. A, 3/14/1862-3/16/1862
Source:
PC, Daniel B. Sanford

181   **Camp Dickerson**

Fayette County, West Virginia

The camp was located on the Dickerson farm at Cotton Hill, south of New River.

Georgia Troops:

13th (Ector's) Regiment Georgia Volunteer Infantry, 10/21/1861-11/12/1861

Phillips' Legion, 10/21/1861-11/12/1861

Sources:

13th GVI, GDAH, CSR, 255/94; 39/70, Charles L. Howard

PL, GDAH, CSR, 258/42; WL, Loc. 05-31 90-19, Dumbleton, Jeanne Humphries Collection, Elisha Humphries letters

Map: O.R. Vol. V, p. 948

182   **Camp Dick Robinson**

Garrard County, Kentucky

The *Confederate Veteran* Magazine, Volume XXIII, page 409, described the camp's location:

> A few days after the battle (Battle of Perryville, Kentucky, October 8, 1862,) Bragg had collected his army at Camp Dick Robinson, about fifteen miles from the battle ground and one year before the chief Federal recruiting camp in Kentucky. The natural strength of this camp for a large army acting on the defensive was very great. To the north was the long line of the Kentucky River cliffs, higher than the Hudson Palisades and reaching from the mountains to below Frankfort, effectually blocking any attacking army from the north. To the west and southwest frowned the Dick's River cliffs, only a little lower than those of the Kentucky and furnishing a secure defense in those quarters. Dick's River pours into the Kentucky a few miles northwest of Camp Dick Robinson and a few hundred yards above the present High Bridge on the Queen and Crescent Railroad. Thus the camp was in an acute angle of the two rivers and unassailable save from the southeast.

The camp was also refered to as Camp Beauregard.

Georgia Troops:

Any of the units involved in the Battle of Perryville could have written a letter from this camp with the caption of either Camp Dick Robinson or Camp Beauregard. It is known that Georgia units were in this camp. They were not identified.

Sources:

O.R., Vol. XVI; CV, XXIII, 409

Map: Atlas, Plate CL.

183   **Camp Direction**

Hamilton County, Tennessee

The camp was located near Chattanooga.

Georgia Troops:

Any Georgia soldier passing through Chattanooga and separated from his unit could have written a letter from this camp. See Chapter IV for the description and purpose of this camp. This camp was used from September, 1862 to April, 1863.

Sources:

CDR, 9/26/1862; SC, 11/11/1862, G.O. #142

Camp Dickerson on the Dickerson farm at Cotton Hill, West Virginia

Map of south central Kentucky showing location of Camp Dick Robinson and Big Hill

184   **Camp Dirt Town**

Chattooga County, Georgia

The camp was located near Dirt Town. See Atlas Plate CXLIX, E 11, for the location of Dirt Town. Also, see the map of Rome, Georgia on page 303.

Georgia Troops:

2nd Regiment Cavalry, Georgia State Guards, 10/3/1863-12/16/1863

Source:

GDAH, CSR, 253/86

185   **Camp Disappointment**

York County, Virginia

This was a picket camp located on the peninsula below Camp Marion, probably near Bethel Church.

Georgia Troops:

Cobb's Legion, Cavalry Battalion, 12/20/1861-12/21/1861

Source:

UGA, Ms. 184, William Gaston Delony

186   **Camp Discipline**

Hanover County, Virginia

The camp was located in an open field near Hanover Court House.

Georgia Troops:

Cobb's Legion, Cavalry Battalion, 7/271862-7/29/1862

Sources:

GDAH, 283/29, William Thomas Huff; UGA, Ms. 184, William Gaston Delony

187   **Camp Dismal**

Charleston County, South Carolina

The camp was located on James Island.

Georgia Troops:

12th Battalion Georgia Volunteers, 12/5/1863, Cos. C & E 3/6/1864

Sources:

SDMN, 12/10/1863; GDAH, CSR, 254/31-34; 171/39, Thomas Carson

188   **Camp Doles**

Portsmouth County, Virginia

The camp was located immediately on the southwestern branch of the Elizabeth River, some four miles from its entrance into the Elizabeth River. See Atlas Plate XXVI, 4.

Georgia Troops:

4th Regiment Georgia Volunteer Infantry, 5/22/1861-5/28/1861

Sources:

GDAH, 194/3, Capt. Cullen R. Ezell & Muster Roll; PC, letter of John, unidentified member of Co. H; EU, #363, David Read Evans Winn

189   **Camp Doles**
Frederick County, Virginia
The camp was located Near Winchester.
Georgia Troops:
Milledge Light Artillery, 10/1862
Source:
ADC&S, 10/21/1862

190   **Camp Doles**
Orange County, Virginia
The camp was located near Orange Courthouse.
Georgia Troops:
4th Regiment Georgia Volunteer Infantry, 2/12/1864-3/12/1864
Sources:
GDAH, 194/3, Capt. Cullen R. Ezell & Muster Roll.

191   **Camp Donelson**
Jasper County, South Carolina
The following is an extract of a letter to the editor of the *Augusta Daily Chronicle and Sentinel*, written on April 7, 1862. It was published in the newspaper on April 9, 1862. The writer was a member of the 48th Regiment Georgia Volunteers and signed the letter, "E." He was probably a member of one of the two companies from Richmond County.

It will be doubtless gratifying to many of your readers, to hear something of the camp and of their friends and relatives who now are here.

It may be found about one mile from Station No. 8, on the Charleston and Savannah Railroad, and a half mile from Grahamsville, on a fine road leading from the station to the village. It is situated on a beautiful spot, slightly elevated above the surrounding country, which has heretofore been used by the good people of the village as a pick-nic ground, where they have erected an extensive shed resembling a "camp-meeting stand," and near by it a small house for the ladies on such occasions to adjust their dresses and beau-catchers. The former is used at present by the Surgeon to dispense his medicines and the latter is the headquarters of the Colonel. Skirting the camp on the East is a beautiful creek, its margin covered with dog-wood, honey-suckle and jessamine in full bloom, casting their fragrance in richness and variety over the entire encampment. On the South are the tents spread out along the roadside, under the cooling shade of magnificent and wide spreading liveoak and cedar trees, profusely and georgeously draped with moss vibrating with the gentlest zephyrs. On the North is the parade ground - the West a pine forest. The camp is supplied by two wells of excellent water, pure and limpid, and nearly, if not quite equal to our own Turknett Spring water. Taking it altogether I think it is a lovely spot, and being in the midst of pine woods must be healthy at all seasons. With the exception of a few cases of measles and mumps, the troops are very healthy, and I have not heard of sickness of any kind in the two companies from Richmond county. The Augusta boys are every one of them, well and while off duty, as at this moment, are wild with exuberance of health and spirits.

The troops have been supplied with first class Enfield rifled muskets of long range, and from what I have seen of this regiment in the field, they will in a very short time be fit to go into battle with credit to themselves and country.

In company with Gen. Donaldson and Col. Gibson, I had, yesterday, the pleasure of witnessing a battalion drill conducted by Lieut. Col. Carswell; the Georgia Guard, commanded by Lieut. Evans, the Wilson Tigers, by Lieut Walker, and the other companies by their respective Captains. It was very creditable to both officers and men , who were highly complimented by Gen. Donaldson. Their proficiency is really wonderful, when we consider that it is only two weeks since their organization.

The companies are required to drill morning and afternoon two hours and a half each, and at five o'clock they have regimental dress parade and drill. It is a fine body of men, and if permited to remain here one month longer, will be as fine a Regiment as Georgia has yet sent into the field.

Their dress parades are graced daily by the presence of the wives and daughters of the chivalry of Carolina.

Georgia Troops:
48th Regiment Georgia Volunteer Infantry, 4/3/1862-5/14/1862
Sources:
GDAH, CSR, 257/47; UDC Books, VIII, 258-262, John Wesley Cheatham; ADC&S, 4/9/1862

192   Camp Dorchester

McIntosh County, Georgia

The camp was located seven to eight miles east of Riceboro post office, near Dorchester.
Georgia Troops;
1st Battalion Georgia Cavalry, Liberty Independent Troop, 11/1862-3/1863 (Later they became Co. G, 5th Regiment Georgia Volunteer Cavalry.)
7th Regiment Georgia Volunteer Cavalry, 3/29/1864-4/7/1864
Sources:
1st Bn GC, GDAH, CSR, 253/79
7th GC, GDAH, CSR, 253/109; 43/79, John D. Carswell

193   Camp Douglass

Randolph County, Georgia

The camp was located near Cuthbert, and probably named after Marcellus Douglass, who was elected Captain of Company E, 13th Regiment Georgia Volunteer Infantry on June 19, 1861, and later served as Colonel of the regiment. He was killed at Sharpsburg, Maryland, on September 17, 1862.
Georgia Troops:
Bartow Guards, 7/30/1861 (They later became Co. E, 31st Regiment Georgia Volunteer Infantry.)
Source:
Not Known

194   **Camp Doyal**
Spalding County, Georgia

The camp was located near Griffin.
Georgia Troops:
53rd Regiment Georgia Volunteer Infantry, 6/11/1862-6/20/1862
Sources:
GDAH, UDC Books, Vol. IV, 114; 194/3, John L. G. Wood

195   **Camp Drayton**
Chatham County, Georgia

The camp was located six miles from Savannah and fourteen miles from Camp Houston.
Georgia Troops:
1st Georgia Regulars, Co. D, Read's Artillery, 5/11/1862-7/23/1862
Source:
GDAH, CSR, 254/67

196   **Camp Drayton**
Chesterfield County, Virginia

The camp was located near Drewry's Bluff on the James River, seven miles below Richmond.
This was a camp of Drayton's Brigade.
Georgia Troops:
50th Regiment Georgia Volunteer Infantry, 8/8/1862
51st Regiment Georgia Volunteer Infantry, 8/8/1862
Source:
Not Known

197   **Camp Dunbar**
Burke County, Georgia

Yesterday morning (May 22, 1862,) on invitation of Mayor May, a number of our citizens, both ladies and gentlemen, made an excursion to Shell Bluff to see the fortifications at that point. The party was a very agreeable one, among which were Majors Rains and Capers, Gen. Gardner, Capt. Allen and other military men, members of the Bar, of the City Council, the medical faculty, the press, clergymen, civilians, &c.

The steamer *Little Edisto*, Capt. Sassard, left the dock about half past 8 o'clock and steamed down the river.

The story, too lengthy, describes the cruise down the river entertained by the music of Mr. Hett's string band, and the scenic beauty of the Savannah River. The artillery on the bluff gave a demonstration described by the unknown writer.

The finest sight, however, at least to novices like ourself, was the shell-firing. --- the first deafening roar as the deadly missile sped from the gun, its appearance for a second far away in the air, it bursting and emitting beautiful wreaths of white smoke, and the final report coming back to us in some time after the explosion. The guns were in several instances fired by some of the ladies of our party - Miss McNatt leading off by firing the columbiad, Miss Doughty and Miss Belle Clayton following, a trial being made also of the six-pounders, sending grape shot among the obstructions which these guns cover.

The writer later describes the walk to Camp Dunbar and their return trip to Augusta.

In company with Lieut. Geo. M. Hood, we paid a visit to Camp Dunbar, on the summit of the Bluff, and were kindly shown about the camp by that gentleman. It is very pleasantly situated in the shelter of the forest, protected from the sun's rays by the foliage of the trees, and the ground cleared of all undergrowth, and sloping off each way from the tents, gives the rains a chance to pass off at once without inconvenience. The tents are laid out handsomely in streets, the Walker Light Artillery and Stevens Battery occuping parallel thoroughfares. --- The trip homeward was pleasantly beguiled by singing, social chat, and dancing by the young folks upon the upper deck. --- We should like to allude to the gradual coming on of twilight, deepening finally into night, as the stars came out and sparkled on the bosom of the river, while sweet music from voice and instruments floated away into purple distance. ---
Just as the clock struck nine, we arrived at the wharf, the excursionists speedily vacated the steamer's decks, and wending their several ways homeward, mutually delighted with the memorable excursion to Shell Bluff.

Georgia Troops:
12th Battalion Georgia Light Artillery, Co. C, Stevens Battery & Co. E, Walker Light Artillery, 5/14/1862-5/22/1862
Sources:
ADC&S, 5/15/1862 & 5/23/1862

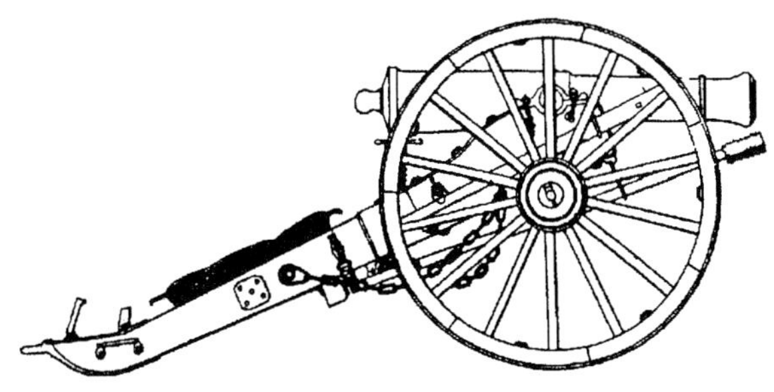

198   **Camp Early**
Prince William County, Virginia
The camp was located near Manassas Junction and Union Mills.
Georgia Troops:
20th Regiment Georgia Volunteer Infantry, 9/1861-1/22/1862
Sources:
SC, 11/8/1861; GDAH, CSR, 256/13; 171/39 George A. Weldon

199   **Camp Easley**
Georgetown County, South Carolina
The camp was located near Georgetown in the old Christ Church Parish.
Georgia Troops:
21st Battalion Georgia Cavalry, Co. B, 2/13/1863-4/1863
Sources:
GHS, *1863 Savannah Digest*; GDAH, CSR, 254/9

200   **Camp Ector**
Spalding County, Georgia
This was a cavalry training camp about one mile below Griffin.
Georgia Troops.
2nd Regiment Georgia Volunteer Cavalry, Cos. D, E, H, J & K, 3/1862-7/1862 (All of the other companies trained at Camp McDonald.)
Capt. Nelson's Independent Company of Partisan Rangers, 5/14/1862
Sources:
2nd GVC, GDAH, MR, 279/64; PC, James Jewell letters
NPR, GDAH, CSR, 254/21

201   **Camp Edla**
Chatham County, Georgia
The camp was located on the southwest common of Savannah and east of Laurel Grove Cemetery, six and one-half miles from Camp Rose on Rose Hill. It was the battalion headquarters at this time.
Georgia Troops:
2nd Battalion Georgia Cavalry, 6/1862-1/1863
2nd Battalion Georgia Cavalry, Co. D, Georgia Hussars, Co. B, 12/10/1862-1/13/1863 (Georgia Hussars, Co. B, became Co. A, 5th Regiment Georgia Volunteer Cavalry on January 22, 1863.)
Sources:
GDAH, CSR, 253/86; EU, #12, John H. Ash

202   **Camp Edray**
Pocahontas County, West Virginia

The camp was located at the springs, five miles above Greenbrier River. William Wood wrote from this camp, "our regiment is scattered all over this country."
Georgia Troops:
14th Regiment Georgia Volunteer Infantry, Co. F, 9/25/1861-10/5/1861
Source:
GDAH, 283/44, William Martin Wood

203   **Camp Ellington**
Quitman County, Georgia

The camp was located eight mile from Georgetown.
Georgia Troops:
Quitman Grays, 5/20/1861 (The company later became Co. I, 11th Regiment Georgia. Volunteer Infantry.)
Source:
MT, 5/24/1861

204   **Camp Elzey**
Jasper County, South Carolina

This camp was located three-fourths mile east of Camp Lee at Hardeeville, on the same side and distance from the railroad.
Georgia Troops:
Phillips' Legion, 5 infantry companies, B, C, L, M & O, 6/8/1862-7/22/1862
Source:
GDAH, 9/79, Ben and Augustus Boyd

205   **Camp Etowah**
Floyd County, Georgia

The camp was located near Rome.
Georgia Troops:
9th Regiment Georgia State Guards, Cos. C, 10/15/1863 & H, 12/15/1863 (The entire regiment was probably here.)
Source:
UGA, Ms. 2345, Ellis Merton Coulter Historical Manuscripts

206   **Camp Evans**
Chatham County, Georgia

The camp was located in the rear of the city jail.
Georgia Troops:
1st (Olmstead's) Volunteer Regiment of Georgia, Montgomery Guards and Washington Volunteers, 11/21/1861
Source:
SDMN, 11/23/1861

207   **Camp Evans**
Cobb County, Georgia
   The camp was probably in north Cobb or west Cherokee County.
Georgia Troops:
1st Battalion Georgia State Cavalry, McCollum's command, 11/1864 or 12/1864
Source:
KMNBPL, G.W. Hunnicutt

208   **Camp Evans**
Charleston County, South Carolina
   The camp was located at Rantowles, twelve miles from the pickets on John's Island. They were
under command of General Nathan G. Evans.
Georgia Troops:
51st Regiment Georgia Volunteer Infantry, 5/25/1862-6/6/1862
Sources:
GDAH, 283/32 W.M. Livingston; USC, J.T. & W. J. Nobles

209   **Camp Evans**
Tazwell County, Tennessee
   The camp was located near Bean Station, and possibly named in honor of Capt. Walter R.
Evans, recently appointed Deputy Provost Marshall for the 4th Military District of East
Tennessee, which included the Tazwell - Bean Station area.
Georgia Troops:
3rd Battalion Georgia Volunteer Infantry, 7/24/1862
Cherokee Light Artillery, 7/24/1862
Source:
KDR, 7/26/1862

210   **Camp Evans**
Shenandoah County, Virginia
   This camp was located near New Market.
Georgia Troops:
26th Regiment Georgia Volunteer Infantry, 8/31/1864
Source:
GDAH, CSR, 256/59

211   **Camp Evansville**
Augusta County, Virginia
   The camp was located near Evansville.
Georgia Troops:
12th Regiment Georgia Volunteer Infantry, 7/11/1861
Source:
EU, #20, John Levi Griffin

212   **Camp Fain**
Loudon County, Tennessee
The camp was located near Loudon.
Georgia Troops:
Smith's Legion, 9/2/1862
Source:
GDAH, CSR, 258/51

213   **Camp Fairfield**
Bedford County, Tennessee
The camp was located four miles north of Wartrace on the Manchester Pike. The troops were in and out of this camp on scouting missions.
Georgia Troops:
3rd Regiment Georgia Volunteer Cavalry, 3/3/1863-4/29/1863
Sources:
RWC, 3/20/1863 & 5/8/1863; *War was the Place, a centenniel collection of Confederate soldier letters*, Chattahoochee Valley Historical Society

214   **Camp Fairfield**
Henrico County, Virginia
The camp was located on the Fairfield Race Course, two and one-half miles from the center of Richmond, on a high beautiful plain.
Georgia Troops:
6th Regiment Georgia Volunteer Infantry, 6/3/1861
10th Regiment Georgia Volunteer Infantry, 5/28/1861-6/20/1861 (The regiment arrived at Yorktown on June 21, 1861.)
20th Regiment Georgia Volunteer Infantry, 6/2/1861-6/171861 & 6/29/1861-7/26/1861
21st Regiment Georgia Volunteer Infantry, 6/22/1861-8/1/1861
Sources:
6th GVI, MT, 6/8/1861
10th GVI, GDAH, CSR, 255/65
20th GVI, MJ&M, 6/19/1861; GDAH, CSR, 256/13
21st GVI, GDAH, 283/20, William M. Butt

215   **Camp Fairground**
Clarke County, Georgia
The camp was located on the north side of the ridge of the fairgrounds near Athens.
Georgia Troops:
30th Battalion Georgia Cavalry, Co. A, 8/7/1864-9/15/1864 (The company returned to this camp for a few days about October 26, 1864.)
Sources:
ASB, 8/17/1864 & 10/26/1864

216   **Camp Fair Ground**
                              Frederick County, Virginia
     See Camp Jackson in Frederick County. This is probably the same camp.
Georgia Troops:
8th Regiment Georgia Volunteer Infantry, 6/8/1861-6/9/1861
Source:
RWC, 6/21/1861

217   **Camp Fancy Bluff**
                              Camden County, Georgia
The camp was located on Fancy Bluff, on Fancy Creek, 17 miles from Camp Wayne.

     Waynesville, March 17.--- The Lincolnites, not satisfied with shelling the deserted town of Brunswick, have turned their guns upon Fancy Bluff. On Tuesday night last, Capt. T.S. Hopkins and Lieutenant J.C. McDonald, of the "Wayne Rangers," drove down in a buggy to the Bluff, on a visit to their pickets. We reached there at 9 o'clock, and as soon as they approached the picket fire, the gunboat opposite in Turtle River, a mile and a half distant, fired a shot at them, which fell to the right of the tent about fifty yards. Very early in the morning, the Capt. and Lieut. with privates Sardis and Geiger, crossed in a small boat to Colonel's Island, and from the top of the dwelling house opened fire on the gunboat with their carbines. At 9 o'clock they returned to Fancy Bluff, where they met Lieut. J.D. Rumph, who had just arrived with a detachment of twenty rangers.

     The appearance of the detachment, and a few carbine shots in the direction of the ship, was followed by four shells and two shots from the cowardly Yankees. The shots were wild, but every shell exploded immediately over the lot where the men were, and their fragments and contents were afterwards picked up in many places, indicating that they must have fallen in the midst of them. Notwithstanding this, "no one was hurt." All the mischief done was the wounding of the Captain's mare, and probably disabled her for a short time. From Colonel's Island three contrabands belonging to Mr. Scarlett, were seen to go on board of the ship. Up to date, that gentleman has lost twenty prime men. The Rangers stood the shelling like men, and with an eye constantly on the enemy as he passed along our coast, long for an opportunity to meet him on land or find him under a bluff.
                    Yours,   Waynesville.

Georgia Troops:
4th (Clinch's) Regiment Georgia Volunteer Cavalry, Cos. A, 3/1862; C, 6/1864; & H, 4/1864
(Other companies were probably here at different times serving picket duty.)
Sources:
ADC&S, 3/22/1862; GDAH, CSR, 253/94

218   **Camp Fannie**
Culpeper County, Virginia

This could be a picket camp of Company B, Georgia Troopers, since the Cavalry Battalion was in Camp Stevensburg at this time. The Infantry Battalion was near Fredericksburg. See Camp Paulina.

Camp Fannie, Virginia
January 31st, 1863,

Miss Paulina Thomas,
Sec'y Ladies Vol. Association

The box shipped to my company, containing clothing, blankets, &c., (corresponding with bill sent,) has been received, and distributed according to your instructions.

I take this the earliest opportunity to return the thanks of the company for the same. We were very much in need of the supplies sent us by your Association, and ever feel grateful to the donors, who thus sympathise with the destitute and suffering soldiers.

Hoping that peace may be returned to our much loved, sunny South, at an early day,
I am , very respectfully, Yours
J.E. Ritch,
Capt. Comd'g Co. "B" Geo. Troopers
Per A.C. Baker, 1st Serg't.
and Secretary of Company.

Georgia Troops:
Cobb's Legion, Cavalry Battalion, Co. B, 1/31/1863
Source:
ASB, 3/18/1863

219   **Camp Fanny H___**
Chatham County, Georgia

This camp was located near Thunderbolt Battery, and was named after a young lady from Savannah that enjoyed visiting the young men in this camp.
Georgia Troops:
The Confederate Signal Corp, mid 1863
Source:
Recollections of a Private in the Signal Corp, Jan.1863 - Apr. 1865, by William Harden

220   **Camp Farley**
Montgomery County, Alabama

The camp was near James A. Farley's residence at Montgomery while attending the inauguration of President Jefferson Davis.

Columbus Guards . . . . Picture.

The Columbus Guards have had a beautiful Ambrotype of the corps taken. The Company stands in front of their tents in open ranks, with officers and non-commissioned officers in inspection order. Near-by is the cannon, the gun squad lying down; while in the rear are the honorary members of the corps and a few ladies and gentlemen on horseback, besides the camp being well filled with visitors. The whole picture is fine and the Guards never looked better in their red uniforms. They present the picture to Mr. Farley, of

Montgomery, as a testimonial of the appreciation of his hospitality to the Guards during their visit to that city.

Georgia Troops:
Columbus Guards, 2/16/1861-2/19/1861 (The company later became Co. G, 2nd Regiment Georgia Volunteer Infantry.)
Sources:
CE, 2/24/1861 & 3/2/1861

221   **Camp Felton**
Gordon County, Georgia

The location of this camp is not known.
Georgia Troops:
Smith's Legion, Infantry Battalion, Co. B, 5/15/1862-5/23/1862
Source:
GDAH, CSR, 258/51

222   **Camp Field**
Prince William County, Virginia

Location not known. Probably named after Col. Charles W. Field of the 6th Virginia Cavalry. The company was attached to the 6th Virginia Cavalry as Company E, from October 17, 1861, to December 13, 1861.
Georgia Troops:
Georgia Hussars, Co. A, 1/26/1862 (On 12/13/1861, the company transferred to Co. F, "Jeff Davis Legion Cavalry".)
Sources:
SR, 2/3/1862; *Roll and Legend of the Georgia Hussars*, by Alexander McC. Duncan

223   **Camp Finnegan**
Duval County, Florida

The camp was located eight miles west of Jacksonville, near Baldwin and Cedar Creek.
Georgia Troops:
4th (Clinch's) Regiment Georgia Volunteer Cavalry, 3/4/1864
5th Regiment Georgia Volunteer Cavalry, 3/2/1864-5/2/1864
1st Georgia Regulars, 4/19/1864-5/1/1864
6th Regiment Georgia Volunteer Infantry, 3/29/1864
30th Regiment Georgia Volunteer Infantry, 10/6/1864-10/11/1864
Sources:
4th GVC, SR, 3/6/1864
5th GVC, EU, #12, John H. Ash; GDAH, 283/24, H. G. Edenfield
1st GR, GDAH, CSR, 254/67
6th GVI, ASB, 4/13/1864
30th GVI, GDAH, MR, 279/83

224   **Camp Fleetwood**

Chatham County, Georgia

The camp was at the Fleetwood Plantation on Whitmarsh Island. See Camp Williams of the 1st Georgia Regulars.

Georgia Troops:

1st (Symon's) Regiment Georgia Infantry Reserves, Cos. D & E, 8/1864

27th Battalion Georgia Volunteer Infantry, 7/17/1864-7/22/1864

Sources:

1st GR, GDAH, CSR, 254/94

27th Bn GVI, GDAH, 283/18, John A. Boyce

225   **Camp Flora**

Henrico County, Virginia

The camp was located near Richmond.

Eli Pinson Landers of the 16th Regiment Georgia Volunteer Infantry wrote his mother from Camp Flora on July 20, 1862. The following is an extract from his letter.

We have been in regular camp for two weeks. No fighting has been done round here since the first though from all reports I think there will be the worst fighting in the course of a month that has ever been yet for the advance pickets report that the Yankeys are advancing a little everyday back towards Richmond. They have been heavily reinforced. I think it is their full intention to destroy our Capital. Let it cost what it may but oh the destruction that will be among men before they do it. They are now exchanging prisoners. We have taken a great many in this last conflict. The number is estimated at 11,000 in all of the fights. Orders has come in since I begun my letter to be ready to move in two hours. I dont know where we will go to but I dont think we will go far. If they do I will not go with them. It is thought we will only go out to a better place to camp. I wish I could write you an interesting letter but not being very well and having to hasten through to get ready to leave you must excuse me this time for you know how it is here.

Private Eli Pinson Landers, Co. H, 16th Regiment Georgia Volunteer Infantry. Eli left home August 11, 1861 for Virginia. On October 27, 1863, he died of disease.

photo courtesy of
Elizabeth Whitley Roberson

Georgia Troops:
16th Regiment Georgia Volunteer Infantry, 7/20/1862
Source:
PC, Letters of Eli Pinson Landers; *Weep Not for Me, Dear Mother*, By Elizabeth Whitley
Roberson

226   **Camp Forest**
Chatham County, Georgia
   The camp was located near Coffee Bluff.
Georgia Troops:
Capt. Anderson Jr's. Company of Partisan Rangers, 11/15/1862-2/24/1862 (Later the company
became Co. B, 24th Battalion Georgia Cavalry. Also known as Randolph Rangers.)
Source:
GDAH, CSR, 254/11

227   **Camp Forest**
Pulaski County, Virginia
   The camp was located near Dublin Depot.
Georgia Troops:
Phillips' Legion, Infantry Battalion, Co. F, 12/21/1862-12/24/1862 (On December 24, 1861, they
received orders to go to South Carolina.)
Source:
GDAH, 283/48 Bibb County file

228   **Camp Forest**
Prince William County, Virginia
   The camp was between Manassas and Centerville, near Camp Georgia of Toomb's Brigade.
Georgia Troops:
11th Battalion Georgia Light Artillery, 1/25/1862-3/1/1862
Sources:
PC, letters of Joseph M. Little; GDAH, 171/39, UDC, Lizzie Rutherford Chapter, Archibald S.
Cameron letters

229   **Camp Fort**
Wayne County, Georgia
   The camp was located near Waynesville.
Georgia Troops:
Capt. Hopkin's Company of mounted partisan rangers, 9/22/1862-10/1862 (Later the company
became Co. A, 24th Battalion Georgia Cavalry.)
Source:
GDAH, CSR, 254/11

230

Camp Fort Powhatan
Prince George County, Virginia

The camp was located at Fort Powhatan, on a bluff of the James River, twenty-two miles below Petersburg.
Georgia Troops:
10th Battalion Georgia Volunteer Infantry, 5/7/1863-6/7/1863
Sources:
GDAH, 78/2 & 283/35, William. J. Moseley

231

Camp Foster
Bartow County, Georgia

The camp was located at the Etowah River railroad bridge, near Etowah Station.
Georgia Troops:
1st (Galt's) Regiment, Georgia State Line Troops, 4/1863-4/3/1864
Sources:
GDAH, AGLB #13; *Joe Brown's Army, The Georgia State Line, 1862-1865*, by William Harris Bragg

232

Camp Fredericks Hall
Louisa County, Virginia

The camp was located near Fredericks Hall Station. Headquarters of Semmes Brigade. It was composed of the 10th, 50th, 51st & 53rd Regiments Georgia Volunteer Infantry. The only record of this camp name came from the 53rd Regiment Georgia Volunteers.
Georgia Troops:
53rd Regiment Georgia Volunteer Infantry, 8/27/1863-9/2/1863
Source:
GDAH, UDC Books, Vol. XIV, Rev. William R. Stillwell

233

Camp Fredericksburg
Spotsylvania County, Virginia

The camp was located near Fredericksburg.
Georgia Troops:
53rd Regiment Georgia Volunteer Infantry, 1/1/1863-6/3/1863
Source:
GDAH, UDC Books, Vol. XIV, Rev. William R. Stillwell

234

Camp Fredericksburg (1st.)
Spotsylvania County, Virginia

The camp was located on Telegraph Road, six miles from Fredericksburg. Also known as Camp McLaws.
Georgia Troops:
Phillips' Legion, Infantry Battalion, 3/29/1863-4/28/1863 & 5/11/1863-5/30/1863 (The Infantry Battalion and Cavalry Batallion separated on April 14, 1863.)
Source:
KMNBPL, Marcus L. Green

235 **Camp Fredericksburg (2nd.)**
Spotsylvania County, Virginia
    The camp was located one mile above Fredericksburg.
Georgia Troops:
Phillips' Legion, Infantry Battalion, 6/1/1863-6/3/1863
Source:
KMNBPL, Marcus L. Green

236 **Camp French**
New Hanover County, North Carolina
    The camp was located about one and one-half miles below Wilmington, down the Cape Fear railroad. An extract from Joshua J. Tinley's letter of May 11, 1861, described the location of the camp.

> We are now encamped about a mile and a half below Wilmington and have gone at our old trade, Viz; that of doing guard duty for the town and the adjacent regions. We did nothing last year but guard every little hovel which could be scared up, and our leaders seem to think that is our proper duty and help us at it.
>
> Our present camp is beautiful beyond description. I feel myself inadequate to the task, and therefore, will not attempt it; however, I will give you one idea and leave you to paint the rest according to your own fancy. Imagine yourself in a desert with a few stunted trees around you and you will have some idea of this beautiful camp.
>
> We look back to those few happy days spent at home with relatives and friends, and wonder if the future has any more such in store for us. I hope there are, and that they are not far ahead. If so I hope we will overtake them about July and take another jaunt to Old Bibb. I speak for Billie, Tom and myself, as we all agree on one thing, and that is, coming home whenever we can get a chance.

Georgia Troops:
2nd Independent Infantry Battalion, 5/1/1861-5/29/1862
Sources:
GDAH, UDC Books, Vol. II, Henry Graves; 283/42, Joshua J. Tinley

237 **Camp French**
Wilson County, North Carolina
    Located near Wilson.
Georgia Troops:
7th Regiment Confederate Cavalry, Co. I, 9/1862 (The company later became a part of the 10th Regiment Georgia Volunteer Cavalry.)
Source:
GDAH, CSR, 258/ 69

Camp French
Prince William County, Virginia

From the 35th Georgia Regiment.
Camp French, Evansport, Va.
February 6th, 1862.

Editors, Southern Confederacy:

The 35th Regiment Georgia Volunteers are stationed at Evansport, Va. midway between the mouths of Aquia and Occoquan Creeks. Our camp is near a mile from the banks of the Potomac, surrounded by several large hills which hide us from the view of the enemy, stationed in large numbers, we presume, on the Maryland side of the river. From the summit of the hills we can see the "Stars and Stripes" floating in the breezes, and hear the shrill notes of the fifes of the enemy playing to the tune of "Yankee Doodle" and "Hail Columbia!" But then as we turn in another direction, from every hill and valley, where Southern troops are encamped, the soul stirring strains of "Dixie" greet the ear.

Private John Rigby, enlisted September 23, 1861, Co. D, 35th Regiment Georgia Volunteer Infantry. He was wounded at Mechanicsville, Virginia, June 26, 1862, captured at Wilderness, Virginia, May 6, 1864, and died of bronchitis at Elmira, New York May 4, 1865.

photo courtesy of
Patricia and Steve Mullinax

Private Jasper Webb, Co. G, 35th Regiment Georgia Volunteer Infantry. He enlisted September 16, 1861, and died at Winchester, Virginia, November 16, 1862.

photo courtesy of Tom Aderhold

Three Miles North of us is Dumfries, a dilapidated cluster of old houses, the ruins of a once populous city. Near its center stands an ancient building now used as a Commissary Store, which the inhabitants say was the Academy in which George Washington acquired the rudiments of an English education. Every one of these old ruins that can be made to stand at all, is crowded with goods of some description, which are sold by these petty merchants to the soldiers at four times their actual worth: but the better part of Dumphries consists in the hospitals for the accomidation of the sick, which are neatly kept, provided with good nurses and under the direction of first class physicians.

But the greatest difficulty with which we have to contend, is getting the sick from camps to the hospitals - the great quantity of rain and snow that has fallen during the last two months, and then the amount of transportation necessary for the use of the army combined, have rendered the roads almost impassible, though I trust ere long we will have no farther use for hospitals, as the health of the Regiment is rapidly improving. Certainly we have had our proportionment of sickness; for today as I look out from my tent, my heart is sad, when I behold upon a neighboring hill those rude pens marking the graves of so many departed Georgians.

Yet every comrad who falls from disease or by the missiles of the enemy I trust will animate our spirits and cause us to be more determined to avenge their noble sacrifice. It is truly gratifying and encouraging to see the spirit of harmony and contentment which pervades the camps of Southern soldiers, and with what alacrity they re enlist as their term of service expires. Surely none intend quitting the service till the flag of the Confederacy can wave without a rival over every Southern State.

Lieut. H.H. Roberts.

Georgia Troops:
35th Regiment Georgia Volunteer Infantry, 11/20/1861-3/8/1862
Sources:
GDAH, CSR, 256/103; 283/34, Benjamin F. Moody; SC, 2/21/1862

239   **Camp Frog**
Beaufort County, South Carolina

Camp Frog, 8 miles from Savannah, Beaufort Dist. S.C.
Sunday Evening June 8th, 1862.

Dear Sister,

Yours of the 2nd inst. came to camp in my absence, on last Tuesday morning about day I left camps with eighty men for a scouting expidition, we went on two Islands Spring Island and Callawassee Island, both of which we thought were occupied by small parties of Yankees. after traveling fifteen miles in small boats we landed on the islands about 2 o'clock wednesday night, but to the great disappointment of all the Yankees had left a day or two before taking every thing of value with them. They left one old negro man who was too old to do them any good; we had a hard time, at least I did; I was detached from the main body on Tuesday evening about dark to take command of forty men who had to approach the Island from an other point, we marched until 12 o'clock that night through the hardest rain I ever saw of all wading swamps where the water was two to three feet deep, I never had a dry thread on me until Thursday night when I returned to camps, I will leave you to imagine my feelings, while in that condition. I had only thirteen of our company on the expidition besides myself; You see from the caption of my letter that we have moved from our old camp, we have four companies here & in at Hardeeville and six at the old camp, but this seperation is only temporary it is best for the health of the men; we are expecting orders to go to some other point every day Either Charleston or Savannah I presume will be our destiny for both of these places are threatened now. Some entertains the idea that we will go to Chattanooga, but I do not think so for our force is too small here. I think we will have some hot work about here before many weeks. I have given up hope of visiting home soon, you can put my shirt in with the boys uniforms. Put my name on them, the name of the camp was suggested by a young lady who lives here to some of our boys and I think it very appropriate. If you were to be here at night and hear the frogs you would think you were surrounded by a legion of dogs barking at you. Tom sends love to all our company is in very good health at present. Much love to all. We are having a great deal of rain every day. I sleep twenty hours in the twenty four. The weather is exceedingly warm.

Write soon. Direct your letters as usual to Hardeeville.

Your Brother
D B Sanford

Georgia Troops:
Phillips' Legion, Infantry Battalion, 4 Companies, including Co. A, 6/8/1862
Source:
PC, Letter of Daniel B. Sanford

240   Camp Frost
Kentucky

Location not known.
Georgia Troops:
1st Regiment Georgia Volunteer Cavalry, 10/17/1862
Source:
RWC, 11/21/1862

241   Camp Fulton
Gordon County, Georgia

Location not known.
Georgia Troops:
Smith's Legion, 5/1862
Source:
GDAH, Original list of camp names

242   **Camp Gardner**

Gadsden County, Florida

The camp was located near Quincy.

Georgia Troops:

28th Battalion Georgia Siege Artillery, 7/1863-12/28/1863

Sources:

GDAH, CSR, 254/43; O.R., XXXV, 334, 339

243   **Camp Gardner**

Fairfax County, Virginia

A letter from a member of the 8th Regiment Georgia Volunteer Infantry describes the camp location, "a little south of a line from Fairfax Station to the Courthouse, about one and one-half miles from the former and two miles from the latter."

        Fairfax County, Virginia   Sept'r 22nd 1861
            Camp Gardner

My Dear Wife:

As it is your special request for me to write soon, and as nothing gives me so much pleasure as to know that I am gratifying you, I seat myself to reply to yours of the 11th inst. which I received yesterday and which I have before said, found me very well as to health and doing very well and very well satisfied.

I had just written a letter to you and was going to mail it this morning, had I not received yours, but I now attempt to write a little more. It made me happy to get your letter and also to get one from nearly all the family to which I am going to reply separately.

You say you have received all my letters. I want to know if you have ever rec'd one mailed from Greensboro or not, and if you have heard from Uncle Jimmy Bruce. I sent $25.00 to him for you and also a short letter which I recon you will get before you do this.

I sent the money to you for you to use just as you see fit. I kept $18.00 with me for fear I might need it, but we have very little use for money in camps.

I sent you word in my last letter to get the things ready to send to me by the time Uncle Bruce came and then have your likeness taken and send them to Greensboro.

As to my being uneasy for fear of your suffering; I am not, for I have every reason to believe that your Father will or would willingly divide his all with you, but I feel it my duty also, to do everyrthing in my power to make you happy and agreeable.

A few words to Mr. William Matthew Brewer:-

My Dear Little Son: I take a great deal of pleasure in replying to your short letter. I am very glad to hear that you are a smart and obedient little boy. It is my earnest desire for you to remain so, and above all things, obey your Mother at every command. Also your Grandpa and Ma. I long to see you, for my whole heart is made up in you and your welfare and I hope if it is my lot ever to see you grown, that I may see you an honorable man and a true Christian. You are almost too small to fight Yankees yet, but if your Uncle T - gives you a gun, you and George had better practice shooting at grasshoppers awhile before you come, and maybe the Yankees will see the evil of their ways by that time.

Tell your Mother she must be sure and get your uniform and Tyre must get your gun, and here is a dollar to get a hat with a feather in it.

Tell Mother Pappy says take good care of his little man and be sure and kiss her for him.

Ed and Bud Bruce sends their love to you and say they want to see little Stephen very bad.

I must close, I remain

Your Father
S.J.G. Brewer

My Dear Wife, I have written so much before this that I have almost run out of anything to say for I believe I write the longest letters of anyone in camps.

Our regiment has just been out shooting the loads out of their guns, and I tell you it made me think of the 21st of July.

I got a letter from Thos. Chapman and one from Uncle Jimmy last week in which they said they had been to see you. I don't recon you would know me now if I was to walk up in the yard, for I have changed a great deal since I left home. I have now got a fine set of moustache on my upper lip and they are very black. My hair is blacker than it was when I left. We are, generally speaking, a hairy set of men for none of us have shaved since we left home.

George and Ed Bruce again sends howdy to you all and say they want to see you, also all the family. Tell Marthy, Ed is the same boy he ever was, that he is dry and behaves himself and often speaks of her and Sarah and Babe and says he wants to see them, and if he ever gets back, he is coming sure. Bud is dry and says nothing; only as the spirit moves him. He is going to write for himself. I must close, hoping you will excuse my bad writing and short letters and believe me to be as ever

Your Loving Husband
S.J.G. Brewer

P.S. Puss, be sure and answer this as soon as you get it for I will be very anxious to hear from you soon.

Georgia Troops:
8th Regiment Georgia Volunteer Infantry, 9/21/1861-10/1/1861
Sources:
GDAH, 283/19, Samuel J. G. Brewer; RWC, 10/11/1861 & 10/18/1861

244   Camp Garnett

Randolph County, West Virginia

"The camp was situated in a gorge just beyond the pass that runs between Rich and another (Laurel Hill) mountain." This was the description of the camp location reported by an unidentified Georgia soldier.

The initial report of Union General George B. McClellan boasts of his victory in the battle near the camp on July 9 through 11, 1861. It was refered to as the battle of Laurel Hill, and is where Confederate General Robert Seldon Garnett was killed.

Washington, Monday, July 15 (1861)
The following dispatch has just been received by the War Department.

Buttonville, Sunday, July 14

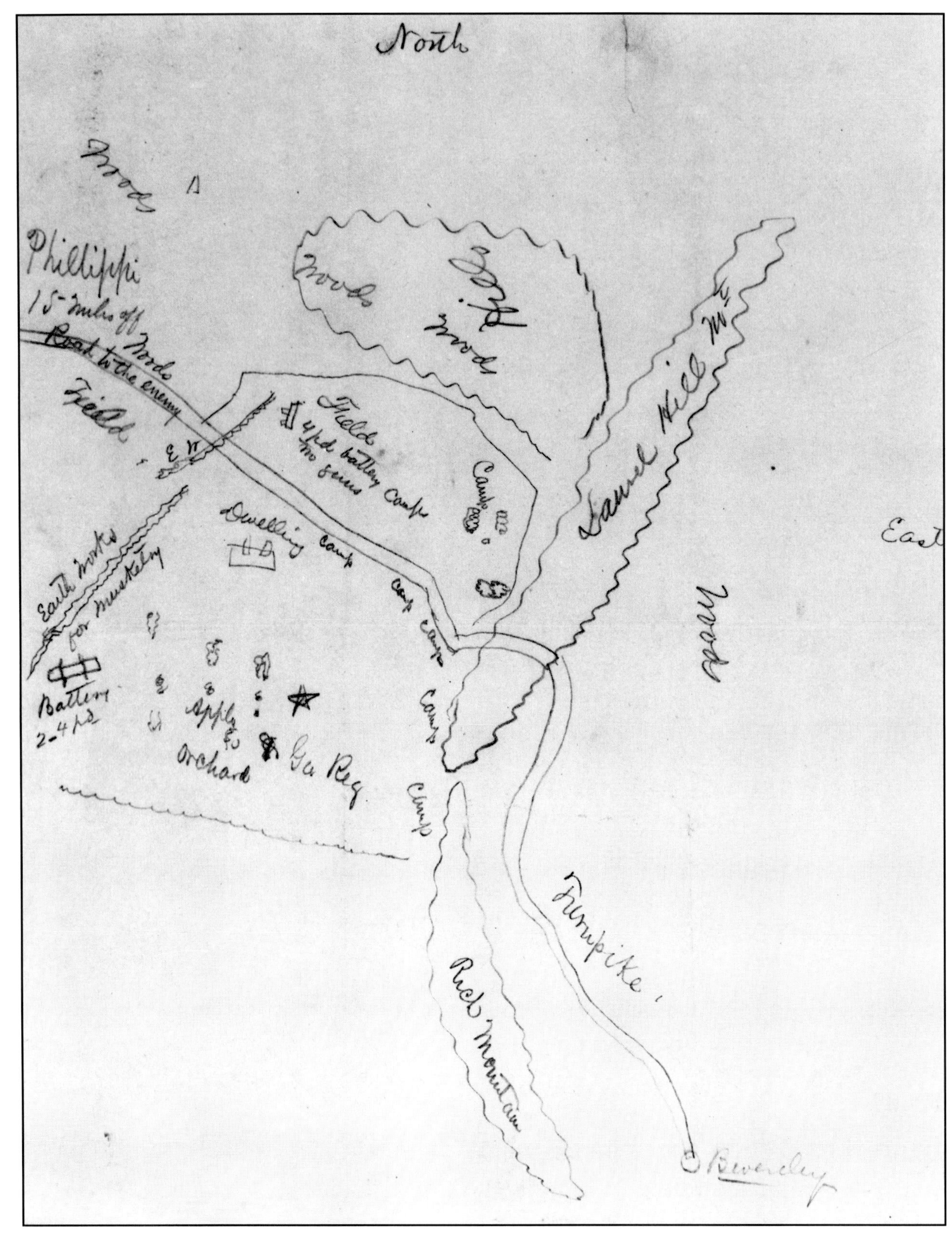

Map of Camp Garnett and area
map courtesy of the Duke University Library, John T. Stephens papers

134

Col. E.D. Townsend, Adjutant General:

Garnett and his forces have been routed: his baggage and one gun taken; his army demoralized and Garnett killed. We have annihilated the enemy in Western Virginia, and have lost 13 killed and not more than 40 wounded.

We have in all killed at least two hundred of the enemy, and the prisoners will amount to at least one thousand. We have taken seven guns in all.

I still look for the capture of the remnant of Garnett's army by Gen. Hill.

The troops defeated are the crack regiments of Eastern Va., aided by Georgians, Tennesseans, and Carolinians.

Our sucess is complete, and secession is killed in this country.   (Signed)
G.B. McClellan, Major General.

Georgia Troops:
1st (Ramsey's) Regiment Georgia Volunteer Infantry, 6/23/1861-7/7/1861 (The Battle of Laurel Hill occured on 7/9/1861-7/11/1861, near the camp.)
Sources:
ADC&S, 7/12/1861; SR, 7/19/1861 & 7/23/1861; *Sketches of the First regiment Ga. vols., together with the history of the 56th regiment Georgia vols., to January 1, 1864, by Lieutenant Oscar A. Cantrell*, By Oscar Alexander Cantrell
Map: Duke University, John T. Stephens

245   **Camp Garrard**
Muscogee County, Georgia

The camp was located near the Opelika Depot on the outskirts of Columbus.
Georgia Troops:
Muscogee Volunteers, Capt. Cooper's Company, 3/13/1862 (Later the company became Co. C, 46th Regiment Georgia Volunteer Infantry.)
Source:
CE, 3/11/1862

246   **Camp Gary**
Dougherty County, Georgia

The camp was located in Albany.
Georgia Troops:
28th Battalion Georgia Siege Artillery, Co. K, 1/27/1864 (The company was known as Mercer Artillery.)
Source:
AP, 1/28/1864

247   **Camp Georgia**
Escambia County, Florida

The *Augusta Daily Chronicle & Sentinel* of April 26, 1861, printed an extract from a letter of "a member of the Oglethorpes" who signed his initials, H.F.C.

* * * * At present our location is in close proximity to the redoubt, near half a mile from the beach, and about the same distance from the Fort. (Ft. Barrancas) As yet we have

engaged at "mule and oxen work," but one day, (yesterday) when we spent most of the time in drawing powder from the wharf to the redoubt in a small car on a track which was entirely covered with sand, the load each trip being three thousand pounds of powder. At the rate of fifty thousand pounds per day, I think we will be supplied with material for a bombardment when the order to attack is given.

In my recent letter, I stated, I think, that there were three thousand men on the Island opposed to us. I should have said this included the men in the war vessels in sight.

We are doing very little at present in building sand batteries. Our Colonel says when the pieces of ordnance arrive that are expected, the batteries can be erected in three days with the force he has at his command. Pike battery is the largest, having two 10-inch Columbiads and a few smaller ones.

Georgia Troops:
1st (Ramsey's) Georgia Volunteer Infantry, 4/13/1861-5/30/1861
Sources:
ADC&S, 4/26/1861; CE, 5/31/1861

248   **Camp Georgia**
Fulton County, Georgia

The camp is located about three miles northeast of Atlanta and six miles from Chattahoochee River among the hills and rocks. The camp is also one and one-half miles from Camp Wayne.
Georgia Troops:
Georgia Militia, 5/21/1864-6/6/1864
Sources:
AHC, Ms. 13, Telemon C. Cuyler & Ms. 116, A.T. Holliday; GDAH, 187/28, Benjamin T. Ray; 283/23, Dickey Family Collection

249   **Camp Georgia**
Dare County, North Carolina

The camp is located on Roanoke Island, four miles from Pork Point batteries near the water on Croatan Sound. One soldier stated in his letter, "the sound is out in front of our encampment." Another letter stated, "We have been clearing up ground about two and one-half miles above this for our winter quarters."
Georgia Troops:
3rd Regiment Georgia Volunteer Infantry, 9/10/1861-12/13/1861.
Sources:
UGA, Ms. 59, Carlton-Newton- Mell Collection; SDMN, 9/28/1861; ASB, 9/18/1861 & 1/1/1862.

250   **Camp Georgia**
Hamilton County, Tennessee

The camp is located one mile down river from Chattanooga and on the railroad. After a day or two in this camp, the name was changed to Camp Harris.
Georgia Troops:
43rd Regiment Georgia Volunteer Infantry, 4/15/1862
Sources:

GDAH, 40/17, Military Records of Georgia; *History of Forsyth County, 1832-1932*, By Garland C. Bagley, letters of Lewis Stovall

251   **Camp Georgia**
Norfolk County, Virginia

The camp was in the rear of Ft. Norfolk, on the bank of the Elizabeth River. Their pickets were located one and one-half miles from camp. See location of Ft. Norfolk on the map accompanying Camp Colquitt.
Georgia Troops:
2nd Independent Infantry Battalion, 4/29/1861-5/16/1861
Sources:
MT, 5/4/61; GDAH, CSR, 254/107

252   **Camp Georgia**
Culpeper County, Virginia

The camp was seven miles from Culpeper Court House.
Georgia Troops:
Cobb's Legion, Cavalry Battalion, 1/23/1863
Source:
UNC, #3353, Noble John Brooke

253   **Camp Georgia**
Henrico County, Virginia

The camp was located at Howard's Grove, about a mile from the center of Richmond, in a beautiful pine grove, and on a high hill. The name of the camp was changed from Camp Howard's Grove on about 6/3/1861, when troops from other States moved out of the camp. See Camp Howard Grove.
Georgia Troops:
2nd Regiment Georgia Volunteer Infantry, 7/27/1861-8/15/1861
8th Regiment Georgia Volunteer Infantry, 6/3/1861-6/5/1861
Sources:
2nd GVI, EU, #20, Dickerson W. Halliday; GDAH, CSR, 254/100
8th GVI, RWC, 6/14/1861

254   **Camp Georgia**
Highland County, Virginia

The camp was located at the foot of Cheat Mountain.
Georgia Troops:
1st (Ramsey's) Regiment Georgia Volunteer Infantry, 6/19/1861
Source:
UNC, #2292, William Oliver Fleming

255   **Camp Georgia**

Prince William County, Virginia

The camp was located between Manassas Junction and Bull Run stone bridge about one mile south of the Manassas battlefield . It was also four and one-half miles west of Camp Steiner. This was the winter camp of Toomb's Brigade.

Georgia Troops:

1st Georgia Regulars, 12/26/1861-3/22/1862

2nd Regiment Georgia Volunteer Infantry, 12/26/1861- 3/22/1862

15th Regiment Georgia Volunteer Infantry, 12/26/1861-3/22/1862

17th Regiment Georgia Volunteer Infantry, 12/26/1861-3/22/1862

20th Regiment Georgia Volunteer Infantry, 12/26/1861-3/22/1862

Sources:

GDAH, CSR, all units; CG, 3/12/1862; CE, 3/11/1862

Private Solomon Mills Cottle, Sr., Co. B, 17th Regiment Georgia Volunteer Infantry. Enlisted August 14, 1861, elected Jr. 2nd Lieut. August 7, 1862, and surrendered at Appomattox, Virginia, on April 9, 1865.

photo courtesy of Charles L. Jackson

256   **Camp Gignilliatt**

McIntosh County, Georgia

The camp was located four miles from the "Ridge" above Darien, and seven miles from White Bluff on the Sapelo River. The camp was in the woods away from the settlement. On August 3, 1864, the camp was destroyed by Yankee raiders. Apparently the camp was used on and off for quite a long time.

Georgia Troops:

1st Battalion Georgia Cavalry, McIntosh Cavalry, 9/1862-4/1863

Sources:

GDAH, CSR, 253/79; SR, 8/11/1864

257   **Camp Gilead**

Fulton County, Georgia

The camp was in Stone's District. The battery received their flag in this camp.
Georgia Troops:
Jo Thompson Artillery, 11/5/1861-11/6/1861
Source:
Atlanta Historical Bulletin, Vol. XIV, "War Diary of Cornelius R. Hanleiter," Edited by Elma S. Kurtz

258   **Camp Golgotha**

Spalding County, Georgia

The camp was located about one and one-half miles south or southeast of Griffin in an old field.
Georgia Troops:
14th Battalion Georgia Light Artillery, Co. A, Southern Rights Battery, Dawson's Battery, Capt. Ferrell's Battery & a battery from Dade County, 5/9/1862-7/9/1862
Sources:
GDAH, CSR, 254/36; 283/31, Thomas Lane; 283/41, William R. Talley

259   **Camp Gordon**

Chatham County, Georgia

The camp was located at Thunderbolt Battery. This camp name was only used when the unit was first organizing. Thereafter they referred to the camp as Camp Thunderbolt or Thunderbolt Battery.
Georgia Troops:
63rd Regiment Georgia Volunteer Infantry, 2/1863
Sources:
GDAH, CSR, 257/120; ADC&S, 8/29/1863

260   **Camp Gordon**

Orange County, Virginia

The camp was in the Orange Courthouse area. The camp was probably named after Col. James B. Gordon, of the 1st Regiment North Carolina Cavalry, commanding their Brigade. His regiment was transferred to another brigade.
Georgia Troops:
Cobb's Legion, Cavalry Battalion, 8/30/1863
Source:
UGA, Ms. 184, William Gaston Delony

261   **Camp Gordon**

Orange County, Virginia

The camp was located four miles northeast of Orange Court House. This was the camp of General Gordon's Brigade.
Georgia Troops:
4th Regiment Georgia Volunteer Infantry, 7/6/1863-8/14/1863
12th Regiment Georgia Volunteer Infantry, 7/6/1863-8/14/1863

21st Regiment Georgia Volunteer Infantry, 7/6/1863-8/14/1863
38th Regiment Georgia Volunteer Infantry, 7/6/1863-8/14/1863
44th Regiment Georgia Volunteer Infantry, 7/6/1863-8/14/1863
Sources:
ADC&S, 8/22/63; *History of the Doles-Cook Brigade, Army of Northern Virginia*, by Henry W. Thomas

262   Camp Graham
Marion County, Tennessee

The camp was located near Nickejack cave which is located close to where the Tennessee, Alabama, and Georgia State lines merge. This description of the site of the camp is from a letter of William N. Swift dated July 10, 1862.

> We had some rain this P.M. and quite a tug to get our camp chest &c. to our selected place in the brier patch by the side of the gentle flowing creek where nearby was a flowing spring water as pure and sweet as Castalia Fount. But we lugged our things there. It is called Camp Graham.

Georgia Troops:
34th Regiment Georgia Volunteer Infantry, 7/4/1862-7/5/1862 & 7/10/1862-7/14/1862
Source:
GDAH, 283/41, William. N. Swift diary

263   Camp Grease Gut
Fulton County, Georgia

The camp was located several miles north of Atlanta
Georgia Troops:
1st Regiment Georgia Militia, 7/11/1864-7/13/1864
Source:
AHC, Ms. 116, A.T. Holliday

264   Camp Greenbrier
Pocohantas County, West Virginia

This is the same as Camp Bartow on the Greenbrier River. It appears this name was used for a day or two before it was changed to Camp Bartow. See Camp Bartow.
Georgia Troops:
12th Regiment Georgia Volunteer Infantry, 8/14/1861-8/16/1861
Source:
GDAH, 283/16, James Atkins

265   **Camp Gregg**

Jasper County, South Carolina

The camp was located near Coosawhatchie. See Camp Calhoun.

Georgia Troops:

46th Regiment Georgia Volunteer Infantry, 4/1862

Source:

GDAH, CSR, 257/35

266   **Camp Gregg**

Spotsylvania County, Virginia

The camp was located about eight miles below Fredericksburg, about eight miles east of Guinea Station, and two miles from the Rappahannock River. The Division Hospital was one mile from the camp, and a church was one and one-half miles from the camp. This was the camp of Thomas's Brigade.

This extract from Sergeant Major Marion Hill Fitzpatrick's letter of March 5, 1863, describes one of the many sad moments in a soldier's life.

> I am also truly glad to hear that Henry's cough was getting well, and that he was so pert. Poor little fellow, no doubt but what he missed his Pa, and looked for him every morning, but alas! in vain as you say, for we are many miles apart now. It looks hard and it almost breaks my heart to think of you and him there alone but, these troubles are upon us and we must try to submit cheerfully. I am in fine health, and am the only man in the Company but what is complaining, more or less.

Georgia Troops:

14th Regiment Georgia Volunteer Infantry, 12/291862-4/29/1863

35th Regiment Georgia Volunteer Infantry, 12/291862-4/29/1863

45th Regiment Georgia Volunteer Infantry, 12/29/1862-4/29/1863

49th Regiment Georgia Volunteer Infantry, 12/29/1862-4/29/1863

Sources:

GDAH, CSRs, 256/103, 257/29, 257/56 & 227/10, Marion Hill Fitzpatrick; GHQ, Vols. 46 & 55, Charles A. Conn

267   **Camp Grice**

Chesterfield County, Virginia

The camp was located "on the Heights, about one mile from Petersburg." The men unofficially named the camp, Camp Heights. See Camp Heights.

Georgia Troops:

3rd Regiment Georgia Volunteer Infantry ,* 5/15/1862-5/22/1862

4th Regiment Georgia Volunteer Infantry, 5/15/1862-5/22/1862

22nd Regiment Georgia Volunteer Infantry ,* 5/15/1862-5/22/1862

* No documents have been found with Camp Grice or Camp Heights on them. Louis Merz and other members of the 4th Georgia Regiment refer to the Brigade in this camp

Sources:

GDAH, UDC Books, Vol. X, 143, Louis Merz

268
Camp Griswold
Jones County, Georgia

The camp was located west of Griswoldville.
Georgia Troops:
30th Regiment Georgia Volunteer Infantry, 12/17/1861-1/22/1862
Sources:
GDAH, CSR 256/85; SR, 1/24/62, 2/1; *Brief History of the Thirtieth Georgia Regiment*, by Augustus Pitts Adamson

269
Camp Guyton
Hinds County, Mississippi

The camp was located near Jackson.
Georgia Troops:
57th Regiment Georgia Volunteer Infantry, 1/19/1863-1/23/1863
Sources:
GDAH, CSR, 257/96, Ruben Huff & 257/97, J. L. Perry

270
Camp Gwynn
Portsmouth County, Virginia

The camp was originally located one hundred yards west of Gosport Navy Yards, but was moved closer to the water on July 4, 1861. See Atlas Plate XXVI, 4.
Georgia Troops:
3rd Regiment Georgia Volunteer Infantry, 4/23/1861-9/19/1861 (The regiment left for Roanoke Island on September 19, 1861, and returned to this camp on December 15, 1861.)
Sources:
GDAH, CSR, 254/114; ASW, 7/10/1861; ASB, 7/17/1861; ADC&S, 12/19/1861

RELICS OF OUR REVOLUTION. -- The holster pistols of the lamented Gen. Barnard E. Bee, one of the heroes of Manassas, have been presented by his widow to the Confederate States; and Captain Childs, of the Ordnance Department, presented them to Col. John H. Morgan, a chieftain worthy to wear them. -- Savh. Repub.

---

271   **Camp Habersham**
                                    Chatham County, Georgia
    The camp was located at White Bluff.
Georgia Troops:
2nd Battalion Georgia Cavalry, Co. F, Chatham Light Horse, 4/12/1862-6/9/1862
Source:
SDMN, 4/14/1862

272   **Camp Hagood**
                               Charleston County, South Carolina
    The camp was probably named after Gen. Johnson Hagood, commander First Sub-Division of
the First Military District of South Carolina.
    The camp was located on James Island.
Georgia Troops:
12th Battalion Georgia Volunteers, Co. D, 11/16/1863
Sources:
GDAH, CSR, 254/33; O.R., XXVIII, 189

273   **Camp Hamilton**
                                      Floyd County, Georgia
    The camp was located near Rome.
Georgia Troops:
2nd Regiment Georgia State Line, Cos., B, I & K, 5/12/1863-5/29/1863
Source:
GDAH, Plunkett-Murdock letters

274   **Camp Hampton**
                                 Beaufort County, South Carolina
    The Camp was located at Bull's Bay.
Georgia Troops.
2nd Battalion Georgia Cavalry, Co. F, Chatham Light Horse, 12/1862-1/24/1863 (The Chatham
Light Horse became Co. B of the 5th Regiment Georgia Volunteer Cavalry on January 22, 1863.)
Source:
GDAH, CSR, 253/87

275   **Camp Hampton**
                                     Greenville County, Virginia
    The camp was located near Bellfield. Probably between Hicks Ford and Bellfield.
Georgia Troops:
8th Regiment Georgia Volunteer Cavalry, 8/1864 & 12/17/1864-12/31/1864
Source:
GDAH, CSR, 253/113

276

Camp Hampton
Culpeper County, Virginia

The camp was located near Culpeper Court House.
Georgia Troops:
Phillip's Legion, Cavalry Battalion, 2/9/1863
Source:
CU, 2/24/1863

277

Camp Wade Hampton
Madison County, Virginia

The location of this camp is not known.
Georgia Troops:
Georgia Hussars, Co. A, Co. F of the Jeff Davis Legion, 2/5/1863
Source:
SR, 2/14/1863

CAMP WADE HAMPTON
Madison Co., Va., Feb 3, 1863
The Georgia Hussars des're to express their gratitude to the young ladies of Madame Lacoste's School, Savannah, Ga., for their kind remembrance of absent friends, as expressed substantially by their gift of one hundred and seventy dollars, ($170.) being a portion of the proceeds of a Fair held by them for the benefit of the soldiers.
DAVID WALDHAUER,
Capt Com'dg "Georgia Hussars,"
feb14   Co. F, Jeff. Davis Legion.

278

Camp Hanover Junction
Hanover County, Virginia, Virginia

Located near the junction of the two railroads known as Hanover Junction.
Georgia Troops:
9th Regiment Georgia Volunteer Infantry, 5/23/1864
Source:
ASB, 6/8/1864

279

Camp Hardee
Chatham County, Georgia

Located one-half mile below Thunderbolt and two and one-half miles from Camp Bartow.
Georgia Troops:
30th Regiment Georgia Volunteer Infantry, 6/12/1862-10/4/1862, 10/15/1862-10/22/1862 & 10/24/1862-11/10/1862
Sources:
GDAH, MR, 279/83; 80/57, Elias Adams; *Brief History of the Thirtieth Georgia Regiment*, by Augustus Pitt Adamson

280   **Camp Hardee**

Chatham County, Georgia

The camp was located in an old field near Ferguson's place, a little over a mile above Bethesda Orphanage.

Georgia Troops:

Chatham Artillery, 4/23/1862-6/8/1862

Source:

Historical Sketch of The Chatham Artillery during The Confederate Struggle for Independence, by Charles C. Jones, Jr.

281   **Camp Hardeman**

Wayne County, North Carolina

The camp is located two miles from Goldsboro, on the New Bern Road.

Georgia Troops:

2nd Independent Infantry Battalion, 3/21/1862-4/1/1862

Sources:

CE, 4/1/1862 & 4/22/1862; TWC, 3/23/62

282   **Camp Hardship**

Pasquotank County, North Carolina

Located between South Mills and a station on the road, three miles from Elizabeth City.

Georgia Troops:

3rd Regiment Georgia Volunteer Infantry, 1/20/1862-4/9/1862

Sources:

MT, X/X/1862; UGA, Ms. 59, Carlton-Newton-Mell Collection; CG, 2/5/1862; DU, James L. Reid

283   **Camp Hard Times**

Frederick County, Virginia

The camp was located near Winchester.

Georgia Troops:

9th Regiment Georgia Volunteer Infantry, 9/21/1862

Source:

UNC, #397, H.C. Kendrick

284   **Camp Hardtimes**

Henrico County, Virginia

The camp was located near Richmond.

Georgia Troops:

Cobb's Legion, 7/3/1862

Source:

GDAH, 21/29, John William. Rheney, Jr.

285   **Camp Harkie**
Chatham County, Georgia

The camp was located four miles from Savannah on Central Railroad.
Georgia Troops:
1st Regiment Georgia State Troops, 12/1/1861-3/31/1862
Sources:
SDMN, 12/3/1861 & 4/1/1862; *Northwest Georgia Historical and Geneological Quarterly*, J. T.
McConnell letters

286   **Camp Harris**
Coastal Georgia

The camp was located along the Georgia coast.
Georgia Troops:
4th (Clinch's) Georgia Volunteer Cavalry, Cos. A, 6/1864; B, 7/30/1864; & G, 8/1862
Source:
GDAH, CSR, 253/94

287   **Camp Harris**
Bibb County, Georgia

Located near Macon.
Georgia Troops:
1st Battalion Georgia Cavalry Reserves, 12/1864-4/11/1865
Sources:
GDAH, CSR, 253/81; 283/48, Bibb Co. file

288   **Camp Harris**
Hamilton County, Tennessee

The camp is located almost a mile down river from Chattanooga, and on the railroad. The camp
was known as Camp Georgia for a few days before being changed to Camp Harris.

Chattanooga, Tenn, May 2d, '62

Mr. Editor: Yesterday was quite an exciting day to the sojourners of our little city. About
8 o'clock blue clouds began to lower o'er us, and in less than fifteen minutes we were
visited by one of the heaviest wind storms I ever witnessed. The atmosphere was for some
time filled with shingles, limbs of trees, and soldiers and citizens hats. The 30th (43rd)
Georgia commanded by Col. Harris, and encamping almost a mile below the town had all
their tents blown down. Two of that regiment were badly wounded by falling limbs and
"that mule" they have so long been endeavoring to find the owner for was seriously killed.
Poor Mewel!

The above article is from the *Knoxville Daily Register* of June 6, 1862.

Georgia Troops:
9th Battalion Georgia Light Artillery, 5/17/1862-5/18/62
43rd Regiment Georgia Volunteer Infantry, 4/18/1862- 5/27/1862
Sources;

9th Bn GA, SC, 5/22/1862
43rd GVI, KDR, 6/6/1862; *History of Forsyth County, 1832-1932*, By Garland C. Bagley, letters of Lewis Stovall; GDAH, 10/82, William A. Fowler; ASB, 5/7/1862

289   **Camp Harrison**
Effingham County, Georgia
   Located between Stations 2 1/2 and 3 on the Central Railroad, near Whitesville (Guyton). This was the original Camp Harrison, training camp of the Georgia State Troops. It was then moved to Screven Station on the Savannah, Albany & Gulf Railroad.

Headquarters 1st Brigade Ga. Vols.
Savannah,   Sept. 23d, 1861.
General Order No. 1.
   For important military reasons the Brigadier General Commanding has determined to remove the Camp of Instruction, ordered to be organized at Station No. 3, on the Central Railroad to a healthy point at or near the Junction of the Savannah and Gulf, and Brunswick and Albany Railroads.
   Companies ordered to the Camp of Instruction will take notice; and those passing through Savannah will proceed at once to the new point designated. The Quartermaster will take measures to provide for the transit of troops through the city.
         By order of   Geo. P. Harrison,
               Brig. Gen. Commanding 1st Brigade Ga. Vols.
      Randolph Spalding, Aide-de-Camp.

Georgia Troops:
Georgia Rangers, later Co. C, 1st Regiment Georgia State Troops, 9/20/1861-9/26/1861
Jackson Avengers, later Co. H, 1st Regiment Georgia State Troops, 9/20/1861-9/26/1861
Dekalb Guards, 9/20/1861-9/26/1861 (Later the Dekalb Guards became Co. B, 26th [Lamar's] Regiment Georgia Volunteer Infantry, then Co. D, 61st Regiment Georgia Volunteer Infantry.)
Sources:
SDMN, 9/23/1861, 9/24/1861, 9/27/1861 & 9/28/1861

290   **Camp Harrison**
Wayne County, Georgia
   This camp was located at Station No. 7, on the Atlantic & Gulf Railroad. This was the Camp of Instruction for the Georgia State Troops, raised for the defence of the coast of Georgia. Three brigades trained or organized in this camp at different times. the 2nd Brigade moved to Camp Satilla after organization, and trained there before moving to Savannah. The three brigades were mustered in for six months service. This camp was used from 10/2/1861-12/26/1861. The following is the organization of the Georgia State Troops.

Major General Henry Rootes Jackson

1st Brigade Georgia State Troops, commanded by Brigadier General George Paul Harrison
1st Regiment Georgia State Troops, Col. C.B. Harkie
2nd Regiment Georgia State Troops, Col. William Barkuloo

5th Regiment Georgia State Troops, Col. George Paul Harrison, Jr.
6th Regiment Georgia State Troops, Col. W. Henderson
1st Batallion Georgia State Troops, Maj. W.A. Ross
Bibb Cavalry, Capt. A.M. Lockett
2nd Brigade Georgia State Troops, commanded by Brigadier Francis W. Capers
3rd Regiment Georgia State Troops, Col. R.J. Cowart
4th Regiment Georgia State Troops, Col. James J. Neely
7th Regiment Georgia State Troops, Col. George P. Hunter
2nd Battalion Georgia State Troops, Maj. Richard S. Taylor
Georgia Light Artillery, Capt. Horatio N. Hollifield
Clayton Dragoons, Capt. F.T. Gayden
Hudson Guards, Capt. Harris, Independent Company
Sunny South, Capt. Williams, Independent Company
Milledgeville Grays, Capt. White, Independent Company
----------- -----------, Capt. Allen, Independent Company

3rd Brigade Georgia State Troops, commanded by Brigadier General W.H.T. Walker,
12/2/1861-12/29/1861
8th Regiment Georgia State Troops, Col. Elijah Webb Chastain
9th Regiment Georgia State Troops, Col. Robert Yerby Harris
10th Regiment Georgia State Troops, Col. W.F. Wright
3rd Battalion Georgia State Troops, Lt. Col. A.D. Nunnally
Macon German Artillery, Capt. F.H. Burghard
Napier Artillery, Capt. Leroy Napier, Jr.
Thomas County Dragoons, Capt. S.B. Spencer
Bibb Cavalry, Capt. F.G. Holt
Sources:
SR, 4/7/1862 & 4/7/1862; GDAH, 200/1, Copeland Collection; UNC, #3349, Joseph Epsey

291 **Camp Harrison**
Georgetown County, South Carolina
   Located at Battery White near Georgetown.
Georgia Troops.
21st Battalion Georgia Cavalry, Co. B, 5/1863, 7/31/1863 & 3/21/1864
Source,
GDAH, CSR, 254/9

292 **Camp Harrison**
Fairfax County, Virginia
   The camp was near Fairfax Court House.
Georgia Troops:
20th Regiment Georgia Volunteer Infantry, 8/23/1861-8/26/1861 & 8/29/1861-10/15/1861
Source:
GDAH, CSR, 256/13

293   **Camp Jennie Hart**
Orange County, Virginia

The camp, located at Madison Run Station, was named in honor of the secretary of the Ladies Volunteer Association of Athens, Georgia.
Georgia Troops:
3rd Regiment Georgia Volunteer Infantry, 4/13/1864-4/28/64
Sources:
GDAH, 283/32, William Luckie; ASB, 4/27/1864

294   **Camp Hatton**
Grainger County, Tennessee

General Alexander W. Reynolds named his encampment, "Camp Hatton," in honor of General Robert Hatton, a Tennesseean, who organized the 7th Regiment Tennessee Infantry, later promoted to Brigadier General, and fell while leading his brigade in the battle of Seven Pines. The camp is located near Lea's Springs near Blains Crossroads. The camp was moved on July 15, 1862, "a mile further up."

2nd Lieutenant, John Lane, Company D, 43rd Regiment Georgia Volunteer Infantry. Some time between July, 1862, and October, 1862, John Lane was on water detail when on his return to camp he was killed by the camp guard. The first shot hit his pocket watch, but instead of falling, he became even more distraught and kept running toward the sentry. The next shot was fatal. The pocket watch was sent home, and John was buried somewhere in Tennessee.

Photo courtesy of Dr. Max E. White

Georgia Troops:
36th Regiment Georgia Volunteer Infantry, 6/30/1862-8/11/1862
39th Regiment Georgia Volunteer Infantry, 7/25/1862-8/4/1862
43rd Regiment Georgia Volunteer Infantry, 6/4/1862-8/4/1862, & 2/20/1863
Sources:
36th GVI, EU, #405, John R. Harris, & #20, Jackson Couch
39th GVI, EU, #278, William H. Brotherton
43rd GVI, GDAH, CSR, 257/18; 10/82, William A. Fowler; AGLB, #14; KDR, 8/7/1862

295   **Camp Hay (Camp Way)**
                         Chatham County, Georgia
   See Camp Way. When the letter of H. G. Edenfield was transcribed from the original letter, an error was made in the letter W. It has been published as Camp Hay in error.
Source:
GDAH, 199/73, H. G. Edenfield

296   **Camp Haynie**
                               Tennessee
   Location not known.
Georgia Troops:
1st Regiment Georgia Volunteer Cavalry, 11/11/1862
Source:
RWC, 11/21/1862

297   **Camp Hazlehurst**
                         Brantley County, Georgia
   The camp was located near Waynesville, probably on the Hazlehurst tract approximately one mile north of the railroad on Browntown Road.
Georgia Troops:
13th (Styles') Regiment Georgia Volunteer Infantry, Co. D, 1/1862 & 3/9/1862-3/12/1862 (The regiment reorganized May 10, 1862, and became the 26th Regiment Georgia Volunteer Infantry.)
Source:
GDAH, CSR, 256/59

298   **Camp Hazzard**
                         Glynn County, Georgia
   The camp was located near Sterling, twenty-two miles from Waynesville.
Georgia Troops:
4th (Clinch's) Regiment Georgia Volunteer Cavalry, Co. C, 1/1864-4/1864
Source:
GDAH, CSR, 253/94

299   **Camp Hebron**
Tennessee

The location is not known.
Georgia Troops:
3rd Regiment Georgia Volunteer Cavalry, 5/20/1863
Source:
ADC&S, 5/24/1863

300   **Camp Hedrick**
New Hanover County, North Carolina

The camp was located near Wilmington.
Georgia Troops:
62nd Regiment Georgia Cavalry, Co. E, 7/23/1862
Source:
GDAH, CSR, 254/15

301   **Camp Heights**
Chesterfield County, Virginia

The camp was located "on the heights, about one mile from Petersburg." The men unofficially named the camp, Camp Heights. The official name was Camp Grice. See Camp Grice. There has been at least one phonetic spelling of height, such as "hits." The 3rd and 22nd Regiments Georgia Volunteer Infantry were in this camp also. No documents have been found for these two regiments with the name Camp Heights or Camp Grice.
Georgia Troops:
4th Regiment Georgia Volunteer Infantry, 5/15/1862-5/22/1862
Sources:
GDAH, UDC Books, Vol. X, 143, Louis Merz; AHC, Ms. 51f, Richard Memminger Campbell; RWC, 5/30/1862

302   **Camp Helen**
Culpeper County, Virginia

The camp was located near Culpeper Court House, and was probably named after Helen Newton who married Captain Henry Hull Carlton of the Troup Artillery.
Georgia Troops:
Troup Artillery, 11/9/1862
Source:
UGA, Ms. 59, Carlton-Newton-Mell Collection, Tom Barrow

303   **Camp Helen**
Caroline County, Virginia

The camp was located ten miles from Hanover Junction and four miles from Chesterfield Depot.
Georgia Troops:
Troup Artillery, 12/29/1862-4/29/1863 (The other batteries of the Artillery Corp were here also.)
Sources:
ASB, 1/14/1863 & 5/27/1863

304   **Camp Henderson**
Dade County, Georgia

The camp was located at Battle Creek.
Georgia Troops:
3rd Regiment Confederate Cavalry, Co. G, 4/17/1862-4/19/1862
Source:
GDAH, CSR, 258/64

305   **Camp Henderson**
DeKalb County, Georgia

The camp was located one mile south of Decatur.
Georgia Troops:
40th Regiment Georgia Volunteer Infantry, 9/27/1863
Source:
EU, #18, William A. Chunn

306   **Camp Hermitage**
Henrico County, Virginia

The camp was located at the Hermitage fairgrounds near Richmond.
Georgia Troops:
20th Regiment Georgia Volunteer Infantry, 8/17/1861-9/30/1861
28th Regiment Georgia Volunteer Infantry, 8/12/1861-8/31/1861
Sources:
20th GVI, GDAH, CSR, 256/13
28th GVI, GDAH, CSR, 256/74

307   **Camp Heth**
Hamilton County, Tennessee

The camp was located at the foot of Lookout Mountain near Chattanooga. The battalion was in Heth's Brigade at this time. All but one company was converted to infantry due to a shortage of horses, and they became known as the 12th Battalion Georgia Volunteers.
Georgia Troops:
12th Battalion Georgia Light Artillery, Cos., A, C & E, 7/9/1862-7/13/62
Sources:
GDAH, CSR, 254/31-34; 283/25, Blanton Fortson

308   **Camp Hill**
Henrico County, Virginia

The Camp was two miles from the James River, four miles from Malvern Hill, and near New Market. It was also seven to eight miles from Camp McIntosh. This was a camp of Toomb's Brigade. No other documentation has been found on this camp.
Georgia Troops:
15th Regiment Georgia Volunteer Infantry, 7/28/62-8/10/62
Source:
GDAH, 53/64, Ivy Duggan

309
Camp D. H. Hill
Northampton County, North Carolina

The camp was near Garysburg. The companies of this unit were in and out of this camp at different times.
Georgia Troops:
62nd Regiment Georgia Cavalry, 9/22/1862-11/2/1862
Source:
GDAH, CSR, 254/15

310
Camp Hite
Chatham County, Georgia

The camp was located near Savannah. The regiment was in this camp for several months.
Georgia Troops:
1st Regiment Georgia Militia, early 1865
Source:
GDAH, 284/43, William Henry Warr

311
Camp Hits
See Camp Heights

Georgia Troops:
4th Regiment Georgia Volunteer Infantry, 5/8/1862
Source:
PC, Letters of Joseph Jackson Felder

312
Camp Hollingsworth
Frederick County, Virginia

Our camp is in sight of the house in which George Washington, the Colonel of a Virginia Regiment, had his quarters in 1760, when fighting the Indians. It is a two story stone house of moderate size, and has neither an antique or ancient appearance The house was erected, but not finished, in the year 1754, by Isaac Hollingsworth. He was driven away from his property by the Indians, and the premises were not occupied in 1760 when Col. Washington was sent here to protect the frontier inhabitants against Indian depredations. He built a fort on the site where the town of Winchester now stands. The timber used in the construction of the breast works, was cut from the field that is now our parade ground. This estate was granted to Isaac Hollingsworth by Lord Fairfax, it has continued in possession of the family ever since, and is now owned by two very interesting young ladies - his great grand daughters - who have in their possession the original grant. It is a coincidence quite remarkable, that Gen. Bartow has his head quarters in the identical room occupied by Washington over a century ago, but how different the circumstances. The savage children of the forest were then in their way repelling the invasion of "pale faces," and the encroachments made upon their hunting grounds, and for the protection of their "peculiar institutions;" and now we are trying to repel an enemy quite as bloody, more vicious and unreasonable than the Indians themselves, and as much more vile and wicked as their superior mental and educational advantages can make them.

On this same Hollingsworth estate and near the residence, is a field in which the Hessian prisoners were encamped after the battle of Trenton, who settled in the Northwestern part of this State, and whose descendants are nearly all Federalists, and I wish we could get a few thousand of them encamped on the same field.

Georgia Troops:
8th Regiment Georgia Volunteer Infantry, 6/26/1861-7/15/1861
Sources:
RWC, 7/12/1861; UGA, Ms. 1737, Barnsley Godfrey papers; SC, 7/2/1861

313   **Camp Holmes**
McIntosh County, Georgia
The camp is located five miles from Camp Hughes at Darien Ridge.
Georgia Troops:
1st Battalion Georgia Cavalry, McIntosh Cavalry, 11/29/1861-12/1861
Source:
GDAH, CSR, 253/79

314   **Camp Holmes**
New Hanover County, North Carolina
The camp was located near Wilmington. While here, the 25th Regiment Georgia Volunteer Infantry was involved in capturing the steamer U. S. S. *Columbia*. For more information on the capture of the steamer U. S. S. *Columbia*, refer to the *Official Records of the Navy*, Series 1, Vol. 8.
Georgia Troops:
25th Regiment Georgia Volunteer Infantry, 1/24/1862
30th Regiment Georgia Volunteer Infantry, 2/2/1863
Sources:
25th GVI, GHS, #874, Claudius C. Wilson
30th GVI, DU, Andrew J. White

315   **Camp Hood**
Fulton County, Georgia
The camp was located near Atlanta.
Georgia Troops:
Georgia Militia, 7/26/1864
Source:
AHC, Ms. 116, A.T. Holliday

Camp Hook
Chatham County, Georgia

The camp is located near Savannah. The camp was named after Captain Edward B. Hook of the 28th Regiment Georgia Volunteer Infantry who died on March 20, 1862.
Georgia Troops:
Sam Robinson Artillery (Capt. Martin's Co.), 6/4/1862-7/11/1862 (The company later became a part of Howell's Battery Georgia Light Artillery.)
Sources:
GDAH, 261/2, Jonas N. Woods; CG, 6/11/1862

317

Camp Hoover
Chatham County, Georgia

The camp was located at the community of Hooverville, at the corner of Gwinnett Street and West Broad Street.

The Georgia Hussars left by train for Richmond, Virginia, on September 17, 1861. The company was not formally mustered into service until after its arrival at Richmond, Va, where it reported for mounted duty, uniformed, armed and equipped in all details of field equipment except mules and wagons. The expenses of railroad transportation, as also equipment, were borne by the company and its friends and amounted to near twenty-five thousand dollars.

The service of the company was accepted under a tender made "to put themselves free at no cost to the government in Richmond, Virginia."

Georgia Troops:
Georgia Hussars, Co. A, 9/6/1861-9/13/1861 (On September 17, 1861, the Georgia Hussars, Co. A, left by train for Virginia.)
Sources:
SDMN, 9/6/1861 & 9/13/1861, SR, 9/10/1861; *Roll and Legend of the Georgia Hussars,* By A. McC. Duncan

318   **Camp Hope**
Chatham County, Georgia

The camp was on the Isle of Hope, near the church.
Georgia Troops:
2nd Battalion Georgia Cavalry, Co. D, Georgia Hussars, Co. B, 3/17/1862-4/22/1862
Sources:
SR, 4/10/1862 & 4/11/1862; EU, #12, John H. Ash

319   **Camp Hope**
New Hanover County, North Carolina

The camp was located near Wilmington.
Georgia Troops:
30th Regiment Georgia Volunteer Infantry, 1/20/1862-1/25/1862 & 1/2/1863-1/29/1863
(Apparently a part of the regiment remained in North Carolina. See Camp Young.)
Source:
DU, Andrew J. White

320   **Camp Hopewell**
Camden County, Georgia

The camp was at Hopewell Point on the Satilla River.
Georgia Troops:
4th (Clinch's) Regiment Georgia Voluntary Cavalry, Co. H, 3/11/1864
Clinch's Battery Georgia Light Artillery, 3/20/1864
Sources:
4th GVC, GDAH, 283/45, Perry W. Ziegler
CBGLA, GDAH, CSR, 258/6

321   **Camp Hopkins**
Duval County, Florida

The camp was two miles from Double Bridges (Double Bridges was six miles from Jacksonville) and eight miles from Camp Milton in East Florida.
Georgia Troops:
1st Georgia Regulars, 5/2/1864-5/7/1864
Source:
GDAH, CSR, 254/67

322   **Camp Hopkins**
Camden County, Georgia

The camp was located between the Great Satilla and Little Satilla Rivers, twenty miles from Camp Fort.
Georgia Troops:
Capt. T. S. Hopkins Company of mounted partisan rangers, 10/1862-11/21/1862 (The company later became Co. A, 24th Battalion Georgia Cavalry.)
Sources:
GDAH, CSR, 254/11; MR, 279/65

323   **Camp Hopkins**
McIntosh County, Georgia
   The camp was located about a mile from the "Ridge" above Darien.
Georgia Troops:
1st Battalion Georgia Cavalry, Mcintosh Cavalry, 4/2/1862-5/12/1862 & 7/1863- 9/7/1863 (The
company later became Co. K, 5th Regiment Georgia Volunteer Cavalry.)
Sources:
GDAH, CSR, 253/79 & 253/101

324   **Camp Houston**
Chatham County, Georgia

   Big Times at Coffee Bluff . - On Friday afternoon (11/7/1862) one of the enemy's
gunboats accended a branch of the Little Ogeechee, near Coffee Bluff, and fired a few shot
and shell at Capt. R. Jacob Read's Camp of light artillery. Capt. R. retired out of range of
the Yankee guns.

Extract from *Savannah Republican*, 11/10/1862.

Georgia Troops:
1st Georgia Regulars, Co. D, Read's Artillery, 7/23/62-11/10/1862
Sources:
GDAH, CSR, 254/67; SR, 11/3/1862 , 11/10/1862 & 11/12/1862

325   **Camp Houston**
New Hanover County, North Carolina
   The camp was located six miles below Wilmington on the Masonboro Sound, three miles from
the Atlantic Ocean.
Georgia Troops:
30th Regiment Georgia Volunteer Infantry, 1/17/1862-1/19/1862
Source:
DU, Andrew J. White

326   **Camp Howard Grove**
Henrico County, Virginia

The camp was located in Howard's Grove, "about a mile from the center of the city (Richmond) in a beautiful pine grove." About June 3, 1861, the name was changed to Camp Georgia. All the troops from other states moved out of the camp and left only Col. Bartow's Regiment in the camp. See Camp Georgia in Howard's Grove. Later Howard's Grove was used as a hospital site.
Georgia Troops:
8th Regiment Georgia Volunteer Infantry, 5/19/1861-6/3/1861

An extract of a letter to the *Rome Weekly Courier* of June 14, 1861, signed M. D. (Melvin Dwinnell) and dated 6/3/1861.

There are now eleven Georgia companies in this encampment, averaging 90 men each. - - - The Arkansas Regiment that was encamped near us left yesterday for Aquia Creek near Fredericksburg.

10th Regiment Georgia Volunteer Infantry, 6/15/1861.

We have remained here longer than expected because some of the companies were dissatisfied in the Regiment which was nearly formed and we had to start another of which Cummings (Alfred Cummings) of Augusta will be appointed Colonel and it is probable that Capt. Mabry will receive an appointment in the same, as Major.   E.J. Prothro.

Sources:
8th GVI, UGA, Ms. 1737, Godfrey Barnsley; RWC, 6/7/1861 & 6/14/1861
10th GVI, GDAH, UDC Books, Vol. X, 125-126, Evan J. Prothro

327   **Camp Huger**
Norfolk County, Virginia

The camp is located on the fairgrounds, one and one-half miles from Norfolk, near the Catholic Cemetery.
Georgia Troops:
2nd Independent Infantry Battalion, 9/6/1861-12/1861
Source:
GDAH, CSR, 254/107

328   **Camp Hughes**
McIntosh County, Georgia

The camp was located at Darien Ridge, five miles from Camp Holmes.
Georgia Troops:
1st Battalion Georgia Cavalry, Liberty Guards, 10/8/1861-10/23/1861 (The company later became Co. D, 5th Regiment Georgia Volunteer Cavalry.)
1st Battalion Georgia Cavalry, McIntosh Cavalry, 10/1861-11/29/1861 (The company later became Co. K, 5th Regiment Georgia Volunteer Cavalry.)
Source:
GDAH, CSR, 253/79

329   **Camp Humphrey's**
                                            Muscogee County, Georgia

The camp was located near Columbus.
Georgia Troops:
Howard's Company Georgia Infantry, non-conscripts, 5/12/1863-11/24/1864 (They became the 27th Battalion Georgia Volunteers, non-conscripts, while in this camp.)
Sources:
GDAH. CSR, 256/73; 258/54

330   **Camp Hunter**
                                            Suffolk County, Virginia

On the 6th of March, we were ordered to Suffolk. On the 7th, most of the men, with the guns, under Capt. Stanley took the steamboat at King's wharf, going by river and rail to Suffolk, via Petersburg - while the drivers and horses, under Lt. Carlton, crossed the James River at Jamestown, and went through the country, via Smithfield. At Suffolk we had a very pleasant time, remaining until the 20th, when we were ordered to Goldsboro, N. C. - the battery being transported by rail and the horses through the country as usual; but left behind us one of our number, to be transferred, we trust, to the army triumphant on high - private John C. Deavors, who died at Suffolk, of typhoid pneumonia, March 31st, 1862.

Extract from *Athens Southern Banner*, 4/13/1864.

Captain Marcellus Stanley, the first commander of the Troup Artillery.

photo courtesy of Lee Joyner

We are encamped about one mile and a half from the centre of the town, immediately on the Norfolk and Petersburg R. R., in a very pleasant locality. The cavalry and infantry of the Legion, and the 16th Ga. occupy one side of the railroad, and our company the other side - we being exactly opposite the 16th. Several trains up and down each day and such a rush as there is to "see the cars!" You would imagine that the men had never "seen the like" before. Anything to break the monotony of camp life, though, and that accounts for it all.

Extract from *Athens Southern Banner*, 3/26/1862.

Additional information about the camp is from this extract of Joel Barnett's letter dated March 23, 1862.

We are still at this place, at present in log cabins, the encampment of the 1st So. Ca. Regiment, waiting for transportation to Goldsboro. We think we will leave in a few hours.

Georgia Troops:
Troup Artillery, 3/8/1862-3/20/1862
16th Regiment Georgia Volunteer Infantry, 3/8/1862-3/22/1862 (See Camp Anners.)
24th Regiment Georgia Volunteer Infantry, 3/14/1862
Cobb's Legion, 3/8/1862-3/23/1862
Sources:
TA, ASB, 3/26/1862 & 4/13/1864
16th GVI, ASB, 3/26/1862
24th GVI, ASB, 3/26/1862
CL, GDAH, 283/17, Joel C. Barnett; 160/74, Samuel A. Burney

331   **Camp Hurricane**
Lott County, Mississippi

The camp was located near Forest Station, probably on Hurricane Creek, four to five miles northeast of the station.
Georgia Troops:
47th Regiment Georgia Volunteer Infantry, 8/6/1863
Source:
DU, Benjamin S. Williams

332   **Camp Ida**

Spotsylvania County, Virginia

The camp was located near Fredericksburg.
Georgia Troops:
8th Regiment Georgia Volunteer Infantry, 1/1/1863
Source:
UGA, Ms. 25, Margaret Branch Sexton Collection

333   **Camp Independence**

Wilkinson County, Georgia

Location not known.
Georgia Troops:
Oconee Grays, 8/4/1861 (They later became Co. B, 2nd Regiment Georgia State Troops.)
Source:
SFU, 8/13/1861

334   **Camp Investment**

Claiborne County, Tennessee

The camp was located near Cumberland Gap.
Leander F. Crumly wrote this about the map enclosed in his letter from Camp Investment,

> I send you a map of our army on this side of the mountain and allso the yankee's camps and you can see wher our company and Some of the Rest thirty in all faut two Regments of yankees for four hours on Indian Creek.

Georgia Troops:
52nd Regiment Georgia Volunteer Infantry, 9/9/1862
Source:
PC, Leander F. Crumly letters

335   **Camp Iverson**

Chatham County, Georgia

The camp was located five miles below Cherokee Hill, near the railroad. On December 8, 1862, the camp was moved to Cherokee Hill.
Georgia Troops:
5th Regiment Georgia State Troops, 11/21/1861-12/8/1861
6th Regiment Georgia State Troops, 11/21/1861-12/8/1861
Sources:
5th GST, SR, 12/3/1861
6th GST, GDAH, 194/3, John L. G. Wood

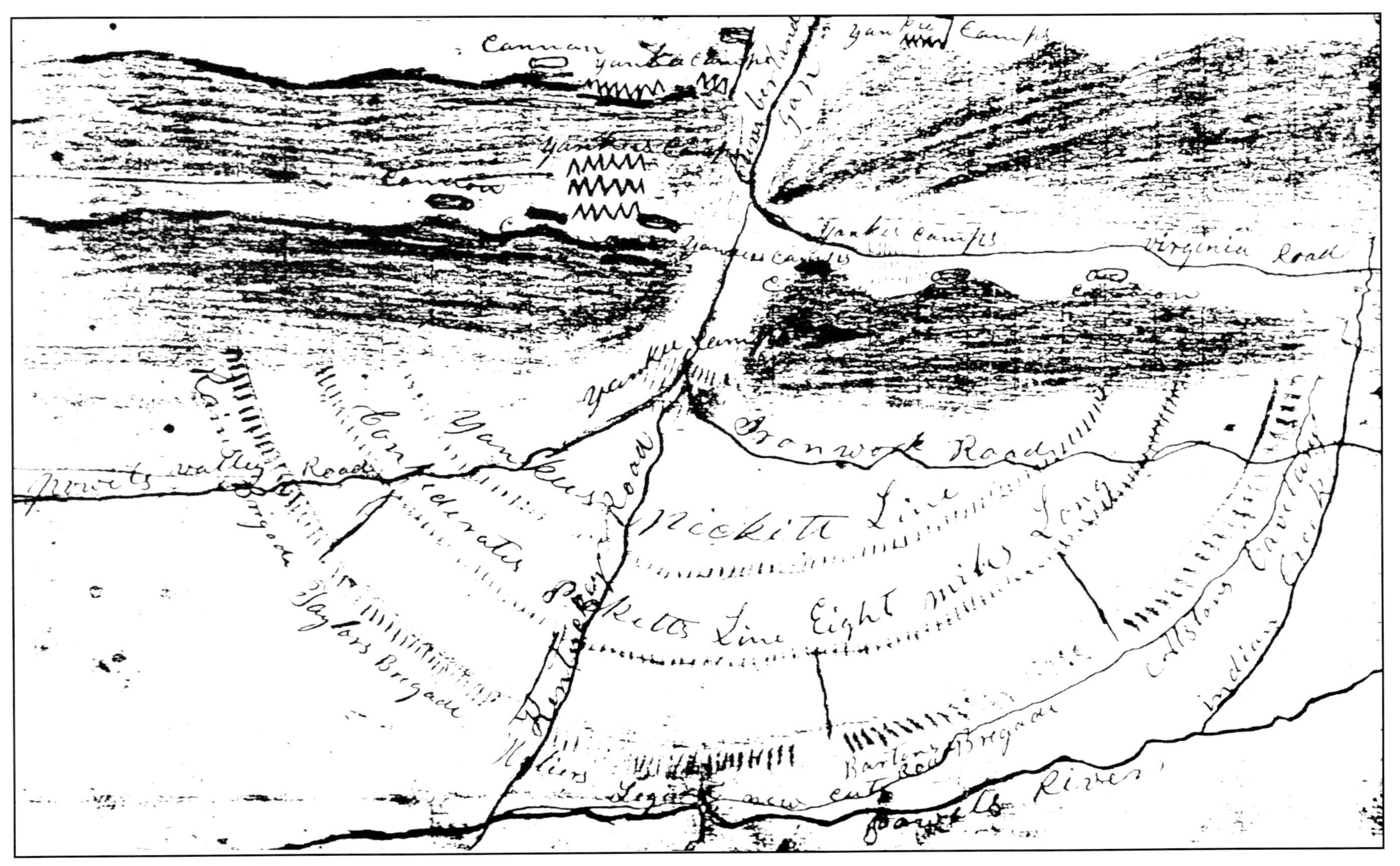

Map of the Cumberland Gap, Tennessee area, drawn by 2nd Corporal Leander F. Crumly, Co. B, 52nd Regiment Georgia Volunteer Infantry, showing Indian Creek and the positions of the Confederate and Union troops.

Map courtesy of Gary Doster

Camp Iverson
Chatham County, Georgia

On December 8, 1861, the Camp was moved to Cherokee Hill, eight miles above Savannah on the Savannah and Charleston railroad. The camp was named in honor of ex-senator Iverson.

> We are now located seven (eight) miles from the city immediately on the Charleston & Savannah Railroad, and about midway between the Savannah River and the Central Railroad on a small elevation. Our present location is from the railroad cut, through the ridge on which we are encamped, some forty feet higher than the surrounding marshs and flats. It is a sand soil, covered with pine and live oak trees festooned with long moss which makes a comfortable bed for the soldier.

Georgia Troops:
3rd Regiment Georgia State Troops, 12/11/1861-2/3/1862
5th Regiment Georgia State Troops, 12/8/1861-2/23/1862
6th Regiment Georgia State Troops, 12/8/1861-2/23/1862
Sources:
3rd GST, GDAH, 91/64, Thomas W. Shine
5th GST, SR, 12/3/1861; SDMN, 1/10/1862
6th GST, SDMN, 1/27/1862; GDAH, 194/3, John L. G. Wood; *Upson Pilot,* 12/7/1861 & 12/14/1861

Camp Iverson
Floyd County, Georgia

The camp was located near Rome.
Georgia Troops:
Floyd's Legion, Co. A, 1/1864
6th Battalion Cavalry, Georgia State Guards, 2/1/1864-2/4/1864 (This was the mustering out camp for 6th Battalion Cavalry, Georgia State Guards.)
Sources:
FL, GDAH, CSR, 258/41
6th Bn GSG, GDAH,.CSR, 253/109

Camp Ivor
Southampton County, Virginia

The 7th Regiment Confederate Cavalry was stationed at Government Depot, Ivor, Virginia, on the Norfolk and Petersburg Railroad. The greater portion of the regiment did picket duty along the Blackwater River over a line of 75 to 100 miles.

The 7th Regiment Confederate Cavalry was organized September 10, 1862. It contained seven companies made up mostly of Georgians, Companies A, B, C, D, E, K & L. On November 31, 1864, these seven companies helped form the 10th Regiment Georgia Cavalry, with the balance of the regiment coming from the 20th Battalion Georgia Cavalry.
Georgia Troops:
7th Regiment Confederate Cavalry, 10/1862 & 12/20/1862
Sources:
GDAH, CSR, 258/69; CE, 1/13/63

339   **Camp Jackson**
Leon County, Florida
    The camp was located twenty miles from Camp Darby.
Georgia Troops:
29th Battalion Georgia Cavalry, Co. E, 9/14/1864
Source:
GDAH, CSR, 254/13

340   **Camp Jackson**
Chatham County, Georgia
    The camp was located on the parade grounds, to the rear of the city park, about one and a half miles from the center of Savannah. Today, the park is known as Forsyth Park. The camp was previously known as Camp Lawton. The name was changed when the 3rd Brigade Georgia State Troops moved into the camp on January 28, 1862, and was probably named for Gen. Henry Rootes Jackson, the commander of the Georgia State Troops.
    See Camp Harrison for the organization of the 3rd Brigade.
Georgia Troops:
3rd Brigade Georgia State Troops, 2/1/1862-4/17/1862
3rd Battalion Georgia State Troops, Co. B, 4/24/1862
7th Regiment Georgia State Troops, Co. H, 3/9/1862
8th Regiment Georgia State Troops, 1/28/1862-4/12/1862
9th Regiment Georgia State Troops, 3/3/1862-3/28/1862
10th Regiment Georgia State Troops, 3/5/1862-3/13/1862
11th Regiment Georgia State Troops, 3/21/1862
8th Battalion Georgia Volunteer Infantry, 3/3/1862-4/12/1862
Sources:
3rd Brig GST, SDMN, 3/14/1862; SC, 1/28/1862 & 4/22/1862
3rd Bn GST, 283/34, Jett T. Mitchell
7th GST, GDAH, 283/38, A. J. Robinett
8th GST, SDMN, 3/28/1862 & 4/1/1862; UNC, #3349, Joseph Epsey
9th GST, SDMN, 3/6/1862; SFU, 4/8/1862; DU, Eugene Verdery, Jr.
10th GST, SDMN, 3/14/1862
11th GST, GDAH, 40/17, Military Records of Georgia
8th Bn GVI, GDAH, CSR, 255/52; SDMN, 4/10/1862

341   **Camp Jackson**
Chatham County, Georgia
    The camp was located on the Thunderbolt Road, near Thunderbolt Battery, within two and one-half miles of Savannah.
Georgia Troops:
Terrell Light Artillery, Brooks Battery, 5/31/1862-10/22/1862
9th Regiment Infantry, Georgia State Guards, 9/16/1863-12/31/1863
Sources:
TLA, BB, GDAH, CSR, 254/47
9th GSG, GDAH, CSR, 255/62

342   **Camp Jackson**
Floyd County, Georgia

The camp was located near Rome. See Camp Lofton. Also, see map of Rome on page 303.
Georgia Troops:
6th Regiment Infantry, Georgia State Guards, 11/9/1863
Lofton's Regiment, 6 month company for local defense, 10/21/1863
Sources:
6th GSG, CG, 12/2/1863
LR, GDAH, AGLB, #20

343   **Camp Jackson**
McIntosh County, Georgia

Location not known.
Georgia Troops:
20th Battalion Georgia Cavalry, Cos. A, B, C & D, 3/1863 & 9/2/1863
Sources:
GDAH, CSR, 254/6 & 7

344   **Camp Jackson**
Richmond County, Georgia

The camp of the 12th Battalion Georgia Light Artillery, was located on the farm of Mr. W. B. Savage on the Carnes Road near Harrisonville, a community near Augusta. The 12th Battalion was formed from a part of the 1st Regiment Georgia Volunteer Infantry, who had disbanded on March 10, 1862.

The battalion was ordered to Tennessee for duty. Enroute, a part of the battalion was involved in a train wreck. The following article is from the *Knoxville Daily Register* of July 9, 1862.

> Accident on the Georgia State Road. -- We learn from the *Atlanta Confederacy* that, on Sunday (7/7/1862,) near Johnson Station, 17 miles from Chattanooga, the locomotives *Excel* and *President* collided, killing Frank Cannon and George Prince, the Engineer and Fireman on the *Excel*, and 12 soldiers - names not learned - belonging to Caper's Battalion, of Augusta, and wounding 30.
>
> The *President* had gone up on Saturday, carrying a train of soldiers and the conductor, H.L. Wing, was trying to bring back the train on Sunday by running *"freight train time,"* instead of waiting till Monday.
>
> The up train was going at full speed and the momentum of the cars forced the tender of the *Excel* over the boiler, causing it's explosion.

Georgia Troops:
12th Battalion Georgia Light Artillery, 5/1/1862-7/9/1862
Sources:
ADC&S, 5/15/1862 & 7/5/1862; *Under the Stars and Bars*, Walter A. Clark; GDAH, CSR, 254/34

345 **Camp Jackson**

Lee County, Mississippi

The camp was located near Saltillo. The name possibly came from Andrew Jackson, who had camped at Saltillo when he was fighting the Indians.
Georgia Troops:
5th Regiment Georgia Volunteer Infantry, 7/22/1862-7/24/1862
Source:
DU, William McCoy

346 **Camp Jackson**

New Hanover County, North Carolina

The camp was located near Ft. Fisher.
Georgia Troops:
7th Regiment Confederate Cavalry, Co. E, 7/1863-1/1864 (The company later became Co. E, 10th Georgia Volunteer Cavalry.)
Source:
GDAH, CSR, 258/69

347 **Camp Jackson**

Georgetown County, South Carolina

The camp was located near Georgetown, South Carolina. This was the headquarters of the cavalry forces in this area.
Georgia Troops:
21st Battalion Georgia Cavalry, Cos. B & E, 7/24/1863-11/8/1863
Sources:
GDAH, CSR, 254/9; SDMN, 9/4/1863

348 **Camp Jackson**

Sullivan County, Tennessee

The camp was located near Zollicoffer, now Bluff City.
Georgia Troops.
6th Regiment Georgia Volunteer Cavalry, 4/15/1863
Source:
GDAH, 186/20, George W. R. Bell

349 **Camp Jackson**

Frederick County, Virginia

The camp was located on the fairgrounds, one-half mile from Winchester. This is probably the same as Camp Fairground.
Georgia Troops:
8th Regiment Georgia Volunteer Infantry, 6/8/1861 & 6/9/1861 (On 6/9/1861, the regiment struck camp for Harper's Ferry.)
Sources:
GDAH, 283/35, Charles & George Norton; RWC, 6/21/1861

Suffolk County, Virginia

The camp was located one-half mile from James River between Bullock (Stritter's) & Hofflar's Creeks. See Atlas Plate XXVI, 4.

The following is an extract from a letter of W. R. Hicks to Mr. Milton Hicks dated March 23, 1862, from Camp Jackson. (Possibly the first recorded ball player on the D.L.)

> Mess No 2 has all gone out to Churchland to Church to day but me. I would have gone but I had a sore foot. I hurt it playing ball yesterday. We have pretty lively times playing ball when we are not drilling.

Georgia Troops:
4th Regiment Georgia Volunteer Infantry, 5/28/1861-5/10/1862
Sources:
MSR, 8/20/1861; GDAH, 185/65; CSR, 254/128; AHC, Ms. 51f, Richard Meminger Campbell
Map: GDAH, 283/20, Terrell A. Cantrell

to the right:
1st Lieut. William C. Wimberly, Co. A, 4th Regiment Georgia Volunteer Infantry. Retired April 26, 1862.

photo courtesy of David Vaughn

to the left:
Capt. Youel G. Rust, Co. E, 4th Regiment Georgia Volunteer Infantry. Resigned April 28, 1862.

photo courtesy of David Vaughn

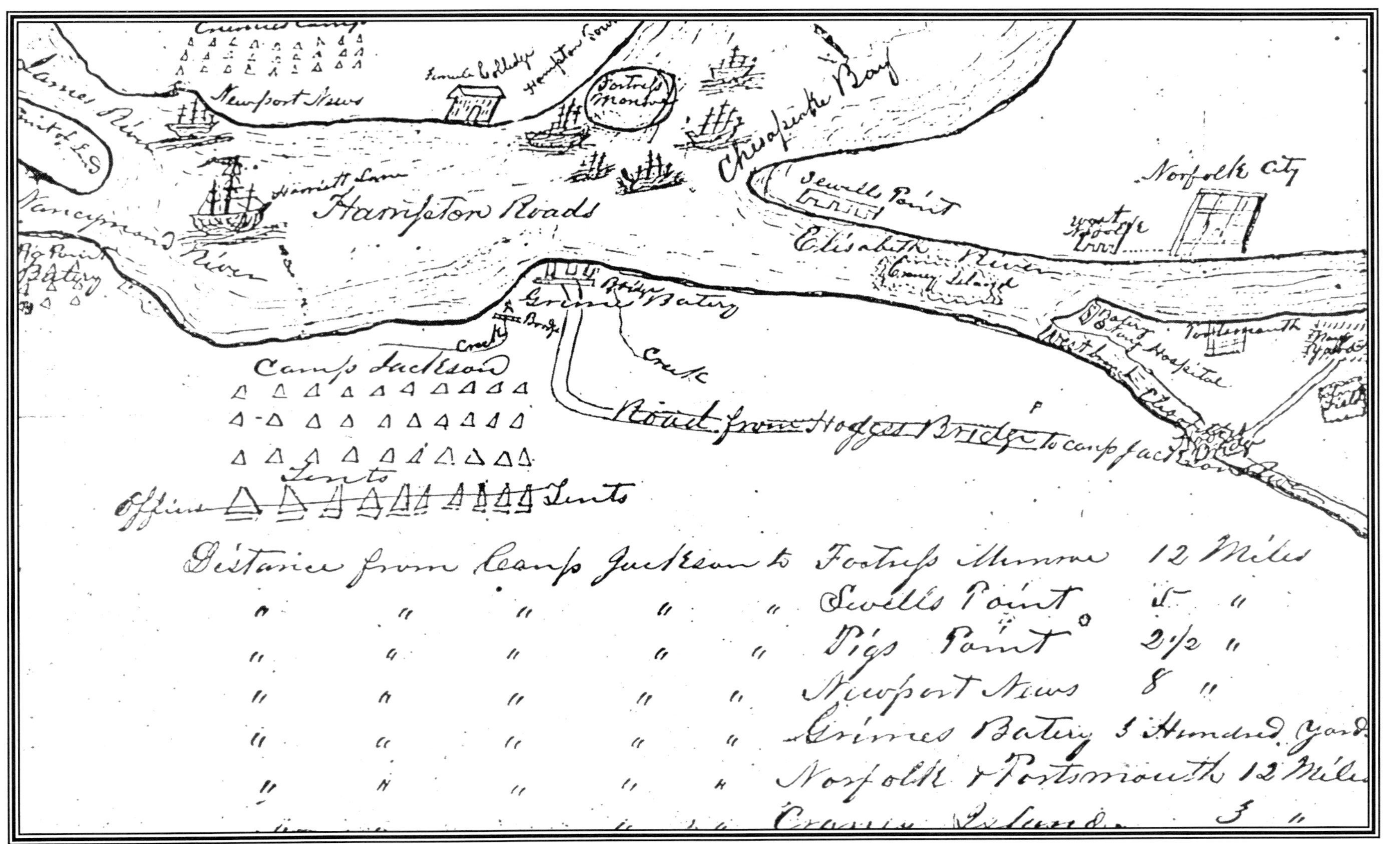

Camp Jackson of the 4th Regiment Georgia Volunteer Infantry
map courtesy of the Georgia Department of Archives and History, Terrell A. Cantrell papers

This 1861 photograph was taken by Mathew Brady and was a part of the Ellsworth
Memorial published by the E. & H. T. Anthony Company of New York.
photo from the collection of George S. Whiteley IV

351   **Camp Jackson of Alexandria**
Chatham County, Georgia
The camp was located three hundred yards behind the lighthouse on Tybee Island.
The following article is from the *Savannah Daily Morning News* of May 29, 1861.

The Killing of Ellsworth by Jackson - Heroism of
Virginia Women

A gentleman who arrived in Richmond last evening, reports as follows:

Ellsworth ascended to the roof of the Marshall House, and secured the (Confederate)
flag. Coming down with the flag wrapped around him, he met Mr. Jackson, when
Ellsworth remarked, "Here, I have got a prize." Jackson replied, "Yes, and here is another
prize" - at the same time levelling his double barrel shot gun, and shooting Ellsworth dead
on the spot.

Jackson was speedily murdered by the Zouaves. The shot that killed him pierced his
brain.

Mrs. Jackson and her sister, as we are informed, took possession of the flag, drew revolvers, and defiled the Zouaves, who endeavored to take it from them. The ladies tore the flag into shreds, determined that it should not pass into the hands of Lincoln's ruffians.

Connected with this affair, we may publish the following copy of a card, which Mr. Jackson had circulated to advertise his business. It shows the spirit of the man:

Marshall House

James W. Jackson, Proprietor.
Corner King and Pett Streets
Alexandria, Virginia.

Georgia Troops:
1st Georgia Regulars, 5/31/1861-6/17/1861
Sources:
SDMN, 5/29/1861; GDAH, CSR, 254/67; *Footprints of a Regiment*, Annotated by Richard M. McMurry

352   Camp Stonewall Jackson
Chatham County, Georgia

The camp was located at Causton's Bluff, and was the former camp of the 47th Regiment Georgia Volunteer Infantry.
Georgia Troops:
Chatham Artillery, 6/10/1862-8/7/1862
Source:
Historical Sketch of The Chatham Artillery During The Confederate Struggle for Independence, by Charles C. Jones, Jr.

353   Camp James Island
Charleston County, South Carolina

The camp was located on James Island.
Georgia Troops;
7th Regiment Georgia Volunteer Infantry, 9/25/1863-9/29/1863 (A number of men from several regiments were sent from Virginia to this camp on wounded furlough.)
19th Regiment Georgia Volunteer Infantry, 5/1863-6/1863 & 12/31/1863-1/21/1864
23rd Regiment Georgia Volunteer Infantry, 2/4/1864
28th Regiment Georgia Volunteer Infantry, 9/24/1863 (A number of men from several regiments were sent from Virginia to this camp on wounded furlough.)
Sources:
7th GVI, GDAH, CSR, 255/33
19th GVI, GDAH, CSR, 256/7; GJ&M, 6/19/1861; PC, Henry Shackelford & John Clegg
23rd GVI, GDAH, CSR, 256/36
28th GVI, GDAH, 283/43, George A. Wiggins

Saturday, December 13th, was a day whose glorius, yet melancholy, history will long remember. The hills, which for some distance ran parallel with the Rappannock a mile above Fredericksburg, swept out in a semi-circle, leaving the town on a comparitive plain between them and the river. The hills in this chain immediately opposite the town and above the Richmond road, are known as Marye's heights; the lower end of the semi-circle, between the Richmond Road and the river, as Howison's hills. On these hills we were situated (Camp Janie). In fact, the hills around the town were pretty well lined with artillery, which - especially that on Marye's hill - was destined to play an important part.

Friday the Yankees had thrown their pontoon bridges across and slowly drove Barksdale's stubborn fellows from the town. Saturday the 13th, the grand attempt was made to carry Marye's hill by storm (it was the key of our position.) The Richmond or Telegraph Road comes straight out of town to the foot of these hills. - then turning to the left, runs along their base for half a mile, having a stone wall next to the town. Behind this wall in front of us, a mile distant but in plain view, our brigade was posted, with Gen. T. R. R. Cobb at their head. Our own position was neither one of much danger or great usefullness; but we could sometimes annoy the enemy, and prevent their massing troops in the old railroad cut in front of Gen. Cobb. By and by, we saw them in two heavy columns, rush to that fatal charge from which so many of them never returned. Bravely did those Irish under Meagher rush into the red arms of death. They only came to add to slaughter. Gen. Cobb cooly maintained his ground until shot down; then left his indomitable spirit to abide in the hearts of his men; and at length the Irish brigade rolled back as rolls a spent wave from a rock bound shore, and left five hundred of their number dead on the field, headless many of them, and many of them dismembered; for the Washington Artillery, from the heights above, had poured upon them shell, case and canister. Truly, it was the very saturnalia of death. --------------

And here I must pause to say, if "death loves a shining mark," he certainly found one in our noble commander. Politically the nation knows him; the prestige of great military success, prevented by the blight of death, shone like the first beams of the rising sun; but of another trait in our General's character I wish to speak - his simple, fervent pietry. We will long remember how gently he stole to an unnoticed place in our prayer meetings; how regularly he arose to present feelingly and forcibly, the claims of religion before us; how sincerely he seemed to be interested in our spiritual, as he had ever shown in our temporal well being. In short, though we admired him as a Jurist, and cannot forget him as a General; yet we loved him and remember him chiefly as the Father of the Troup Artillery.

Georgia Troops:
Troup Artillery, 11/28/1862-12/13/1862
Sources:
GDAH, 283/17, Thomas A. Barrow; ASB, 4/27/1864

Chatham County, Georgia

Also known as Camp Race Course. Located about two miles northwest of Savannah and about 200 yards northeast of the railroad tracks, on and around the Ten Broeck race course, and near Jasper Spring. The race course was owned by Charles A. L. Lamar, once president of the Savannah Jockey Club, who organized the Lamar Mounted Rifles at the race track, December 31, 1860. In an 1862 letter from C. A. L. Lamar to his father, Gazaway Bugg Lamar, he complained about the soldiers (Georgia State Troops) who had encamped there for the winter of 1861-1862, and built their campfires next to the fence surrounding the race track which burnt and scorched it to the point it would have to be replaced.

Private John L. G. Wood, Company G, 6th Regiment Georgia State Troops, wrote his father, William Wood, a letter dated November 15, 1861, while "encamped at the race track in a corn field in a low marshy looking place." He also stated, "We use water out of the spring where Jasper and Newton, two heros of the revolution and brave doers of General Francis Marion, performed one of the most noble and daring deeds of the Revolutionary War by slipping upon the British and Tories while they were eating and drinking and refreshing themselves, taking possession of their arms which they had stacked, killed two officers, took several prisoners and releasing some of ours."

General Henry Rootes Jackson, commanding the Georgia State Troops in Savannah, issued GENERAL ORDER No 8, dated January 9, 1862, changing the names of four camps of the Georgia State Troops, including Camp Jasper, to Camp Lee. In a letter of William J. Moseley, Company A., 1st Battalion (Ross' Battalion,) Georgia State Troops, to Father and Mother, dated January 23, 1862, he wrote, "We have moved from where we was and how far do you reckon we moved? We just moved six feet. We are very well fixed up now, we have got our tents floored and some of us has got shelters to cook under." In his letter of February 4, 1862, he writes, " The name of our camp changed from Jasper to Lee named after the old General Lee." ("Light-Horse" Harry Lee, hero of the Revolution and father of Gen. Robert E. Lee)

Georgia Troops:
1st Regiment Georgia State Troops, 11/23/1861
2nd Regiment Georgia State Troops, 11/11/1861-1/20/1862
3rd Regiment Georgia State Troops, 11/11/1861- 12/11/1861
6th Regiment Georgia State Troops, 11/13/1861-11/19/1861
1st Battalion Georgia State Troops, or Ross' Bn., 11/29/1861-1/10/1862
Bibb County Cavalry, 12/4/1861
25th Regiment Georgia Volunteer Infantry, Co. K, Wise Guards, 8/31/1862-10/31/1862 (On 11/26/1862, the company became the 23rd Battalion Georgia Siege Artillery.)
Sources:
1st GST, CG, 11/27/1861
2nd GST, SR, 11/22/1861; SDMN, 1/24/1862
3rd GST, SDMN, 11/19/1861; GDAH, 91/64, Thomas W. Shine
6th GST, GDAH, 194/3, John L.G. Wood
1st Bn. GST, SDMN, 11/23/1861; GDAH, 78/2, William J. Moseley
Bibb Co. Cav., GDAH, 283/48, Bibb Co. file
25th GVI, GHQ, (1917), 106-107

356

Camp Johnson
Bibb County, Georgia

The camp was located on the old academy lot near Macon.
Georgia Troops:
Goode's Battalion of Partisan Rangers, 8/20/1862 (Maj. Charles T. Goode of Houston County)
Source:
ADC&S, 8/22/1862

357

Camp Johnson
Chatham County, Georgia

This picket camp was located near the residence of Mr. Barclay near the Little Ogeechee River bridge on the Savannah Albany and Gulf Railroad.
Georgia Troops:
25th Regiment Georgia Volunteer Infantry, 1st Co. I, 7/16/1862
Source:
SDMN, 7/17/1862

358

Camp Johnson
Morgan County, Georgia

The camp was located near Madison.
Georgia Troops:
Home Guards, 3/1861 (The company later became Co D, 3rd Regiment Georgia Volunteer Infantry. Other companies from Morgan County probably organized here also.)
Source:
GDAH, 283/33, Tatham Massey

359

Camp Johnson
Hamilton County, Tennessee

The camp was located about one mile from Chattanooga on the Nashville Railroad. See Camp Harris at this same location.
Georgia Troops:
34th Regiment Georgia Volunteer Infantry, 6/16/1862-6/20/1862
Source:
Chickamauga & Chattanooga National Military Park Library, letters of George Burns

360

Camp Johnson
Augusta County, Virginia

The camp was located in a beautiful valley, about three miles to the south (east) side of the Shenandoah Mountain.
Georgia Troops:
12th Regiment Georgia Volunteer Infantry, 4/5/1862-4/8/1862
Source:
EU, #20, John Levi Griffin

361   **Camp Johnson**
Frederick County, Virginia
The camp was located near Winchester.
Georgia Troops:
8th Regiment Georgia Volunteer Infantry, 6/28/1861
Source:
SDMN, 7/4/1861

362   **Camp Johnson**
Pocahontas County, West Virginia
The camp was located near Occoquan.
Georgia Troops:
19th Regiment Georgia Volunteer Infantry,
1/1/1862-3/1/1862
Sources:
GDAH, CSR, 256/7-9

Private Francis Eugenius Hart, Co.
I, 19th Regiment Georgia Volunteer
Infantry. Died of typhoid fever in
Farmville, Virginia, on May 23,
1862, and buried in Hollywood
cemetery at Richmond, Virginia.

photo courtesy of Lee Joyner

363   **Camp Jeff Johnson**
Tennessee
Location not known. It is probably in middle Tennessee near Tullahoma.
Georgia Troops:
12th (Avery's) Regiment Georgia Volunteer Cavalry, Co. D, 3/28/1863 (Avery's 4th Georgia
Volunteer Cavalry became the 12th Regiment Georgia Volunteer Cavalry on 1/30/1863.)
Source:
GDAH, CSR, 253/122

364   **Camp Sidney Johnson**
Wakulla County, Florida
The camp was located about ten miles southwest of St. Marks. See map with Camp Brokaw.
Georgia Troops:
Echols' Light Artillery, 8/10/1863-11/17/1863
Source:
PC, James Jewell letters

365   **Camp Johnston**
Prince William County, Virginia

The camp was located near Manassas.
Georgia Troops:
17th Regiment Georgia Volunteer Infantry, 9/27/1861-9/29/1861
Sources:
SFU, 10/8/1861; ADC&S, 10/9/1861

366   **Camp Jones**
Chatham County, Georgia

The camp was located near White Bluff.
Georgia Troops:
Guerard's Battery Georgia Light Artillery, 8/1864
Source:
GDAH, CSR, 254/53

367   **Camp Jones**
Cobb County, Georgia

The camp was the headquarters of the Georgia Military Cadets. Probably located near the
G.M.I. Academy below Marietta.
Georgia Troops:
Georgia Military Institute Cadet Battalion, 6/21/1864
Source:
KMNBPL, Ga-13, letter of Francis W. Capers

368   **Camp Jones**
Henrico County, Virginia

The camp was located near Richmond.
Georgia Troops:
20th Regiment Georgia Volunteer Infantry, 6/27/1861
Source:
GDAH, CSR, 256/13

369   **Camp Sam Jones**
Fairfax County, Virginia

Camp Sam Jones, 8th Ga. Reg.,
Feb. 21, 1862.

Dear Courier: - As there is nothing of particular interest to write about, I propose in this
letter to give your readers a brief description of our camp, and, perhaps, a little peep inside
the cabins.

Camp Jones lies on the East bank of Cub Run. When the camp was laid off it was in the
midst of a forest of oak, hickory, poplar, gum, &c., &c., but now, between obtaining
lumber for the cabins and the consumption of firewood, a belt of about three fourths of a
mile in width, has been all cut away, leaving a rocky, hilly, rough and stumpy clearing,
containing about four hundred cabins and some two hundred tents.

The ground around here is so rocky in many places, that were it desirable to plant wheat, it would have to be shot from a gun into the crevices between the rocks; and if grass should grow in these little interstices, sheep noses would have to be rasped down to a point, in order to enable them to nibble it off.

The non-commisioned officers and privates all have comfortable cabins, while most of the officers are still in tents. The reason why the officers have not cabins, is, because they were left for the last, and, before those for the men were completed, the supply of lumber, suitable and on hand, gave out - and it has not yet been possible to get more hauled - there being hardly horses to transport provisions and forage. The cabins made of rough logs, with stone and mud chimneys, present rather a rude and crude appearance, but each Regiment is laid off in regular streets, a street containing on either side four or five double cabins, and accomodating the men of one company. Each room in these is fifteen feet square, with a large fireplace, dirt floor, rude beds for eight or ten men, a tolerable looking table, covered with oil cloth, and a grotesque lot of rough chairs, or stools, and a mess chest. Around the spacious fireplace may be seen pots and kettles, ovens and bake pans, spiders and frying pans, tea kettles and coffee pots,and whatever deemed indispensible in a cook room. The groups that assemble round these fires, particularly after supper, at night, are all dressed in the dull, dingy suits of soldier clothes, but, though there is none of the bandboxy appearance of town fops, there are cheerful, honest faces and a high-toned manliness of bearing that mere dressing would not give them anywhere. Some spend these long winter evenings in reading and writing, others in little interesting games, and still others, who are more socially disposed, in telling long yarns, singing songs, and occassionally, by way of variety, we have fiddling and dancing, and "a good time generally."

For the past two weeks it has been horrid walking about this camp - so awful muddy that one can hardly get about at all. And the new road between here and the Junction - about two feet below the old one - is litterally strewn with wrecks of wagons and the unsightly remains of faithful steeds.

There is no news here worth mentioning, unless, perhaps to those who love to "whirl in the dizzy mazes of the dance," it may be "interesting to learn that there is to be a grand military ball at or near Manassas; on the 25th inst." I know of no place there or "therabouts," but a mud puddle - vast and deep - that might suit *webb-footed* ducks - nor where any *ducks* are to come from for such a frolic, at such a time. This Regiment was paid off, up to 1st Jan., last Wednesday, so money is quite plenty here, just now, and the *sutlers* are doing a firstrate business.

Most of the boxes that came in car No. 4 are still at the Junction, and are likely to be, until they get a better engine and more cars on the Centreville track, which is now completed to within a mile and a half of this camp.
M . D. (Melvin Dwinnell)

From the *Rome Weekly Courier* of March 14, 1862.

Georgia Troops:
7th Regiment Georgia Volunteer Infantry, 1/22/1862-3/8/1862
8th Regiment Georgia Volunteer Infantry, 1/22/1862-3/8/1862
9th Regiment Georgia Volunteer Infantry, 1/22/1862-3/8/1862
11th Regiment Georgia Volunteer Infantry, 1/22/1862-3/8/1862

Sources:
7th GVI, GDAH, CSR, 255/33
8th GVI, GDAH, CSR, 255/44; RWC, 3/14/1862
9th GVI, GDAH, CSR, 255/56
11th GVI, GDAH, CSR, 25/77; 283/42, James Thomas Thompson

370   **Camp Jordan**
Chatham County, Georgia
   The camp was located near Savannah. This could possibly be Camp Gordon.
Georgia Troops:
1st Battalion Georgia Sharpshooters, 2/15/1863-4/1863
Sources:
GDAH, CSR, 254/96; UDC Books, Vol. II, 396, Cornelius M. Hardy; PC, John Isom Royal
letters

371   **Camp Julia**
Frederick County, Virginia
   The camp was located near Brucetown and between Winchester and Brucetown.
Georgia Troops:
Troup Artillery, 8/28/1862-10/27/1862
Sources:
UGA, Ms. 59, Carlton-Newton-Mell Collection; ASB, 4/27/1864

372   **Camp Kelly**

Roane County, Tennessee

The camp was near Mouse Creek, near Kingston.

Georgia Troops:

1st Regiment Georgia Volunteer Cavalry, 4/4/1863

Source:

GDAH, *Letters Written by Lavender R. Ray of Newnan, Georgia, During the War Between the States,* Compiled by Ruby F. Ray

373   **Camp Kilkenny**

Bryan County, Georgia

The camp was probably located at or near Kilkenny Bluff on the coast below Ft. McAllister.

Georgia Troops:

24th Battalion Georgia Cavalry, Co. B, 4/1863

Source:

GDAH, CSR, 254/11

374   **Camp King**

Sullivan County, Tennessee

The camp was located near Bristol. On May 2nd, 1863, the battalion left Bristol for Knoxville. See article from the *Southern Confederacy* newspaper of November 19, 1862, in Chapter II.

Georgia Troops:

9th Battalion Georgia Light Artillery, 3/26/1863-4/16/1863 & 4/19/1863-5/1/1863

Sources:

Letters to Lucinda, 1862-1864, James Addison McMurtrey; EU, #57, Richard B. Jett; SC, 11/19/1862

375   **Camp Kingston**

Fulton County, Georgia

The camp was located near Atlanta.

Georgia Troops:

Georgia Militia camp for sick & wounded, 5/29/1864

Source:

AHC, #13, Telemon Cuyler Collection

376   **Camp Kirby**

Bradley County, Tennessee

The camp was located near Charleston, Tennessee.

3rd Regiment Confederate Cavalry, Cos. A, C & I, 5/31/1862-7/31/1862

Source:

GDAH, CSR, 258/64

Camp Kirkpatrick
DeKalb County, Georgia

The camp was located in Kirkpatrick's Grove, two miles west of Decatur and four miles east of Atlanta on the Georgia Railroad.

Trial of Guns.

Atlanta, Oct. 10th, 1861.

Messr. Editor: It was my priviledge, in company with a number of other gentlemen, to witness on yesterday, the trial of the improved breech-loading cannon and swivel made by Mr. Wm. Rushton, of this city.

The trial took place at the Stone Mountain, under the direction of Capt. G.W. Lee, of the Wright Legion. The reputation of Capt. G.W. Lee as a most skillful gunner was fully sustained by the results of the day. The target was placed on the side of the mountain, at about 1,500 yards from the gun. Nine shots were fired, all of which were remarkably fine - three of them striking within a few inches of each other, and almost touching the target; a fourth penetrated the target within a few inches of the centre. Three shots were then fired over the tower on the summit of the mountain, at a distance of about a mile and a half, and an elevation of over *fourteen hundred feet.* The whole result was the most complete demonstration of the superiority of the gun. And everyone present felt like congratulating the skillful and energetic inventor for the perfect success of his effort. The swivel, owing to the lateness of the hour, received a more hurried trial, but enough to satisfy us that in power, range and accuracy, it will probably be unsurpassed by any gun of the kind now in use, We are gratified to learn that the Confederate Government has ordered a number of these guns for arming the Wright Legion, under the command of Col. A.R. Wright. We venture that no regiment will have more effective arms.

On our return we stopped at the encampment of the Legion and took supper. Everything about the encampment made a most favorable impression on our minds. The health of the men, the order and neatness of the camp, and above all, the sobriety and morality that prevail, are most pleasant and encouraging features. Soon after supper, the evening prayers were held in front of one of the tents, at which a very large portion of the men were present. And this, I learn, is their regular practice every evening, besides divine service on Sabbath.

With such men for our soldiers as compose this Legion, and with such mechanical genius as that of Mr. Rushton to furnish them with arms, we have no fears for the result of our contest.

SPECTATOR.

Georgia Troops:
Wright's Legion, 9/17/1861-11/16/1861 (Wright's Legion included the Chestatee Artillery and Jo Thompson Artillery.)
Chestatee Artillery, 9/26/1861-11/16/1861
Jo Thompson Artillery, 11/6/1861-11/16/1861
9th Battalion Georgia Light Artillery, 3/26/1862-5/16/1862
Sources:
WL, SC, 10/11/1861; GDAH, CSR, 256/121; ADC&S, 9/21/1861; RWC, 9/27/1861; *Atlanta Historical Bulletin*, "War Diary of Cornelius R. Hanleiter," Elma S. Kurtz
9th Bn GA, SC, 3/27/1862 & 5/16/1862

     Camp Knoxville
Knox County, Tennessee

The camp was near Knoxville.
Georgia Troops:
Phillips' Legion, Infantry Battalion, 11/28/1863-11/30/1863
Source:
KMNBPL, Marcus L. Green

379   **Camp Lamar**

Effingham County, Georgia

The camp was near Whitesville (Guyton, Station No. 3, Central Railroad).

Georgia Troops:

26th (Lamar's) Regiment Georgia Volunteer Infantry, Irwin Cow Boys, Tatnall Rangers, Montgomery Sharpshooters, Wiregrass Rifles, Dekalb Guards, 9/17/1861-9/27/1861 (The 26th Regiment later became the 7th Infantry Battalion, then the 61st Regt. Ga. Vol. Inf.)

Sources:

SR, 9/19/1861, 9/21/1861 & 9/28/1861

380   **Camp Lamar**

York County, Virginia

The camp was on the Yorktown-Williamsburg Road, less than two miles from Yorktown. The camp was named in honor of Mrs. Cobb's brother, John B. Lamar.

Georgia Troops:

16th Regiment Georgia Volunteer Infantry, 12/12/1861-3/6/1862

Sources:

Howell Cobb's Confederate Career, by Horace Montgomery, Confederate Centennial Studies, Number Ten; GDAH, CSR, 255/115; 283/17, William T. Bailey

381   **Camp Lamb**

New Hanover County, North Carolina

The camp, located near Wilmington, was possibly named after Col. William Lamb, commanding North Carolina troops, or at the Lamb residence, one and a half miles east of Wilmington. See Atlas Plate CXXXII, 1.

Georgia Troops:

46th Regiment Georgia Volunteer Infantry, 12/16/1862-12/27/1862

Source:

GDAH, CSR, 257/35

382   **Camp Lane**

Floyd County, Georgia

The camp was located near Rome, and was the mustering out camp of this unit.

Georgia Troops:

2nd Regiment Cavalry, Georgia State Guards, 1/28/1864-1/31/1864

Source:

GDAH, CSR, 253/86

383   **Camp Lang**

Camden County, Georgia

The camp was located at or near Jeffersonton, on the Satilla river.

Georgia Troops:

4th (Clinch's) Georgia Volunteer Cavalry, Co. D, 1/1862-5/1862

Source:

GDAH, CSR, 253/94

Camp Lawton
Chatham County, Georgia

The camp was located on the parade grounds to the rear of the city park, now Forsyth Park, one and a half miles from the center of Savannah. It was named in honor of Alexander Robert Lawton, Commander of the Military District of Georgia. The camp was used by many units passing through Savannah. The name of this camp changed two times. On about February 1, 1862, it was changed to Camp Jackson, probably in honor of Gen. Henry Rootes Jackson, Commander of the Georgia State Troops. Shortly after the death of General William Duncan Smith, on October 4, 1862, the name was changed to Camp William Duncan Smith by the 32nd Georgia Volunteer Infantry.

An extract from a letter of a member of the Troup Artillery from Athens, Georgia, describes their camp:

> The place we are encamped on seems as if it was designed by nature for an encampment. In the near or back of our camp stands three large oaks beautifully laden with moss, and indeed quite a beautiful ornament it is. Well underneath the center one stands Captain Stanley's tent, Frank Pope with him on the left. Under another stately moss decorated oak stands E.P. Lumpkin & H. H. Carlton's tent. On the right of the Captain's is Pope Barrow's, his bro. Tim our instructor with him. His tent also having the natural & beautiful advantages of the others. Then to the right & left of these three tents, running down to the front is the privates tents. Ten on either side. Then little to the left of the left row of tents, & at the head of the row, stands our provision tent or Quartermaster's Department, it also accomodated with the elegant shade of a most beautiful & highly appreciated old oak. Here our cooking is done on our camp fire stands, also the dinner table at which the privates eat. The officers not being allowed so to do. They have to eat to themselves & provide for themselves. Then just in front of the camp & in the center of the space (or the street of the camp as we call it) between the row of tents which space is about 40 or 50 yards, & underneath another, by no means shaby oak stands our guard tent. Then to either side of this tent is placed our guns with their muzzles wide gapping all the while, which indeed would indeed speak Danger to any opposing foe, & victory to the Troup Artillery.

Georgia Troops:
2nd Regiment Georgia Volunteer Infantry, Co. A, 4/27/1861-5/30/1861
2nd Regiment Georgia Volunteer Infantry, 7/25/1861 (The regiment had left Brunswick a few days earlier and was passing through Savannah enroute to Richmond, Virginia.)
7th Battalion Georgia Volunteer Infantry, Cos. A, B, D, E & F, 9/27/1861-10/2/1861 (These companies left for Brunswick on October 2, 1861.)
13th (Styles') Regiment Georgia Volunteer Infantry, 9/3/1861-10/18/1861 (This regiment became the 26th Regiment Georgia Volunteer Infantry, on May 10, 1862.)
29th Regiment Georgia Volunteer Infantry, 9/12/1861-12/2/1861
Georgia Foresters, 9/9/1861 (The company later became Co. F, 29th Regiment Georgia Volunteer Infantry.)
Georgia Sapers and Miners (Engineers), 7/27/1861
Irish Volunteers, 9/12/1861 (The Irish Volunteers later became Co. B, 1st Volunteer Regiment of Georgia.)

1st Volunteer Regiment of Georgia, Montgomery Guards, 9/10/1861 (Guilmartin's Company later became Co. E, 22nd Battalion Georgia Siege Artillery.)

Ocklocknee Light Infantry, 7/27/1861 (This company later became a company with the 13th [Styles'] Regiment Georgia Volunteer Infantry. Then upon reorganization they became Co. B, 29th Regiment Georgia Volunteer Infantry. They were enroute from Thomasville to Brunswick to join the 13th Regiment.)

Oglethorpe Light Infantry, Co. B, 8/30/1861-9/29/1861 (The O.L.I., Co. B, moved to Ft. Pulaski on September 29, 1861, and was captured when Ft. Pulaski surrendered April 11, 1862.)

Troup Artillery, 4/27/1861-7/1/1861 (The Troup Artillery moved to Virginia on July 1, 1861.)

Thomasville Guards, 7/27/1861 (This company later became a company with the 13th [Styles'] Regiment Georgia Volunteer Infantry. Then upon reorganization they became Co. F, 29th Regiment Georgia Volunteer Infantry. They were enroute from Thomasville to Brunswick to join the 13th Regiment.)

Sources:

2nd GVI, Co. A, ASB, 5/8/1861

2nd GVI, GDAH, CSR, 254/100; SR, 7/26/1861

7th Bn GVI, SR, 9/28/1861; SDMN, 10/2/1861

13th GVI, RWC, 10/11/1861 & 10/25/1861

29th GVI, GDAH, CSR, 256/79; RWC, 11/15/1861 & 12/6/1861

GF, SDMN, 9/11/1861

GS&M, SDMN, 8/1/1861

IV, SR, 9/12/1861

1st VRG, SR, 9/11/1861

OckLI, SR, 7/27/1861

OLI Co. B, SDMN, 9/4/1861 & 9/29/1861

TA, ASB, 5/8/1861 & 7/17/1861; UGA, Ms. 59, Carlton-Newton-Mell Collection

TG, SR, 7/27/1861

385   **Camp Lawton**
Jenkins County, Georgia

The camp was located at what is now Magnolia State Park near Millen, Georgia. See the view of the exterior of the stockade on page 302.

Georgia Troops:

1st Regiment (Fannin's) Georgia Reserves, 9/1864-11/11/1864

2nd Regiment Georgia Reserves, 9/1864-11/11/1864

3rd Regiment Georgia Reserves, 9/1864-11/11/1864

55th Regiment Georgia Volunteer Infantry, 10/31/1864 (Those who were not captured at Cumberland Gap on September 9, 1863)

Sources:

1st, 2nd & 3rd GR, GDAH, CSRs, 254/77, 254/105 & 254/121; 171/39, Thomas J. Hand; 283/48, Unit files; GHQ, 24 (1) : 75-76

55th GVI, GDAH, CSR, 257/87

386   **Camp Lawton**
McIntosh County, Georgia
The camp was located near Darien.
Georgia Troops:
1st Battalion Georgia Cavalry, McIntosh Cavalry, Captain O. C. Hopkin's Company, 5/21/1862
(They later became Co. K, 5th Regiment Georgia Volunteer Cavalry.)
Source:
GDAH, MR, 279/66

387   **Camp Lawton**
Spalding County, Georgia
The camp was located near Griffin.
Georgia Troops:
2nd Regiment Georgia Cavalry, Decatur Cavalry, Capt. J. E. Dunlop, Co. K, 6/4/1862
Source:
SR, 6/16/1862

388   **Camp Lawton**
Wayne County, Georgia
The camp was located on the St. Savilla Bluff, across the Altamaha River from Fort Barrington.
Georgia Troops:
25th Regiment Georgia Volunteer Infantry, Co. B, 3/22/1862-4/29/1862
Source:
GDAH, CSR, 256/49

389   **Camp Ledbetter**
Catoosa County, Georgia
The camp was located twelve to thirteen miles below Chattanooga on the railroad. It was described as near three springs and surrounded by mountains.
Georgia Troops:
56th Regiment Georgia Volunteer Infantry, 7/7/1862-7/13/1862
Sources:
GDAH, 283/30, James M. Kuglar; 171/7, Alvin Chandler; *Saddle Bag and Spinning Wheel*, Edited by George Peddy Cuttino

390   **Camp Lee**
Bryan County, Georgia
The camp was located near Way's Station, No. 1 1/2 on the Savannah, Albany & Gulf Railroad.
Georgia Troops:
24th Battalion Georgia Cavalry, 3/17/1863-10/17/1863
Sources:
GDAH, CSR, 254/11; SDMN, 8/27/1863

391
Camp Lee
Chatham County, Georgia

The camp was located on Skidaway Road, three and a half miles below Savannah.
Georgia Troops:
Chestatee Artillery, 11/18/1862-2/1863
Sources:
GHQ, Vol. 1, 266; GDAH, CSR, 256/121

392
Camp Lee
Chatham County, Georgia

This camp was the headquarters of the 2nd Brigade Georgia State Troops at this time. It was located two miles from Savannah on White Bluff Road and in sight of the Batteries. The duty of the Georgia State Troops in this camp was to assist in building Battery Harrison. See Camp Battery Harrison.

See map of Camp Lee on page 186

John Wood wrote this description of the work at the battery in his letter to his father, February 25, 1862.

> You ought to see the Savannah Militia at work especially the wealthy speculators who would seem to be a commissioned officer but not persuaded to be a private with their broad cloth coats, silk cravat, fine starched linen shirts, calf skin boots on half knee-deep in mud and water, spade in hand throwing sand and mud like a piney woods salamander much to the amusement of our Newton County boys. The boys plug them sometimes, I think too much, by calling them "Militia." When the volunteers see them walking about they are sure to holler out,'"Left, Left, Left, Left."

Georgia Troops:
2nd Battalion Georgia State Troops, Taylor's Battalion, 1/30/1862
2nd Regiment Georgia State Troops, 1/13/1862-1/31/1862
6th Regiment Georgia State Troops, 3/3/1862
7th Regiment Georgia State Troops, 11/1862-2/1863
Sources:
2nd Bn GST, GDAH, 194/3, John L.G. Wood; UGA, Ms. 2345, E. Merton Coulter Collection
2nd GST, 283/34, Andrew J. Miller.
6th GST, SDMN; 283/32, John T. McLane

393
Camp Lee
Fulton County, Georgia

The camp was near Atlanta.
Georgia Troops:
Col. John L. Hardee's Regiment, possibly local defense troops, 3/20/1863-3/25/1863
Sources:
SC, 3/24/63; AGLB, #14

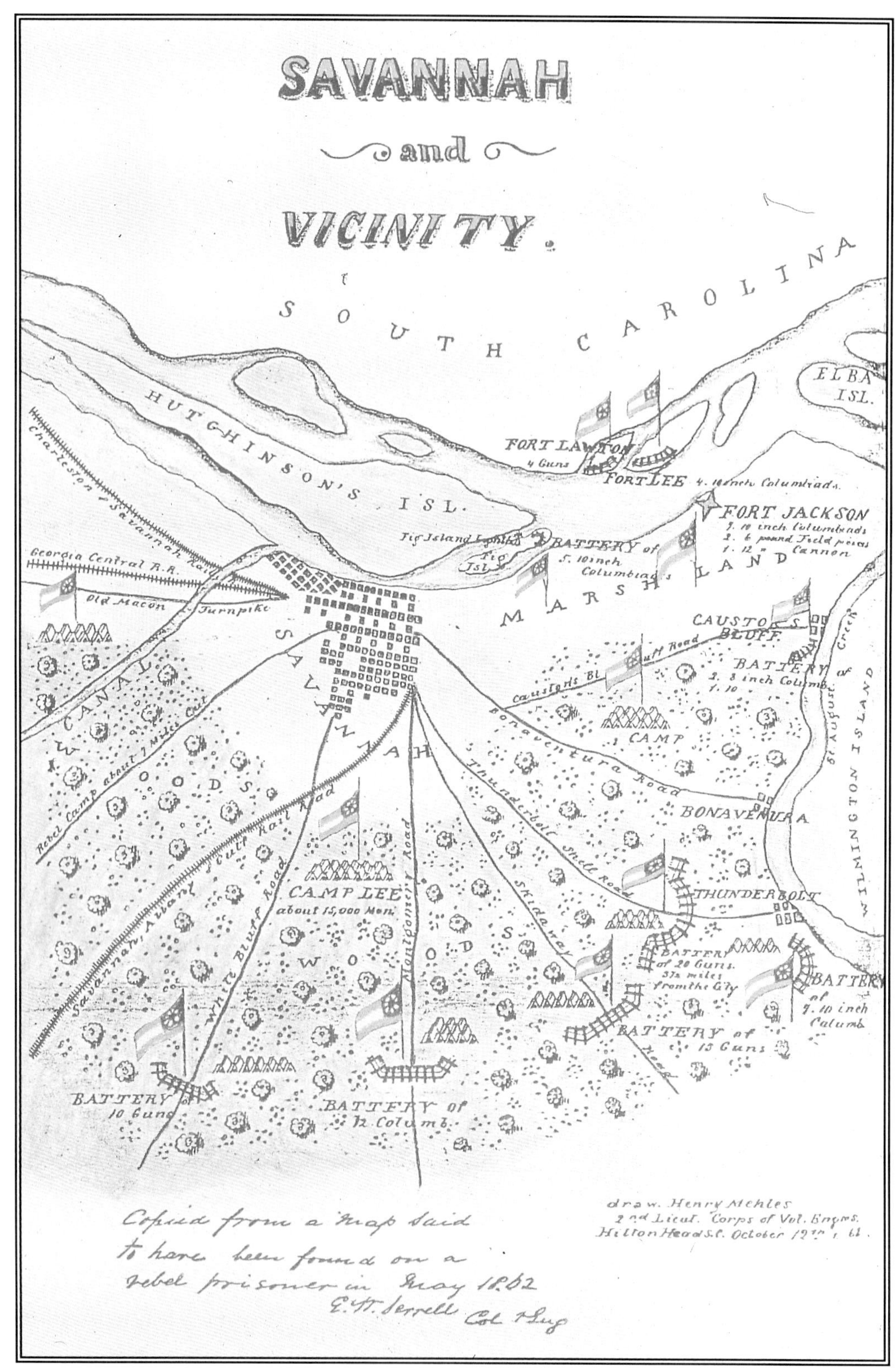

This map of Camp Lee, two miles from Savannah on the White Bluff Road, may have been "intentially captured" by the Union troops on Hilton Head Island. Note the caption below Camp Lee, "about 15,000 men." At no time during the war was there any camp in Savannah with 15,000 men. Map Courtesy of the Atlanta History Center. *Atlanta Historical Bulletin,* War Diary of Cornelius R. Hanleiter, Edited by Elma S. Kurtz

394   **Camp Lee**
Lee County, Georgia

The camp was probably near Starkville.
Georgia Troops:
Lee County Volunteers, 6/1/1861-6/28/1861 (The company later became Co. B, 11th Regiment
Georgia Volunteer Infantry.)
Sources:
AP, 6/6/1861 & 7/1/1861

395   **Camp Lee**
Wayne County, Georgia

Location not known.
Georgia Troops:
4th (Clinch's) Regiment Georgia Volunteer Cavalry, 8/1863
Source:
GDAH, CSR, 253/94

396   **Camp Lee**
Jasper County, South Carolina

The camp was located two to three miles from the Savannah River, near the Savannah &
Charleston Railroad at Hardeeville, on a pine hill. It was also three-fourths mile west of Camp
Elzey.
Georgia Troops:
Phillips' Legion, Infantry and Cavalry Battalions, 1/4/1862-2/10/1862, Co. B, Infantry Battalion,
3/8/1862
Sources:
GDAH, 9/79, Ben & Augustus Boyd; SC, 1/12/1862 & 2/21/1862; UNC, #3015, John Alexander
Barry

397   **Camp Lee**
Hamilton County, Tennessee

The camp was located near Chattanooga.
Georgia Troops:
5th Regiment Georgia Volunteer Infantry, 8/11/1863
Source:
ADC&S, 8/18/1863

398   **Camp Lee**
Campbell County, Virginia

The camp was located near Lynchburg. See Camp Davis.
Georgia Troops:
17th Regiment Georgia Volunteer Infantry, 8/23/1861-9/2/1861
Source:
UNC, #2292, William Oliver Fleming

399   **Camp Lee**
Chesterfield County, Virginia

The camp was located near Petersburg.
Georgia Troops:
2nd Independent Infantry Battalion, 6/25/1862-7/30/1862
Sources:
GDAH, 283/17, John Thomas Bass; CE, 8/12/1862

400   **Camp Lee**
Henrico County, Virginia

The camp was located at the Hermitage Plantation about two miles north of Richmond. The present site is on the north side of Broad Street at the intersecton of Davis Avenue, the present site of Broad Street Station. The camp was named for Robert E. Lee's father, "Light-Horse" Harry Lee. The camp was a major training camp for troops from many states.
Georgia Troops:
11th Battalion Georgia Light Artillery, 5/5/1862-5/23/1862
Cherokee Light Artillery, 10/24/1861-10/25/1861
3rd Battalion Georgia Volunteer Infantry, 10/23/1861-10/25/1861
8th Regiment Georgia Volunteer Infantry, 8/24/1863-8/31/1863
13th (Ector's) Regiment Georgia Volunteer Infantry, 9/1/1862-9/4/1862
22nd Regiment Georgia Volunteer Infantry, 11/15/1861-11/23/61
24th Regiment Georgia Volunteer Infantry, 7/14/1862-8/21/62, & 11/9/1862-11/10/1862
27th Regiment Georgia Volunteer Infantry, 3/1/1862 & 11/20/1862
35th Regiment Georgia Volunteer Infantry, 8/12/1861, 10/31/1861, 6/23/1863 & 8/11/1863
41st Regiment Georgia Volunteer Infantry, 7/19/1863 (The men from this regiment were captured at Baker's Creek or Vicksburg, paroled, and exchanged in Virginia.)
50th Regiment Georgia Volunteer Infantry, 7/24/1862-7/29/1862
51st Regiment Georgia Volunteer Infantry, 8/2/1862
52nd Regiment Georgia Volunteer Infantry, 6/23/1863-6/30/1863 (The men from this regiment were captured at Baker's Creek, paroled, and exchanged in Virginia.)
56th Regiment Georgia Volunteer Infantry, 7/19/1863 (The men from this regiment were captured at Vicksburg, paroled, and exchanged in Virginia.)
Sources:
Descriptive location of camp, *Moore's Complete Civil War Guide to Richmond*, By Samuel J. T. Moore, Jr.
11th Bn GLA, UGA, Ms. 15, Florence Hodgson Heidler Collection, Frank M. C. Coker letters; GDAH, *Civil War Letters of Jessee Sumner Battle and James Norman Battle*, Edited by John D. Battle, Jr., M. D.,
CLA, RWC, 11/1/1861 & 11/8/1861
3rd Bn GVI, RWC, 11/1/1861 & 11/8/1861
8th GVI, GDAH, CSR, 255/44; 283/48, Bibb County File
13th GVI, GDAH, 171/40, Richard W. Milner
22nd GVI, GDAH, CSR, 256/28
24th GVI, GDAH, CSR. 256/43; 263/60, W. K. Hadaway
27th GVI, GDAH, 194/3, James Matt Jordan

35th GVI, GDAH, CSR, 256/103; PC, letters of George B. Pass
41st GVI, GDAH, CSR, 257/9
50th GVI, GDAH, CSR, 257/63
51st GVI, GDAH, CSR, 257/69
52nd GVI, GDAH, CSR, 257/74
56th GVI, GDAH, CSR, 257/92

401   **Camp Lee**
Norfolk County, Virginia

The camp was at Tanner's Creek Crossroads, in an open field with trees all around them. It was also seven miles from Sewell's Point. See Atlas Plate XXVI, 4.
Georgia Troops:
2nd Independent Infantry Battalion, Co. A, 5/17/1861-5/19/1861, Cos. B, C & D, 5/16/1861-6/10/1861
Sources:
GDAH, CSR, 254/107; MT, 5/24/61

402   **Camp Lees Mill**
York County, Virginia

The camp was located at Lee's Mill on the Warwick River, about six mile from Yorktown.
Georgia Troops:
Fraser's Battery Georgia Light Artillery, 4/1862 (The Battery was attached as Co. I, 1st Regiment Virginia Artillery.)
Source:
GDAH, CSR, 254/52

403   **Camp Legares Point**
Charleston County, South Carolina

The camp was at Legare's Point on James Island.
Georgia Troops:
27th Regiment Georgia Volunteer Infantry, 5/6/1864
Source:
GDAH, 283/31, Israel Lindler

404   **Camp Leon**
Leon County, Florida

The camp was located about six miles south of Tallahassee, on both sides of the road. See map to accompany Camp Brokaw for the location of the camp.
Georgia Troops:
Echols' Light Artillery, 3/22/1863-4/1/1863 & 11/17/1863-6/1/1864 (On May 24, 1864, the battery turned in their guns, took up muskets, and became infantry.)
Sources:
PC, James Jewell letters; EU, #20, James Jewell; GDAH, CSR, 254/63

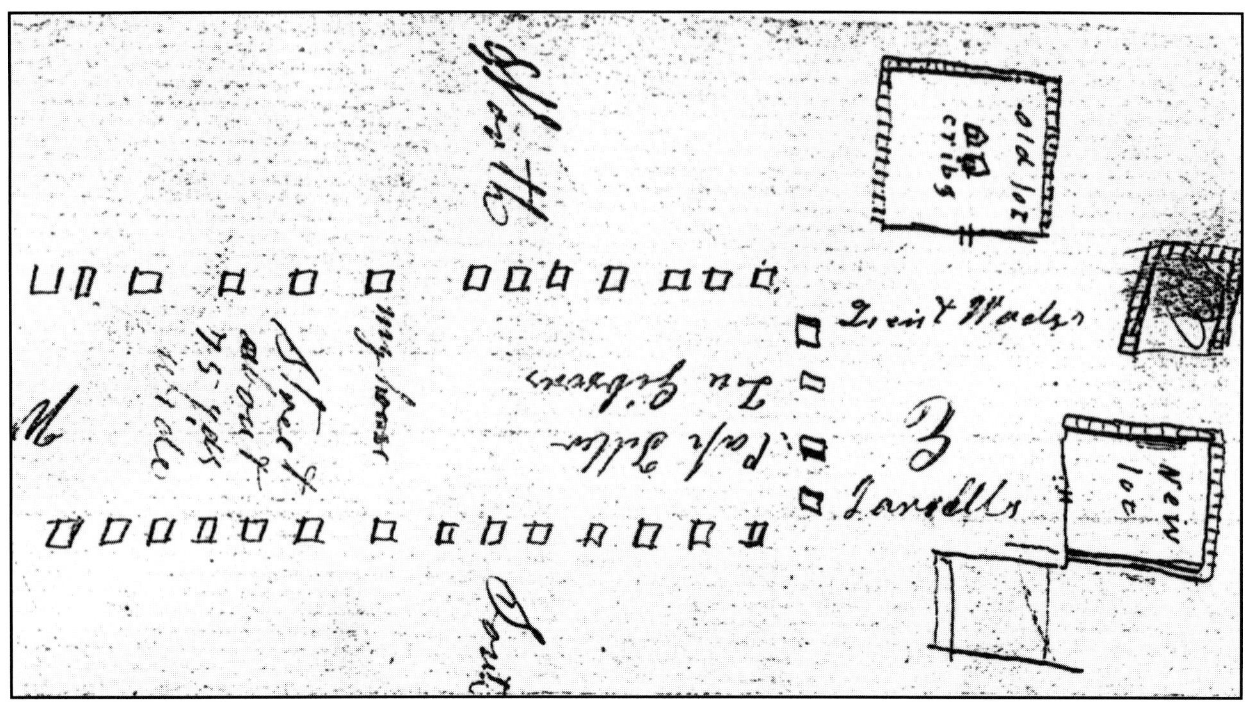

This layout of the camp of Echols' Artillery shows how the artillery camp was organized. The men were apparently in houses since James Jewell indicates on the map, "my house."

James Jewell wrote a note to accompany the map which read, "This is sorter of sketch of our camps. The railroad and public roads pas at the west end of the encampment."

405   **Camp Letcher**
Fairfax County, Virginia

The camp was located at Fairfax railroad station.
Georgia Troops:
Georgia Hussars, Co. E, 6th Virginia Cavalry, 10/23/1861-12/7/1861 (On December 13, 1861, the company was transfered to the Jeff Davis Legion, as Co. F.)
Sources:
GDAH, CSR, 254/22; SDMN, 12/14/1861; *Roll and Legend of the Georgia Hussars*, By A. McC. Duncan

406   **Camp Liberty**
Wilkinson County, Georgia

Location not known.
Georgia Troops:
Oconee Grays, 7/21/1861 (The company later became Co. B, 2nd Regiment Georgia State Troops.)
Source:
MSR, 7/30/1861

407   **Camp Lick Skillet**
Fulton County, Georgia
   The camp was located in the woods about one-fourth mile from the forks of Lick Skillet Road in
the direction of the Chattahoochee River. The name of the camp changed to Camp Carswell on
June 22, 1864.
Georgia Troops:
Georgia Militia, 6/21/1864-6/22/1864
Sources:
GDAH, m87-019, letter no. 9; AHC, Ms. 116, A. T. Holliday

408   **Camp Linton**
Lafayette County, Florida
   The camp was located on Mr. Linton's farm near Hammock's Landing on the Apalachicola
River, sixteen miles below Quincy.
   Fishing at the landing was quite a sport and an alternate to the steady diet of beef. This extract
from the February 20th, 1864 letter of O. T. Smith to his Mother, tells a little about their success.

> if you think you can fix up a box and Send it to me by express I think it will come Safe as
> Some of the company have got boxes from home we get Male here twist a week if you
> Send me the Box pleas Send me som fish hooks mi bige hooks and tell Kitey and Lovey to
> make me some long line about 20 feet long and about as bige as will hold a fish that will
> way 50 pounds Some of the boys catch fish every morning they way 30 pounds we can
> catch a plenty if we had hooks and lines

Georgia Troops:
1st Georgia Regulars, 11/10/1863-2/8/1864
12th Battalion Georgia Volunteers, 3/27/1864
29th Battalion Georgia Cavalry, Cos. A, B & C, 12/31/1863-5/18/1864
Sources:
1st GR, GDAH, CSR, 254/67; *Footprints of a Regiment*, Annotated by Richard M. McMurry;
O.R., Vol. LIII, 316
12th Bn GV, O.R., Vol. LIII, 316
29th Bn GC, GDAH, CSR, 254/13; GDAH, *Diary and Letters of Charles Alden Rowland*,
294.A9 R69

409   **Camp Linwood**
Muscogee County, Georgia
   The camp was located near the residence of Mr. A. C. Flewellan near Columbus.
Georgia Troops:
Semmes Guards, 7/11/1861 (The company later became 2nd Co. C, 2nd Regiment Georgia
Volunteer Infantry.
Source:
CDT, 7/11/61

410   **Camp Lizzie**
Berkeley County, West Virginia
The camp was located south of the Potomac River, two miles from Martinsburg.
Georgia Troops:
16th Regiment Georgia Volunteer Infantry, 9/20/1862-10/1862
24th Regiment Georgia Volunteer Infantry, 9/20/1862-10/1862
Cobb's Legion, Infantry Battalion, 9/20/1862-10/1862
Source:
Howell Cobb's Confederate Career, by Horace Montgomery, Confederate Centennial Studies, Number Ten

411   **Camp Lofton**
Fulton County, Georgia
The camp was located near Atlanta. See Camp Jackson in Floyd County.
Georgia Troops:
6th Regiment Infantry, Georgia State Guards, 9/16/1863-9/28/1863 (This unit was organized on 9/19/1863, by a combination of Maj. Lofton's Battalion and Maj. Mangham's Battalion. It was ordered to Rome on 9/25/1863 to report to Gen. Jackson and guard prisoners, stores, etc.)
Source:
CU, 10/6/1863

412   **Camp Look Out**
Tazewell County, Virginia
The camp was near Jeffersonville, now Tazewell.
Georgia Troops:
9th Battalion Georgia Light Artillery, 11/30/1862-12/2/1862
Source:
Letters To Lucinda, 1862-1864, written by James Addison McMurtrey

413   **Camp Lookout**
Suffolk County, Virginia
The camp was located a few hundred yards from Pigs Point Battery, and was probably used by the pickets of the 4th Georgia Regiment the entire time they were in Camp Jackson.
Georgia Troops:
4th Regiment Georgia Volunteer Infantry, 8/12/1861-8/30/1861 (Different companies rotated picket duty at Pigs Point.)
Sources:
MT, 8/15/1861 & 9/5/1861

414   **Camp Lookout (Mountain)**
Hamilton County, Tennessee
The camp was located near the foot and on the south side of Lookout Mountain, about one and one-half mile from Chattanooga.
Georgia Troops:
3rd Battalion Georgia Sharpshooters, 10/16/1863-10/24/1863

8th Regiment Georgia Volunteer Infantry, 11/20/1863-11/25/1863
Sources:
3rd Bn SS, C&CNMPL, W. R. Montgomery; RWC, 10/30/1863
8th GVI, GDAH, CSR, 255/44; 65/54, Thomas Wesley Asbury; RWC, 10/30/1863

415   **Camp Lovejoy**
Clayton County, Georgia
The camp was near Lovejoy. This could be the same as Camp Bald Head.
Georgia Troops:
Georgia Militia, 11/11/1864-11/13/1864
Source:
Not Known

416   **Camp Lovers Lane**
Chatham County, Georgia
The camp was located on Lover's Lane below Savannah.
Georgia Troops:
1st (Olmstead's) Volunteer Regiment of Georgia, 11/9/1862 (This was the headquarters of the
regiment at this time.)
Source:
GDAH, CSR, 254/81

417   **Camp Lucas**
Georgetown County, South Carolina
The camp was on the North Santee River, one mile below Managault's Ferry.
Georgia Troops:
20th Battalion Georgia Cavalry, Co. E, 6/15/1863-2/1864
Source:
GDAH, CSR, 254/9

418   **Camp Luckie**
Fulton County, Georgia
The camp was located in Atlanta.
Georgia Troops:
9th Battalion Georgia Light Artillery, Co. D, 4/1862-11/19/1862 (Company D had no arms or
accoutrements, and was guarding government stores.)
Sources:
GDAH, CSR, 254/23; SC, 11/20/1862

419   **Camp Mackey**
Chatham County, Georgia

The camp was at Mackey's Point in the middle of a rice plantation on a piece of high ground surrounded by stagnant water. Mackey's point is at the intersection of the Savannah River and St. Augustine Creek. This was used as a picket post for an extended period of time. See Camp Troup.
Georgia Troops:
25th Regiment Georgia Volunteer Infantry, Co. A, 6/1862, 7/20/1862
29th Regiment Georgia Volunteer Infantry, 3/17/1862, 4/2/1862, 5/21/1862
47th Regiment Georgia Volunteer Infantry, Co. D, 6/17/1862 & Co. H, 7/15/1862-8/17/1862
Sources:
25th GVI, GDAH, CSR, 256/49
29th GVI, GDAH, 283/23, Dickey Family Collection
47th GVI, GDAH, CSR, 257/42; SDMN, 6/17/1862

420   **Camp Madison**
Orange County, Virginia

The camp was located two miles west of Orange Court House, not far from Montpelier, the home of President James Madison.
Georgia Troops:
7th Regiment Georgia Volunteer Infantry, 3/18/1862-4/11/1862 (Part of the regiment left two to three days earlier.)
Sources:
GDAH, CSR, 255/33; 71/77 George W. Hopkins

1st Sgt. Moses Liddell Brown, Co. E, 7th Regiment Georgia Volunteer Infantry. He was wounded at 1st Manassas, Virginia, on July 21, 1861. He was discharged, disability, at Camp Madison, Virginia, March 22, 1862. He was then elected Captain of Co. E, 66th Regiment Georgia Volunteer Infantry August 22, 1863.

photo courtesy of Jerry Coody

421
Camp Magnolia
Escambia County, Florida

The camp was located a few miles west of Ft. Barrancas. See map on page 184.
Georgia Troops:
36th (Villepigue's) Regiment Georgia Volunteer Infantry, Co. I, 4/16/1861-7/28/1861
Source:
GDAH, CSR, 256/116

422
Camp Magon
Berkeley County, West Virginia

The camp was located near Martinsburg.

Camp "Magon"
August 24th, 1862

Miss Helen,

You will see from the name of our camp that it was named by the Gen'l (Gen. Howell Cobb) after Mary Ann.

We are camped about one mile north of the Junction between there, and the North Anna River.

I went over to see George this evening and took supper with him. I have just come from there and he is very well; but I forgot to tell you about his horse.

He has got a very nice horse named Stonewall, and I tell you if George does not stop giving him so much medicine, he will be a walking apothecary shop; already agriptions are appearing, George gave him a large dose of calomel and it raining on him liked to have saturated him.

If any man in the Battery wants any medicine he goes to George and he commences unpacking his medicine chest and after a while he scares all the disease out of the poor fellow by his show of medicines.

When you write to him make him tell you about that Circus Jacket of his that he has made as a Confederate uniform. Owing however to the display of buttons on it and the fancy red trimmings it looks more like a clowns suit in a circus.

You must not think that I mean anything by writing this about George for I like him better than any boy I know.

I tease him half to death about his horse and tell him he is not worth a cent when in reality he is a splendid horse.

I am keeping one of the gayest diaries you ever saw.
You must make some of them either Sister or Mary Hamilton show you that beautiful poem
"The Serenade."

It is one of the prettiest little tricks I ever saw; and besides all its other beauties its appropriateness.

Our Brigade Is camped very well all but water.

I find that the opinion about war is the same here as it is in Athens all agree for it to end right now.

All well.

Give my respects to all.
Your Friend,
Tom. (Thomas A. Barrow)

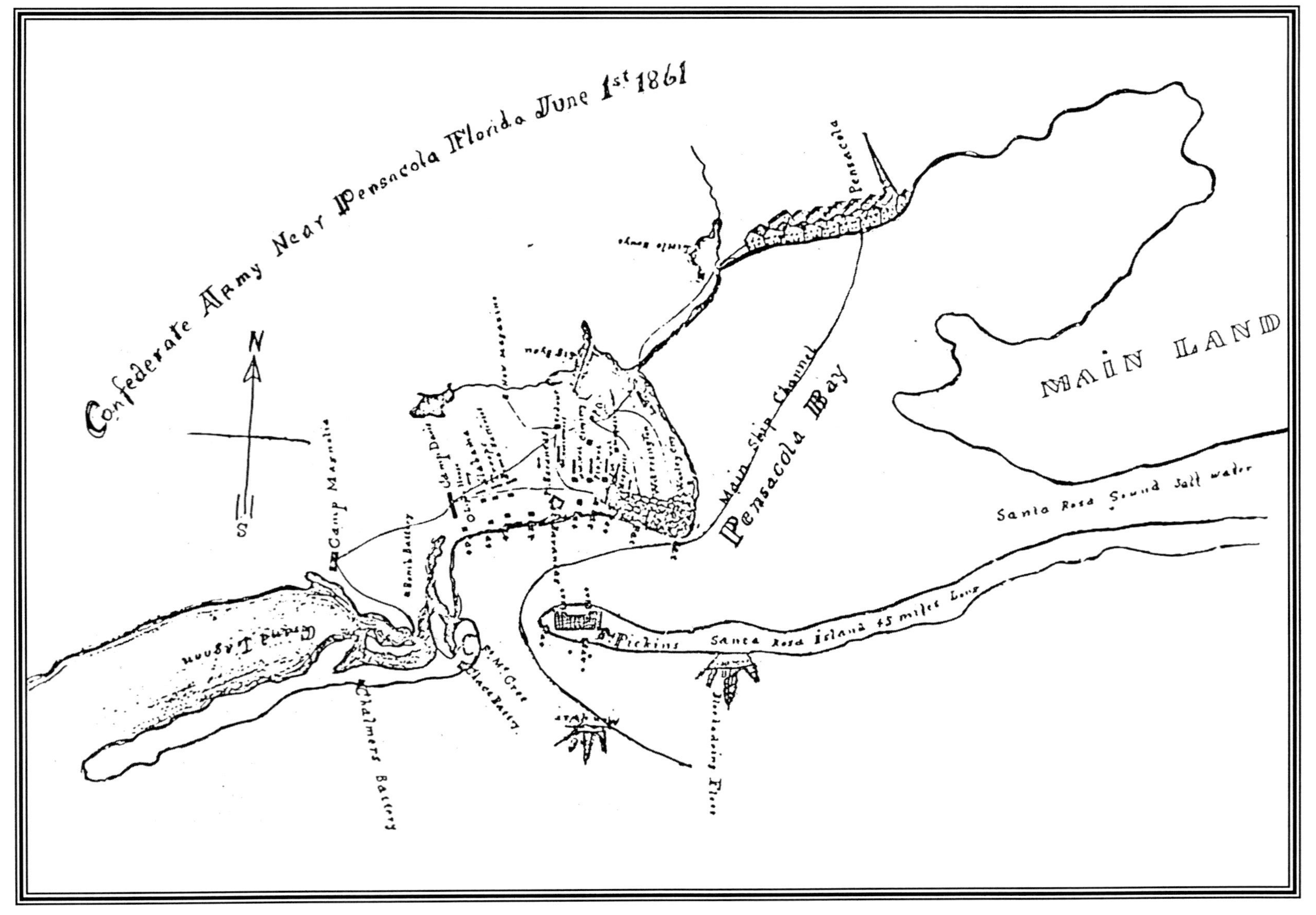

Map of the Pensacola area showing Camp Magnolia to the northwest of Ft. McRae and west of the lighthouse. map courtesy of the Mississippi Department of Archives and History

Georgia Troops:
Troup Artillery, 8/22/1862-8/28/1862
Sources:
UGA, Ms. 59, Carlton-Newton-Mell Collection; ASB, 4/27/1864

423   **Camp Magruder**
Hamilton County, Tennessee
The camp was located near and below Chattanooga.
Georgia Troops:
41st Regiment Georgia Volunteer Infantry, 4/2/1862-4/10/1862
Source:
GDAH, 160/57, John C. Curtwright

424   **Camp Magruder**
Muscogee County, Georgia.
The camp was located near Columbus.
Georgia Troops:
Georgia Light Infantry, 8/29/1861-9/12/1861 (They later became Co. A, 31st Regt. Ga. Vol. Inf.)
Sources:
CDT, 8/28/1861 & 9/13/1861

425   **Camp Mangham**
Jasper County, South Carolina
The camp was located near Pocataligo.
Georgia Troops:
30th Regiment Georgia Volunteer Infantry, 4/27/1863-5/4/1863
Sources:
GDAH, MR, 279/83; *Brief History of the Thirtieth Georgia Regiment*, by Augustus Pitt Adamson

426   **Camp Marietta**
Fulton County, Georgia
The camp was located near Atlanta, and was a hospital camp for the sick and wounded.
Georgia Troops:
Georgia Militia, 5/29/1864-6/24/1864
Sources:
GDAH, CSR, 254/55; AHC, Ms. #13, Telemon Cuyler Collection

427   **Camp Marina**
Columbia County, Florida
The camp was near Lake City.
Georgia Troops:
29th Battalion Georgia Cavalry, Co. D, 10/21/1864
Source:
GDAH, CSR, 254/13

428   **Camp Marion**
                                    Spotsylvania County, Virginia
   The camp was located near Fredericksburg.
Georgia Troops:
Cobb's Legion, Cavalry Battalion, 4/4/1864
Source:
GDAH, 283/29, Henry Francis Jones

429   **Camp Marion**
                                    York County, Virginia
   The camp was located seven miles below Yorktown, two miles from Cockletown, six miles from Bethel Church, and three miles from Winn's Mill on the Warwick River.
Georgia Troops:
Cobb's Legion, Infantry & Cavalry, 10/10/1861-1/9/1862 & 1/18/1862-3/4/1862
Troup Artillery, 12/15/1861-3/2/1862
Sources:
CL, GDAH, CSR, 254/49; 283/29 Henry Francis Jones; 160/74, Samuel A. Burney; EU, #75, Benjamin L. Mobley; ASB, 3/26/1862
TA, GDAH, CSR, 254/49; ASB, 3/26/1862;
283/29 Henry Francis Jones;
160/74, Samuel A. Burney

Jr. 1st Lieut. A. Franklin Pope,
Troup Artillery

photo courtesy of Lee Joyner

430   **Camp Marshall**
                                    Chatham County, Georgia
The camp was located near Coffee Bluff.
Georgia Troops:
1st Georgia Regulars, Co D, Read's Artillery, 11/18/1861-1/11/1862
Sources:
GDAH, CSR, 254/67; SDMN, 1/11/1862

431   **Camp Martin**

Washington County, Virginia

The camp was located near Abingdon.

Georgia Troops:

9th Battalion Georgia Light Artillery, 10/8/1862

Sources:

GDAH, CSR, 254/23-25

432   **Camp Mason**

Wayne County, North Carolina

The camp was located near Goldsboro.

Georgia Troops:

45th Regiment Georgia Volunteer Infantry, 4/17/1862-4/22/1862

49th Regiment Georgia Volunteer Infantry, Cos. C, H & I, 4/9/1862-5/24/1862 (All the other companies were at Camp McIntosh at this time.)

Sources:

45th GVI, GHQ, Vols. 46 & 55, Charles A. Conn

49th GVI, GDAH, CSR, 257/56; SFU, 4/29/1862

433   **Camp Mason**

Frederick County, Virginia

The camp was located two miles northwest of Winchester on the road to Romney.

Georgia Troops:

1st (Ramsey's) Regiment Georgia Volunteer Infantry, 12/16/1861-1/1/1862 & 2/10/1862-2/20/1862

Sources:

GDAH, CSR, 254/91; SC, 12/29/1861, 2/20/1862 & 3/8/1862

pvt. William McD. Felder, Co. D, 1st Regiment Georgia Volunteer Infantry Enlisted March 18, 1861, mustered out March 18, 1862.

photo courtesy of Jerry Coody

Camp Mason's Hill
Fairfax County, Virginia

The camp was located one mile west of Munson's Hill and seven miles west of Alexandria. The regiment was on picket duty.

The following article is from the *Columbus Times* newspaper of November 8, 1861.

"Firstrate - Fine." - We learn that while the 8th Georgia Regiment were on picket duty at Munson's or Mason's Hill, a member of the Oglethorpe Light Infantry was put on duty about two hours before day. When daylight came he saw the warlike line of Federal pickets off two or three hundred yards - the following dialogue ensued:

Oglethorpe (at the top of his voice.) - How are you?

Yankee. - Good morning - how are you, this morning?

Oglethorpe. - You are a pretty *darn* rascal to be out here fighting for money.

Yankee. - You are a liar! I'm fighting for the *promise* of it!

Georgia Troops:
8th Regiment Georgia Volunteer Infantry, 9/16/1861-9/19/1861
Sources:
RWC, 9/27/1861 & 10/4/1861

Camp Maxey
McNairy County, Tennessee

The camp was located at Bethel Springs, on a hill near the railroad and about four miles from Purdy. See Camp Bethel.

Georgia Troops:
41st Regiment Georgia Volunteer Infantry, 4/14/1862-4/24/1862 (The 5th Regiment Georgia Volunteer Infantry arrived in camp April 15, 1862.)
Source:
GDAH, 160/57, John C. Curtwright

Camp Bob May
Burke County, Georgia

The camp was located on Shell Bluff, on the Savannah River, in a pine thicket adjacent to an open field. The camp was named for the mayor of Augusta.

Georgia Troops:
48th Regiment Georgia Volunteer Infantry, Co. C, 3/12/1862-3/27/1862 (The company left for Grahamville, South Carolina, on March 30, 1862.)
Sources:
ADC&S, 3/12/1862 & 3/27/1862; TWC, 3/23/1862

437
Camp Maynard
Virginia

The location of this camp is not known. It is probably a picket camp near Stevensburg. See Camp Stevensburg.
Georgia Troops:
Cobb's Legion, Cavalry Battalion, Co. K, 2/15/1863
Source:
GDAH, CSR, 258/8

438
Camp Mayson
Fulton County, Georgia

The camp was located on Mayson's Hill, about one mile from the rail car shed.
Georgia Troops:
9th Regiment Infantry, Georgia State Guards, de Leaperriere's Company, 9/25/1863
Source:
ASB, 5/27/1863

439
Camp McAllister
Bryan County, Georgia

The camp was located three miles above Ft. McAllister on the Ogeechee River at Hardwick.
Georgia Troops:
Howell's Battery Georgia Light Artillery, 9/18/1862-10/12/1862
Sources:
Memoirs of a Confederate Veteran, By I. Hermann; GDAH, CSR, 254/55; 261/2, Jonas N. Wood

440
Camp McAlpin
Chatham County, Georgia

The camp was probably located near Savannah. It was the headquarters of the 3rd Brigade State Troops who were involved in the battle at Griswoldville.
Georgia Troops:
3rd Brigade State Troops, 12/16/1864 (The brigade was commanded by Brig. Gen. C. D. Anderson, which included in part Hartridge's Battalion and Pruden's Battery.)
Source:
SR, 12/10/1864

441
Camp McDonald
Cobb County, Georgia

This was the largest of Georgia's camps of instruction. It was first used June 11, 1861, by the 4th Brigade Georgia Volunteers, and was named for Georgia's past Governor, Charles J. McDonald who had recently passed away. The camp was located just west of the Big Shanty (Kennesaw) railroad depot. The map of Camp McDonald was drawn by topographical engineer, G. Wadsworth, and sold for the benefit of the soldiers in Camp McDonald.
Georgia Troops:
Georgia Military Institute Cadet Battalion, 6/11/1861 (The cadets assisted in training the raw recruits for the 4th Brigade Georgia Volunteers.)

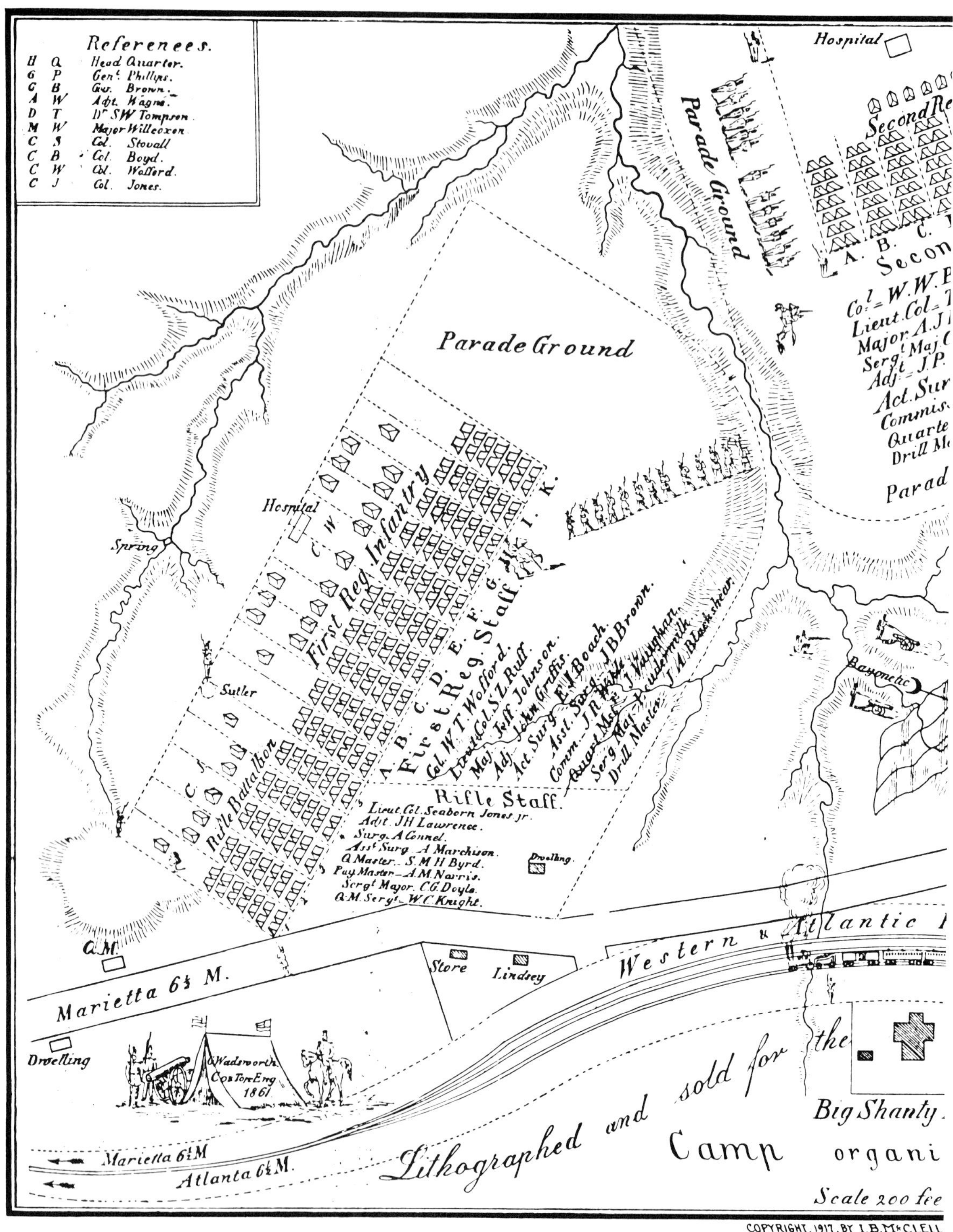

The Georgia Military Institute was organized at Marietta, Georgia, in 1851, by Colonel A. V. Brumby; chartered at the session of the General Assembly in the winter of 1851-1852, and modeled after the U.S. Military Academy at West Point.

During the war between the states CAMP McDONALD was established, including the Georgia Military Institute

CAMP M

A School of Instruction for the

His Excellency Governor Joseph

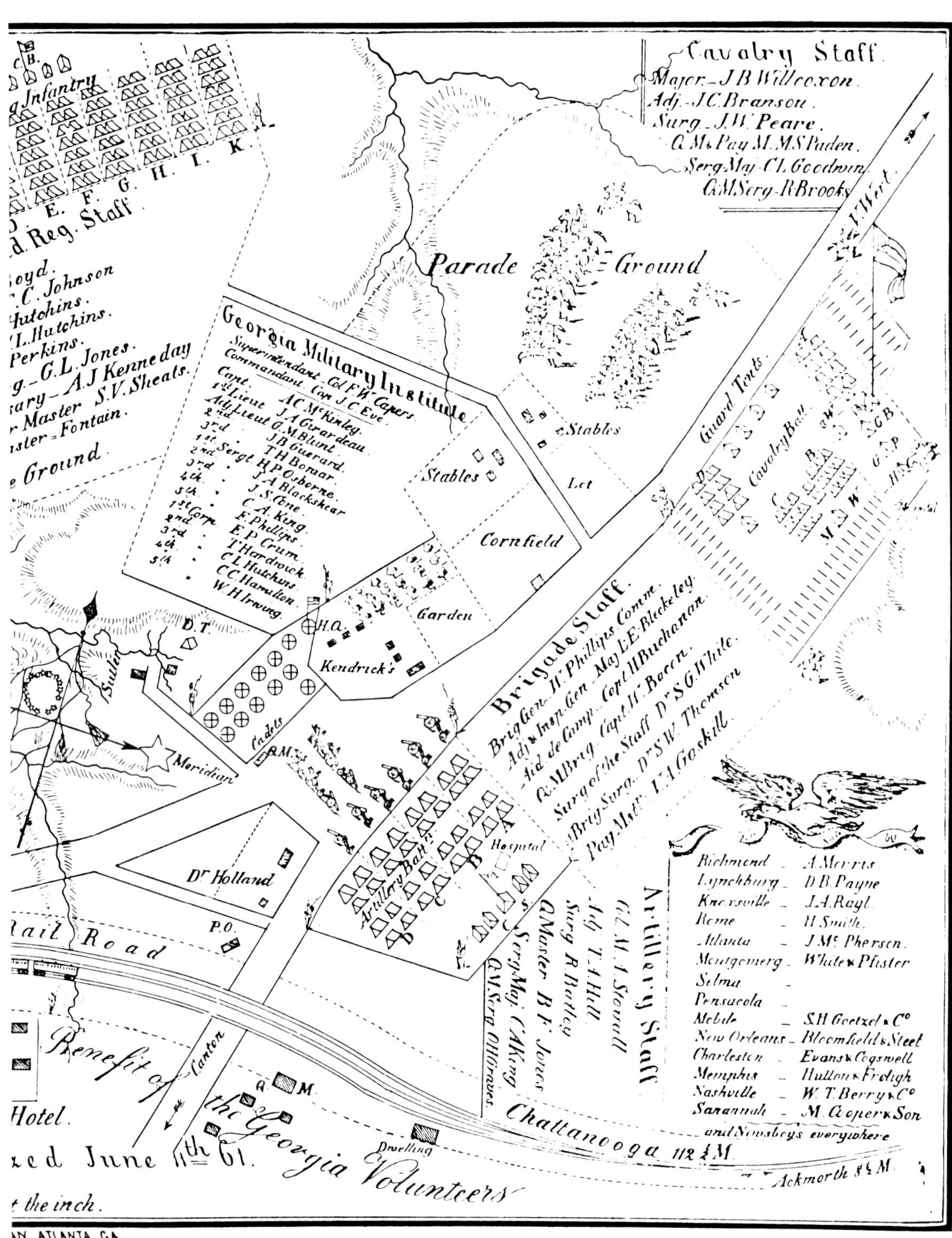

ᶜDONALD

4th Brigade Georgia Volunteers.

E. Brown, Commander in Chief.

grounds and extending to Big Shanty (now called Kennesaw). Here recruits for the Confederate Army were drilled by the cadets and new regiments organized.

During the campaign from Dalton to the sea in 1864 the Georgia Military Institute cadets served with great credit. Camp McDonald was destroyed by Sherman and the school was never revived.   **Joseph Tyrone Derry.**

DITION, 1917

4th Brigade Georgia Volunteers, 6/11/1861-7/10/1861 (The 4th Brigade later became the 18th & 19th Regiments Georgia Volunteer Infantry, Phillip's Legion, the 3rd Battalion Georgia Volunteer Infantry and the Cherokee Light Artillery.)

Georgia Artillery Battalion, 6/11/1861-7/10/1861 (This was a part of the 4th Brigade Georgia Volunteers. This unit later becomes Stovall's 3rd Battalion Georgia Volunteer Infantry, with the Cherokee Light Artillery attached.)

Cherokee Light Artillery, 6/11/1861-7/10/1861 (They were a part of the Georgia Artillery Bn.)

1st Regiment Georgia Volunteer Cavalry, Co. G, 4/29/1862

3rd Regiment Georgia Volunteer Cavalry, Co. F, 6/11/1862

3rd Battalion Georgia Volunteer Infantry, 6/29/1861-8/7/1861

9th Battalion Georgia Volunteer Infantry, 3/18/1862-4/18/1862

1st (Galt's) Regiment Georgia State Line, 2/16/1863-2/20/1863 (The unit organized here.)

7th Regiment Infantry Georgia State Guards, 8/1/1863

18th Regiment Georgia Volunteer Infantry, 6/23/1861-8/3/1861

19th Regiment Georgia Volunteer Infantry, 7/25/1861

22nd Regiment Georgia Volunteer Infantry, 8/27/1861-11/15/1861

23rd Regiment Georgia Volunteer Infantry, 8/27/1861-11/15/1861

24th Regiment Georgia Volunteer Infantry, Co. A, 9/4/1861 (The order for the 24th Georgia to report to Camp McDonald was rescinded and they were ordered straight to Virginia. See Camp Randolph.)

34th Regiment Georgia Volunteer Infantry, 5/13/1862-6/5/1862

39th Regiment Georgia Volunteer Infantry, 3/18/1862-4/18/1862

40th Regiment Georgia Volunteer Infantry, 3/10/1862-4/18/1862

41st Regiment Georgia Volunteer Infantry, 3/15/1862-4/18/1862

42nd Regiment Georgia Volunteer Infantry, 3/10/1862-4/13/1862

43rd Regiment Georgia Volunteer Infantry, 3/10/1862-4/10/1862

52nd Regiment Georgia Volunteer Infantry, 3/13/1862-4/18/1862

56th Regiment Georgia Volunteer Infantry, 5/13/1862-6/15/1862 (Part of the regiment left on June 2, 1862.)

Phillips' Legion, Infantry Battalion & Cavalry Battalion, 7/5/1861-8/3/1861 (The Legion moved directly to Camp Davis, Lynchburg, Virginia, on August 3, 1861.)

Sources:

GMI Cadets, *History of the Atlanta Ladies Memorial Association, 1866-1946, Markers and Monuments*, By Alberta Malone

4th Brig GV, RWC, 6/7/1861 & 8/9/1861

GABn, RWC, 6/7/1861 & 8/9/1861

CLA, RWC, 6/7/1861 & 8/9/1861

1st GVC, GDAH, CSR, 253/74

3rd GVC, GDAH, 283/24, Julius L. Dowda

3rd Bn GVI, GDAH, CSR, 254/123

9th Bn GVI, GDAH, 283/32, Hezekiah M. McCorkle

1st GSL, GDAH, AGLB, #13

7th GSG, GDAH, CSR, 255/42

18th GVI, EU, #20, Tom Dowtin

19th GVI, GDAH, CSR, 256/7

22nd GVI, GDAH, CSR, 256/28; RWC, 11/8/1861; O.R., Series IV, Vol. 1, 575
23rd GVI, GDAH, 283/25 William. W. Fisher; RWC, 11/8/1861
24th GVI, ASB, 9/4/1861 & 9/18/1861
34th GVI, GDAH, CSR, 256/100; SC, 6/8/1862
39th GVI, GDAH, 283/32, Hezekiah M. McCorkle
40th GVI, GDAH, 283/32, Hezekiah M. McCorkle
41st GVI, GDAH, 160/57, John C. Curtwright; 283/32, Hezekiah M. McCorkle
42nd GVI, GDAH, CSR, 257/13; SC, 4/22/1862
43rd GVI, *Men & Things*, By Hiram Parks Bell; GDAH, CSR, 257/18
52nd GVI, GDAH, 9/79, Col. Wier Boyd
56th GVI, GDAH, 171/7, Alvin Chandler; 283/30, James M. Kugler
PL, GDAH, 283/44, J. S. Wood; 9/79, Ben & Augustus Boyd

442   Camp McEnery
Chatham County, Georgia

The camp was located two miles from Savannah.
Georgia Troops:
1st Georgia Regulars, Co. D, Read's Artillery, 11/10/1862-12/31/1862
Source:
GDAH, CSR, 254/67

443   Camp McHenry
Beaufort County, South Carolina

The camp was located about one mile from Red Bluff and four or five miles from Proctor's Point. This is probably the same as Camp Red Bluff.
Georgia Troops:
47th Regiment Georgia Volunteer Infantry, 2/26/1863-4/13/1863 (Companies A, B & K left Camp McHenry on April 13, 1863, and camped three miles west of Hardeeville, at the battery by the side of the Savannah River. Their camp was right by the side of the railroad, 300-400 yards from where the train stopped.)
Sources:
GDAH, CSR, 257/42; 199/74, Eli and Jonas Proctor

444   Camp McIntosh
Wayne County, North Carolina

The camp was located three miles east of Goldsboro near the Atlantic & North Carolina Railroad. The camp was named after Gen. James McIntosh who fell at the battle of Elkhorn, Arkansas.
Georgia Troops:
44th Regiment Georgia Volunteer Infantry, 4/11/1862-5/28/1862
49th Regiment Georgia Volunteer Infantry, Cos. A, B, D, E, F, G & K, 4/9/1862-5/24/1862 (All the other companies were at Camp Mason.)
Troup Artillery, 3/21/1862-4/5/1862
Sources:

44th GVI, *History of the Doles-Cook Brigade, Army of Northern Virginia, 1861-1865*, By Henry W. Thomas
49th GVI, GDAH, CSR, 257/56; SFU, 4/29/1862; CG, 4/23/1862
TA, ASB, 4/9/1862

445   **Camp McIntosh**
Henrico County, Virginia
   The camp was located two miles below Richmond on the Darbytown Road, near a cool spring.
Georgia Troops:
15th Regiment Georgia Volunteer Infantry, 7/8/1862-7/28/1862 & 8/10/1862-8/13/1862 (On August 13, 1862, Toomb's Brigade moved by train to Gordonsville.)
Sources:
GDAH, CSR, 255/108; 53/64, Ivy Duggan

446   **Camp McIntyre**
Chatham County, Georgia
   The camp was located near Savannah.
Georgia Troops:
12th Regiment Georgia Militia, 1/24/1864
Source:
GDAH, 283/23, Dickey Family Collection

447   **Camp McKee**
Camden County, Georgia
   The camp was located four miles from St. Marys and twenty miles from Camp Fort.
Georgia Troops:
Capt. Hopkins Company of mounted partisan rangers, 11/20/1862-11/28/1862 (The company later became Co. A, 24th Battalion Georgia Cavalry.)
Source:
GDAH, CSR, 254/11

448   **Camp McLaws**
James County, Virginia
   The camp was located near Williamsburg.
Georgia Troops:
10th Regiment Georgia Volunteer Infantry, 6/25/1861
Source:
DU, Andrew J. McBride

449   **Camp McLaws**
Spotsylvania County, Virginia
   The camp was located near Fredericksburg. This camp was also refered to as Camp Fredericksburg, No. 1. The infantry and cavalry battalions permanently separated on April 14, 1863.

Georgia Troops:
Phillips' Legion, Infantry Battalion, 3/29/1863-4/28/1863
Sources:
KMNBPL, Ga.-2, W.R. Montgomery and Marcus L. Green

450   Camp McPace
Dougherty County, Georgia

The camp was located near Albany.
Georgia Troops:
Dougherty Hussars, 7/2/1861 (The company later became Co. D, Cobb's Legion, Cavalry Battalion.)
Source:
AP, 7/4/1861

451   Camp McTavis
Hamblen County, Tennessee

The camp was located near Russellville. This was the winter camp of the 16th Georgia while they were with Gen. Longstreet in East Tennessee.
Georgia Troops:
16th Regiment Georgia Volunteer Infantry, 2/2/1864
Source:
GDAH, UDC Books, Vol. II, 158

452   Camp Meadow
Henrico County, Virginia

The camp was located three miles north of Richmond.
Georgia Troops:
Cobb's Legion, Cavalry Battalion, 6/8/1862-6/25/1862, 7/5/1862-7/7/1862 &
7/20/1862-7/21/1862
Sources:
GDAH, 283/38, Jeremiah E. Ritch; 283/29, William Thomas Huff; AHC, Maj. Zachariah A. Rice;
Sketch of Cobb Legion Cavalry and Some Scenes Remembered, By Wiley C. Howard

453   Camp Mercer
Appling County, Georgia

Location not known. It is probably near Waynesville.
Georgia Troops:
4th (Clinch's) Regiment Georgia Volunteer Cavalry, 9/1863-12/1863 (This was the headquarters of the 4th Georgia Cavalry up to June, 1864.)
Clinch's Light Battery, 2/23/1864
Sources:
4th GVC, GDAH, CSR, 253/94
CLB, GDAH, CSR, 258/6

454   **Camp Mercer**
Chatham County, Georgia

This camp was located on Tybee Island and at this time was the regimental headquarters of the 1st Volunteer Regiment of Georgia.

Georgia Troops:

1st (Olmstead's) Volunteer Regiment of Georgia, 7/1861-10/26/1861

25th Regiment Georgia Volunteer Infantry, 7/22/1861-11/10/1861

2nd Battalion Georgia Cavalry, Co. A, Effingham Hussars, 9/7/1861-10/31/1861

Sources:

1st VRG, GDAH, CSR, 254/81; SR, 8/24/1861 & 10/17/1861; UNC, #1856, Charles H. Olmstead

25th GVI, GHS, #875, Claudius C. Wilson; GDAH, CSR, 256/49; SR, 8/26/1861

2nd Bn GC, GDAH, CSR, 253/87

455   **Camp Mercer**
Chatham County, Georgia

The camp was located, "on the East and near the Toll Gate of the White Bluff Road." This is at or near Camp Berrien.

Georgia Troops:

38th Regiment Georgia Volunter Infantry, 4/24/1862-6/6/1862

38th Regiment Georgia Volunter Infantry, Co. M, Jo Thompson Artillery, 4/24/1862

38th Regiment Georgia Volunter Infantry, Co. N, Chestatee Artillery, 4/24/1862 (The Chestatee Artillery and Jo Thompson Artillery were detached from the 38th Georgia Infantry on 6/6/1862, when the 38th Georgia left by train for Virginia.)

Sources:

GDAH, CSR, 256/121; SR, 6/4/1862; *Atlanta Historical Bulletin*, "War Diary of Cornelius R. Hanleiter," Edited by Elma S. Kurtz

456   **Camp Mercer**
Chatham County, Georgia

This camp was located near Battery Walker.

Georgia Troops:

50th Regiment Georgia Volunteer Infantry, detachment, 6/25/1862-7/20/1862

Source:

GDAH, 215/40, Curry Hill Plantation Records

457   **Camp Mercer**
Chatham County, Georgia
The location of the camp was near Savannah. The exact location is not known.
Georgia Troops:
21st Battalion Georgia Cavalry, 8/1862-11/26/1862
Source:
GDAH, CSR, 254/9

458   **Camp Mercer**
Chatham County, Georgia
The camp was located three and one-half miles from Savannah, on the Skidaway Road.
Georgia Troops:
Columbus Artillery, Croft's Battery Georgia Light Artillery, 11/17/1862-4/11/1863
Sources:
GDAH, CSR, 254/50; SR, 1/5/1863

459   **Camp Mercer**
Chatham County, Georgia
William H. Hill wrote in his letter of December 5, 1862, from Camp Mercer, "We are camped about 400 yards from our old camp, (Camp Brown near Ft. Brown and behind the Cathedral Cemetery) about one and one-half miles from town."
12th Battalion Georgia Volunteers, 11/25/1862-4/14/1863
Sources:
GDAH, CSR, 254/31-34; WL, Loc. 05-31 87-06, William H. Hill Collection

460   **Camp Mercer**
Chatham County, Georgia
The exact location of this camp is not known. This may be the same as Camp Mercer, Appling County.
Georgia Troops:
Clinch's Battery Georgia Light Artillery, 12/18/1863-5/1864
Sources:
GDAH, CSR, 254/50

461   **Camp Mercer**
Liberty County, Georgia
The camp was located near Riceboro. The 24th Battalion Georgia Cavalry apparently organized in this camp.
Georgia Troops;
24th Battalion Georgia Cavalry, 1/11/1863-3/17/1863
Capt. Anderson's Co. Partisan Rangers, 7/21/62-8/31/62
Capt. T. S. Hopkin's Co., Mercer Partisan Rangers, 12/1862 (The company became Co. A of the 24th Bn. Ga. Cav. while in this camp.)
Sources:
GDAH, CSR, 254/11; SR, 5/7/1863

462   **Camp Mercer**
Prince William County, Virginia
   The camp was located near Manassas Junction.
Georgia Troops:
21st Regiment Georgia Volunteer Infantry, 8/24/1861
Source:
GDAH, 283/20, William M. Butt

463   **Camp Meredith**
Henrico County, Virginia
   The camp was Located near Richmond. "We named our camp in honor of our fellow townsman,
James W. Meredith."
Georgia Troops:
10th Regiment Georgia Volunteer Infantry, Co. D, 6/4/1861
Source:
ADC&S, 6/11/1861

464   **Camp Milledge**
Culpeper County, Virginia
   The camp was located near Stevensburg.
Georgia Troops:
Milledge's Battery Georgia Light Artillery, 9/1863 & 11/4/1863 (formerly Blodget Flying
Artillery)
Source:
GDAH, CSR, 254/59

465   **Camp Millen**
Chatham County, Georgia
   The camp was located on a bluff one-half mile towards Ft. Jackson from Causton's Bluff.
Georgia Troops:
20th Battalion Georgia Cavalry, most companies, 6/4/1862-10/16/1862
Sources:
GDAH, CSR, 254/6; 283/23, Dickey Family Letters

466   **Camp Miller**
Chatham County, Georgia
   The camp was located one mile from Miller Station, Station No. 1, on the Savannah, Albany &
Gulf Railroad, and on the west side of the Grove River. This camp was three miles from Camp
Croft.
Georgia Troops:
Columbus Artillery, Croft's Battery Georgia Light Artillery, 8/13/1862-11/17/1862
Source:
GDAH, CSR, 254/50

467   **Camp Miller**

Chatham County, Georgia

The camp was located near the Gulf Railroad Depot. This is possibly the same camp as the previous Camp Miller at Miller Station.

Georgia Troops:

20th Battalion Georgia Cavalry, Co. C, 6/25/1862

21st Battalion Georgia Cavalry, Co. C, 6/27/1862

Sources:

20th Bn GC, SDMN, 6/27/1862

21st Bn GC, SDMN, 6/28/1862

STRAYED,

FROM the camp of Capt R. G. Miller, known as Camp Miller, near the Gulf Depot, Savannah, a medium sized roan HORSE, about fourteen and a half or fifteen hands high, both hind feet and right fore foot white, stands a little bent in the fore legs, and feet very flat. Any one finding him will be suitably rewarded by conveying intelligence of the fact to me.

G. O. WARNOCK,

Je28—3   Lieutenant Miller Rangers.

468   **Camp Miller**

Henrico County, Virginia

The camp was located near Richmond. See Camp Cobb.

Georgia Troops:

Cobb's Legion Infantry Battalion, Co. E, 8/10/1861-8/14/1861 (Company E, had just arrived in Richmond on August 10, 1861, and possibly had not joined the Cobb Legion in Camp Cobb.)

Source:

GDAH, 21/29, John William Rheney, Jr.

469   **Camp Milton**

Duval County, Florida

The camp was located at McGirt's Creek, about ten miles west of Jacksonville, six miles below Baldwin.

Georgia Troops:

28th Battalion Georgia Siege Artillery, 2/27/1864-4/29/1864

1st Georgia Regulars, 2/21/1864-4/1/1864 & 4/3/1864-4/19/1864

12th Battalion Georgia Volunteers, 4/5/1864-4/18/1864

23rd Regiment Georgia Volunteer Infantry, 2/26/1864-4/19/1864

27th Regiment Georgia Volunteer Infantry, 2/26/1864-4/19/1864

28th Regiment Georgia Volunteer Infantry, 4/10/1864

32nd Regiment Georgia Vomunteer Infantry, 2/26/1864-4/19/1864

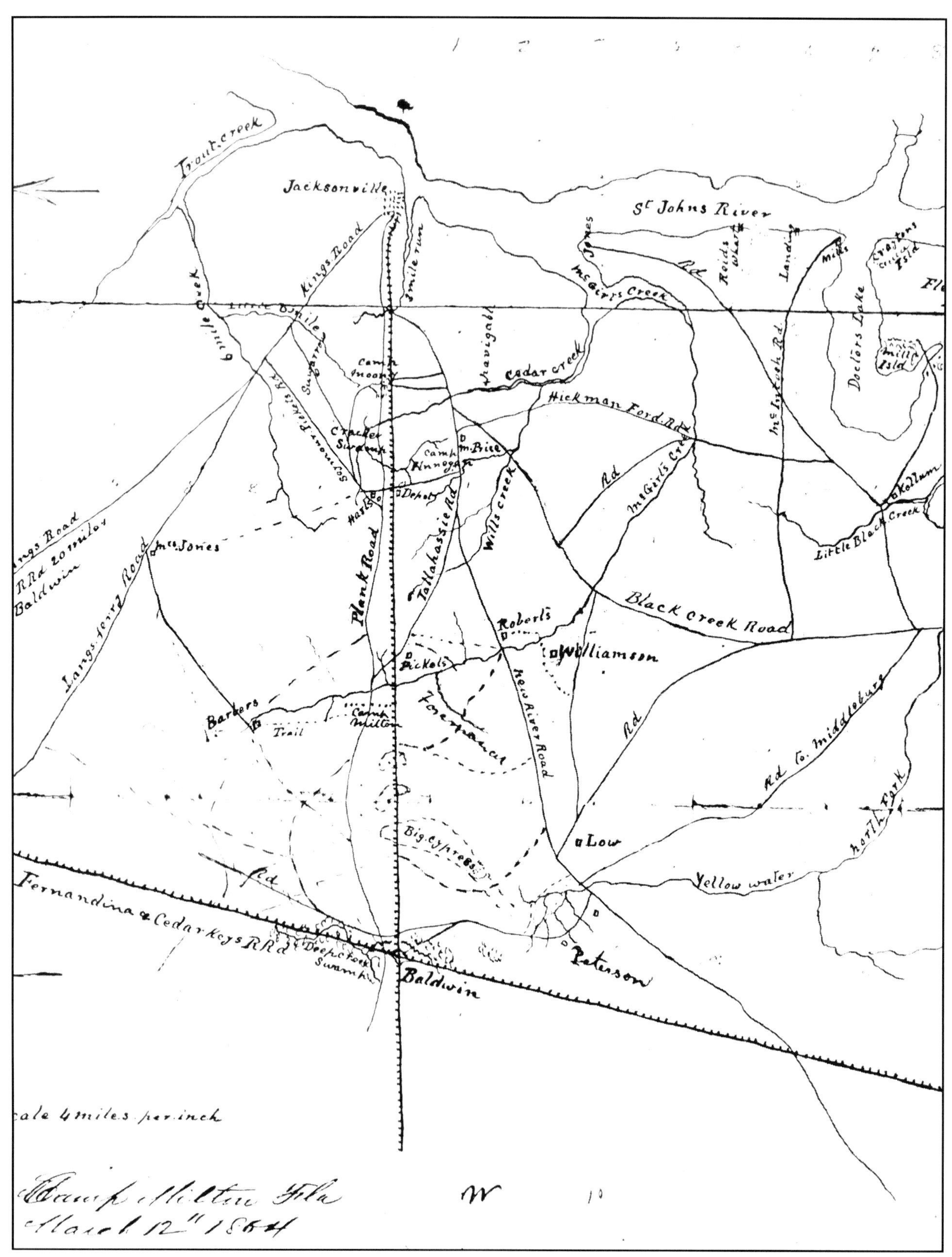

Map of the Jacksonville, Florida area and Camp Milton
map courtesy of The Florida State Archives

64th Regiment Georgia Volunteer Infantry, 2/26/1864-4/19/1864
Sources:
28th Bn GSA, GDAH, CSR, 254/43
1st GR, GDAH, CSR, 254/67
12th Bn GV, GDAH, CSR, 254/33
23rd GV, GDAH, CSR, 256/36
27th GVI, GDAH, CSR, 256/66
28th GVI, CDT, 4/26/1864
32nd GVI, O.R., Vol. 35
64th GVI, O.R., Vol. 35

Private James Leckie, Co. D, 27th Regiment Georgia Volunteer Infantry. Enlisted February 23, 1862. In 1864 he enlisted in Graham's Battalion Georgia Militia.

photo courtesy of Kerry Elliott

470 **Camp Miserable**
Orange County, Virginia

The camp was near Orange Court House.
Georgia Troops:
11th Battalion Georgia Light Artillery, 3/25/1862
Source:
P.C., letter of Joseph M. Little

471 **Camp Misery.**
Claiborne County, Tennessee.

The camp was located near Cumberland Gap.
Georgia Troops:
5th Regiment Georgia Volunteer Infantry, 3/17/1862
Source:
DU, William McCoy

472 **Camp Mobley**
Floyd County, Georgia

The camp was located three miles below Rome on the Cave Springs Road. See map of Rome.
Georgia Troops:
10th Regiment Cavalry, Georgia State Guards, Floyd's Regiment, 10/2/1863-2/2/1864
Source:
Dekalb County Historical Society, Diary of Benjamin T. Hunter

473   **Camp Montgomery**

Muscogee County, Georgia

The camp was located near Columbus.

Georgia Troops:

Jackson Avengers, 6/29/1861-7/9/1861 (The company later became Co. F, 3rd Battalion Georgia Volunteer Infantry.)

Gen. Imboden's Command, recruits from the Columbus area, 1/10/1864 (Capt. F. P. Crutchfield was recruiting men for a company of mounted riflemen in this camp.)

Sources:

JA, CDT, 6/29/1861 & 7/9/1861

IC, CDT, 1/29/1864

474   **Camp Montpelier**

Orange County, Virginia

The camp was near Montpelier, the estate of President James Madison, about seven miles west of Orange Court House.

Georgia Troops:

2nd Regiment Georgia Volunteer Infantry, 4/4/1862-4/11/1862 (The regiment left on April 11, 1862, for Yorktown with the 1st Brigade.)

Sources:

CE, 4/22/1862; RWC, 4/18/1862

475   **Camp Moore**

Bibb County, Georgia

The camp was located near Macon.

Georgia Troops:

Blount's Cavalry, 2/6/1864

Source:

GDAH, 283/48, Bibb County file

476   **Camp Moore**

Rockingham County, Virginia

The camp was located on the farm of Thomas Moore, four miles southwest of New Market, and three-fourths mile west of Valley Pike (1864). This was a camp of Gordon's Division which included Evan's Brigade of Georgians, Terry's Brigade of Virginians and York's Brigade of Louisianians.

Georgia Troops:

13th Regiment Georgia Volunteer Infantry, 11/8/1864-11/10/1864 & 11/14/1864-12/1864

26th Regiment Georgia Volunteer Infantry, 11/8/1864-11/10/1864 & 11/14/1864-12/1864

31st Regiment georgia Volunteer Infantry, 11/8/1864-11/10/1864 & 11/14/1864-12/1864

38th Regiment Georgia Volunteer Infantry, 11/8/1864-11/10/1864 & 11/14/1864-12/1864

60th Regiment Georgia Volunteer Infantry, 11/8/1864-11/10/1864 & 11/14/1864-12/1864

61st Regiment Georgia Volunteer Infantry, 11/8/1864-11/10/1864 & 11/14/1864-12/1864

12th Battalion Georgia Volunteers, 11/8/1864-11/10/1864 & 11/14/1864-12/1864

Source:

Intrepid Warrior, Compiled and Edited by Robert Grier Stephens, Jr.

477   **Camp Morgan**

Chatham County, Georgia

The camp was located near Savannah.

Georgia Troops:

18th Infantry Battalion, 7/1862-12/14/1862 (Savannah Volunteer Guards)

Sources:

GDAH, 32/56, Muster Roll; CSR, 256/3

478   **Camp Morris**

Henrico County, Virginia

The camp was in a farm yard, five miles from Richmond. Captain Joel C. Barnett, Co. B, Cobb's Legion, Infantry Battalion, was writing a letter when the opening shots were fired in one of the seven days battles May 27, 1862, and described what he heard.

> I hear the booming of cannon now on our left perhaps 2 miles - We go on picket - to night after a respite of 2 days - We still without tents - I have a fly - it rained all last night It is now clear & pleasant - We are in a farm yard. The cannon has ceased & I now hear the pop of musketry - I suppose it is near Mechanicsville I judge it pretty sharp skirmish - it does not appear to be a very large force engaged, but quite determined as it very regular & continued -

Georgia Troops:

Cobb's Legion, Infantry Battalion, 5/27/1862

Source:

GDAH, 160/74, Joel Crawford Barnett

479   **Camp Morrison**
                                     Bartow County, Georgia
     The camp was located near Cartersville.
Georgia Troops:
1st Regiment Georgia Volunteer Cavalry, 3/31/1862-4/4/1862
Source:
GDAH, CSR, 253/74; MR, 279/64

480   **Camp Morton**
                                   Scott County, Mississippi
     The camp was located near Morton.
Georgia Troops:
47th Regiment Georgia Volunteer Infantry, 7/19/1863-8/27/1863
Source:
Not Known

481   **Camp Morton's Ford**
                                    Orange County, Virginia
     The camp was near Morton's Ford on the Rapidan River, about fifteen miles northeast of
Orange Court House.
Georgia Troops:
12th Regiment Georgia Volunteer Infantry, 9/15/1863-10/7/1863 (The 12th Georgia was on
picket duty.)
Sources:
SDMN, 10/20/1863; GDAH, CSR, 255/86; *A Post of Honor, The Pryor Letters, 1861-1863*,
Edited and narrated by Charles R. Adams, Jr.

482   **Camp Mossy Creek**
                                    White County, Georgia
     The camp was on the Mossy Creek Campground on the Hall and White County lines.
Georgia Troops:
11th Regiment Georgia Volunteer Cavalry, Co. E, 5/2/1864-5/4/1864
13th Battalion Georgia Cavalry, 5/20/1864
Sources:
11th GVC, GDAH, CSR, 253/119
13th Bn GC, ASB, 4/27/1864

483   **Camp Mountain Run**
                                    Orange County, Virginia
     The camp was on Mountain Run, east of Orange Court House.
Georgia Troops:
Milledge's Battery Georgia Light Artillery, 1/1864
Source:
GDAH, CSR, 254/59

484   **Camp Mud Hole**
York County, Virginia

   The camp was a temporary camp while the men were building huts for winter quarters at Camp
Marion.
Georgia Troops:
Cobb's Legion, Cavalry Battalion, 10/21/1861
Source:
GDAH, 283/29, Henry Francis Jones

485   **Camp Murphy**
Upson County, Georgia

   The camp was located on the Upson County Campground, seven miles east of Thomaston and
one mile south of The Rock, Georgia. It is likely that other companies from Upson County, or the
surrounding area used this camp also.
Georgia Troops:
Holloway Grays, Summer 1861 (The company later became Co. E, 3rd Battalion Georgia
Volunteer Infantry, then later Co. C, 37th Regiment Georgia Volunteer Infantry.)
Source:
GDAH, 283/33, J. E. F. Matthews

486   **Camp Neely**
Chatham County, Georgia
The camp was located near the Catholic Cemetery (Cathedral Cemetery) east of Savannah.
Georgia Troops:
1st (Olmstead's) Volunteer Regiment of Georgia, DeKalb Riflemen and three other companies, 1/9/1863
Source:
GDAH, CSR, 254/81

487   **Camp Nelson**
Gordon County, Georgia
The camp was located near Calhoun.
Georgia Troops:
Smith's Legion, 6/30/1862-7/1/1862
Source:
GDAH, CSR, 258/51

488   **Camp News**
Henrico County, Virginia
The camp was located five miles from Richmond within the Confederate lines. A letter of January 1, 1865, states, " we have been here nearly three months."
Georgia Troops:
9th Regiment Georgia Volunteer Infantry, 10/1864-1/7/1865 (The 9th Georgia was in Anderson's Brigade. The brigade included the 7th, 8th, 9th, 11th & 59th Regiments from Georgia.)
Sources:
GDAH, 194/3, Will F. Montgomery; EU, #483, Jonathan LaFayette Oxford

489   **Camp Ninevah**
Warren County, Virginia
The camp was near Nineva, seven miles from Front Royal and eleven miles from Winchester. See Atlas Plate V, 5.
Georgia Troops:
11th Battalion Georgia Light Artillery, 10/5/1862-11/1/1862
Sources:
GDAH, CSR, 254/26; UGA, Ms. 15, Florence Hodgson Heidler Collection, Frank M. C. Coker letters

490   **Camp Nix**
Chatham County, Georgia
This was a picket camp located at the Great Ogeechee River railroad bridge.
Georgia Troops:
25th Regiment Georgia Volunteer Infantry, Co. D, detachment, 8/23/1862-10/1862
Sources:
PC, letter of James W. Rogers; GDAH, CSR, 256/54, James W. Rogers

Camp Norman
Fairfax County, Virginia

The camp was located near Centreville.

Georgia Troops:

11th Battalion Georgia Light Artillery, Lane's Battery, 1/10/1862-3/8/1862 (This battery was previously Co. A, 9th Regiment Georgia Volunteer Infantry, and was converted to artillery on December 13, 1861.)

Source:

PC, *Diary of James Hillhouse Alexander*

492   **Camp Oakwood Cemetery**
                                  Henrico County, Virginia
The camp was near Richmond's Oakwood Cemetery.
Georgia Troops:
11th Battalion Georgia Light Artillery, 6/25/1862-8/19/1862 (Different batteries of this battalion
were in and out of this camp during this time period.)
Sources:
EU, #122, Morgan Callaway letters; PC, various sources

493   **Camp Ogeechee**
                                  Chatham County, Georgia
    This camp was located near the Ogeechee River railroad bridge.
Georgia Troops:
Terrell Light Artillery, Brooks Battery, 12/1/1862-4/5/1863
Source:
GDAH, CSR, 254/47

494   **Camp Oglethorpe**
                                  Escambia County, Florida
    The camp was located one mile from the beach across the Pensacola Bay from Ft. Pickens.
Georgia Troops:
Washington Artillery, 4/27/1861-5/1/1861
Source:
GJ&M, 5/8/1861

495   **Camp Oglethorpe**
                                   Bibb County, Georgia
    The camp faced 7th Street on the northwest, Pine Street on the northeast, Hawthorne Street on
the southwest, and a swamp on the southeast. The camp covered twelve acres and was the site of
the old fairgrounds in Macon. See Chapter II, and the story written about Camp Oglethorpe.
    A number of other companies and units used this camp for short periods of time while stopping
overnight in Macon.
    The camp was also used as a prison camp for Federal officers for a period of time. The
following article from *The Columbus Daily Times* of June 30, 1864, describes an attempted
escape by the Federal prisoners.

> Escape of Prisoners. - On Sunday night, says the *Macon Confederate*, the Yankee
> officers confined in Camp Oglethorpe succeeded in completing a subterranean tunnel they
> have supposed to have been working on for some time. - But it had not been finished many
> moments before it was discovered, It was supposed yesterday that only one man succeeded
> in getting away, although it was not positively known. We heard it stated yesterday that the
> officers of the guard knew all about the progress of the tunnel long before it was completed
> but suffered it to go on in order to administer to those who might attempt to make an
> escape through it, a wholesome lesson.

Vincent's New Map of Macon dated 1854 shows Camp Oglethorpe on the Fairgrounds
map courtesy of Joey Seguin

Georgia Troops:
Washington Artillery, 4/3/1861-4/13/1861
1st Independent Battalion of Georgia Volunteers, 4/3/1861-4/5/1861
1st (Ramsey's) Georgia Volunteer Infantry, 4/2/1861-4/5/1861
3rd Regiment Georgia Infantry Reserves, 4/1864 & 5/1864 (This unit was guarding federal prisoners.)
5th Regiment Georgia Infantry Reserves, 12/21/1863-6/7/1864 (This unit was guarding federal prisoners.)
5th Regiment Georgia Volunteer Infantry, 5/7/1861-5/9/1861
10th Battalion Georgia Volunteer Infantry, 5/28/1862-12/1862 (This unit was guarding federal prisoners.)
Sources:
WA, CG, 4/3/1861; ADC&S, 4/13/1861
1st Ind Bn GVI, SDMN, 4/6/1861; GJ&M, 4/10/1861
1st GVI, SDMN, 4/6/1861; RWC, 4/12/1861; UNC, #510, A. J. Miller
10th Bn GVI, GDAH, 283/26, Martin Hambrick; 78/2, William J. Moseley; TCE, 12/2/1862
3rd Bn GIR, GDAH, CSR, 254/121
5th GIR, GDAH, CSR, 255/18
5th GVI, FU, 5/7/1861; UP, 6/1/1861

496   Camp Olmstead
Chatham County, Georgia

   The camp was located near Savannah.
Georgia Troops:
1st (Olmstead's) Volunteer Regiment of Georgia, DeKalb Riflemen, 11/9/1862-12/6/1862
Source:
GDAH, CSR, 254/81

497   Camp Orange Court House
Orange County, Virginia
The following extract is from a letter of W. S. Moore to his sister, Miss Huldah Annie Fain.

> Our camp is situated on a little mountain called Clarks Mountain, an elevation of some hundred feet from the level with extensive vallies on either side affords a splendid view of the surounding country. Have a cool breeze all the time & the best of cold mountain water. There being no enemy near here our duty only consists in drilling & Guard details which is reasonably light. The time is past very pleasantly. Have preaching every day & prayer meeting at night in a large church near camps. The house a large brick building furnished with Louis floor & gallery sufficient to contain three or four hundred people is crowded to over flowing each hour since much good may be accomplished even here in the Army where wickness has so richly abounded.

Georgia Troops:
44th Regiment Georgia Volunteer Infantry, 5/22/1863
Source:
DU, Huldah Annie (Fain) Briant letters

498   **Camp Palmyra**

Liberty County, Georgia

The camp was located at the Palmyra plantation on the banks of Dickinson Creek, eight and one-half miles from Riceboro post office.

Georgia Troops:

1st Cavalry Battalion, Liberty Independent Troop, 5/17/1862-11/1/1862 & 7/1/1863-8/16/1863

20th Battalion Georgia Cavalry, Headquarters, 8/1863-10/1863, Cos. A, B, E & F, 10/1863

Sources:

1st CBn, GDAH, CSR, 253/79

20th Bn GC, GDAH, CSR, 254/6-8

499   **Camp Patterson**

Bryan County, Georgia

The camp was located on the Patterson plantation north of Fort McAllister. See Atlas Plate LXIX, 4.

Georgia Troops:

Howell's Battery Georgia Light Artillery, 11/26/1862

Sources:

GDAH, 261/2, Jonas N. Wood

500   **Camp Paulina**

Spotsylvania County, Virginia

Camp "Paulina," near Fredericksburg, Va.

May 11th, 1863.

You will perceive we have named this camp in honor of the accomplished and patriotic Secretary of the "Ladies Volunteer Association" of Athens. It is a compliment richly merited, not only by her indefatigable energy in our behalf, but by the graceful and eloquent terms in which she has been pleased to convey to us the willing zeal of the Association to aid us with all their resources. She and her fair coworkers have nobly "illustrated Georgia," at home. May heaven's choicest blessings rest upon them all, and may all survive to see and enjoy the glorious fruition of their prayers and works in a free, happy, prosperous people - with their sons, their husbands, their brothers, their fathers, and their *sweethearts* safely return to the loving voices and bright smiles of "Home sweet Home."

The above is an extract from a letter published in the *Athens Southern Banner*, May 27, 1863, and signed by A. W. R. (Reese)

Georgia Troops:

Troup Artillery, 5/11/1863-5/21/1863

Sources:

ASB, 5/27/1863 & 5/18/1864

501   **Camp Peace**

McIntosh County, Georgia

The camp was located near Darien.

Georgia Troops:

1st Battalion Georgia Cavalry, McIntosh Cavalry, 5/12/1862-8/31/1862

Source:

GDAH, CSR, 253/79

502   **Camp Pegram**

Tennessee

Location not known. It is believed to be near Kingston or Loudon.

Georgia Troops:

1st Regiment Georgia Volunteer Cavalry, Co. H, 4/19/1862-6/30/1862

Sources:

GDAH, CSR, 253/74; MR, 279/64

503   **Camp Pemberton**

Charleston County, South Carolina

The camp was located at White Point Battery, White Point Garden, Charleston.

Georgia Troops:

26th Regiment Georgia Volunteer Infantry, 7/21/1862 (Lawton's Brigade was passing through Charleston enroute to Virginia.)

46th Regiment Georgia Volunteer Infantry, 5/17/1862-10/23/1862 & 2/12/1863-5/6/1863

Sources:

26th GVI, GDAH, 283/44, John W. Wilkinson

46th GVI, GDAH, CSR, 257/35; AGLB # 15; ADC&S, 5/20/1862

504   **Camp Pembroke (Pembrook)**

Chatham County, Georgia

The camp was located six and one-half miles below Savannah, directly on the river. See Camp Bartow in Chatham County.

Private William A. Moseley of Capt. Barnwell's Battery, Georgia Light Artillery described the camp in an extract of his letter of February 1, 1864.

> We are on the Savannah River or a branch of it - 16 miles from the Atlantic Ocean. The country is level and swampy, a considerable portion covered with water at this season of the year, the growth is principally pine and the most beautiful evergreens, but not withstanding this, it has a gloomy sombre aspect, from the fact that almost every tree is clothed in a drapery of long hanging moss sweeping to every wind.

Georgia Troops:

30th Regiment Georgia Volunteer Infantry, Co. D, 4/1862

Maxwell's Battalion Georgia Light Artillery, (This was the Battalion headquarters at this time.)

Maxwell's Battalion included:

Barnwell's Battery, 1/11/1864-2/21/1864

Daniel's Battery, 3/12/1864

Maxwell's Battery Georgia Light Artillery, 10/23/1863-10/26/63 & 5/2/1864 (The Battery was also known as Regular Battery Georgia Artillery.)

Sources:

30th GVI, GDAH, CSR, 256/85

MBn GLA, GDAH, CSRs, 254/47, 254/51, 254/58, 256/85 & 258/6; 291/79, William A. Moseley

505   **Camp Pender**

Orange County, Virginia

The camp was located near Orange Court House.

Georgia Troops:

45th Regiment Georgia Volunteer Infantry, 9/5/1863-10/4/1863

Sources:

MCU, 9/22/1863; WL, Loc. 05-31 90-19, Dumbleton, Jeanne-Humphries Collection, Thomas Turner Raines letters

506   **Camp Pendleton**

Fairfax County, Virginia

The camp was located one mile from Centreville.

Georgia Troops:

11th Battalion Georgia Light Artillery, 1/1862 & 2/1862

Source:

GDAH, CSR, 254/26

507   **Camp Perdido**

Escambia County, Florida

The camp was located near Perdido Sound.

Georgia Troops:

36th (Villegipues) Regiment Georgia Volunteer Infantry, Co. K, 10/31/1861

Source:

GDAH, CSR, 256/116

508   **Camp Philips**

Chatham County, Georgia

The camp was located at Beaulieu plantation, on the Vernon River, ten miles below Savannah. See Camp Beaulieu.

Georgia Troops:

7th Battalion Georgia Volunteer Infantry, 2/21/1862-3/1/1862 (Previously the 7th Battalion was the 26th [Lamar's] Regiment Georgia Infantry. On 5/31/1862, the 7th Battalion became a part of the 61st Regiment Georgia Volunteer Infantry.)

27th Regiment Georgia Volunteer Infantry, 1/16/1862-5/29/1862 (The 27th Regiment became the 31st Regiment Georgia Volunteer Infantry in March, 1862.)

Sources:

27th GVI, GDAH, CSR, 256/89; 283/27, William W. Head

7th Bn GVI, GDAH, CSR, 257/113

509   **Camp Philips**

Glynn County, Georgia

The camp was located on St. Simons Island. This could be the the same as Camp Styles.
Georgia Troops:
27th Regiment Georgia Volunter Infantry, Co. A, 11/12/1861-12/1/1861
Source:
CDT, 11/18/1861

510   **Camp Phillips**

Henrico County, Virginia

The camp was located a few miles from Richmond.
Georgia Troops:
Phillips' Legion, Cavalry Battalion, 8/23/1862
Source:
GDAH, 57/65, John F. Milhollin

511   **Camp Pickens**

Prince William County, Virginia

The camp was located one and one-half miles from Manassas Junction on the road to Centreville.

The following letter was written to the mother of Henry Shackelford by Henry and two of his mess mates. Henry was appointed Regimental Musician and in Company A, 19th Regiment Georgia Volunteer Infantry. John Clegg drowned while skating January 4, 1862. W. H. Owen was 4th Sergeant and discharged, disability at Lynchburg General Hospital February 18, 1863.

Camp Pickens
Sept. 28th, 1861
My Dear Mother,

I now seat myself in my tent this beautiful morning to comply with your request relative to the nice and much needed little presents. They all come safe and sound after being 12 days on the road. They came in good time as did the money from father and brother. We have not been paid off yet by the Government. I read the letter over to my esteemed friends Clegg and Owens. I gave Owens a pair of the drawers and Clegg the socks. You cannot have the least conseption how glad it makes us poor boys to get letters and presents from our dear old home & far off friends. You know I used to dislike to get long letters but things have now changed entirely.

I wished I could get a long letter everyday. I wrote Bro. W. a long letter and mailed it today thanking him for his brotherly kindness. Those little favors I never can forget.

Col. Boyd is going to move our encampment 2 1/2 miles nearer to Centreville on tomorrow then we are going to build small houses for winter quarters. We had a terrible storm yesterday which blew one half of the tents down in the reg. As for my tent it is as comfortable as a parlor. My health was never better and I am in good spirits. My friend, Clegg will write you a few lines. Direct your letters to me at this place care Co. A, 19th Ga. reg. Manassas Va. Col W.W. Boyd, Jr.

Your Son,
Henry Shackelford

Marry - they came in the "nick of time" and have added greatly to my comfort. I am looking for a box from my dear Mother and will divide with him.

Mrs. Shackelford,

I take great pleasure in writting a few lines to you in your sons Henrys letter and thank you kindly for your present to me and also for your wishes for our welfare. Together we are getting along well with the exception of disagreeable weather. We have had very warm weather until yesterday when it was very strong & cold & did quite considerable damage to our encampments but I am glad to say that the sun has shown out this morning with warm and cheering rays and we feel in better spirits and am use to these tricks and hardships which a soldier has to encounter in times of war. We are in hopes that the war will soon be at an end although there is not much prospect as we are constantly receiving news to be in readiness to march forward to meet the invading foe who are coming to battle against us again. Hoping you will pardon my short epistle and wishing you the best of health & prosperity, I remain yours truly,

John Clegg

Mrs Shackelford

Dear Madam

My friends Henry and John have by writting first anticipated me in all I could say as regards to our camp & its incidents - but while they were at their agreeable employment I found out something and did not comunicate in time to be of use to them orders where issued last evening for all citizens, sutlers (that are not connected with regiments) & such person that are not one of the army to leave by 10 O'clk of this morning and I assure you there is quite a stir of preparation amonst those itinerant hucksters & peddlers when have since the occupation of this place been on hand to swindle the Georgia Volunteers by selling them mean articles at exorbitant prices - I for your edification site one article - common negro brogans - price in Ga. $1.25 per pr. - worth here $3.50 - I am glad they have received marching orders - as it rids us of them - and also indicates the rapid approach of the enemy - a hotely contested engagement is confidently expected by our commanding officer - it is thought that the enemy will use every effort to drive back our brave boys redeem their estchions from the front strain placed upon it by the disgracefull defeat of July 21st - In this dear madam they will again be badly decimated - for all of our army are more eager than ever to get at them - our regt. the quick 19th will I am confident will give a good account of themselves - and I can only say to yourself and Mr. S that Mr. Clegg and myself will look after Henry - We three are comrads in battle and will together in the "Trig of War" and if any of the three get wounded the two will protect him with life - allow me in conclusion to thank you for the nice & much needed present received! Through owing to your thoughtfull kindness we can get on comfortably. Henry and I have a nice bedspread made by ourselves - cedar posts & plank top matress we do not want it would be to troublesome to keep house, the post are not a very handsome pattern not being so elaborately carved as some we have seen but answers the purpose. The sheet is now consumed and I have written you a very silly letter and would say by way of opology that I never write any but my Mother but will in the course of my correspondence try and improve. Best respects to Mrs. S.

Very Respectfully
W.H. Owen

Georgia Troops:
14th Regiment Georgia Volunteer Infantry, 12/5/1862
19th Regiment Georgia Volunteer Infantry, 9/19/1861-11/9/1861
27th Regiment Georgia Volunteer Infantry, 12/1/1861-3/9/1862
28th Regiment Georgia Volunteer Infantry, 12/9/1861-3/9/1862
Sources:
14th GVI, GDAH, 40/17, Adj. Gen. Commission books
19th GVI, GDAH, CSR, 256/7; GJ&M, 6/19/1861; PC, Letter of Henry P. Shackelford
27th GVI, GDAH, CSR, 256/66-69
28th GVI, GDAH, 283/45, William Wood; CG, 12/18/1861

512   **Camp Pinch Gut**
Fulton County, Georgia
   The camp was located nine miles above Atlanta and fifteen miles from Camp Georgia.
Georgia Troops:
1st Regiment Georgia Militia, 7/9/1864
Source:
AHC, Ms. 116, A. T. Holliday

513   **Camp Pine Creek**
Fairfax County, Virginia
   The camp was located on Old Braddock Road, four miles from Centreville, on a red clay hill near Piney Creek. This was the camp of Toomb's Brigade. The Regiments in this camp rotated picket duty to Munson's Hill and were in Camp Advance for a part of this time.
Georgia Troops:
1st Georgia Regulars, 9/16/1861, 9/26/1861-10/6/1861, 10/10/1861-10/15/1861
2nd Regiment Georgia Volunteer Infantry, 9/16/1861-9/23/1861 & 9/30/1861-10/15/1861
15th Regiment Georgia Volunter infantry,* 9/16/1861-10/15/1861
17th Regiment Georgia Volunteer Infantry,* 9/16/1861-10/15/1861
20th Regiment Georgia Volunteer Infantry,* 9/16/1861-10/15/1861
* No letters or documents with this camp name have been found for these units. It is known they were in this camp.
Sources:
1st GR, *Footprints of a Regiment,* Annotated By Richard M. McMurry
2nd GVI, GDAH, CSR, 254/100
15th GVI, GDAH, 53/64, Ivy Duggan
17th GVI, GDAH, 53/64, Ivy Duggan
20th GVI, GDAH, 53/64, Ivy Duggan

514   **Camp Pine Thicket**

Spotsylvania County, Virginia

The camp was probably located near Fredericksburg, and is probably the samp as Camp Pinewood.

Georgia Troops:

11th Battalion Georgia Light Artillery, 2/20/1863

Source:

PC, letter of Joseph M. Little

515   **Camp Pinewood**

Spotsylvania County, Virginia

The camp is located near Fredericksburg.

Georgia Troops:

11th Battalion Georgia Light Artillery, 1/3/1863-4/29/1863

Source:

UGA, Ms. 15, Florence Hodgson Heidler Collection, Frank M.C. Coker letters.

516   **Camp Pleasant**

Orange County, Virginia

The camp was located near Orange Court House.

Georgia Troops:

45th Regiment Georgia Volunteer Infantry, 12/9/1863

Source:

GHQ, Vols. 46 & 55, Charles A. Conn letters

517   **Camp Plenty**

Pierce County, Georgia

The camp was probably located near Blackshear.

Georgia Troops:

Blackshear Guards, later Co. H, 14th Regiment Georgia Volunteer Infantry, 7/10/1861

Source:

MSR, 7/16/1861

518   **Camp Pole Cat**

Orange County, Virginia

The camp was located about three miles above Deersville, and about six miles from Summerton's Ford on the Rapidan River. Summerton's Ford is two to three miles above Racoon Ford. This was the camp of Benning's Brigade.

Georgia Troops:

15th Regiment Georgia Volunteer Infantry, 8/2/1863-8/5/1863

Source:

Pryor Gardner Veazey and Some of his Ancestors and Decendants, By John Veazey Chapman

519   **Camp Poplar Spring**
Fulton County, Georgia
   The camp was located two miles east of Atlanta at Poplar Spring.
Georgia Troops:
Georgia Militia, 7/16/1864-7/24/1864
Source:
GDAH, 283/30, Jack H. King

520   **Camp Precarious**
Union County, Tennessee
   The camp was in an apple orchard near Maynardville.
Georgia Troops:
1st Regiment Georgia Volunteer Cavalry, 6/28/1862
Source:
GDAH, *Letters Written by Lavender R. Ray of Newnan, Georgia, During the War Between the States*, compiled by Ruby F. Ray

521   **Camp Price**
Chatham County, Georgia
   The camp was located near Savannah.
Georgia Troops:
30th Regiment Georgia Volunteer Infantry, Co. C, 11/22/1862-12/14/1862
Source:
DU, Andrew J. White

522   **Camp Price**
McIntosh County, Georgia
   The camp was located near Darien.
Georgia Troops:
20th Battalion Georgia Cavalry, Co. C, 9/1863-12/1863
Source:
GDAH, CSR, 254/6

523   **Camp Pritchard**
Beaufort County, South Carolina
   The camp was located about two miles from the New River bridge near Capt. Pritchard's house.
Georgia Troops:
Phillips' Legion, Infantry Battalion, 3/26/1862-6/8/1862 (The Cavalry Battalion was in this camp for a short time in early June and remained in the camp after the Infantry Battalion left on June 8, 1862.)
Source:
GDAH, 9/79, Ben & Augustus Boyd

Camp Pryor
Prince William County, Virginia

The camp was located near Manassas.

Georgia Troops:

19th Regiment Georgia Volunteer Infantry, 11/6/1861-12/1/1861

Sources:

GDAH, CSR, 256/7-9

Trophies from the Battle-field

At the drug store of Mr. J. W. Brooks may be found several souvenirs of the late battle of Manassas, sent here by Capt. R. A. Hardaway. One is a crimson sash - a very fine one - taken from the body of a Federal officer who was killed on the field. Another is a red skull cap ventillated with a bullet hole in the rear, which was once the property of a Fire Zouave. The third and last is a small United States flag, made of silk, and was taken by Capt. Hardaway, after the battle, from its position on one of the guns of Sherman's battery.

Columbus Daily Times, 8/6/61

---

525   **Camp Race Course**

Chatham County, Georgia

This is the same as Camp Jasper. Almost all references to Camp Race Course are during the early stages of the camp.

526   **Camp Rains**

Richmond County, Georgia

The camp was in a field near Milledge Springs, on the Sand Hills near Augusta. It was probably named after Maj. George W. Rains, commander at the Augusta Arsenal.

Georgia Troops:

1st Regiment Local Defense Troops, Augusta Volunteers, Co. B, 9/2/1863-9/12/1863

1st Regiment Local Defense Troops, Augusta Volunteer Artillery, 9/12/1863-9/25/1863

1st Regiment Local Defense Troops, Wheeler Dragoons, 9/24/1863-10/8/1863

1st Regiment Local Defense Troops, The City Guard, 10/9/1863-10/22/1863

Sources:

AV, Co B, ADC&S, 9/2/1863 & 9/12/1863

AVA, ADC&S, 9/12/1863 & 9/25/1863

WD, ADC&S, 9/24/1863 & 10/9/1863

TCG, ADC&S, 10/9/1863 & 10/22/1863

527   **Camp Randolph**

Wakulla County, Florida

The camp was located fifteen miles south of Tallahassee, six miles from St. Marks and five miles from Newport.

Georgia Troops:

29th Battalion Georgia Cavalry, 12/1863-4/1864

64th Regiment Georgia Volunteer Infantry, 8/1863 & 9/1863

Sources:

29th Bn GC, GDAH, CSR, 254/13; O.R., Vol. XXXV, pt. 1, 585

64th GVI, GDAH, CSR, 257/126

528   **Camp Randolph**

Chatham County, Georgia

The camp was probably located near Savannah.

Georgia Troops:

1st Battalion Georgia Sharpshooters, 9/2/1862 & 12/16/1862

Source:

GDAH, 283/58, Misc. file

529   **Camp Randolph**

Decatur County, Georgia

The camp was probably located near the Chattahoochee Arsenal.

Georgia Troops:

29th Battalion Georgia Cavalry, 9/23/1863-11/1/1863

Source:

GDAH, CSR, 254/13

530   **Camp Randolph**

DeKalb County, Georgia

The camp was located four miles west of Atlanta and two miles east of Decatur just north of the railroad, also known as Camp of Instruction No. 2. See Atlas plate XC, 3, for conscript camp. More information on this camp is in Chapter II.

Georgia Troops:

27th Regiment Georgia Volunteer Infantry, new recruits to Cos. A & E, 8/13/1862-9/28/1862 (The regiment was in Virginia at this time. A recruiter was sent from Virginia to sign up men out of this camp. A number of other regiments did the same thing.)

Barnwell's Battery, Georgia Light Artillery, conscripts, 1/1/1864

Georgia State Line, 1/7/1863.

23rd Battalion Georgia Cavalry, Headquarters, 11/19/1862. (About the end of January, 1863, this battalion became a part of Avery's 4th Regiment Georgia Volunteer Cavalry.)

2nd Battalion Infantry, Georgia State Guards, 3/4/1864

Sources:

27th GVI, GDAH, CSR, 256/66-69

BB, GDAH, 291/79, William. A. Mosley

GSL, ASB, 11/26/1862 & 1/7/1863; GDAH, AGLB, #15

23rd Bn GC, GDAH, CSR, 253/122

2nd Bn GSG, GDAH, CSR, 254/113

531   **Camp Randolph**

Gordon County, Georgia

This group of camps referred to as Camp Randolph was in the neighborhood of Calhoun. This camp was also used for conscripts.

The following is an extract from a citizen from Rome Georgia, who signed his letter to the editor of the *Rome Weekly Courier* as "H." It appeared in the issue of July 18, 1862.

Camp Randolph.

It is hard to locate precisely this camp, there are several encampments in the vicinity of Calhoun going by this general name. Major Dunwoody commands the post with control especially of conscripts. At their camp we saw Lieut. Col. Clark, chief in authority there - he belonged to the late 1st Georgia Regiment (Ramsey's,) and was in the memorable affair of Laurel Hill, but fortunately was neither killed, lost, nor captured. He is a fine looking, polite officer. From him we learned that the recruits would very soon be sent forward to fill up the wanted ranks of our heroic Georgians. Smith's Legion, Harkie's (55th Regiment Georgia Volunteer Infantry) and Buckaleu's (Barkaloo's 54th, later 57th, Regiment

Georgia Volunteer Infantry) regiments had just left for an important point. But the most important feature of the camp is the 3rd Ga. Cavalry.

Georgia Troops:
Griffin Light Artillery, Capt. Obadiah C. Gibson's Battery, 8/15/1862
Griffin Light Artillery, Capt. John Scogin's Battery Georgia Light Artillery, 8/22/1862-8/26/1862
Montgomery's Battalion Georgia Artillery, 8/15/1862 (Later became 14th Battalion Georgia Light Artillery.)
14th Battalion Georgia Light Artillery, 9/30/1862-10/7/1862
3rd Regiment Georgia Volunteer Cavalry, 6/14/1862-8/19/1862
14th Battalion Georgia Cavalry, 4/1862-10/1862
24th Regiment Georgia Volunteer Infantry, 8/8/1861-8/17/1861
54th Regiment Georgia Volunteer Infantry, 6/14/1862-7/4/1862 (In January, 1863, the designation was changed to the 57th Regiment Georgia Volunteer Infantry.)
55th Regiment Georgia Volunteer Infantry, early July, 1862 (No document with the name "Camp Randolph" has been found for this regiment.)
Smith's Legion, early July, 1862 (No document with the name "Camp Randolph" has been found for this unit.)
Sources:
GLA, ADC&S, 8/20/1862; GDAH, CSR, 254/61
M Bn GA, ADC&S, 8/20/1862
14th Bn GLA, GDAH, CSR, 254/36
3rd GVC, GDAH, 283/24, Julius L. Dowda; CE, 6/24/1862 & 9/9/1862
14th Bn GC, GDAH, CSR, 253/89
24th GVI, GDAH, 263/60, W. K. Hadaway
54th GVI, CG, 11/5/1862; GDAH, 283/22, Tralona Edwin Davis
55th GVI, RWC, 7/18/1862
SL, RWC, 7/18/1862

532   **Camp Randolph**
Wayne County, North Carolina
This camp was located in a pine grove beside the railroad, four miles below Goldsboro. It is believed that name Camp Randolph was changed to Camp McIntosh.
Georgia Troops:
16th Regiment Georgia Volunteer Infantry, 3/22/1862-4/4/1862
24th Regiment Georgia Volunteer Infantry, 3/22/1862-4/4/1862
Cobb's Legion, 3/22/1862-4/4/1862
Sources:
ASB, 4/9/1862 & 4/23/1862; *Howell Cobb's Confederate Career*, By Horace Montgomery, Confederate Centennial Studies, Number Ten

533   **Camp Rapidan**

Orange County, Virginia

The camp was near Racoon Ford on the Rapidan River.
Georgia Troops:
Cobb's Legion, Cavalry Battalion, 10/1862 & 12/1862
Phillips' Legion, Cavalry Battalion, 11/24/1862
Sources:
CLCB, ADC&S, 12/9/1862; GDAH, CSR, 258/8
PLCB, GDAH, 283/41, John T. Swan

534   **Camp Rapidan Station**

Orange County, Virginia

The camp was at Rapidan Railroad Station near the Rapidan River.
Georgia Troops:
35th Regiment Georgia Volunteer Infantry, 8/31/1861
48th Regiment Georgia Volunteer Infantry, 12/12/1863
Sources:
35th GVI, GDAH, 283/32, James T. McElvaney
48th GVI, DU, James Paul Verdery

535   **Camp Read**

Chatham County, Georgia

The camp was located three miles from Adam's Point on Skidaway Island.
Georgia Troops:
2nd Battalion Georgia Cavalry, Co. D, Georgia Hussars, Co. B, 3/3/1862-3/17/1862
Source:
EU, #12, John H. Ash

536   **Camp Readdick**

Georgia

The camp was on the coast of Georgia.
Georgia Troops:
4th (Clinch's) Regiment Georgia Volunteer Cavalry, Cos. D & F, 6/1862-9/1862
Source:
GDAH, CSR, 253/94

537   **Camp Recovery**

Campbell County, Virginia

This hospital camp was probably at Lynchburg., since this was the location of a number of Confederate hospitals. The writer reported the location as near Lynchville. It is possible that a number of Georgia units could have used this hospital camp name.
Georgia Troops:
26th Regiment Georgia Volunteer Infantry, Co. B, 9/15/1862
Source:
GDAH, 283/26, Daniel Gillis

538   **Camp Red Bluff**

Beaufort County, South Carolina

   The camp was located near Red Bluff on New River. This is either the same camp as Camp McHenry, or the picket camp for Camp McHenry.

Georgia Troops:

1st Battalion Georgia Sharpshooters, 5/11/1864

47th Regiment Georgia Volunteer Infantry, Co. H, 3/2/1863

Sources:

1st Bn SS, GDAH, 194/3, Joseph J. Hardy

47th GVI, DU, Benjamin S. Williams

539   **Camp Refuge**

Camden County, Georgia

   The camp was probably located at the Refuge Plantation.

Georgia Troops:

4th (Clinch's) Regiment Georgia Volunteer Cavalry, Co. E, 1/1864-4/1864

Source:

GDAH, CSR, 253/94

540   **Camp Regina**

Escambia County, Florida

   The camp was located near Pensacola.

Georgia Troops:

36th (Villepigue's) Regiment Georgia Volunteer Infantry, Co. F, 2/5/1862

Source;

GDAH, CSR, 256/116

541   **Camp Reppard**

Ware County, Georgia

   The camp was located near Tebeauville, which is now Waycross.

Georgia Troops:

3rd Battalion Georgia Cavalry, Co. A, Atlantic & Gulf Guards, 2/20/1862-3/4/1862 (The 3rd Battalion became a part of the 4th [Clinch's] Regiment Georgia Volunteer Cavalry.)

Source:

GDAH, CSR, 254/21

542   **Camp Republic**

Rockingham County, Virginia

   The camp was located near Port Republic. See Atlas Plate LXXXV, 5.

Georgia Troops:

12th Regiment Georgia Volunteer Infantry, 6/12/1862-6/16/1862

Source:

EU, #20, John Levi Griffin

543   **Camp Rescue**
Bibb County, Georgia
The camp was located in Macon opposite Rose Hill Cemetery, in a grove of trees . The camp was established in June 1864, and on September 12, 1864, was broken up per the following orders.

State of Georgia
Adjutatnt & Inspector Gen's. Office
Milledgeville, Sept. 12, 1864

Special Orders
No. 124.
The Camp at Macon for the Militia known as Camp Rescue, is broken up, and the Militia will. until further orders, report to Maj. F.W. Capers, Post Commandant Milledgeville.
Aides-de-Camp, and other officers instructed to look up laggards and skulkers, will continue their duties, notwithstanding the furlough granted for the first Division, and send the men forward to Major Capers at Milledgeville.
Men who have failed to come forward promptly in their country's hour of need, are not entitled to indulgencies, and will receive none.
By order of the Commander-in-Chief:
Henry C. Wayne,
Adj. & Ins. General.

Georgia Troops:
Georgia Militia Reserve, 6/1864-9/12/1864
Sources:
ASB, 9/21/1864; *The Historical Record of Macon and Central Georgia*, By John C. Butler

544   **Camp Rescue**
Dare County, North Carolina
The camp was located on Roanoke Island, three to four miles from the seven gun battery guarding the channel. See Camp Georgia on Roanoke Island.
Georgia Troops:
3rd Regiment Georgia Volunteer Infantry, 9/1/1861-9/10/1861
Sources:
ASB, 9/18/1861; ADC&S, 9/13/1861

545   **Camp Rescue**
Caroline County, Virginia
The camp was located on the Fredericksburg railroad near Guinea's Station, in huts previously occupied by other troops.
Georgia Troops:
3rd Regiment Georgia Volunteer Infantry, Co. K, 3/10/1863-4/2/1863
22nd Regiment Georgia Volunteer Infantry, 2/16/1863-4/1863
Sources:
GDAH, 283/29, Henry Jackson; 283/37, Marquis D. L. Pittman

546   **Camp Reservoir**
Henrico County, Virginia
   The camp was located near the city reservoir, two miles from Richmond.
Georgia Troops:
12th Regiment Georgia Volunteer Infantry, 6/23/1861-7/7/1861
16th Regiment Georgia Volunteer Infantry, 7/27/1861 (The regiment remained in this camp until formed, then moved to Camp Cobb.)
Sources:
12th GVI, *A Post of Honor, The Pryor Letters, 1861-1863*, Edited and narrated by Charles R. Adams, Jr.
16th GVI, ASB, 10/16/1861

547   **Camp Rice**
Charleston County, South Carolina
   The camp was probably located near Charleston.
Georgia Troops:
54th Regiment Georgia Volunteer Infantry, Co. K, 2/1/1864
Source:
GDAH, CSR, 257/83

548   **Camp Ripley**
Chatham County, Georgia
   This camp was located on the Isle of Hope.
Georgia Troops:
1st (Olmstead's) Volunteer Regiment of Georgia, 6/15/1863
Source:
SR, 9/17/1863

549   **Camp Ripley**
Charleston County, South Carolina
   The camp was near Mt. Pleasant.
Georgia Troops:
32nd Regiment Georgia Volunteer Infantry, 11/9/1864-12/1864
Source:
GDAH, CSR, 356/96

550   **Camp Ripley**
Chesterfield County, Virginia
   The camp of Ripley's Brigade was located on Petersburg Road near Richmond.
   This extract from the *Augusta Daily Chronicle & Sentinel* of July 29, 1862, describes apparent problems the Georgia troops had with medical treatment.

Camp Ripley, near Richmond, Virginia.
July 23d, 1862.

Since the fights the health of the regiment has been bad, though there has not been a great deal of mortality considering the number of cases reported on the sick list.

The daily change of water on the march, the diet which consists solely of hard crackers and broiled bacon, with sleeping on the bare ground, and open air without blankets even, had the tendency to provoke dysentary and fever from which many have been suffering ever since having failed in some regiments to get that attention from Surgeons that their duty to the Government and humanity demanded of them. Is it not hard that volunteers, should contract diseases, in doing service for their country and then should be neglected, and accused of hypocracy &c,?

Such has been the case I am informed in some Georgia regiments, but as it is said the M. D's. to whom they applied have resigned, it is believed that their successors will not be so inhumane. These things will be remembered by Georgians who have had sick relatives in the regiment. ---

There are others however in Richmond whose kindness to the sick and wounded deserve the highest commendations and are doing anything they can (as they can not take up arms,) to further the consommation or our purpose of our gaining our independence. The ladies of Richmond and indeed of Virginia generally are all that could be desired.

They are untiring in their efforts and when a sick or wounded soldier falls in their hands he is treated like a mother would treat him, and he almost feels as though he were at home. If we gain our Independence, Mr. Editor, woman's farter kindnesses and other acts should be entitled to nearly as much credit as those who fought amid the cannons loud and deafening roar. ---

Signed "N" of Greene County Volunteers

Georgia Troops:
4th Regiment Georgia Volunteer Infantry, 7/20/1862-8/18/1862
44th Regiment Georgia Volunteer Infantry, 7/23/1862
Sources:
4th GVI, EU, #363, David Read Evans Winn
44th GVI, ADC&S, 7/29/1862

551   **Camp Roberts**

Chatham County, Georgia

The camp was near Thunderbolt Battery, four miles below Savannah.
Georgia Troops:
22nd Battalion Georgia Heavy Artillery, 5/1863-10/1863
1st Volunteer Regiment of Georgia, Co. E, 8/18/1863
Sources:
22nd Bn GHA, GDAH, CSR, 254/38
1st VRG, SDMN, 8/20/1863

552   **Camp Robertson**

Greene County, North Carolina

The camp was located near Snow Hill.

Georgia Troops:

7th Regiment Confederate Cavalry, headquarters, 4/16/1863

Source:

GDAH, CSR, 258/69

553   **Camp Rockingham**

Rockingham County, Virginia.

The camp was located sixteen miles from Staunton.

Georgia Troops:

Phillips' Legion, Cavalry Battalion, 3/8/1863-3/23/1863

Source:

GDAH, 39/69, John T. Swan

554   **Camp Rocky Run**

Fairfax County, Virginia

The camp was located on Rocky Run, between Rocky Run and Cub Run, near Centreville, and one-half mile east of Camp Steiner.

Georgia Troops:

1st Georgia Regulars, 11/5/1861-11/14/1861

2nd Regiment Georgia Volunteer Infantry, 11/5/1861-11/14/1861

15th Regiment Georgia Volunteer Infantry, 10/31/1861-11/4/1861

Sources:

1st GR, GDAH, CSR, 254/67

2nd GVI, GDAH, CSR, 254/100

15th GVI, GDAH, CSR, 255/108; MR, 279/78

555   **Camp Rodes**

Chesterfield County, Virginia

The camp was located a few miles from Petersburg.

The following is an extract from a letter of Thomas M. Hightower of the 21st Regiment Georgia Volunteer Infantry headed Camp Rodes and dated February 13, 1865.

> Well, Lou, we have moved into our winter quarters but we have not had the chance to go home yet. The men got in theirs nearly a month ago but I only moved into mine a few days ago and you ought to see how I have it furnished. In one corner by the fireplace I have a Georgia bedstead reared up and you know it looks stylish. I have four planks before the fire for a floor and that would be a great place for Twistification, if I only had anybody to Twistify with me; and upon this platform I have one nail keg and two boxes for seats, by this time you know what size crowd I could entertain. My house is quite roomy as I keep my furniture close to the fire to keep it from getting dusty. There are portions of it that look very lonesome -- those parts I never visit, much. It being so much larger room than I have been used to staying in I am afraid I will get lost unless I have someone to look after me.

Georgia Troops:

4th Regiment Georgia Volunteer Infantry,* 12/1864-1/1865

12th Regiment Georgia Volunteer Infantry,* 12/1864-1/1865

21st Regiment Georgia Volunteer Infantry, 1/13/1865-2/19/1865

44th Regiment Georgia Volunteer Infantry, 1/30/1865

* No letters or documents have been found for these units with this camp name. It is known they were in this camp.

Sources:

4th GVI, Part of Cook's Brigade, Rodes' (Late) Division

12th GVI, Part of Cook's Brigade, Rodes' (Late) Division

21st GVI, GDAH, 40/50, Capt. Thomas M. Hightower

44th GVI, GDAH, CSR, 257/36, Dr. Augustus Taylor

556   **Camp Rogers**
Bryan County, Georgia

Military Meeting.

At a meeting of the non-commisioned officers and privates of the Hardwick Mounted Rifles, held at their encampment this day, the following resolutions were adopted:

1st. *Resolved*, That tender to our Captain, J. L. McAllister, our sincere thanks for his many kindnesses to us during our encampment at Genesis Point.

2d. *Resolved*, That we duly appreciate the kindness of Mr. Thos. C. Arnold, for certain privelidges granted us in forming our new encampment.

3d. Resolved, That in the establishment of our new encampment, we call it Camp Rogers, in compliments to our highly esteemed and liberal fellow-citizen W. M. Rogers, Esq.

4th. *Resolved*, That we tender to Captain McAllister and the little girls of Augusta, Ga., our grateful acknowledgements for their very generous contributions for the benefit of our sick soldiers.

5th. *Resolved*, That the money, the sum of ninety dollars this day contributed by the officers and privates of our troop, for the benefit of our comrads in arms in the State of Virginia, be placed in the hands of our Quartermaster, W. M. Duphene, to be forwarded through the proper channel, for their benefit.

Camp Rogers, Nov. 4th, 1862.

Georgia Troops:

4th (Clinch's) Regiment Georgia Volunteer Cavalry, 12/1863 & 10/1864

29th Battalion Georgia Cavalry, Co. H, 8/1/1864 & 10/1864

Coast Guard Battalion, Georgia Militia, 9/29/1864-10/31/1864

Hardwick Mounted Rifles, Cos. A & B, 11/4/1862 & 4/13/1864 (They left on April 13, 1864, for Virginia, with the rest of the 7th Regiment Georgia Cavalry.)

Sources:

4th GVC, GDAH, CSR, 253/94

29th Bn GC, Co. H, GDAH, CSR, 254/13; ECN, 8/17/64

CGB, GM, GDAH, CSR, 258/5

HMR, GDAH, CSR, 254/20, SR, 11/17/1862

557
                                      Camp Rose
Chatham County, Georgia

The camp is located on Rose Hill, three and one-half miles from White Bluff, five and one-half miles from Coffee Bluff and six and one-half miles from Savannah.
Georgia Troops:
2nd Battalion Georgia Cavalry, 5/1862-12/10/1862 (This was the headquarters of the battalion for this period of time. Different companies entered and left this camp at different times.)
Sources:
GDAH, CSR, 253/87; EU, #12, John H. Ash

558
                                      Camp Ross
Portsmouth County, Virginia

The camp was located one to two miles west of Gosport Navy Yard, and six to seven miles from Hodges Bridge and Ferry on the western branch of the Elizabeth River, also referred to as Camp Clover as the camp was in a clover field.
Georgia Troops:
4th Regiment Georgia Volunteer Infantry, 5/18/1861-5/22/1861
Sources:
GDAH, CSR, 254/128; MR, 194/3; AP, 6/13/1861

559
                                      Camp Ruff
Fulton County, Georgia

The camp was located on the Western & Atlantic Railroad, near Boltonville. (Bolton Station) This could be the same as Camp Bolton.
Georgia Troops:
2nd Regiment Georgia State Line, 12/1863-4/2/1864 & 6/6/1864
Georgia Militia, 3/9/1864
Sources:
GSL, AHC, #13, Telemon Cuyler Collection; GDAH, AGLB #20; 199/58, Clontz Family GM, GDAH, 283/34, J. J. Lee; 171/40, Misc.

560
                                      Camp Rushton
Fulton County, Georgia

The camp was located near Atlanta.
Georgia Troops:
9th Battalion Georgia Light Artillery, Co. E, Wyly's Battery, 6/5/1862-6/7/1862
Source:
SC, 6/8/1862

Camp Sandtown
Fulton County, Georgia

The camp was located near Sandtown on the Chattahoochee River.
Georgia Troops:
3rd Regiment Georgia Militia, 6/25/1864-7/8/1864
Source:
Letters of Jonathan Bridges, a Confederate Soldier of Stewart County, Georgia, By Richard M. Patchin & Deborah Dean Patchin

Camp Sans
Chatham County, Georgia

The camp was probably near Savannah.
Georgia Troops:
12th Battalion Georgia Volunteers, 6/7/1863
Source:
A Calendar of Confederate Papers, Edited by Douglas Southall Freeman

Camp Sansavilla
Wayne County, Georgia

The camp was on the Sansavilla or St. Savilla Bluff, on the Altamaha River across from Fort Barrington.

In a letter from A.W. Smith to Col. Claudius C. Wilson dated April 1st, 1862, Smith expresses his dissatisfaction with just about everything that has to do with this picket duty.

Camp Sansavilla Wayne Co. April 1st 1862

Col. C. C. Wilson
      Col.
           The Flies are numerous in our Camp. We are quite Busy Both day and night Ridding ourselves of the Little Biting Devils.

This Detachment of the 25th Regt is Becoming very much Dissatisfied With This Camp, And There Commander.

We are almost entirely Without Communication from Savannah. The Bridge at Jim Holoway is partly Gone, and the obstruction above us in the River is nearly Complete. As Soon as it is Completed We Will have to be moved by Land to any point on the Railroad and the nearest point is 20 miles with a Bad Road.

We have Know Conveniences here for the sick, and it is almost impossible to get them of. We have not got a mail for four days past and I do not Know When We Will be able to get one, all of these inconveniences is doing your Regt harm. It has turned the feeling of the men to wards home after this Term. I feel Sure that there is but few men in this Detachment that will reenlist be fore June next and if We are to Suffer for the use of the Mail and the sick have to remain in Camp from the cause of communication being so bad There Will be but few Reenlist. I have 4 four that has Reenlisted, and I Believe that I will be able to Reenlist the Majority of my Comd. If We are properly Situated I have been informed but I do not Know how True it is that We Will be moved to bug Suck Where the obstruction is. I hope it is not True. for while we might do some good Where We are. We could do nothing at Bug Suck for We Would be on a Small Bluff Surrounded by Swamp and Water and the Course of the River Would give the Enemy all advantage. We Could go there and stop for until We saw the Enemy advancing. And then We Would have to Leave or be Sheled of the hill and I do not Like to be placed Were I canot do any Damage to the Enemy. Below you Will find the program of Bug Suck. We have Some Sickness in Camp This is a Sickly place.

I am Well

Your friend

A. W. Smith

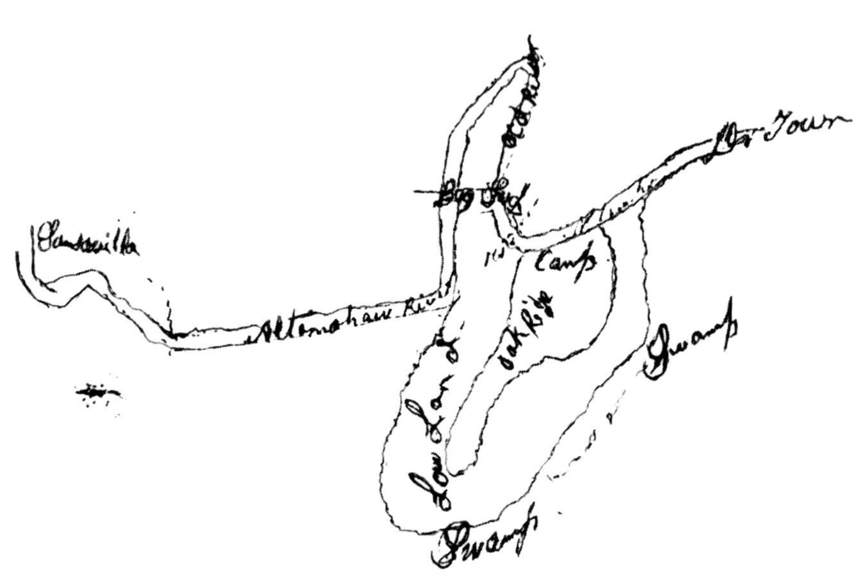

Georgia Troops:
25th Regiment Georgia Volunteer Infantry, Cos. B, D & I, 3/22/1862-4/29/1862
Sources:
GHS, #874, Claudius C. Wilson; GDAH, CSR, 256/49

564   Camp Sarah

Loudoun County, Virginia

The camp was located a few miles from Leesburg, just south of the Potomac River.
Georgia Troops:
16th Regiment Georgia Volunteer Infantry, 9/3/1862-9/5/1862
24th Regiment Georgia Volunteer Infantry, 9/3/1862-9/5/1862
Sources:
16th GVI, *Johnny Cobb: Confederate Aristocrat*, By Horace Montgomery; *Howell Cobb's Confederate Career*, By Horace Montgomery, Confederate Centennial Studies, Number Ten
24th GVI, *Grand Pa's War Stories*, Written by E. H. Sutton

565   **Camp Satilla**
Brantley County, Georgia

"Our new camp will be on the Satilla at Atkinson's place, three and one-half miles from Waynesville. I have made arrangements for a switch and siding at that place." Gen. Capers.

The camp was about two miles east of the Satilla River.

Georgia Troops:

2nd Brigade Georgia State Troops, 11/29/1861-1/3/1862 (See the organization for this brigade under Camp Harrison.)

Sources:

GDAH, 3133-07, Gen. Caper's letter to Adj. Gen. Wayne.; SC, 1/15/1862; DU, Eugene Verdery, Jr.

566   **Camp Sawyer**
Virginia

The location is not known.

Georgia Troops:

Cobb's Legion, Infantry Battalion, 1861

Source:

GDAH, 160/74, Joel Crawford Barnett

567   **Camp Scott**
Gadsden County, Florida

The camp was located near Quincy, six miles from the battery at Hammock's Landing, and about one mile from Mr. Hawkin's house.

Georgia Troops:

28th (Bonaud's) Battalion Georgia Siege Artillery, 9/1863-10/30/1863

Source:

GDAH, CSR, 254/43

568   **Camp Scott**
Madison County, Kentucky

The camp was located on a big hill below Richmond. See Camp Big Hill. Also, see map with Camp Dick Robinson.

Georgia Troops:

1st Regiment Georgia Volunteer Cavalry, 8/26/1862

Source:

RWC, 9/26/1862

569   **Camp Screven**
Chatham County, Georgia

The camp was located on the Isle of Hope.

Georgia Troops:

18th Infantry Battalion (Savannah Volunteer Guards,) 5/12/1863-6/1/1863 (This was the battalion headquarters at this time.)

25th Regiment Georgia Volunteer Infantry, Co. C, 11/1861-1/5/1862

Sources:
18th IB, SDMN, 6/17/1863; *A Calendar of Confederate Papers*, Edited by Douglas Southall
Freeman
25th GVI, GDAH, CSR, 256/49 & 54

570   **Camp Secessionville**
Charleston County, South Carolina
The camp was located on James Island, near Secessionville.
Georgia Troops:
28th Battalion Georgia Siege Artillery, 6/1864
Source:
GDAH, CSR, 254/43

571   **Camp Security**
McIntosh County, Georgia
The camp was located near Darien.
Georgia Troops:
13th (Style's) Regiment Georgia Volunteer Infantry, Thomasville Guards, 1/1/1862-1/5/1862
(The company later became Company F, 29th Regiment Georgia Volunteer Infantry.)
Source:
GDAH, 283/23, Dickey Family

572   **Camp Semmes**
Chatham County, Georgia
The camp was located on the Isle of Hope, nine miles from Savannah.
Georgia Troops:
24th Battalion Georgia Cavalry, 1/12/1863-2/24/1863 & 10/18/1863-3/7/1864
Sources:
GDAH, CSR, 253/109 & 254/11; MR, 279/65; UNC, #1498, George W. & E. C. Anderson

573   **Camp Semmes**
Glynn County, Georgia
The camp was located on the ridge about one mile south of Brunswick, and one hundred feet
from the water.
The following extract is from a letter written by a citizen of Savannah who visited Camp
Semmes. It appeared in the *Savannah Daily Morning News* on September 5, 1861.

The Thirteenth Regiment
I see, from the report of the election of officers in the News, this regiment is called the
12th. I was told by the officers in command that it was the 13th, but whether they be
mistaken, or the reporter, I am unable to say. I shall, however, for the present, call it the
13th. Here, too, is a fact which may greatly embarrass the future historian in recording the
exploits of the soldiers of Georgia, inasmuch as there are two regiments of Georgia troops
called the 13th. ---
The tents are pitched in an open space sufficiently near to the water to get the full benefit
of the fresh sea breezes and the salt water baths. Of the latter, the soldiers seem remarkibly

fond, a greater part of them making it a daily business to perform this "sacred right of oblation." Most of the tents have good plank floors raised a few inchs above the damp soil upon which are spread the soldiers beds, composed of Palmetto leaves, pine boughs and other articles of convenience and economy. East, and in the rear of the tents, from the water and marsh which streches out for miles. On the Western side, is the "campus meritus" of the 13th Regiment, which is a beautiful green turf covered field perfectly level and free from hills, trees, stumps, roots &c., upon which the soldiers perform their daily evolutions under the instruction of their officers. The soldiers are well cared for at present in the Commissariat Department, it being no uncommon thing to see a soldier with a chunk of beef nearly as large as his head, going down the bay "to catch crabs."

August 28, 1861   Frank Highwater

Georgia Troops:
Jackson Artillery, 10/1/1861
2nd Regiment Georgia Volunteer Infantry, 6/25/1861-7/24/1861 (Part of the regiment was in Camp Styles on St. Simons at this time.)
Wiregrass Minutemen, 6/11/1861 (The company later became Co. B, 2nd Regiment Georgia Volunteer Infantry.)
13th (Styles') Regiment Georgia Volunteer Infantry, 8/19/1861-10/24/1861 (The regiment reorganized 5/10/1862, in Savannah and became the 26th Regiment Georgia Volunteer Infantry.)
Sources:
JA, GDAH, 283/48, Bibb County file
2nd GVI, SDMN, 7/11/1861; GDAH, CSR, 254/100
WG MM, SDMN, 6/29/1861
13th GVI, GDAH, CSR, 256/59; 283/44, John W. Wilkinson; SDMN, 9/5/1861

574   **Camp Seven Pines**
                                          Henrico County, Virginia
   The camp was located at Seven Pines, east of Richmond.
Georgia Troops:
28th Regiment Georgia Volunteer Infantry, 6/20/1862
Source:
GDAH, 283/39, James A. Rowe

575   **Camp Sewell**
                                          Jackson County, Alabama
   The camp was located near the Tennessee River opposite Bridgeport. See Camp Davis in Jackson County, Alabama.
Georgia Troops:
3rd Regiment Georgia Volunteer Cavalry, 8/27/1862
Source:
TCE, 9/9/1862

576   **Camp Sewell**
Jasper County, South Carolina
The camp was located four miles below Hardeeville on Screven Ferry Road.
Georgia Troops:
Phillips' Legion, Infantry Battalion, 2/6/1862-3/26/1862
Source:
GDAH, 186/31, A. J. Reese

577   **Camp Sheibly**
Floyd County, Georgia
The camp was located at Sheibly's School house, about one mile from Rome.
Georgia Troops:
Floyd County Sharpshooters, 6/10/1861-6/24/1861 (The Floyd Sharpshooters later became Co. B, 21st Regiment Georgia Volunteer Infantry.)
Floyd Infantry, 5/13/61-5/23/61 (They became Co. H, 8th Regiment Georgia Volunteer Infantry.)
Sources:
FCSS, RWC, 6/7/1861, 6/14/1861 & 6/24/1861
FI, RWC, 5/17/1861 & 5/24/1861

578   **Camp Shenandoah**
Augusta County, Virginia
The camp was located in a beautiful valley on the south side of the Shenandoah Mountains.
Georgia Troops:
12th Regiment Georgia Volunteer Infantry, 4/8/1862-4/18/1862
Source:
EU, #20, John Levi Griffin

579   **Camp Shiloh**
Pierce County, Georgia
The camp was located near Blackshear.
Georgia Troops:
3rd Battalion Georgia Cavalry, Co. A, Atlantic & Gulf Guards, 9/22/1861-10/2/1861 (They later became Co. G, 4th [Clinch's] Regiment Georgia Volunteer Cavalry.)
Source:
GDAH, CSR, 254/21

580   **Camp Shirley**
Shenandoah County, Virginia
The camp was located three-fourths mile northwest of New Market, on Zachariah Shirley's land. This was the camp of Evan's Brigade.
Georgia Troops:
13th, 26th, 31st, 38th, 60th, 61st, Regiments Georgia Volunteer Infantry, and 12th Battalion Georgia Volunteers, 10/8/1864-10/11/1864 & 10/21/1864-11/7/1864
Source:
Intrepid Warrior, Compiled and edited by Robert Grier Stephens, Jr.

581   **Camp Shorter**
Chatham County, Georgia

The camp was located near Ft. Brown behind the Catholic Cemetery on the road to Causton's Bluff.
Georgia Troops:
Napier Artillery, 3/1862 (At this time the Napier Artillery was attached to the 3rd Brigade Georgia State Troops.)
Source:
Not known

582   **Camp Siege Train**
Chatham County, Georgia

The camp was located seven miles south of Savannah at Harrack's place near the Isle of Hope.
Georgia Troops:
Siege Train Georgia Artillery, 10/20/1863-4/30/1864
12th Battalion Georgia Volunteers, Co. C, 2/5/1863-4/6/1863 (The company was detached from the battalion and attached to Siege Train Georgia Artillery.)
54th Regiment Georgia Volunteer Infantry, Co. A, 6/1863-4/3/1864
Source:
STGA, GDAH, CSR, 254/61
12th Bn GV, GDAH, CSR, 254/31
54th GVI, GDAH, CSR, 257/83

583   **Camp Simonton**
Charleston County, South Carolina

The camp was not far from Secessionville on James Island.
Georgia Troops:
Chatham Artillery, 7/11/1863.
Source:
Historical Sketch of The Chatham Artillery during The Confederate Struggle for Independence, by Charles C. Jones, Jr.

584   **Camp Simpkins**
Wakulla County, Florida

The camp was located about one mile below Newport, on the east side of the St. Marks River. The men built cabins to live in. See the map to accompany Camp Brokaw for the location of Camp Simpkins.
Georgia Troops:
Echols' Light Artillery, 7/17/1864
Source:
PC, James Jewell letters

585   **Camp Simpson**
Hancock County, Georgia

The camp was located near Sparta.
Georgia Troops:
Georgia Guards, 10/1861 (The company was possibly a local defense company.)
Source:
GDAH, original list of camps

586   **Camp Sims**
Dougherty County, Georgia

The camp was located near Albany.
Georgia Troops:
Davis Invincibles, 6/7/1861-7/1861 (The company later became Co. D, 18th Regiment Georgia Volunteer Infantry.)
Sources:
AP, 8/8/1861; MT, 6/10/1861

587   **Camp Skidaway**
Chatham County, Georgia

The camp was located on the north end of Skidaway Island, at the batteries on Skidaway River.
Georgia Troops:
Georgia Hussars, Co. A, 6/1/1861-7/1/1861
1st (Olmstead's) Volunteer Regiment of Georgia, Co. F, 8/1861-2/1862 (Capt. Pritchard's Co.)
4th Battalion Georgia Volunteer Infantry, 10/1861-11/6/1861 & 11/8/1861-3/16/1862 (The 4th Battalion became a part of the 60th Regiment Georgia Volunteer Infantry on April 25, 1862. See Camp Calhoun.)
Sources:
GH, GDAH, CSR, 254/22
1st VRG, GDAH, original camp list
4th Bn GVI, GDAH, CSR, 257/105

588   **Camp Smith**
Mobile County, Alabama

The camp was located at Choctaw Bluff about thirty-five miles above Mobile on the Alabama River. See Atlas Plate CX, 1.
Georgia Troops:
1st Confederate Regiment Georgia Volunteers, 12/1862
Source:
1st Confederate Regiment, Compiled by C. Pat Cates

589

Camp Smith
Leon County, Florida

The camp was located near Tallahassee.
Georgia Troops:
29th Battalion Georgia Cavalry, Co. C, 1/9/1864-1/20/1864
64th Regiment Georgia Volunteer Infantry, Co. K, 8/1863
Sources:
29th Bn GC, GDAH, CSR, 254/13
64th GVI, GDAH, CSR, 257/126

590

Camp Smith
Bibb County, Georgia

The camp was located three miles west of Macon.
Georgia Troops:
Georgia Militia, 1st Division Headquarters, 10/16/1864-11/20/1864
Sources:
GDAH, 283/26, Horatio J. Goss; SR, 10/21/1864

591

Camp Smith
Chatham County, Georgia

The camp was located four miles from Causton's Bluff on Thunderbolt Road.
Georgia Troops:
8th Battalion Georgia Infantry, 5/7/1862-6/11/1862
25th Regiment Georgia Volunteer Infantry, 5/16/1862-6/8/1862 & 6/14/1862-6/17/1862
Sources:
8th Bn GVI, GDAH, CSR, 255/52
25th GVI, GDAH, CSR, 256/49; SR, 5/20/1862

592

Camp Smith
Floyd County, Georgia

The camp was located near Rome. See map of Rome on page 303.
Georgia Troops:
Cherokee Legion, Georgia State Guards, 12/5/1863
Source:
Cherokee Legion, Georgia State Guards, Compiled by C. Pat Cates

593

Camp Smith
Whitfield County, Georgia

The camp was located at Gordon Springs.
Georgia Troops:
Smith's Legion, Partisan Rangers, 8/3/1862-8/23/1862, also 9/26/1862
Sources:
SC, 8/26/1862; DU, Huldah Annie (Fain) Briant; 9/26/1862, source not known.

594   **Camp E. Kirby Smith**
Fairfax County, Virginia

The camp was located near Centreville.
Georgia Troops:
21st Regiment Georgia Volunteer Infantry, 11/28/1861-12/13/1861
Sources:
GDAH, CSR, 256/21; 40/50, Thomas M. Hightower

595   **Camp Kirby Smith**
Anderson County, Tennessee

The camp was located about one mile from the Clinch River, near Clinton.
Georgia Troops:
39th Regiment Georgia Volunteer Infantry, 5/13/1862-5/19/1862 & 6/7/1862-6/8/1862
Source:
Personal Reminiscences of a Confederate Soldier Boy in Company F, 39th Georgia Infantry, By Robert M. Magill

596   **Camp William Duncan Smith**
Chatham County, Georgia

The camp was located in the rear of the Savannah City Park, two and one-half miles from Battery Harrison on White Bluff Road, the headquarters for the 32nd Georgia Regiment. The camp was named after Gen. William Duncan Smith, former Colonel of the 20th Regiment Georgia Volunteer Infantry, who died of yellow fever in Charleston, South Carolina, on October 4, 1862. The camp was previously known as Camp Lawton and Camp Jackson.
Georgia Troops:
32nd Regiment Georgia Volunteer Infantry, 10/17/1862-10/21/1862, 10/24/1862-11/21/1862 & 3/5/1863-5/21/1863
Sources:
GDAH, CSR, 256/96; 283/29, William H. Ivey; SDMN, 5/22/1863 & 6/17/1863; DU, William S. Benjamin

597   **Camp Smyrna**
Cobb County, Georgia

The camp was located on the Smyrna Campgrounds, about five miles below Marietta. After only a day or two, the camp name was changed to Camp Brown in honor of Governor Joseph E. Brown.
Georgia Troops:
4th Brigade of Georgia Volunteers, 4/23/1861
Sources:
RWC, 4/26/1861 & 5/30/1861

598   **Camp South May River**

Beaufort County, South Carolina

The camp was located near Bluffton, fifteen miles from Hardeeville, and about six miles from Foot Point.

Georgia Troops:

Phillips' Legion, Cavalry Battalion, Cos. D & F, 6/6/1862-7/18/1862

Source:

GDAH, 283/41, John T. Swan

599   **Camp South Newport**

McIntosh County, Georgia

The camp was located near South Newport.

Georgia Troops:

20th Battalion Georgia Cavalry, Co. A, 4/1863

29th Battalion Georgia Cavalry, Co. C, 10/1864

Sources:

20th Bn GC, GDAH, CSR, 254/6

29th Bn GC, GDAH, CSR, 254/13

600   **Camp Spalding**

Liberty County, Georgia

The camp was located near Riceboro, ten and one-half miles from Sunbury.

Georgia Troops:

1st Battalion Georgia Cavalry, Liberty Independent Troop, 11/8/1861-2/1862

Source:

GDAH, CSR, 253/79

601   **Camp Spalding**

McIntosh County, Georgia

The camp was located near the Spalding residence on the "Ridge," three miles above Darien.

Georgia Troops:

Wiregrass Minutemen, 6/27/1861-7/22/1861 (The company later became Co. B, 2nd Regiment Georgia Volunteer Infantry, then later, they became Co. C, 26th [Lamar's] Regiment Georgia Volunteer Infantry.)

Sources:

SDMN, 6/29/1861 & 8/9/1861

602   **Camp Springs**

Marion County, Tennessee

Location not known.

Georgia Troops:

1st Regiment Georgia Volunteer Cavalry, 5/4/1863

Sources:

GDAH, 283/58, Unit File; SC, 5/9/63

603   **Camp Starke**
Chatham County, Georgia

The camp was located near Savannah.
Georgia Troops:
2nd Regiment Georgia State Troops, Co. F, Georgia Rangers, 1/6/1862
Source:
SDMN, 1/7/1862

604   **Camp Starvation**
Frederick County, Virginia

See Camp Washington at Winchester.
Georgia Troops:
8th Regiment Georgia Volunteer Infantry, 6/26/1861-6/27/1861
Source:
UGA, Ms. 25, Margaret Branch Sexton Collection

605   **Camp Steiner**
Fairfax County, Georgia

The camp was located on Cub Run, one-half mile west of Camp Rocky Run, and four and one-half miles east of Camp Georgia..
Georgia Troops:
15th Regiment Georgia Volunteer Infantry, 11/28/1861-12/24/1861
Sources:
GDAH, CSR, 255/108; UNC, #2097, Alexander H. Stephens

606   **Camp Stephens**
Escambia County, Florida

The camp was located on a hill about one mile above Pensacola on the Florida & Alabama Railroad, and about one and one-half miles from the bay. The parade grounds were just north of camp. See Camp White at this same location.

On October 8, 1861, a detachment of the 5th Georgia prepared for the night attack of Billy Wilson's camp on Santa Rosa Island, across the bay from Pensacola. Private Richard A. Clayton was one of the seventeen chosen from Company F, 5th Regiment Georgia Volunteer Infantry to participate in this expedition. This letter to his father, Dr. Samuel Clayton of Cuthbert, Georgia, describes the attack.

                                        Camp Stephens Oct 24th - 61
        Dear Father
                Your kind favor of the 17th inst. was received and would have been answered yesterday had I not been on guard. The cold wind whistled around my ears last night and of course I feel somewhat dull this morning.
      You asked me for a "circumstantial account" of the "Santa Rosa Expedition." I don't know how to start about giving such an account. I'll not try to tell a polished tale - only a straight forward one in pure English. You have no doubt read many accounts of it in the various newspapers - more interesting than any I could write but since you ask I'll try to give you the truth (as I know it). I'll begin with the beginning and take it all the way through -. Late

on the evening of the 8th Col. Jackson ordered the various companies to be formed in their respective camps. He came to ours (from the Clinch's). He said, "I want 17 men (privates) from this company. I want volunteers. I want them for hazardous work to night. All who are willing to go shoulder arms." The whole company I believe quickly brought their muskets to their shoulders. He then says "Lieut. give me 17 men." Lieut. Douglas then detailed 17 men from the right. I and Milt were (to our joy) included. We prepared - left Camp Stephens 8 O'clock - marched to the wharf - where we waited for the troops from the Navy Yard. (150 men were taken from each Regiment - Each company had it's proportionate number. - These 150 were divided into three companies, viz 1st, 2nd, & 3rd. The first composed of the detachments from the Clinch Rifles - Cuthbert Rifles and Georgia Grays was commanded by Captain Manghum - Lieut. James & Lieut. Hundley. The first company occupied the right of the Battalion.) We waited until about 11 O'clock when the steamer "Time" camp from the Navy Yard. We were about an hour fixing up and getting aboard the "flat boats" - open concerns - we had to stand up on them so thick that if I had fallen he would have knocked down a half dozen. At 12 O'clock precisely - the propeller McAffie - guard boat (now the Nelms) and the steamer Ewing - (now being converted into a gun boat to be called the Bradford) left the 1st wharf each carrying 2 or 3 of the "flat boats" (The whole force 1250 men were placed on these flat concerns). The lights were extinguished at a given signal. Some of us had curious feelings while we were gliding across the bay. I thought of you - my sisters - brothers and friends - prayed God to bless you and them and words. We landed on the Island at 2 O'clock - formed into line - loaded our guns - fixed our bayonets and started up the beach. I will be compelled to confine myself to our own little 5th Regiment - because I don't know much about the balance. We marched very fast - way down next to the water. Sometimes the waves would roll high up above our shoes - sometimes almost to our knees. We had marched about 3 1/2 miles when Col. Jackson cried out "Down men and wait well for the word." We were on our knees in a moment, our pieces cocked ready to fire. The body of men that we had supposed to be the enemy proved to be the Miss. boys. Dreadful would have been the slaughter if we had fired - few if any would have escaped. We started off again - marched about a mile when a shot was heard - one of our scouts had sent one of the scamps - a sentinel to his long home. We marched on when we halted a body of men numbering between 12 & 15. They fired upon us. We returned the fire and not one of them escaped. 2 of our men were killed. Milt had his musket shot by one of the balls so that he could not load it. He dropped it and seized another - (which he loaded). We turned across the Island - found a large wagon road - followed it up - We soon came in sight of Billy Wilson's camps. We marched to within about 20 yards of the camp when we were ordered to "fire" and charge. We fired a volley and with a deafening yell rushed into the camp. The rascals had fled to the fort - leaving guns clothing &c. behind. We killed many while they were running - took about 10 prisoners. We put fire to the tents - burned everything - The Miss. & Florida boys came up and gave us three cheers. After destroying everything we started to march forward when Gen. Bragg fired a gun at the Navy Yard, a signal for the retreat. Gen Anderson had the retreat sounded and we turned our course for our boats. We marched down the beach the same way that we had marched up -
After we had gone some distance - we heard firing ahead.- Our scouts had been fired upon by Major Bodge (Vogdes) and his regulars whom he had led down on the other side of the Island. Here we lost most (that we had killed). The troops rushed up fired and charged. We killed many of them, the balance ran like dogs. I wish you could have seen them. They would stand very well until the command "Charge Bayonets" was given - then they would run - run as Yankees alone can run, Major Bodge was taken Prisoner by Capt. Hallonquist

and Lieut. Nelms. Seven or eight of his men were taken also. We got along very well - until we had got on board our boats - when 2 or three companies of their regulars came up and fired on us with their "long range minnie muskets." 2 or 3 of our men were killed and Gen Anderson was wounded in the arm by their fire. We got off at last. They fired several shots from a battery near the fort at our boats. The balls would pass above and fall in the water. We lost Lieut. Nelms, a fine officer - & a perfect gentleman. Another brave Georgian gone. One of the Yankees fired on him the ball pierced him through the breast. He cried McDuffie's rally (He was Lieut. of the McDuffie Rifles). One of his men standing near rushed on the man who killed Nelms. The fellow cried for mercy - The McDuffie threw him to the ground jumped on him - and says, "Yes, I'll show you mercy" - He raised his "large knife" and came down with a lick which cut the Yanks "heart out." He then cut the fellows throat telling him at the same time, "If I had 3 thousand of you I'd do with them all just as I have done with you." (His words as near as I remember.) Capt. Bradford of the Floridians was killed also. We lost no other officers. We had 2 or 3 officers taken prisoner and several privates. Lieut. C. Layne of the C. S. Marine Corps was taken. He was badly wounded in his leg. He was taken to the Fort - treated well by Col. Wilson. He was sent over to us on condition that when he gets well he is to return to the Fort. Our men taken by them have been sent to New York or Tortugas . We have sent theirs with Major Bodge to Montgomery. I don't know where they will be sent from there. The Expedition was a complete success on our side. We accomplished everything that we were sent for. I have heard the balls whistle - have seen friends fall pierced by the "death" - ball - have heard the dying groan - and then I have heard the victorious shout.

War is an awful thing but can't be helped with us. We are fighting in self defense, and it is a crowd of scamps we are fighting. While our men are in the field - their lowest - meanest scrapings are in opposition to us. Talk about whipping us that can't be done. "Three million of (our) people fighting for their country - their firesides are invincible."

But I must cease. I sent you a letter by Mr. Guismaine. Please send the articles as soon as you can. Excuse my dullness this morning. I will say more about the S. Rosa Affair hereafter. Tell Sis to write to me.   Goodbye

Excuse mistakes &c.   Write soon to
                                                 Your son   R A Clayton

Georgia Troops:
5th Regiment Georgia Volunteer Infantry, 5/25/1861-2/10/1862
Sources:
MT, 6/3/1861; GDAH, CSR, 255/12; SC, 1/28/1862; SDMN, 2/19/1862; PC, letter of Richard A. Clayton

607   **Camp Stephens**
                                 Fulton County, Georgia

    The camp was located near Atlanta.
Georgia Troops:
8th Battalion Cavalry, Georgia State Guards, late 1863
Source:
GDAH, CSR, 253/115

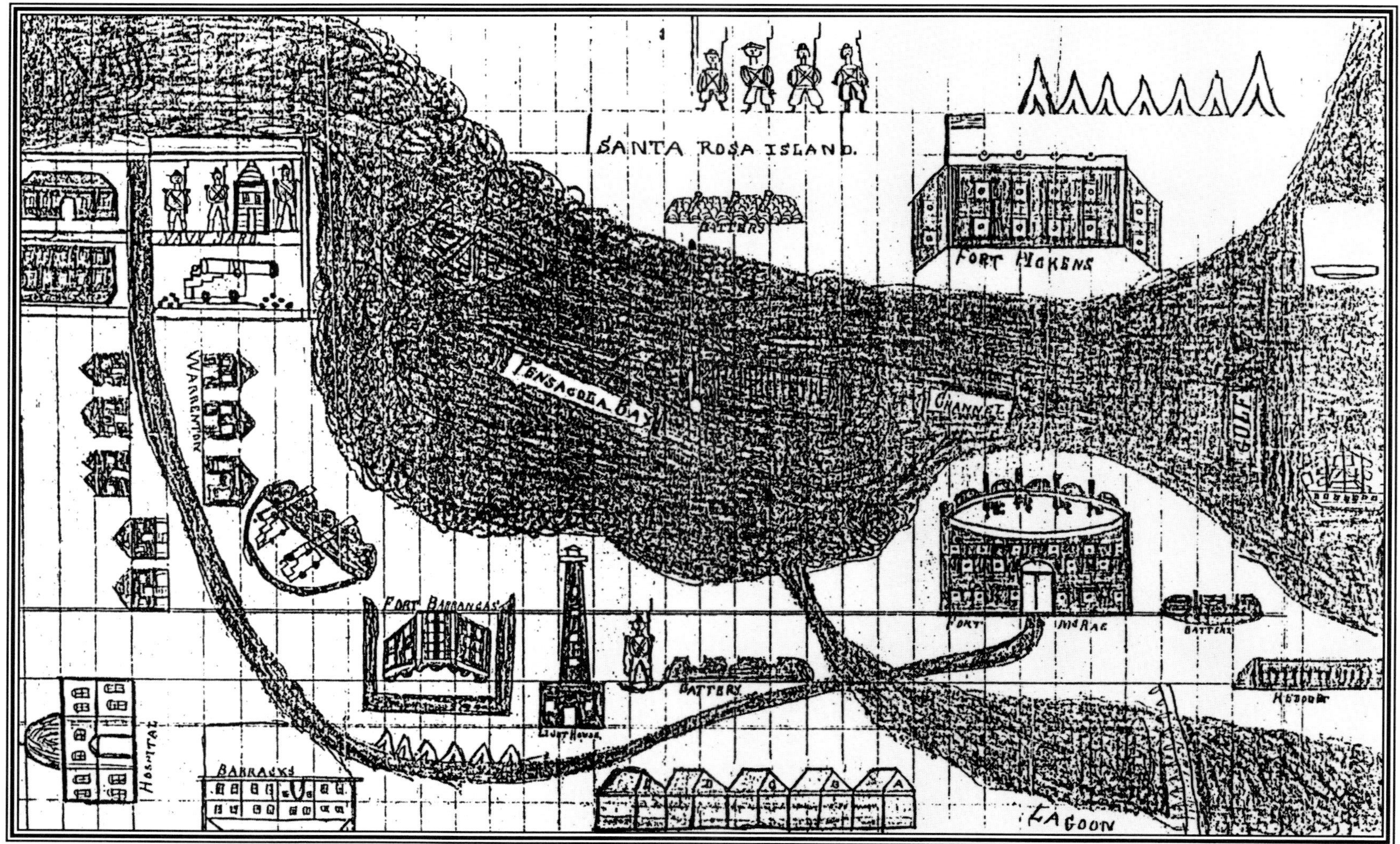

Pensacola Bay area showing the location of Billy Wilson's camp on Santa Rosa Island behind Ft. Pickens
Map courtesy of the Mississippi Department of Archives and History, John R. Rietti papers

MEN OF THE FIFTH GEORGIA
CLINCH RIFLES
photo courtesy of L. C. Mathis, Jr.

Camp Stephens
Spalding County, Georgia

The camp was located one-half mile east of the railroad, two miles north of Griffin, and was about one thousand yards long. This was also the grounds of the Georgia experiment farm in 1905.

The following extract is from a letter of Asbury Hull Jackson of the 44th Georgia, dated March 16th, 1862, written to mother and family.

We are still in our same chicken coops which are about 6 by 8 feet; we got 15 of them at first. Since we got 4 more; and yesterday evening our Capt. got two large wall tents with flies to them which they took for officers tents. So we have now 21 tents for 113 men. We still wish for our (old Clark) tents. Send them on.

There are about 4,000 Soldiers here now. They have been coming in every day this week. I do not know whether all have come or not.

This camp is situated 1/2 mile East of the railroad which runs from Atlanta to Macon, is about 1,000 yards long and a road running through from W to E, all old field except 200 yards of the East end, in which is our, or the third division; our camp is the extreme East one. Our street runs North and South with the Capt. tent on the side of the road. Ours is the prettiest location in camps with the woods on the East and North, and down a slant 150 yards north is a very good spring 12 feet long 2 feet wide and 1 1/2 feet deep and below the spring is a box of the same size for washing etc. West of our camp are located four other companies, located like ours facing the side of the road, in (it) is a great deal of passing. The one next to ours is the Putnam Company, Capt. Hitchcock. Next Cpt. Alliston of Morgan composed of two squads united, one was his, the other was from Henry, next the Baldwin Com. lastly is the Com. from Greene, Capt. Beal.

South of us is the 10th division is more extensive composed of 11 companies in which are some very large tents which they brought from. I have seen Decatur and Columbus Dismukes who are from Webster and Harrison and Johnson Lanier from Marion. Charlie Copeland and Willis Gunn are in the Morgan Company. On the extreme north is the 5 divisions (some 600 yds from us) on the extreme West is the 8th division in which is Charley Allen from Pike. I believe these are all the acquaintances I have seen though I have been around but once. We have company and squad drills every day.

Our Regiment was formed Friday, composed of the following Counties, Clarke, Putnam, Morgan, Greene, Jasper, Henry, Fayette, Pike, Clayton, Spalding.

We elected yesterday the three first officers of the Reg. Cpt. Smith of Macon Col, Capt. Estis of Jonesborough Lieut. Col. and Cpt Banks of Pike Maj, Cpt Beck ran against Estis , and Hitchcock against Banks. The other Field officers are to be appointed to morrow. There is much electioneering here, they come to see our Cpt almost every hour, some for Adjutant, some for Surgeon, and so on.

We had preaching in our division today (at Cpt Allison's tent) by Cpt Hitchcock and again this evening by Rev Wm Sanders who is preaching now. I do not go on account of writing. I went this morning. Our Company as afore said is generally very civil but some other companies are very noisy, hollering at every body that passes, but they are improving.

Georgia Troops:

Bartow Artillery, 8/21/1861 (Later became Co. A, 4th [Stiles'] Infantry Battalion, then Co. A, 22nd Battalion Georgia Heavy Artillery.)

Echols' Light Artillery, 4/7/1862-5/19/1862

Griffin Light Artillery, 5/7/1862-5/23/1862

Joe Thompson Lancers, 9/26/1861-11/5/1861 (Later in camp they changed their designation to Jo Thompson Artillery.)

10th Battalion Georgia Volunteer Infantry, 3/11/1862-5/18/1862

13th (Ector's) Regiment Georgia Volunteer Infantry, 7/13/1861-7/15/1861 (This was their rendezvous point only. They left in a day or two and passed through Atlanta July 16, 1861. See Camp Decatur.)

27th Regiment Georgia Volunteer Infantry, 8/27/1861-11/7/1861 (The regiment was originally refered to as the 21st Regiment Georgia Volunteer Infantry.)

28th Regiment Georgia Volunteer Infantry, 8/27/1861-11/7/1861 (The regiment was originally referred to as the 20th Regiment Georgia Volunteer Infantry.)

44th Regiment Georgia Volunteer Infantry, 3/11/1862-4/7/1862

45th Regiment Georgia Volunteer Infantry, 3/4/1862-4/4/1862 (On 4/4/1862, Col. Hardeman was ordered to Goldsboro.)

46th Regiment Georgia Volunteer Infantry, 3/11/1862-3/21/1862

53rd Regiment Georgia Volunteer Infantry, 5/13/1862-6/23/1862

55th Regiment Georgia Volunteer Infantry, 5/3/1862-5/16/1862

59th Regiment Georgia Volunteer Infantry, 5/8/1862-6/1862 (The 59th Georgia was formed from the 7th Regiment Georgia State Troops.)

7th Battalion Georgia Volunteer Infantry, Irwin Cowboys, Co. A, 8/27/1861-9/18/1861 (The 7th Battalion later became the 61st Regiment Georgia Volunteer Infantry.)

Georgia Militia, 1st Brigade, 9/7/1864, 10/29/1864 & 11/16/1864

Sources:

BA, GDAH, CSR, 257/105

ELA, GDAH, 78/2, provision return in William. J. Moseley file; PC, James Jewell letters.

GLA, GDAH, CSR, 254/61

JTL, AHB, Vol. 14, No. 3

10th Bn GVI, GDAH, 283/17, A. S. Avant; 283/20, Levi R. Cason; 283/26, Martin Hambrick; MCU, 8/12/1862; ASB, 3/26/1862

13th GVI, SFU, 7/16/1861 & 7/23/1861

27th GVI, ADC&S, 8/18/1861 & 10/31/1861; GDAH, CSR, 256/66; 283/32, James McDonald; GDAH, CSR, 256/66

28th GVI, ADC&S, 8/18/1861 & 10/31/1861; ASB, 3/26/1862; SR, 8/27/1861 & 10/18/1861; GDAH, CSR, 257/74

44th GVI, *History of the Doles-Cook Brigade, Army of Northern Virginia*, By Henry W. Thomas; DU, Harden Collection, Asbury Hull Jackson

45th GVI, GDAH, CSR, 257/29

46th GVI, GDAH, CSR, 257/35, DU, Harden Collection

53rd GVI, ADC&S, 5/17/1862; GDAH, CSR, 257/78; SC, 5/6/1862

55th GVI, *A Georgia Soldier in the Civil War*, By R. D. Chapman; GDAH, CSR, 257/87

59th GVI, GDAH, CSR, 257/99

IC, GDAH, CSR, 257/113

GM, GDAH, 283/26, Horatio H. Goss; 283/43, William Henry Warr; SFU, 11/8/1864

609   **Camp Stephens**
New Hanover County, North Carolina
This camp was possibly near Ft. Fisher.
Georgia Troops:
7th Regiment Confederate Cavalry, Co. E, 1/1864-4/1864
Source:
GDAH, CSR, 258/69

610   **Camp A. H. Stephens**
Prince William County, Virginia
The camp was located near Manassas.
Georgia Troops:
21st Regiment Georgia Volunteer Infantry, 11/1861-3/9/1862
Source:
GDAH, CSR, 256/21

611   **Camp Stevensburg**
Culpeper County, Virginia
The camp was in the Stevensburg area. This unit was also in the Stevensburg area from August 17, 1863, until they moved to the Orange Courthouse area on August 28 or 29, 1863.
Georgia Troops:
Cobb's Legion, Cavalry Battalion, 1/26/1863-2/16/1863
Sources:
GDAH, 283/37, Marquis D. L. Pittman; 283/38, Jeremiah E. Ritch; ADC&S, 3/8/1863; UGA, Ms. 184, William Gaston Delony

612   **Camp Stoddard**
Liberty County, Georgia
The camp was located near Hinesville.

Camp Stoddard, Liberty County, Ga.
October 5th, 1861.
At a called meeting of the Bartow Light Infantry, Faulk Invincibles and Coffee Rangers, Capt. Griffin of the Faulk Invincibles was called to the chair, and Sergeant Liles, of the Bartow Light Infantry, was requested to act as secretary, The following resolutions were unanimously adopted:

Resolved, That in desolving our military connection with Col. Gaulden, we take pleasure in testifying to his universal kindness while here.

Resolved, That we as volunteers, tender him our thanks for the same, with the assurance that we shall ever rejoice at his success for all his efforts; and we believe his Regiment would have been formed but for the fact he was only authorized a Regiment for the war, while other Regiments are being formed for twelve months.

Resolved, That the thanks of the companies be tendered Messrs. _____ Fraser, _____ Harrison and the ladies of Hindsville to us while in camp.

On motion, it was ordered that the above be published in the Savannah papers.

A. J. Liles, Sec'y.   Capt. Griffin, Ch'mn.

Georgia Troops:
Bartow Light Infantry, Faulk Invincibles, Coffee Rangers & Mount Vernon Rifles, 9/1861-10/8/1861 (The Bartow Light Infantry and the Faulk Invincibles became a part of the 13th [Styles'] Regiment Georgia Volunteer Infantry. The Mount Vernon Rifles became Co. A, 2nd Regiment Georgia State Troops, then later Co. G, 57th Regiment Georgia Volunteer Infantry.)
Sources:
SR, 10/8/1861; SDMN, 10/10/1861; GDAH, CSR, 256/59

613 **Camp Strurbury (Strawberry)**
Henrico County, Virginia
   The camp was located within two miles of Richmond, possibly on Strawberry Hill.
Georgia Troops:
21st Regiment Georgia Volunteer Infantry, 7/12/1862
Source:
GDAH, 71/7, Sidney J. Richardson

614 **Camp Stuart (Stewart)**
Chatham County, Georgia
   The camp was located near Savannah.
Georgia Troops:
Columbus Artillery, Croft's Battery Georgia Light Artillery, 6/1863
Source:
GDAH, CSR, 254/50

615 **Camp Styles**
Glynn County, Georgia
   The camp was located on St. Simon's Island.
Georgia Troops:
Jackson Artillery, 11/8/1861-11/26/1861
3rd Battalion Georgia Cavalry, Co. A, Atlantic & Gulf Guards, 10/19/1861-2/16/1862 (This battalion became part of the 4th [Clinch's] Regiment Georgia Volunteer Cavalry.)
1st Volunteer Regiment of Georgia, Irish Volunteers, Co. E, 12/31/1861
13th (Styles') Regiment Georgia Volunteer Infantry, 8/19/1861-2/16/1862 (The regiment reorganized 5/10/1862 in Savannah and became the 26th Regiment Georgia Volunteer Infantry.)
27th Georgia Infantry Regiment, 10/10/1861-12/7/1861 (This regiment became the 31st Regiment Georgia Volunteer Infantry in March 1862.)
Sources:
JA, GDAH, CSR, 254/58
3rd Bn GC, GDAH, CSR, 254/21
1st VRG, IV, GDAH, MR, 279/68
13th GVI, GDAH, CSR, 256/59
27th GIR, GDAH, 283/39, William L. Scaife; GDAH, CSR, 256/89

Camp Sugar Loaf
New Hanover County, North Carolina

The camp was located near Sugar Loaf, about fifteen miles below Wilmington, and six miles above Ft. Fisher. See Atlas Plate CXXXII, 1.

This extract is from a letter written by Green M. Fain to his cousin, Huldah Annie Fain, on January 30, 1865.

"I have no news of interest to write you, war never is unimportant in this part; We have a great talk of peace hear and I have great faith in believing that this war will have a speedy termination one way or the other."

Georgia Troops:
23rd Regiment Georgia Volunteer Infantry, 1/30/1865
Source:
DU, Huldah Annie (Fain) Briant letters

Camp Sumter
Macon County, Georgia

This camp was located at Andersonville prison. See the plan view of the Andersonville prison area and the camps of the guards on page 302.
Georgia Troops:
1st, 2nd, 3rd & 4th Regiments of Georgia Infantry Reserves, 1/26/1864-9/1864
55th Regiment Georgia Volunteer Infantry, 6/30/1863-10/30/1864 (The men from the 55th Georgia were those who were sick or on detached duty at Cumberland Gap on September 9, 1863, when the regiment was captured.)
57th Regiment Georgia Volunteer Infantry, Cos. A, B, C, D, E, F, H, I & K, 4/22/1864
Furlow's Battalion, 7/27/1864
Sources:
GIR, GDAH, CSR, 254/77, 254/105, 254/121 & 255/8
55th GVI, GDAH, CSR, 257/87
57th GVI, GDAH, CSR, 257/95
FB, ECN, 8/3/1864
Map: *Century Magazine*, Vol. 40, p. 452

Camp Sumter
Chesterfield County, Virginia

The camp was located near Chesterfield Station on the Richmond, Fredericksburg, & Potomac Railroad.
Georgia Troops:
11th Battalion Georgia Light Artillery, 12/26/1862-4/30/1863
Sources:
SDMN, 5/1/1863; PC, James Hillhouse Alexander

619   **Camp Sweetwater**
Monroe County, Tennessee
   The camp was located at Sweetwater.
Georgia Troops:
53rd Regiment Georgia Volunteer Infantry, 11/7/1863-11/10/1863
Phillips' Legion, Infantry Battalion, 11/7/1863-11/8/1863
Sources:
53rd GVI, GDAH, UDC Books, Vol. XIV, Rev. William R. Stillwell
PL, KMNBPL, Marcus L. Green

620   **Camp Symons**
Chatham County, Georgia
   The camp was located at Battery Harrison, three and one-half miles from Savannah on the
White Bluff Road. See Camp Battery Harrison.
Georgia Troops:
Chatham Siege Artillery, 4/30/1862-5/10/1862
Sources:
SDMN, 4/30/1862 & 5/30/1862

621
Camp Taliaferro
Chatham County, Georgia

The camp was located seven miles from Savannah, one-half mile from the left of the Isle of Hope defenses.
Georgia Troops:
32nd Regiment Georgia Volunteer Infantry, 3/27/1863
Source:
A Calendar of Confederate Papers, Edited by Douglas Southall Freeman

622
Camp Taliaferro
Chatham County, Georgia

The camp was located near the city hospital near Savannah.
Georgia Troops:
18th Infantry Battalion, Savannah Volunteer Guards, 6/6/1863-7/3/1863
Sources:
GDAH, CSR, 256/3; SDMN, 7/4/1863

623
Camp Taliaferro
Greene County, North Carolina

The camp was located near Snow Hill.
Georgia Troops:
7th Regiment Confederate Cavalry, Headquarters, 7/27/1863
Source:
GDAH, CSR, 258/69

624
Camp Tatnall
Fairfax County, Virginia

The camp was located near Fairfax.
Georgia Troops:
21st Regiment Georgia Volunteer Infantry, 9/16/1861
Source:
RWC, 10/4/1861

625
Camp Tattnall
Camden County, Georgia

The camp was located about five miles south of Woodbine, across from Cole's Cemetery.
Georgia Troops:
4th (Clinch's) Regiment Georgia Volunteer Cavalry, 1/1863-4/1863
29th Battalion Georgia Cavalry, Co. E, 10/1864
Sources:
4th GVC, GDAH, CSR, 253/94
29th Bn GC, GDAH, CSR, 254/13

626 **Camp Tattnall**

Chatham County, Georgia

The camp was located near Savannah and is possibly the same camp as Camp Tattnall of the 29th Regiment Georgia Volunteer Infantry.
Georgia Troops:
Savannah Volunteer Guards, 6/5/1861 (Later they became part of the 18th Infantry Battalion.)
Source:
SDMN, 6/6/1861

627 **Camp Tattnall**

Chatham County, Georgia

The camp was located on the right of White Bluff Road, one mile from Camp Lawton, and one mile from Camp Wilson, above where the Gulf Road (Railroad) crosses.
Georgia Troops:
29th Regiment Georgia Volunteer Infantry, 2/22/1862-4/16/1862
Sources:
RWC, 3/7/1862 & 5/2/1862

628 **Camp Taylor**

Jackson County, Alabama

The camp was located on Long Island on the Tennessee River in front of Bridgeport.
Georgia Troops:
3rd Regiment Georgia Volunteer Cavalry, 8/25/1862-8/29/1862
Sources:
KMNBPL, William N. Thompson; *War was the Place, a centenniel collection of Confederate soldier letters*, Chattahoochee Valley Historical Society, letter of John David Johnson

629 **Camp Taylor**

Chatham County, Georgia

The camp was located east of Laurel Grove Cemetery.
Georgia Troops:
2nd Battalion Georgia Cavalry, Co. F, Chatham Light Horse, 1/29/1862
Source:
SDMN, 2/19/1862

630 **Camp Taylor**

Clarke County, Georgia

The camp was located near Thibodaux.
Georgia Troops:
Athens Reserve Corp, Georgia Infantry (Light Duty), 9/30/1862
Source:
GDAH, CSR, 258/52

631   **Camp Taylor**
                                  Warren County, Mississippi

The camp was located near Vicksburg.
Georgia Troops:
57th Regiment Georgia Volunteer Infantry, 2/9/1863-3/12/1863 (The 57th Georgia was in Gen. Thomas H. Taylor's Brigade at this time.)
Source:
GDAH, CSR, 257/97

632   **Camp Taylor**
                                    Fairfax County, Virginia

The camp was near Taylor's house, near Centreville. This was a camp of Toomb's Brigade.

In a letter to the *Central Georgian* newspaper dated September 13, 1861, Ivy Duggan of the 15th Georgia describes what they found on their camp grounds when they arrived at Camp Taylor.

> After marching about six or seven miles, we arrived at our present locality, Camp Taylor. This place is about one-half mile south-east of Centreville, and immediately on the old "Bradock Road." We are camped on a high open field, convenient to three or four springs of good water, and are on the very spot where thousands of the enemy camped a few days before the Manassas battle. Among the articles we have found on their old camping ground are canteens, tin cups and plates, knives, old clothes, gun locks, bayonets, two or three pistols, decks of cards, parts of letters, envelopes representing in glowing colors a New York Zouave leading a charge and bearing a staff with a sign-board pointing "To Richmond."
>
> The citizens here say it was indeed a powerful army, well equipped, and humanly speaking, seemed perfectly irresistable. The idea that they might be defeated by the "Southern barbarians" seems never to have entered their minds.

Georgia Troops:
1st Georgia Regulars, 9/10/1861-9/16/1861
2nd Regiment Georgia Volunteer Infantry, 9/10/1861-9/16/1861
15th Regiment Georgia Volunteer Infantry, 9/11/1861-9/18/1861
Sources:
1st GR, *Diary of W. H. Andrews, 1st Sergt. Co. M, 1st Georgia Regulars, from February, 1861, to May 2, 1865.* By W. H. Andrews
2nd GVI, GDAH, CSR, 254/100
15th GVI, GDAH, 53/64, CG, Ivy Duggan; 17/78, John M. Tilley

633   **Camp Tazewell**
                                   Claiborne County, Tennessee

The camp was located near Tazewell.
Georgia Troops:
9th Battalion Georgia Volunteer Infantry, 8/15/1862
Source:
GDAH, CSR, 255/63

634   **Camp Terrell**
                                    Orange County, Virginia
The camp was located near Orange Court House.
Georgia Troops:
44th Regiment Georgia Volunteer Infantry, 4/1/1864-5/4/1864
Source:
GDAH, CSR, 257/23

635   **Camp Thomas**
                                    Fulton County, Georgia
     The boys in Camp Thomas said they received soup and milk from Mrs. Isaac Winship. Isaac
Winship lived on Harris Street, between Orme and Hayden Streets in Atlanta. This is now about
one-quarter mile to the southwest of little five points in down-town Atlanta. Mr Isaac Winship
was a partner with his two brothers George and Robert in the Winship Iron Works at the corner
of the Western & Atlantic Railroad and Foundry Street in Atlanta.
Georgia Troops:
Stephens Battalion Georgia State Guards & Bartow Invincibles, 10/7/1861
Source:
SC, 10/7/1861; GDAH, Atlanta City directory of 1859-1860 on microfiche

636   **Camp Thomas**
                                    Orange County, Virginia
The camp was located near Orange Court House.
Georgia Troops:
35th Regiment Georgia Volunteer Infantry, 3/28/1864-5/4/1864
Sources:
EU, # 340, Aaron M. Sewell; GDAH, CSR, 256/103

637   **Camp Thomson**
                                    Glynn County, Georgia
The camp was located near Brunswick.
Georgia Troops:
Thomson Guards, 12/10/1861 (The company was originally part of Lamar's 26th Regiment
Georgia Infantry.)
Source:
MT, 12/25/1861

638   **Camp Thorpe**
                                    McIntosh County, Georgia
The camp was located near South Newport.
Georgia Troops:
1st Battalion Georgia Cavalry, Lamar Mounted Rifles, 12/21/1861
Source:
SR, 1/8/1862

Camp Thunderbolt
Chatham County, Georgia

The camp was located near Thunderbolt.

Camp Thunderbolt May the 13th 1862
Dear Sister

I seat myself down this morning to write you a few lines to let you know that I am tolerable well hopeing they may find you all enjoying good health Sister I have nothing of importance to write more than to let you know how I am geting allong and all about them the 13th Geo. pickit fore of them took fifteen yankies last sunday without fireing a gun the yankies were unharmed they took them on whitmarsh Island the yankies sayed they going on a pleasure trip to forte pulaska but I supose they have found a lodgeing some whers else they were sent to Macon for safe keeping I have been vacinated and when the scab comes off I will send it home in a leter so if any of you wants to try it you coan have the chance I hear that the yankies have got Norfolk Va it come in the papers this morng it may be so and may not. I want you to save me some butter a caist I come home I will hav try to come up next Saturday if I can I don want you to get look for me for I dont expect to get off So nothing more at the present but remain

Your Affectionate
Brother A P Thompson

Georgia Troops:
25th Regiment Georgia Volunteer Infantry, 2/5/1862-4/5/1862 (The Regiment moved to Camp Young, then back on 5/3/1862-5/13/1862.)
Sources:
Letters and Papers of Archibald P. Thompson and James S. Thompson, Two Confederate Soldiers of Screven County, Georgia, Compiled by Rabun A. Lee, Jr.; GHS, #874, Claudius C. Wilson

640   **Camp Thunderbolt Battery**
Chatham County, Georgia

The camp was located at Thunderbolt Battery on St. Augustine Creek, four miles southeast of Savannah.

An unidentified soldier from Augusta wrote a letter to the *Augusta Chronicle & Sentinel* describing their accommodations. This extract from the letter gives an idea of their activities and needs.The 63rd Regiment Georgia Volunteer Infantry was located at the Thunderbolt Battery until they left for a short time to participate in the Atlanta Campaign the end of April, 1864.

We are comfortably quartered in log houses immediately in the rear of the battery. These are kept very neat; this contributes to no small degree to the health of the men. We have prayer meeting among ourselves twice a week, which are largely attended, and a general interest taken in the meeting. We experience some inconvenience from want of hymn books.

Our rations invariably run short and we would fare poorly indeed, did not our relatives and friends at home send us boxes. Mr. Jesse Ansley has more than once liberally contributed vegetables and other necessaries to our corps, all of which has been most highly appreciated and will be most gratefully remembered.

Georgia Troops:
63rd Regiment Georgia Volunteer Infantry, 1/1862-4/1862 & 4/1863-12/1863
Sources:
UGA, Ms. 15, Florence Hodgson Heidler Collection, John M. & Will B. C. Coker letters; GDAH, CSR, 256/49; ADC&S, 8/29/1863

641   **Camp Tiller**
Spalding County, Georgia
The camp was located on a hill about one-half mile and in full view of Griffin. The camp was also seven miles from the Flint River, and in a few letters referred to as Camp Stephens.
Georgia Troops:
Echols' Light Artillery, 5/19/1862-8/19/1862
Source:
PC, James Jewell letters

642   **Camp Tolo**
Madison County, Florida
The camp was located about twenty miles from Monticello near Station No. 5 on the Georgia and Pensacola Railroad.
Georgia Troops:
29th Battalion Georgia Cavalry, Co. C, 1/23/1864-2/1/1864
Source:
GDAH, CSR, 254/13

643   **Camp Tom**
Frederick County, Virginia
This was the camp of Cobb's Brigade, and was located seven miles west of Winchester. The camp was named after Gen. Howell Cobb's younger brother, Gen. Thomas (Tom or T. R. R.) Cobb, who had taken over his command while he nursed an infected foot.
Georgia Troops:
16th Regiment Georgia Volunteer Infantry, 9/30/1862-10/9/1862
24th Regiment Georgia Volunteer Infantry, 9/30/1862-10/9/1862
Cobb's Legion, 9/30/1862-10/9/1862
Sources:
Cobb's Brigade; GDAH, 283/17, Thomas A. Barrow; *Howell Cobb's Confederate Career*, By Horace Montgomery, Confederate Centennial Studies, Number Ten; UGA, Ms. 69, David C. Barrow Papers

644   **Camp Toombs**
Jasper County, South Carolina
The camp was located near Hardeeville.
Georgia Troops:
Phillips' Legion, Cavalry Battalion, Co. A, 4/5/1862-4/29/1862
Source:
GDAH, 283/16, James R. Andrews; SFU, 4/15/1862

645   **Camp Toombs**

Culpeper County, Virginia

The camp was at Warrenton Springs, near Culpeper Court House, where the troops were quartered in the resort buildings. It also served as a hospital the entire war.

Georgia Troops:

15th Regiment Georgia Volunteer Infantry, 3/15/1862

Source:

The Granite Farm Letters, Edited by John Rozier

646   **Camp Toombs**

Fairfax County, Virginia

The camp was located on a field near Fairfax Court House.

Georgia Troops:

21st Regiment Georgia Volunteer Infantry, 8/1861 & 10/1/1861-10/2/1861

Sources:

GDAH, UDC Books, Vol. VIII, 186; RWC, 11/8/1861

647   **Camp Toombs**

Henrico County, Virginia

The camp of Toomb's Brigade was located about two miles from the center of Richmond, near the reservoir, on a hill with no trees. At the same time, this same camp was known as Camp Winder by several other Georgia Regiments. See Camp Winder near the reservoir. Also, see Camp Reservoir.

Georgia Troops:

Troup Artillery, 7/4/1861-7/25/1861

Sources:

ASB, 7/17/1861 & 7/31/1861

648   **Camp Toombs**

Henrico County, Virginia

The camp was located on Meadows' Ridge on the Chickahominy River. This was the camp of Toomb's Brigade.

Georgia Troops:

1st Georgia Regulars, 5/19/1862-6/1/1862

2nd Regiment Georgia Volunteer Infantry,* 5/19/1862-6/1/1862

15th Regiment Georgia Volunteer Infantry,* 5/19/1862-6/1/1862

17th Regiment Georgia Volunteer Infantry,* 5/19/1862-6/1/1862

20th Regiment Georgia Volunteer Infantry, 5/19/1862-6/1/1862 (On 5/2/1862, the 20th Georgia was detached from Gen. Early's Brigade and permanently assigned to Gen. Toomb's Brigade.)

* No letters or documents have been found for these units with this camp name. It is known they were in this camp.

Sources:

1st GR: *Diary of W. H. Andrews, 1st Sergt. Co. M, 1st Georgia Regulars, from February, 1861 to May 2, 1865*, By W. H. Andrews

2nd GVI, Same references to Brigade as 1st Ga. Regs. and 20th Ga. Vol. Inf.

15th GVI, Same references to Brigade as 1st Ga. Regs. and 20th Ga. Vol. Inf.
17th GVI, Same references to Brigade as 1st Ga. Regs. and 20th Ga. Vol. Inf.
20th GVI, GDAH, 171/39, UDC, Lizzie Rutherford Chapter, letter # 11, George A. Weldon;
CE, 5/27/1862; FU, 6/17/1862

649   **Camp Toombs**
Louisa County, Virginia
   The camp was located a few miles southwest of Gordonsville.
Georgia Troops:
20th Regiment Georgia Volunteer Infantry, 8/13/1862-8/16/1862
Source:
GDAH, 171/39, UDC, Lizzie Rutherford Chapter, letter # 14, George A. Weldon

650   **Camp Toombs**
Prince William County, Virginia
   The camp was located near Manassas. See Camp Georgia, No. 255. This may be the same
camp.
Georgia Troops:
15th Regiment Georgia Volunteer Infantry, Co. D, 12/31/1861-1/31/1862
Source:
GDAH, 19/79, John M. Tilley

651   **Camp Top Sail**
New Hanover County, Virginia
   The camp was located at Top Sail Sound and near the mouth of Cape Fear River, seventeen
miles from Wilmington.
Georgia Troops:
47th Regiment Georgia Volunteer Infantry, 1/4/1863-2/23/1863
Sources:
GDAH, CSR, 257/42; *The Barefoot Confederate*, By Dixon Hollingsworth

652   **Camp Trapier**
Georgetown County, South Carolina
   The camp was located near Georgetown. This was the headquarters of the Waccamaw cavalry
forces. On March 13, 1864, the 21st Battalion Georgia Cavalry was ordered to Savannah.
Georgia Troops:
21st Battalion Georgia Cavalry, 12/14/1863-3/13/1864
Sources:
GDAH, CSR, 254/9; SR, 3/19/1864

653   **Camp Trouble**
                                          Coastal Georgia

   The location of this camp is not known.
Georgia Troops:
4th (Clinch's) Regiment Georgia Volunteer Cavalry, Co. D, 5/1863 & 6/1863
Source:
GDAH, CSR, 253/94

654   **Camp Troup (Troupe)**
                                       Chatham County, Georgia

   The camp was located three and one-half miles east of Savannah on the road to Causton's Bluff,
and about six miles from McKay's Point. Duty was to support Battery Lee and picket McKay's
Point. See Camp Mackey. This is the same location spelled differently.
Georgia Troops:
25th Regiment Georgia Volunteer Infantry, Cos. C & E, 8/1862-10/29/1862 (Various companies,
one or two at a time would be sent to picket McKay's Point.)
29th Regiment Georgia Volunteer Infantry, Co. I, 9/1862-10/29/1862 (Various companies, one or
two at a time would be sent to picket McKay's Point.)
47th Regiment Georgia Volunteer Infantry, Co. D, 9/6/1863-9/13/1863
Sources:
25th GVI, GDAH, CSR, 256/49; RWC, 10/10/1862
29th GVI, GDAH, CSR, 256/79; RWC, 10/10/1862
47th GVI, GDAH, CSR, 257/42; RWC, 10/10/1862

655   **Camp Troupe**
                                        Ware County, Georgia

   The camp was located at Tebeauville, now Waycross, at Station # 9 on the Savannah, Albany &
Gulf Railroad. The troops in this camp were enroute to Florida.
Georgia Troops:
12th Battalion Georgia Volunteers, 2/26/1864-3/9/1864
Sources:
GDAH, CSR, 254/31-34

656   **Camp Truesdale**
                                      Sumner County, Tennessee

   The camp was located near Pritchettville, close to the Kentucky state line. Camp Truesdale was
one of the major training camps of Tennessee troops.

                              From North Georgia and Tennessee.
   At Camp Truesdale the other day one of the companies of the Georgia State Guard went
   to receive their arms. One of the men, who was a veteran of the Mexican War, had his
   attention called to the fact of his name being cut on the stock of the gun he had drawn, and
   looking at it recognized it as the identical weapon he had used in the Mexican war, and on
   which he had cut his name with his pocket knife.

Georgia Troops:
Georgia State Guards, 10/1863
Source:
ADC&S, 10/20/1863

657   **Camp Tucker**
Georgetown County, South Carolina
   The location of this camp is not known.
Georgia Troops:
21st Battalion Georgia Cavalry, Co. E, 6/15/1863 (By Special Order No. 75, this company left
Camp Tucker and encamped on the North Santee River, one mile below Managault's Ferry. See
Camp Lucas.)
Source:
GDAH, CSR, 254/9

658   **Camp Turner**
Orange County, Virginia
   The camp was located near Orange Court House.
Georgia Troops:
4th Regiment Georgia Volunteer Infantry, 4/1/1864
Source:
GDAH, CSR, 254/128

659   **Camp Tybee**
Chatham County, Georgia
   The camp was located about one-half mile from King Landing on Tybee Island.
Georgia Troops:
Columbus Guards, later Co. G, 2nd Regiment Georgia Volunteer Infantry, 4/20/1861-4/23/1861
Source:
CE, 4/25/1861

[COMMUNICATED]
Effingham Speaks for Herself
Mount Pleasant, August 1, 1961.
   At a fish party on the 26th ultimo, at Mount Pleasant, Effingham County, the ladies
(about fifty in number) made up and formed a company styling themselves the "Mount
Pleasant Rangers." The company was duly organized, and the gallant and truly patriotic A.
H. Malory was chosen as their Captain. Their number is still increasing and I expect they
will soon make their appearance in full uniform, which will be made of homespun. They
bid to excel some of the militia companies; and, should an invasion come, you may depend
on the Mount Pleasant Rangers. Success to the fair soldiers.   B. FLETCHER.

SDMN 8/8/61

---

660   **Camp Vallambrosa**
Henrico County, Virginia
The camp was located on Mechanicsville turnpike, three miles from Richmond on the Wilkin's farm.
Georgia Troops:
Troup Artillery, 5/22/1862-5/25/1862
Cobb's Legion, Infantry Battalion, 5/22/1862-5/25/1862
Sources:
TA, ASB, 4/20/64; GDAH, 283/17, Thomas A. Barrow
CL, GDAH, 160/74, Capt. Joel Crawford Barnett

661   **Camp Van Dorn**
Knox County, Tennessee
The camp was located one and one-half miles from Knoxville in a pine grove. "most of the regiments from Big Shanty (Camp McDonald) are here," Hezekiah M. McCorkle.
Georgia Troops:
9th Battalion Georgia Volunteer Infantry, 4/19/1862-4/28/1862
40th Regiment Georgia Volunteer Infantry, 5/17/1862-5/24/1862
52nd Regiment Georgia Volunteer Infantry, 4/19/1862-5/21/1862 & 6/21/1862-6/23/1862
Sources:
9th Bn GVI, GDAH, 40/17, Military Records of Georgia; 283/32, Hezekiah M. McCorkle
40th GVI, GDAH, 199/58, Clontz Family Papers
52nd GVI, ADC&S, 6/28/1862; GDAH, 9/79, Augustus and Wier Boyd; EU, # 346, Andrew Edge; PC, Leander F. Crumly

662   **Camp Vason**
Lee County, Georgia
The camp was located on the railroad near Starkeville.
Georgia Troops:
Lee County Volunteers, 5/15/1861-5/20/1861 (The company later became Co. B, 11th Regiment Georgia Volunteer Infantry.)
Sources:
AP, 5/16/1861 & 5/23/1861

663   **Camp Vason**
Worth County, Georgia
The camp was located at Isabella.
Georgia Troops:
Yancey Independents, 6/10/1861 (The company later became Co. G, 14th Regiment Georgia Volunteer Infantry.)
Source:
AP, 6/13/1861

664   **Camp Verdery**

Gordon County, Georgia

The camp was probably on the Western & Atlantic Railroad, near Resaca.
Georgia Troops:
2nd (Storey's) Regiment Infantry, Georgia State Line, Co. I, 6/1863 & 7/1863
Source:
Not Known

665   **Camp Vernon**

Chatham County, Georgia

The camp was located at Beaulieu plantation on the Vernon River.
Georgia Troops:
2nd Battalion Georgia Cavalry, Co. D, Georgia Hussars, Co. B, 4/24/1862-7/24/1862
Sources:
SR, 6/4/62; SDMN, 5/29/1862; EU, #12, John H. Ash; GDAH, CSR, 253/86

666   **Camp Victory**

Prince William County, Virginia

The camp was located near the hospital camp near Manassas.
Georgia Troops:
8th Regiment Georgia Volunteer Infantry, 7/27/1861
Source:
EU, #13, Godfrey Barnsley

667   **Camp Vincent**

Suffolk County, Virginia

The camp was located six miles west of Camp Blanchard in the forks of the Elizabeth, Nansemond and James Rivers. See Atlas Plate XXVI, 4.
Georgia Troops:
22nd Regiment Georgia Volunteer Infantry, 4/1862-5/1862 & 7/1862-10/1862
Sources:
GDAH, CSR, 256/28; 283/20, Alexander H. Campbell

668   **Camp Wade**
Randolph County, Georgia

The camp was located near Cuthbert, and probably named after Capt. R. W. Wade of Company H.
Georgia Troops:
29th Battalion Georgia Cavalry, Cos. G & H, 2/12/1864-2/16/1864 (The companies were here on conscript duty.)
Sources:
ECN, 2/17/1864; GDAH, CSR, 254/14

669   **Camp Wakefield**
Sussex County, Virginia

The camp was located near Wakefield.
Georgia Troops:
7th Regiment Confederate Cavalry, Cos. D, G & K, 7/1862-10/1862 (Companies. D & K of the 7th Confederate Cavalry later became companies D & K of the 10th Georgia Cavalry, Company G later became Co. D of the 16th Battalion North Carolina Cavalry.)
Source:
GDAH, CSR, 258/69

670   **Camp Walker**
Escambia County, Florida

The camp was near Warrenton Navy Yard, two miles from the new light house, and near the General Hospital.
Georgia Troops:
1st Independent Battalion of Georgia Volunteers, 4/1861-10/1861 (Later the 1st Battalion became the Georgia and Mississippi Regiment, then the 36th [Villigipue's] Regiment Georgia Volunteer Infantry, and finally the 1st Confederate Regiment Georgia Infantry.)
Source:
GDAH, CSR, 256/116

671   **Camp Walker**
Chatham County, Georgia

This camp was named for Gen. W. H. T. Walker, Commander of the 3rd Brigade Georgia State Troops, who were in this camp.

> Camp Walker, our present station, is situated four and a half miles above Savannah, and about midway between the Central and Charleston Railroads. The location is on a flat of Ground, dubbed with the refreshing name of "Biscuit Hill," which resembles about as much as turnip resembles a bar of music; for like Camp Harrison, the situation is level and sandy, and I think, as the water is good and healthy.

The above extract is from the *Rome Weekly Courier*, January 16, 1862, signed, NEMO.

The following letter is from the *Southern Confederacy*, January 24, 1862.

Camp Walker, Savannah,
Jan. 20, 1862.

Dear Confederacy: You must be weary of the monotonous sketches of general evolutions and revolutions, pagean tries and paraphernalia of military encampments, but I must forward you the latest camp "dots."

As it is latest in date, I'll tell you first - We were honored to-day with a visit by his Excellency, Joseph E. The entire command near Savannah was called into line, dressed in the best uniforms, fixed and fitted, armed and harnessed for any emergency. Infantry, Artillery, and Cavalry, each, in its own parade ground, passed in review before the Governor and his aids with burnished guns and glittering bayonets, presenting a grand array of patriots The whole programme was an entire success. Some regiments vocalized the camps with noisy cheers for the Chief Executive of Georgia, while others did not think it prudent to act so foolishly.

The visit of the Governor, the very strict orders daily renewed and enforced, the getting together of muskets, Enfield rifles, and ammunition, may be ominous of a spicy change in the excercises of the camp. If the Burnside fleet lands on the north shore of the Ogeechee and attempts to take Savannah by land, we will have some pretty exercise for a few hours, but the only thing about this programme that we hate is, they do not all come on us this way at once, so we can kill them up and be done with it.

This powerful fleet, which is to be so effective (!) will end in gasconade as the others, and we will have to sheathe our swords in dissapointment again. This is my prediction.

Our company, the "J. L. Calhoun Guards," has been some days without a Captain, the first one having resigned. On last Saturday, 18th inst., we elected Mr J. M. Hill, of Newnan, to take the command. His election was entirely unanimous, for all knew him to be every inch a *man*, a man in body, heart and head. This leads us to believe that all things will work together for our good.

Col. Chastain's regiment buried another one of its brave patriots on the 16th inst., a Mr. Smith from Union County. He died in his tent, without a kind sister, devoted wife or mother to sooth the last moments of his stay on earth. Is it superstition to think that the beings of brightest glory, spirits from the mansions of perfect love, stay with and comfort the dying soldier and feast his mind on the themes and scenery of Heaven? May that God, who is Love, make the scanty bed for the sick soldier and preserve him from every want.

His comrades followed him to the grave and buried him with martial honors, near the old vault of the English Telfair and Gibbon family, where have slept for 70 years, over 200 brave patriots of revolutionary distinction. Close by his grave, too, are resting in the arms of Death over 500 red men of the forest, who were killed on the same spot, in 1778. Poor, wearied soldier! He sleeps in a historic cemetery, with those who died in gaining the liberty that he sacrificed his life in defending. Rest on, departed! and while the agony wrung hearts of the loved ones at home call loudly for their lost companion, may thy spirit be enjoying the rich fruition of that bright land beyond the veil which death alone can tear asunder.

Soldiers should be allowed to go to their homes or to some good private residence and spend the days of their sickness, where they can be attended to and restored to health and strength. This would be economy in the truest sense of the word - economy in money, in labor, and in human life.

Respectfully,   J. H. H.

Georgia Troops:

3rd Brigade Georgia State Troops, Walkers Brigade, 12/27/1861-1/28/1862 (See the organization of the 3rd Brigade under Camp Harrison.)

Sources:

GDAH, 283/16, James D. Alexander; RWC, 1/17/1862; SR, 12/31/1861, 12/28/1861 & 1/7/1862; SDMN, 1/3/1862 & 1/10/1862

672   **Camp Walker**
Glynn County, Georgia

The camp was located at Waynesville.

Georgia Troops:

4th (Clinch's) Regiment Georgia Volunteer Cavalry, Cos. B, D, G, I & K, 1/1863-6/1863 & 2/1864

Sources:

GDAH, CSR, 253/94; 283/27

673   **Camp Walker**
Jasper County, South Carolina

The camp was located at Coosawhatchie Station.

Georgia Troops:

12th Battalion Georgia Volunteers, Co. A, 12/26/1863-2/11/1864

Source:

GDAH, CSR, 254/31

674   **Camp Walker**
Jasper County, South Carolina

The camp was located at Pocataligo.

Georgia Troops:

12th Battalion Georgia Volunteers, Cos. C & E, 2/19/1864 & 2/20/1864

Sources:

SR, 3/3/1864; GDAH, CSR, 254/31-35

675   **Camp Walker**
Georgetown County, South Carolina

The camp was located at Battery White, near Georgetown.

Georgia Troops:

21st Battalion Georgia Cavalry, Co. E, 7/31/1863

Source:

GDAH, CSR, 254/9

676   **Camp Walker**
Chesterfield County, Virginia
The camp was located near Drewry's Bluff on the James River, seven miles below Richmond.
Georgia Troops:
2nd Independent Infantry Battalion, 6/6/1862-7/4/1862
Sources:
GDAH, UDC Books, Vol. II, 228-230 & Vol. II, 265-268

677   **Camp Walker**
Prince William County, Virginia
The camp was located four miles from Manassas Junction on the road to Alexandria, between quarries of red stone. This was the camp of Toomb's Brigade. Only three regiments of Toomb's Brigade were present in this camp.

Ivy Duggan of the 15th Georgia sent the following tribute to the *Central Georgian* newspaper, and was published on September 4, 1861.

My Mother.

My Mother! Sweet Name! The first word lisped from my Infant tongue! Before hunger placed its first complaints upon my grieving lips; my mother fed me. Before restless hours came, her sweet voice sang me to rest. The frequent pain always found her a ministering angel to sooth, and the fretful cries were turned into peaceful slumbers by the sweet charms of her lullaby. Childhood hid all its troubles in her open heart and our little faults were so purified and buried there that they put forth new resolutions to err no more. Her sweet influence and meek patience prepared me for the temptations of youth and the trials of early manhood. Her christian walk, pious counsels and ernest prayers were burning lights, shining along the path that leads to "Our Father who art in Heaven."

But my mother is dead.

Last night a letter brought me to the sad news that I am motherless.

A dark cloud has cast its shadow over my heart. Were I at home with friends, sympathy would lighten my burden; but I am far away in camps. The soldier pities me when he learns my mother is dead; but he can only pass on and leave me to bear the burden all alone. My father's house is desolate. Should I ever return home, it is so sad to think I shall not find mother there.

But tears have washed away my grief now, and I find consolation in the assurance that my mother is in Heaven. Her mouldering dust at Bethlehem is another tie binding me to that spot where I too hope to rest when the toils of life are over. Her sainted spirit is another tie binding me to that home where the wicked cease from troubling and the weary are at rest.

May We, who tempers the wind to the shorn lamb, comfort the withered heart of my bereaved father, sanctify this sore affliction to the good of children and friends, and by the influences of His spirit prepare us all to meet mother in Heaven.

Manassas, Va., August 18th, 1861.   Ivy W. Duggan.

Georgia Troops:
1st Georgia Regulars, 7/31/1861-9/10/1861
2nd Regiment Georgia Volunteer Infantry, 8/26/1861-9/10/1861
15th Regiment Georgia Volunteer Infantry, 7/31/1861-9/11/1861

21st Regiment Georgia Volunteer Infantry, 1/11/62-3/6/62
Sources:
1st GR, GDAH, CSR, 254/67; *Footprints of a Regiment*, Annotated by Richard M. McMurry
2nd GVI, GDAH, CSR, 254/100
15th GVI, GDAH, 53/64, *Central Georgian* newspaper, letters of Ivy Duggan; *The Granite Farm Letters*, Edited by John Rozier; CG, 9/4/1861
21st GVI, GDAH, 40/50, Capt. Thomas M. Hightower

678   **Camp W. H. T. Walker**
Lee County, Mississippi
The camp was located near Tupelo.
Georgia Troops:
2nd Battalion Georgia Sharpshooters, 6/30/1862-7/5/1862
5th Regiment Georgia Volunteer Infantry, 6/8/1862-7/31/1862
Sources:
2nd Bn Ga SS, GDAH, CSR, 254/111
5th GVI, GDAH, CSR, 255/12; DU, William McCoy

679   **Camp W. H. T. Walker**
Charleston County, South Carolina
The camp was located on James Island.
Georgia Troops:
Chatham Artillery, 7/10/1863-2/8/1864
32nd Regiment Georgia Volunteer Infantry, Co. D, 2/8/1864
Sources:
CA, *Historical Sketch of The Chatham Artillery During The Confederate Struggle for Independence*, By Charles C. Jones, Jr.
32nd GVI, GDAH, CSR, 256/96

680   **Camp Waller's Tavern**
Spotsylvania County, Virginia
The camp was located near Waller's Tavern, twenty miles south of Zovar Church, 30 miles southeast of Fredericksburg and nine miles from the Virginia Central Railroad.
Georgia Troops:
10th Regiment Georgia Volunteer Infantry, 8/28/1863
Phillips' Legion, Infantry Battalion, 9/1/1863-9/7/1863 (The Legion had been in this camp several days previous to this earlier date.)
Sources:
10th GVI, 283/37, Evan J. Prothro
PL, KMNBPL, Marcus L. Green

681   **Camp Walnut Ridge**

Rutherford County, Tennessee

Benjamin P. Weaver with the 42nd Regiment Georgia Volunteer Infantry stopped for a break when they were twenty-two miles northwest of Manchester, enroute to Readyville. Weaver wrote a letter while on this two hour break and captioned this spot, Camp Walnut Ridge.

Georgia Troops;

42nd Regiment Georgia Volunteer Infantry, 12/8/1862

Source:

GDAH, 283/43, Benjamin P. Weaver

682   **Camp Walton**

Colleton County, South Carolina

The camp was located near Green Pond, fifteen miles from Tar Bluff on the Combahee River, and twenty miles from Adams Run. The drill grounds were in an old field, one-half to three-fourths mile from the camp.

Georgia Troops:

5th Regiment Georgia Volunteer Cavalry, 12/14/1863-2/15/1864

Sources:

GDAH, MR, 279/65; EU, #12, John H. Ash

683   **Camp Wappoo**

Charleston County, South Carolina

The camp was located at the Wappoo Bridge over the Wappoo Creek above James Island.

Georgia Troops:

Augusta Volunteers, Co. C, Thomas' Battalion of Columbia, South Carolina, 4/10/1862-4/15/1862 (The company was temporarily attached to Thomas' Battalion. After these five days in Confederate service, the Augusta Volunteers returned to Augusta and served as local defense troops for the rest of the war.)

Sources:

ADC&S, 4/8/1862 & 4/17/1862

684   **Camp Warner**

Chatham County, Georgia

The camp was located near Savannah.

Georgia Troops:

1st (Olmstead's) Volunteer Regiment of Georgia, 4/17/1864

Source:

GDAH, UDC Books, Vol. VII, 255

685   **Camp Warren**
                                        Cobb County, Georgia
   The camp was probably in north Cobb County or west Cherokee County.
Georgia Troops:
1st Battalion Georgia State Cavalry, McCollum's command, 1/16/1863
Source:
KMNBPL, Ga-9, Diary of G. W. Hunnicutt

686   **Camp Washington**
                                    Beaufort County, North Carolina
   The camp was located near the Pamlico River below Washington, North Carolina.
Georgia Troops:
24th Regiment Georgia Volunteer Infantry, 10/12/1861-2/12/1862
Sources:
GDAH, 283/31, J. L. Leonard; ASB, 1/8/1862

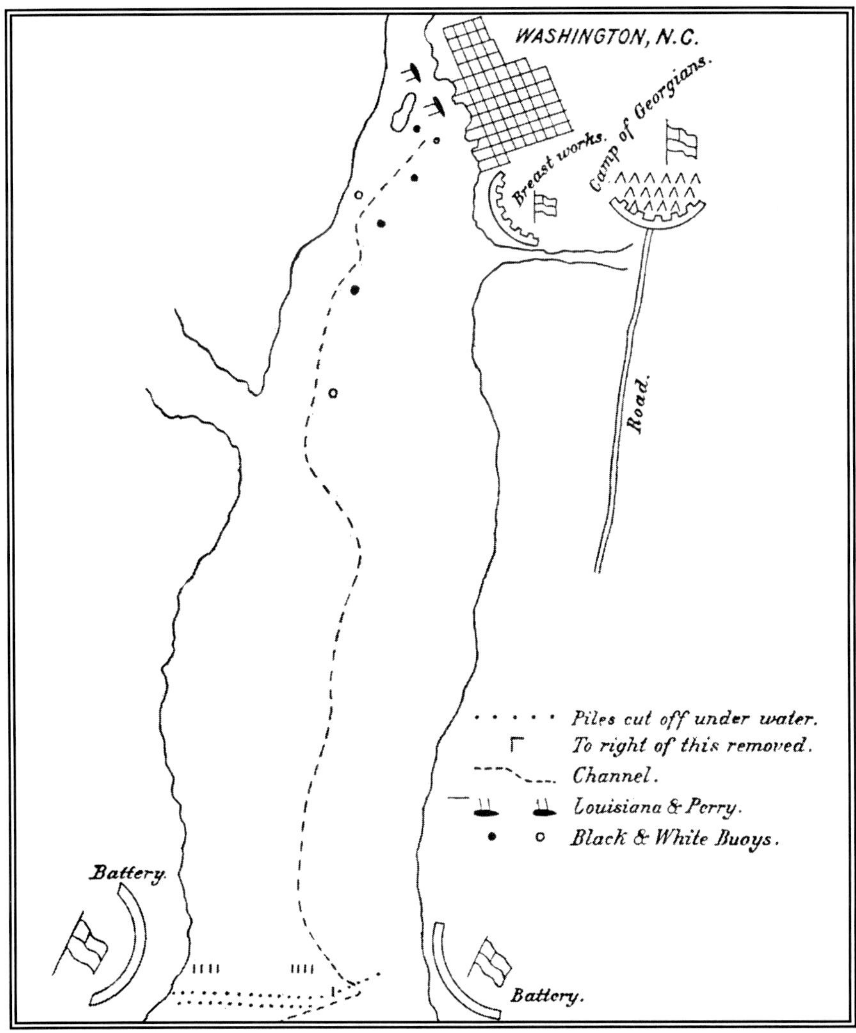

Map showing the location of Camp Washington from the *Official Records of the Union and Confederate Navies*, Vol. 4, page 152

687   **Camp Washington**
Frederick County, Virginia

The camp was located in a grove, one mile east of Winchester, on the Hollingsworth estate. This is the same as Camp Starvation. Also, see Camp Hollingsworth.
Georgia Troops:
8th Regiment Georgia Volunteer Infantry, 6/26/1861-7/2/1861 & 7/7/1861-7/15/1861
Sources:
GDAH, 283/35 & 239/38, Charles & George Norton; RWC, 7/5/1861

688   **Camp Washington**
York County, Virginia

The camp was located about two miles southeast of Yorktown, within one hundred yards of the house on the Temple Farm. The spot where Cornwallis surrendered to Gen. George Washington was one mile from the camp. A monument marks the spot. The Temple house is where Gen. Washington had his headquarters during the Revolution. See Atlas Plate XVII, 1.

Camp Washington Yorktown, Va.
Oct 8' 1861 Thursday 11'oclk A.M

Dearest Wife,

It seems that I cannot hear from you, but you shall hear from me; at least I will do my part, I will start there. I cannot think you have delayed so long. It must be in the mails as the package of letters just handed us for the "Panola Guards" bear date - some of them 10 days ago. You ought to have seen me just now, jumping up and running to see if I had a letter. I had none, and so I came back, determined to write to you. Dear one, If the fault be yours, do correct it. To morrow (Friday) will be two week since I have been in Yorktown and I have heard from you only once. I am well at time of writing with the exception of a sore throat, which is but a trifle. It is better today than it was yesterday. I think I caught cold. The most particular care of one's self will not, cannot keep away colds, where we are exposed to the damp night air, and often rain. Last night it commenced to rain about dark, and it poured down in torrents till morning. The tents all washed some. I slept perfectly dry myself. To day it is perfectly clear and hotter than it has been since I have been here. The soldiers are all airing their tents, and spreading out wet blankets &c. to dry. After a hard rain, a good sunshine day is of immence benefit. In your letter you wrote the baby had the thrash. I can only repeat the hope expressed in my last, that he may recover speedily. I hope my dear wife that you have had no more attacks of the head-ache. I know how you suffer from them, and I often pray that you may be freed from any further attacks. Oh! how I hope that you are sustained by the Divine arm. It is a support upon which you may repose, and never feel disturbed. Let the Lord be your helper and you shall not faint. Wife, I guess you think that I have much to say in my letters about trusting in God. It is true and I shall continue to speak of it. It is upper-most in my heart, and it is manifested from the mouth, and by the pen. Oh! that God would bless you and comfort you - may you be kept as the apple of the eye, and hid under the shadow of his wing. I pray God that he would be a husband to my wife and a father to my son. I love to trust in God, for I know I shall never be deceived - my reward is as certain as the Eternal Throne -.

I think we have had about half dozen days appointed upon which we would leave this place. I can say that we are here, and no more. Cobb knows no more when we will leave, than I do. I will write to you and let it be known after we have moved. This much is true -

we expect to leave every day. I know that the little babe is as sweet as ever. I earnestly hope that he is well and I fancy now that I can see his sweet little laughing eyes & his dimpled rosy cheeks. Sometimes I paint him before me asleep - with his little hands seizing each ear - the very quintessence of infant beauty innocence and love. When I think of you & him, and then myself I can but re-commit us all into God's holy hands.

The war will have this good effect I think; it will cause a fresher love for home to spring up in the hearts of many whose dissolute habits forbade their staying there. It will make husbands more attentive, kind & affectionate. It will humble the proud, and be a source of benefit to all those who feel the chastening hand of God. How do you get on at night with the baby; I often lay awake in my tent at night, and wander in imagination back to my distant home - I wonder if my dear wife is asleep, or is she up nursing the baby and trying to get him asleep - The baby is one month old now; I guess he has changed his looks some. I recollect how he looked, exactly, when I left you and him. You will soon be able to walk about the yard if not already. You must go up and see our family when you get strength enough. I know that they all love you as they do me. My dear Mother I know feels so tenderly to you as the Mother that bore you; She will exhaust her energies in ministering to your comfort. If you need anything you must send and get it; while I do not believe in excess in anything, I believe that God has given us what we have, richly to enjoy while we may. Tell your Mother that we have some of the finest horses in our cavalry campanies, she ever saw. She could get any kind of a pair here, she would wish. I wish she could have the pick of them. I shall ever cherish a feeling of the deepest and most lasting gratitude towards your Mother, for her uniform kindness to me, and for her unremitting attention bestowed upon our little boy. She has proven herself a Mother to me - a most gracious <u>Grandmother</u> to the little darling boy -

Dinner hour is approaching and I will close. Now wife, I hope you will write to me often. I do not believe you have neglected to do it - I must think the irregularity of the mails accounted for it. You know that situated as I am, I am delighted to hear from you. Give my love to all the family, and to all my friend of me. Jim Johnson & Matt Sheppard are well - say this much to their respective kinship - Matt is anxious to hear how his Mother is. And now my dear wife, I pray the Lord's blessings upon you and our precious little one. Oh! may God bless you.

Your affectionate husband
Saml. A. Burney

Georgia Troops:
Cobb's Legion, Infantry & Cavalry, 9/15/1861-10/10/1861
Sources:
SC, 10/9/1861; AHC, Zachariah Rice letters; GDAH, 106/74, Samuel A. Burney

689 **Camp Watchout**
Union County, Tennessee

The camp was located near Maynardville, about twenty miles from Knoxville and thirty miles from Big Creek Gap.
Georgia Troops:
1st Regiment Georgia Volunteer Cavalry, 6/22/1862
Source:

690   **Camp Watts**
                          Bibb County, Georgia
   The camp was located near Macon.
Georgia Troops:
Conscripts on special duty, employed by Chewacla Lime Company at the Macon arsenal, 4/27/1864-6/24/1864
Source:
GDAH, CSR, 258/53

691   **Camp Way**
                         Chatham County, Georgia
   The camp was located on White Bluff Road.
Georgia Troops:
54th Regiment Georgia Volunteer Infantry, 5/15/1862-6/28/1862
Sources:
SDMN, 5/24/1862; GDAH, MR, 257/83

692   **Camp Wayne**
                          Bibb County, Georgia
   The camp was located nine miles below Macon on the Central Railroad and near Griswoldville.
Georgia Troops:
2nd (Storey's) Regiment Infantry, Georgia State Line, 2/16/1863-2/20/1863, 2/1864 & 3/1864 (The unit organized in this camp and was then sent to Savannah.)
Source:
GDAH, AGLB, # 13, 320

693   **Camp Wayne**
                         Baldwin County, Georgia
   The camp was located at Milledgeville.
Georgia Troops:
Georgia Militia, 8/18/1864 & 8/27/1864
Source:
GDAH, 283/31, George Washington Lee

694   **Camp Wayne**
                        Brantley County, Georgia
   The camp was located one and one-half miles from Waynesville on the old Savannah Road. It is believed the site is where the race track is now located.
Georgia Troops:
4th (Clinch's) Regiment Georgia Volunteer Cavalry, 6/1862-9/1862
Source:
GDAH, CSR, 253/94

695   **Camp Wayne**
Fulton County, Georgia
The camp was located about three miles from the railroad depot in Atlanta.
Georgia Troops:
Georgia Militia, 5/24/1864-6/17/1864
Sources:
GDAH, 283/37, Benjamin T. Ray; AHC, Ms. 116, A. T. Holliday; UNC, #2292, William Oliver Fleming

696   **Camp Wayne**
Glynn County, Georgia
The camp was located on Jekyl Island.
Georgia Troops:
7th Battalion Georgia Volunteer Infantry, 10/8/1861-2/15/1862
Source:
GDAH, CSR, 257/113

697   **Camp Wayne**
Gordon County, Georgia
The camp was located near Resaca.
Georgia Troops:
1st Regiment Infantry, Georgia State Guards, Cos. B, C, D, E, F, H, I & K, 9/11/1863-11/17/1863
1st (Galt's) Regiment Infantry, Georgia State Line, 2/23/1864-2/26/1864 & 4/1/1864
Sources:
1st SG, GDAH, CSR, 254/77
1st GSL, GDAH

698   **Camp Wayne**
Troup County, Georgia
The camp was located near West Point.
Georgia Troops:
37th Regiment Georgia Militia, 11/1864
Source:
Not Known

699   **Camp Weems**
McMinn County, Tennessee
The camp was located two miles from Athens.
Georgia Troops:
1st Regiment Georgia Volunteer Cavalry, 6/12/1863-6/25/1863
Sources:
GDAH, *Letters Written by Lavender R. Ray of Newnan, Georgia, During the War Between the States*, Compiled by Ruby F. Ray; SC, 6/27/1863

700   **Camp Wees**
Roane County, Tennessee
    The camp was located near Kingston.
Georgia Troops:
1st Regiment Georgia Volunteer Cavalry, 1/29/1863
Source:
GDAH, CSR, 253/74

701   **Camp Werner**
Chatham County, Georgia
    The camp was located four miles from Ft. Bartow, which was on Causton's Bluff, and was named after Capt. Claus Werner of the German Volunteers.
Georgia Troops:
1st (Olmstead's) Volunteer Regiment of Georgia, 5 companies at various times, 11/1863-4/17/1864 (This included the City Light Guards, Tattnall Guards, Co. B of the Oglethorpe Light Infantry, the German Volunteers and the Washington Volunteers.)
Sources:
GDAH, CSR, 254/81; UDC Books, Vol. VII, 255

702   **Camp Wheaton**
Chatham County, Georgia
    The camp was located eleven miles from Coffee Bluff, four miles from Ft. Bartow and seven miles from Whitmarsh Island.
Georgia Troops:
1st (Olmstead's) Volunteer Regiment of Georgia, five companies at various times, 3/6/1864-5/8/1864 (This includes Company D and the same companies that were at Camp Werner.)
Sources:
GDAH, CSR, 254/81; 283/27, Lindsey Henderson

703   **Camp Wheaton**
Charleston County, South Carolina
    The camp was near Royal's place on James Island. See Camp Colquitt on James Island.
Georgia Troops:
Chatham Artillery, 1/4/1864-2/8/1864
Sources:
SR, 1/6/1864; *Historical Sketch of The Chatham Artillery During The Confederate Struggle for Independence*, by Charles C. Jones, Jr.

704   **Camp Wheeler**
Claiborne County, Tennessee
The camp was located two to three miles from Cumberland Gap, on the south side of the mountain, and on the road to Big Creek Gap. Different companies were in and out of this camp at different times on scouting duty.
Georgia Troops:
6th Regiment Georgia Volunteer Cavalry, 1/1863-7/8/1863 (The 6th Georgia Cavalry was formed in March, 1863, from seven companies of Smith's Legion Cavalry Battalion and four other companies.)
Sources:
GDAH, CSR, 253/106; 186/20, George W. R. Bell; RWC, 5/15/1863

705   **Camp Whitaker**
Bartow County, Georgia
The camp was north of the Etowah River at Kingston, near the railroad spur to Rome.
Georgia Troops:
2nd (Storey's) Regiment Infantry, Georgia State Line, 4/1863-7/19/1863
Source:
GDAH, AGLB, # 15

706   **Camp White**
Escambia County, Florida
The Upson Guards, Company K, 5th Regiment Georgia Volunteer Infantry, left Camp Oglethorpe in Macon on May 13, 1861, and they were the first company of the regiment to set up their tents in Pensacola. Since they were the first of the regiment to arrive, they named their camp "Camp White." When the rest of the regiment arrived, the regiment named the camp "Camp Stephens" in honor of Vice President, Alexander H. Stephens of Georgia. The Upson Guards refered to this camp as "Camp White within Camp Stephens." See Camp Stephens for the location of the camp.
Georgia Troops:
5th Regiment Georgia Volunteer Infantry, Company K, 5/16/1861-9/1861
Sources:
UP, 6/1/1861, 6/22/1861 & 9/28/1861

707   **Camp Whiting**
New Hanover County, North Carolina
The camp was located near Wilmington.
Georgia Troops:
27th Regiment Georgia Volunteer Infantry, 12/31/1864-1/25/1865
Sources:
GDAH, CSR, 256/66; UDC Books Vol. II, 64-66

708   **Camp Whitmarsh Island**
Chatham County, Georgia
The camp was located on Whitmarsh Island.
Georgia Troops;
Maxwell's Battalion Georgia Light Artillery, 10/20/1864-11/25/1864 (See Camp Pembroke.)
Sources:
GDAH, 283/35, William A. Mosley; 291/79, William A. Moseley

709   **Camp Whittle**
Glynn County, Georgia
The camp was located on St. Simons Island.
Georgia Troops:
Jackson Artillery, 1/18/1862
Source:
MT, 1/29/1862

710   **Camp Wigfall**
Prince William County, Virginia
The camp was located three miles east of Dumfries on the Potomac River. This was the winter quarters of Gen. Wigfall's Brigade.
Georgia Troops:
18th Regiment Georgia Volunteer Infantry, 12/1861-3/21/1862
Sources:
SDMN, 12/11/1861; O.R., Vol. V, 534

711   **Camp Wigfall**
Spotsylvania County, Virginia
The camp was located near Fredericksburg.
Georgia Troops:
18th Regiment Georgia Volunteer Infantry, with Hood's Brigade, 4/1/1863
Sources:
GDAH, 283/28, Hood's Brigade; 49/74, W. W. White letters

712   **Camp Wild Cat Church**
Jefferson County, Florida
The camp was located twenty miles from Camp Tolo, which was near Station No. 5 on the Pensacola & Gulf Railroad. It was possibly near Monticello.
Georgia Troops:
29th Battalion Georgia Cavalry, Co. C, 2/1/1864-2/8/1864 (This company returned to Camp Linton on February 23, 1864.)
Source:
GDAH, CSR, 254/13

713   **Camp Willcoxon**
Fulton County, Georgia

The camp was located near Atlanta. The camp was named after Col. John B. Willcoxon, previously the major of Phillips' Legion, Cavalry Battalion.
Georgia Troops:
2nd Regiment Cavalry, Georgia State Guards, 9/10/1863-9/28/1863
Source:
GDAH, CSR, 253/86

714   **Camp Willcoxon**
Beaufort County, South Carolina

The camp was located two miles above Bluffton, on the bluff, ten feet from the May River.
Georgia Troops:
Phillips' Legion, Cavalry Battalion, Co. A, 6/26/1862-7/19/1862 (Phillips' Legion was ordered to Richmond on July 18, 1862. Maj. John B. Willcoxon resigned on January 4, 1862.)
Source:
WL, Loc. 05-31 90-19, Dumbleton, Jeanne Humphries Collection, Elisha Humphries letters

715   **Camp Williams**
Chatham County, Georgia

The camp was located on Tybee Island.
Georgia Troops:
1st Georgia Regulars, 7/11/1861-7/17/1861
Source:
SDMN, 7/12/1861

716   **Camp Williams**
Chatham County, Georgia

The camp was located one and one-half miles from Savannah near the Charleston & Savannah Railroad bridge.
Georgia Troops:
47th Regiment Georgia Volunteer Infantry, 5/1862-10/22/1862, 10/24/1862-12/14/1862 & 2/20/1863
54th Regiment Georgia Volunteer Infantry, Cos. A & H, 3/7/1863
Sources:
47th GVI: GDAH, CSR, 257/42; DU, William S. Benjamin
54th GVI: GDAH, 283/28, Seaborn J. Hightower

717   **Camp Williams**
Chatham County, Georgia
     The camp was located at Fleetwood Plantation on Whitmarsh Island, eight miles from
Greenwich Point. See Camp Fleetwood.
Georgia Troops:
1st Georgia Regulars, 5/25/1864-6/30/1864
Source:
GDAH, CSR, 254/67

718   **Camp Williams**
McIntosh County, Georgia
     The camp was located seven miles from Camp Brailsford and near South Newport. See Camp
Brailsford.
Georgia Troops:
1st Battalion Georgia Cavalry, Lamar Mounted Rifles, 6/8/1862-11/11/1862 (The Lamar
Mounted Rifles became Co. H, 5th Regiment Georgia Volunteer Cavalry on January 22, 1863.)
Sources:
GDAH, CSR, 253/ 79 & 253/101; O.R., Vol. XIV, 192

719   **Camp Wilson**
Catoosa County, Georgia
     The camp was located near Catoosa platform about one mile south of Ringold on the Western
& Atlantic Railroad.
Georgia Troops:
2nd (Storey's) Regiment Infantry, Georgia State Line, Co. B, 6/1863-8/10/1863
Sources:
GDAH, Original list of camps; CG, 9/2/1863

720   **Camp Wilson**
Chatham County, Georgia
     The camp was located three and one-half miles below Savannah on White Bluff Road, two miles
from Camp Lawton, and one mile from Camp Tattnall.
Georgia Troops:
25th Regiment Georgia Volunteer Infantry, 11/10/1861-1/17/1862 & 1/25/1862-2/4/1862
27th Regiment Georgia Volunteer Infantry, 11/14/1861-1/16/1862 (In March, 1862, the 27th
Georgia became the 31st Regiment Georgia Volunteer Infantry.)
29th Regiment Georgia Volunteer Infantry, 12/12/1861-2/22/1862
Sources:
25th GVI, GDAH, CSR, 256/49; *Letters & Papers of Archibald P. Thompson and James S.
Thompson, Two Confederate Soldiers from Screven County, Georgia*, Compiled by Rabun A Lee,
Jr.
27th GVI, GDAH, 283/27, William W. Head letters; RWC, 1/24/1862
29th GVI, GDAH, CSR, 256/79; RWC, 3/7/1862

721   **Camp Winchester**

Frederick County, Virginia

The camp was located one and one-half miles north of Winchester. This was a camp of Bartow's Brigade.

Georgia Troops;

7th Regiment Georgia Volunteer Infantry,* 6/20/1861-6/26/1861

8th Regiment Georgia Volunteer Infantry, 6/20/1861-6/26/1861

9th Regiment Georgia Volunteer Infantry,* 6/20/1861-6/26/1861

* No letters or documents have been found for these regiments with this camp name. It is known they were in this camp.

Sources:

GDAH, 239/38, Charles B. Norton; RWC, 7/5/1861

722   **Camp Winder**

Henrico County, Virginia

The camp was located near the Richmond reservoir and Hollywood Cemetery, about one mile northwest of Richmond. In May, 1862, the camp was made into a hospital camp.

Georgia Troops:

11th Battalion Georgia Light Artillery, 4/14/1862-5/4/1862

1st Georgia Regulars, 7/23/1861-7/25/1861

7th Regiment Georgia Volunteer Infantry, 4/10/1862-4/14/1862

8th Regiment Georgia Volunteer Infantry, 5/12/1862

11th Regiment Georgia Volunteer Infantry, 4/12/1862

15th Regiment Georgia Volunteer Infantry, 4/11/1862 & 4/12/1862

17th Regiment Georgia Volunteer Infantry, 4/1862

18th Regiment Georgia Volunteer Infantry, 10/21/1861-10/24/1861 (On October 24, 1861, the 18th Georgia left for North Carolina.)

Cobb's Legion, Cavalry Battalion, 5/24/1862

Sources:

11th BnGLA, GDAH, CSR, 254/26; UGA, Ms. 15, Florence Hodgson Heidler Collection, Frank M. C. Coker letters

1st GR, *Footprints of a Regiment*, Annotated by Richard M. McMurry

7th GVI, GDAH, CSR, 255/33; 71/77, George W. Hopkins

8th GVI, GDAH, 283/18, Samuel J. G. Brewer

11th GVI, GDAH, 283/42, James Thomas Thompson

15th GVI, CG, 5/7/1862

17th GVI, GDAH, CSR, 255/121

18th GVI, AP, 10/31/1861; SR, 10/30/1861

CLCBn, UNC, #3353, Noble John Brooks

723 **Camp Womble (Wamble)**

Gordon County, Georgia

The camp was located near Resaca. The original list of camp names shows this as Camp Womble. It is most likely Camp Wamble named after Major D. W. Wamble of the 2nd Georgia State Line.

Georgia Troops:

2nd (Storey's) Regiment Infantry, Georgia State Line, Co. H, 7/1863-9/1863

Source:

GDAH, original camp list

724 **Camp Woodlawn**

Hawkins County, Tennessee

The camp was located near Rogersville.

Georgia Troops:

1st Regiment Georgia Volunteer Cavalry, 1/29/1863-2/14/1863

Sources:

GDAH, MR, 279/64; *Letters Written by Lavender R. Ray of Newnan, Georgia, During the War Between the States*, Compiled by Ruby F. Ray

725 **Camp Wright**

Bibb County, Georgia

The camp was located near Ft. Hawkins in east Macon.

Georgia Troops:

1st (Brooks) Regiment Local Defense Troops, 12/1864

2nd Battalion Local Defense Troops, 12/1864

Confederate Headquarters in Macon, 12/1864

Convalescent camp, 12/1864

Sources:

1st LDT, GDAH, CSR, 254/99

2nd LDT, GDAH, CSR, 254/113

Confed HQ, GDAH, CSR, 254/113; *Historical Record of Macon and Central Georgia*, by John C. Butler

Conv, GDAH, CSR, 254/113; *Historical Record of Macon and Central Georgia*, by John C. Butler

726 **Camp Wright**

Chatham County, Georgia

The camp was located near Savannah.

Georgia Troops:

12th (Wright's) Regiment Cavalry, Georgia State Guards, 1/1/1864-1/31/1864

Source:

GDAH, CSR, 253/126

727   **Camp Wright**
Prince William County, Virginia

The camp was located near Gainesville.
Georgia Troops:
21st Regiment Georgia Volunteer Infantry, 9/6/1861-9/7/1861 (Only part of the regiment was here, which included the Sardis Volunteers.)
Source:
RWC, 9/20/1861

728   **Camp Wright**
Chesterfield County, Virginia

The camp was located near Falling Creek.
Georgia Troops:
48th Regiment Georgia Volunteer Infantry, 8/2/1862-8/4/1862
Sources:
ADC&S, 8/5/1862 & 8/8/1862

729   **Camp Yeaby**
                                    Spotsylvania County, Virginia
The camp was located near Fredericksburg.
Georgia Troops:
8th Regiment Georgia Volunteer Infantry, 1/7/1863
Source:
UGA, Ms. 25, Margaret Branch Sexton Collection

730   **Camp Yeager**
                                  Pocahantas County, West Virginia
    The camp was located nine miles from Greenbrier River on Allegheny Mountain. This is the
same as Camp Allegheny. See Camp Allegheny.
Georgia Troops:
12th Regiment Georgia Volunteer Infantry, 7/22/1861-7/28/1861 (James Atkins and John W. Ellis
began using the name Camp Allegheny on their letters August 2, 1861.)
Sources:
GDAH, 283/16, James Atkins; 283/24, John W. Ellis

731   **Camp Yeiser**
                                       Floyd County, Georgia
    The camp was located nine miles from Rome and nineteen miles from Camp Bush Arbor.
Georgia Troops:
Floyd's Legion, Georgia State Guards, 8/1863-11/9/1863 & 12/7/1863
Sources:
GDAH, CSR, 258/41; AGLB, # 20; SDMN, 12/16/1863

732   **Camp Yorktown**
                                       York County, Virginia
    The camp was located near Dam # 1 on the Warwick River, near Yorktown.
Georgia Troops:
7th Regiment Georgia Volunteer Infantry, 4/17/1862-5/4/1862
Source:
GDAH, CSR, 255/33

733   **Camp Young**
                                     Chatham County, Georgia
    The camp was located near Savannah.
Georgia Troops:
2nd (Storey's) Regiment Infantry, Georgia State Line, 2/27/1863-3/9/1863
25th Regiment Georgia Volunteer Infantry, 4/5/1862-5/3/1862 & 7/1862-2/23/1863
29th Regiment Georgia Volunteer Infantry, 3/1862-5/6/1862 & 9/1862-3/12/1863
30th Regiment Georgia Volunteer Infantry, 11/10/1862-12/14/1862, 1/3/1863-1/18/1863,
2/9/1863-4/9/1863, 4/19/1863-4/27/1863 & 5/4/1863-5/8/1863 (Apparently a part of the
regiment remained in North Carolina while the rest of the regiment returned to Savannah. See
Camp Hope.)

Sources:
2nd GSL, GDAH, 227/10, Moses Bunn; CU, 3/10/1863
25th GVI, GDAH, CSR, 256/49
29th GVI, GDAH, CSR, 256/79; SR, 5/7/1863
30th GVI, *Brief History of the Thirtieth Georgia Regiment*, By Augustus Pitt Adamson

734   **Camp Young**

McIntosh County, Georgia

The camp was located near Darien.

Georgia Troops:

29th Regiment Georgia Volunteer Infantry, 9/12/1861 (The compiled service records shows there were several companies of the 29th Georgia at Darien until 12/31/1861.)

Sources:

GDAH, CSR, 256/79; MR, 279/83; 283/23, Dickey Family letters

735   **Camp Young**

Louisa County, Virginia

The camp was located near Louisa Court House. This was the camp of Young's Cavalry Brigade.

Georgia Troops:

7th Regiment Georgia Volunteer
Cavalry, 6/11/1864

Sources:

SR, 7/8/1864; GDAH, CSR, 253/109

Gen. Pierce Manning Butler Young held the rank of major during the period of Camp Young in June, 1862. After several promotions, he served as Brigadier General while in the Camp Young of June, 1864. He received a promotion to Major General as of December 30, 1864, and is pictured in this uniform.

photo courtesy of Jerry Coody

Camp Young
Henrico County, Virginia

The camp was located in an oak grove, about two and one-half miles from Richmond, and about two and one-half miles from the enemy's pickets.
Georgia Troops:
Cobb's Legion, Cavalry Battalion, Co. I, 6/7/1862
Source:
ADC&S, 6/12/1862

Rosecrans Soliloquy:
That fellow Wheeler's ruined all
My sour krout and beans -
Who ever heard of taking boats
With rebel *horse-marines.*
Spirit of the South

Camp Zollicoffer
Chatham County, Georgia

The camp was located on Skidaway Island, between the old mansion west of the Batteries and Waring's Landing, which was one mile from camp. The camp was also one-quarter mile from the lower Battery.

Georgia Troops:

Jo Thompson Artillery, 1/31/1862-2/13/1862

Source:

Atlanta Historical Bulletin, "War Diary of Cornelius R. Hanleiter," Edited by Elma S. Kurtz

Map from p. 53 of AHB

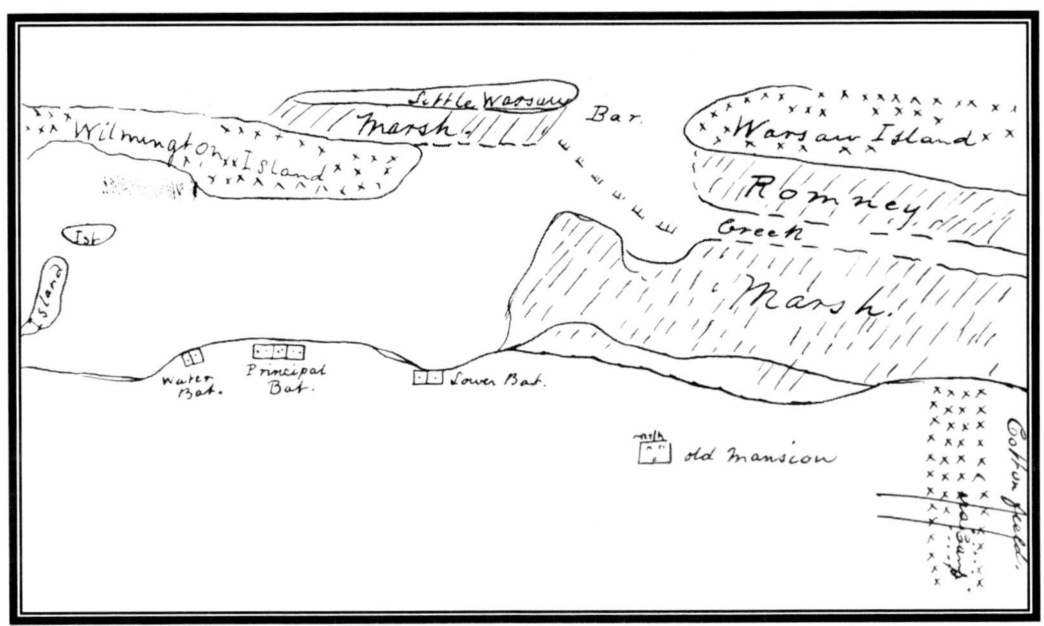

Map showing the location of Camp Zollicoffer on Skidaway Island
courtesy of the Atlanta History Center, *Atlanta Historical Bulletin*, "War Diary of Cornelius R. Hanleiter," Edited by Elma S. Kurtz

ADDENDUM

The following camp names were received too late to be included in the main part of the book. Very little research has been done on these camps.

Camp Belton
Bradley County, Tennessee

The camp was located near Cleveland, Tennessee.
Georgia Troops:
3rd Regiment Confederate Cavalry, Co. E, 8/31/1862
Source:
GDAH, CSR, 258/64

Camp Breckenridge
Hamilton County, Tennessee

The camp was located near Chattanooga.
Georgia Troops:
19th Battalion Georgia Cavalry, Co. B, 12/25/1862-12/27/1862 (Company B of the 19th Battalion Georgia Cavalry became Co. G of the 10th Regiment Confederate Cavalry on December 30, 1862, when they consolidated with the 5th Alabama Battalion of cavalry [Hilliard's Legion Cavalry]. The 19th Battalion Georgia Cavalry was also referred to as the 2nd Battalion Georgia Partisan Rangers.)
Source:
PC, Letters of Bennett Pate

Camp Charleston
Bradley County, Tennessee

The camp was located at Charleston.
Georgia Troops:
19th Battalion Georgia Cavalry, 9/19/1862
Source:
PC, Letters of Bennett Pate

Camp Fleming
Liberty County, Georgia

The location is not known.
Georgia Troops:
1st Battalion Georgia Cavalry, Liberty Independent Troop, 8/23/1861
Source:
GDAH, CSR, 253/80

Camp Henderson
Georgia or Tennessee

The camp was located near Battle Creek. The camp could be on either the Battle Creek in Dade County, Georgia, or Battle Creek in Hamilton County, Tennessee.
Georgia Troops:
3rd Regiment Confederate Cavalry, Co. G, 4/17/1862
Source:
GDAH, CSR, 258/64

Camp Johnson
Tennessee

Location not known.
Georgia Troops:
19th Battalion Georgia Cavalry, 8/20/1862
Source:
PC, Letters of Bennett Pate

Camp Lowery

The location of the camp is not known. It is in either northwest Georgia or east Tennessee.
Georgia Troops:
3rd Regiment Confederate Cavalry, Co. H
Source:
GDAH, CSR, 258/64

Camp Maxey
Clinton County, Kentucky

The camp was located near Albany, Kentucky.
Georgia Troops:
3rd Regiment Confederate Cavalry, 9/1862
Source:
GDAH, CSR, 258/64

Camp Smith

The location of the camp is not known. It is in either Florida or Georgia.
Georgia Troops:
64th Regiment Georgia Volunteer Infantry, Co. K, 8/1863
Source:
GDAH, CSR, 254/63

Camp Smith
Bradley County, Tennessee

The camp was located near Cleveland, Tennessee.
Georgia Troops:
3rd Regiment Confederate Cavalry, Co. E, 5/16/1862
Source:
GDAH, CSR, 258/64

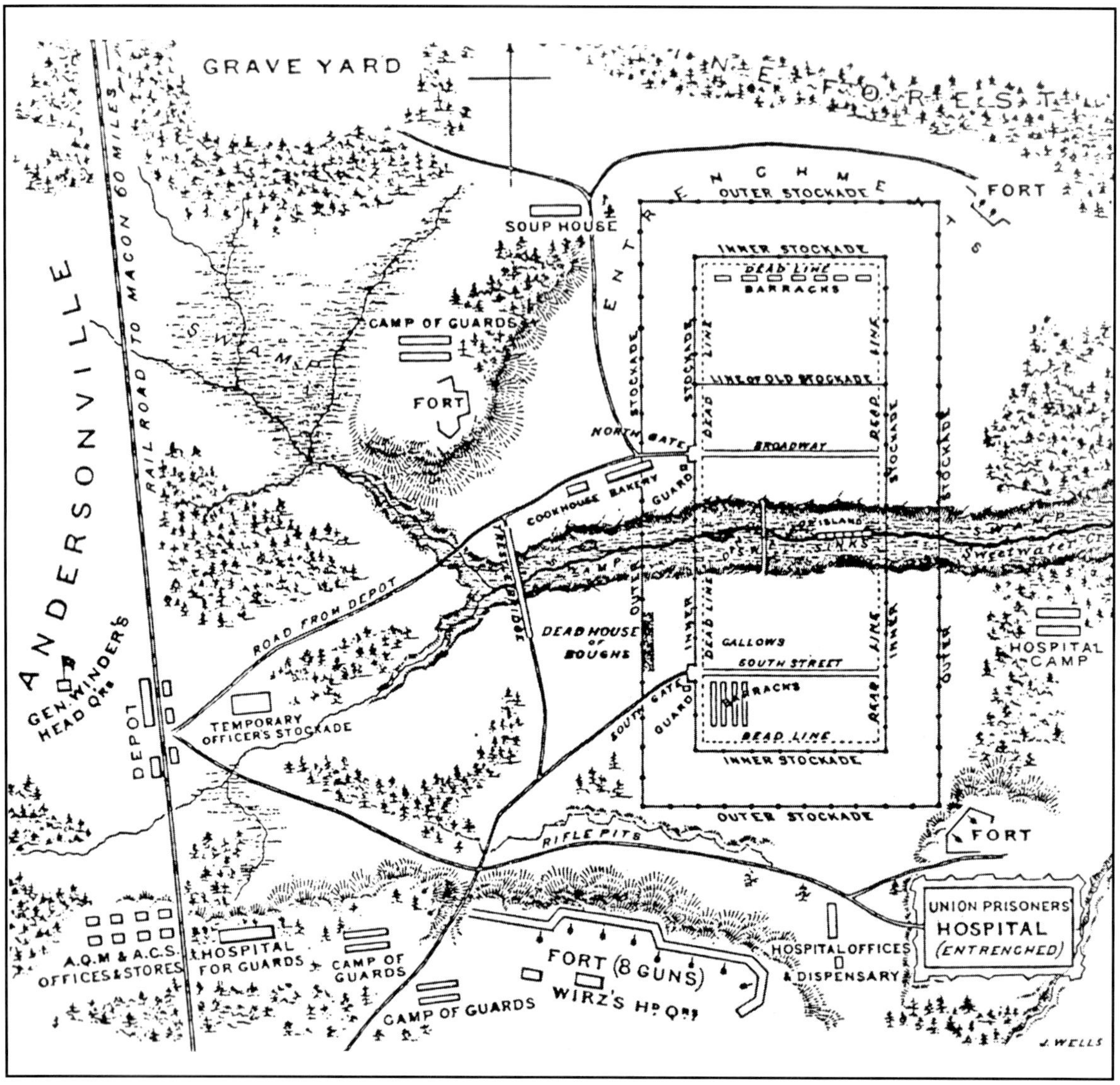

Plan of the stockade and surroundings at Andersonville from the *Century Magazine*, Vol. 40, p. 452

Exterior view of the prison pen at Millen, Georgia (Camp Lawton) from *Harper's Weekly*, Jan. 7, 1865

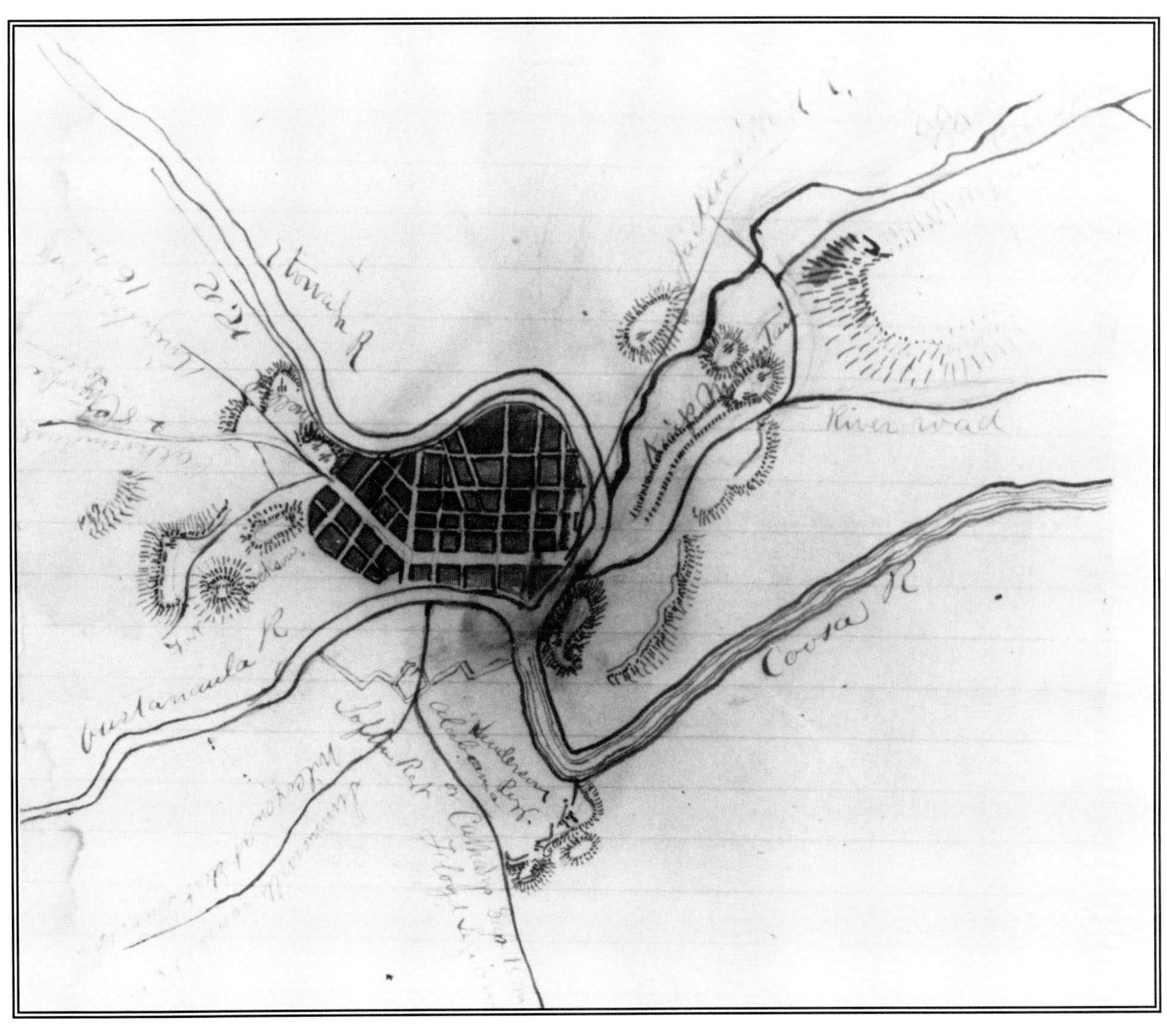

This map of Rome, Georgia and vicinity was drawn between October 3, 1863 and December 16, 1863.
Note on map that Wilcoxon was at Dirt Town. Then see Camp Dirt Town of the 2nd Regiment Cavalry,
Georgia State Guards. Also, see Camps Jackson, Yeiser and all of the other camps of the Georgia State
Guards in Floyd County.
Map courtesy of the Hargrett Library, University of Georgia. The map
is from Ms 1376, Howell Cobb's papers, Box 67, folder 21.

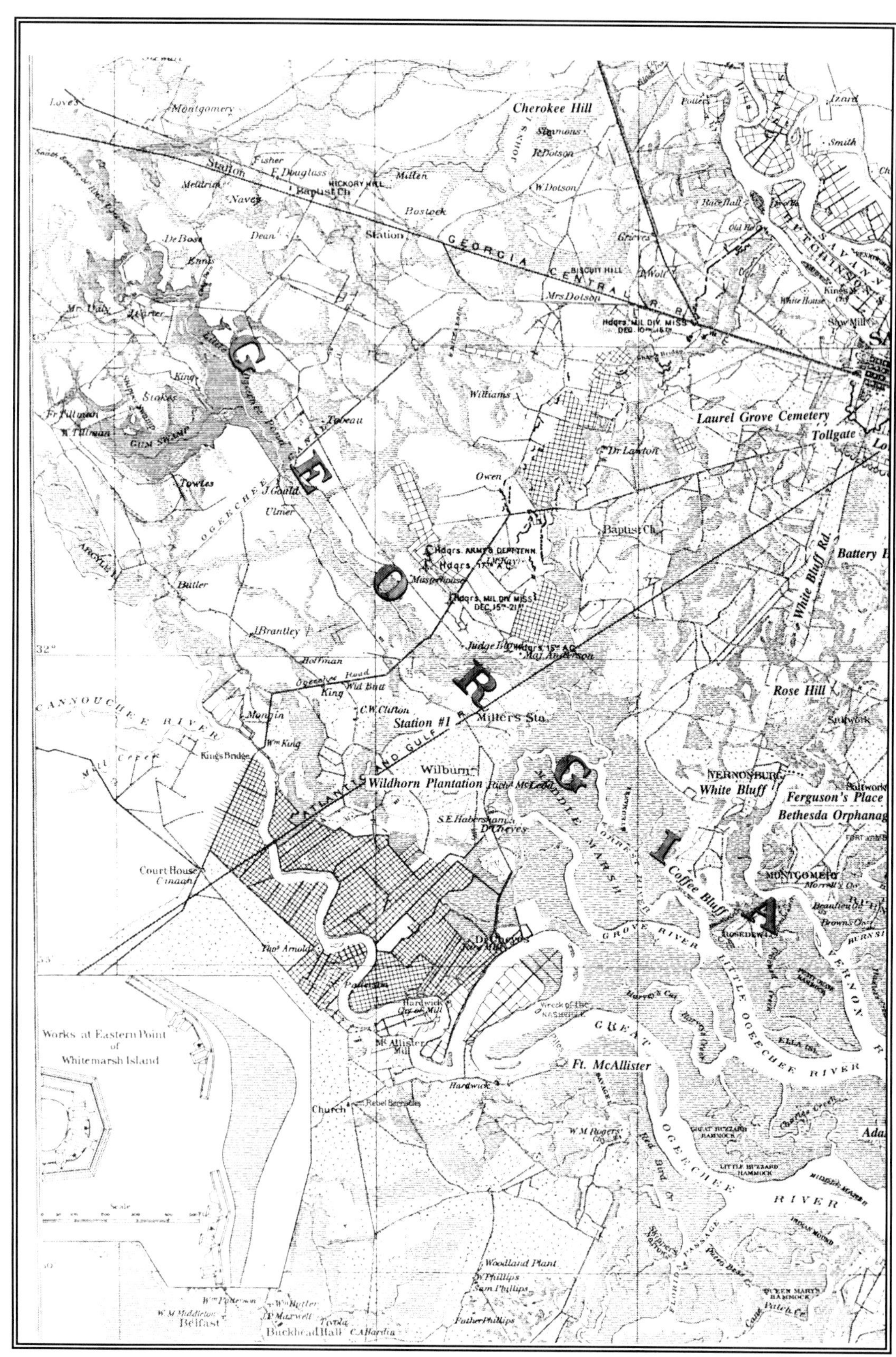

Map of Savannah, Georgia and vicinity with many additional names and places
All of the names added to the map are mentioned

added to the map from *The Official Military Atlas of the Civil War.*
in the descriptive locations of the camps.

Index Of Proper Names

Index Of **Proper Names**

Index Of Proper Names

Index Of Proper Names

Index Of Proper Names

Index Of Proper Names

Index Of **Proper Names**

Index By Unit In Chronological Order

Index By Unit In Chronological Order

Index By Unit In Chronological Order

Index By State And County In Alphabetical Order

All listings are by the camp number.

ALABAMA

Jackson Co., 20, 159, 575

Mobile Co., 152, 588

Montgomery Co., 220

FLORIDA

Columbia Co., 42, 427

Decatur Co., 529

Duval Co., 223, 321, 469

Escambia Co., 114, 247, 421, 495, 507, 540, 606, 670, 706

Gadsden Co., 132, 242, 567

LaFayette Co., 408

Leon Co., 26, 72, 339, 404, 589

Madison Co., 642, 712

Wakulla Co., 77, 157, 364, 527, 584

GEORGIA

Counties unknown, 286, 536

Appling Co., 453, 454

Baldwin Co., 693

Bartow Co., 205, 231, 479, 705

Bibb Co., 5, 38, 80, 128, 144, 156, 287, 356, 475, 495, 543, 590, 690, 692, 725

Brantley Co., 297, 565, 694

Bryan Co., 17, 99, 373, 390, 439, 499, 556

Burke Co., 197, 436

Camden Co., 19, 27, 43, 217, 320, 322, 383, 447, 539, 625, 561

Carroll Co., 105

Catoosa Co., 389, 719

Chatham Co., 1, 10, 18, 25, 28, 37, 41, 47, 53, 56, 63, 71, 79, 81, 89, 93, 98, 100, 101, 108, 109, 121, 129, 138, 139, 150, 151, 153, 158, 160, 173, 175, 179, 195, 201, 206, 219, 224, 226, 259, 271, 279, 280, 285, 310, 316, 317, 318, 324, 335, 336, 340, 341, 351, 352, 355, 357, 266, 370, 384, 391, 392, 416, 419, 430, 440, 442, 446, 454, 455, 456, 457, 458, 459, 460, 465, 466, 467, 477, 486, 490, 493, 496, 504, 508, 521, 528, 535, 548, 551, 557, 562, 569, 572, 581, 582, 587, 591, 596, 603, 614, 620, 621, 622, 626, 627, 629, 639, 640, 654, 659, 665, 671, 684, 691, 701, 702, 708, 716, 717, 720, 726, 733, 737

Chattooga Co., 184

Clarke Co., 215, 630

Clayton Co., 23, 415

Cobb Co., 82, 148, 207, 367, 441, 597, 685

Dade Co., 304

Dawson Co., 62

DeKalb Co., 161, 174, 305, 377, 530

Dougherty Co., 69, 246, 450, 586

Effingham Co., 162, 289, 379

Floyd Co., 40, 92, 273, 337, 342, 382, 472, 577, 592, 731

Fulton Co., 22, 70, 83, 106, 248, 257, 263, 315, 375, 393, 407, 411, 418, 426, 438, 512, 519, 559, 560, 607, 635, 695, 713

Glynn Co., 73, 78, 107, 122, 298, 509, 573, 615, 637, 672, 696, 709

Gordon Co., 65, 94, 149, 221, 487, 531, 664, 697, 723

Habersham Co., 29

Hancock Co., 163, 585

Jenkins Co., 385

Jones Co., 268

Lee Co., 394, 662

Liberty, Co., 11, 74, 133, 461, 498, 600, 612

Long Co., 123

Macon Co., 9, 617

McIntosh Co., 76, 134, 192, 256, 313, 323, 328, 343, 386, 501, 522, 571, 599, 601, 638, 718, 734

Morgan Co., 358

Muscogee Co., 30, 52, 164, 245, 329, 409, 424, 473

Pierce Co., 517, 579

Pike Co., 165

Quitman Co., 203

Randolph Co., 193, 668

Richmond Co., 344, 526

Spalding Co., 166, 194, 200, 258, 387, 608, 641

Sumter Co., 167

Index By State And County In Alphabetical Order

Index By State And County In Alphabetical Order